INDIGENOUS PEOPLES' WISDOM AND POWER

Capturing the narratives of indigenes, this book presents a unique anthology on global Indigenous peoples' wisdoms and ways of knowing. Covering issues of religion, cultural self-determination, philosophy, spirituality, sacred sites, oppression, gender and the suppressed voices of women, the diverse global contexts across Africa, Asia, the Middle East, North and South America, and Oceania are highlighted. The contributions represent heart-felt expressions of Indigenous peoples from various contexts – their triumphs and struggles, their gains and losses, their reflections on the past, present, and future – telling their accounts in their own voices.

Opening new vistas for understanding historical ancient knowledge, preserved and practiced by Indigenous people for millennia, this innovative anthology illuminates areas of philosophy, science, medicine, health, architecture, and botany to reveal knowledge suppressed by Western academic studies.

VITALITY OF INDIGENOUS RELIGIONS

Series Editors
Graham Harvey, Open University, UK
Lawrence Martin, University of Wisconsin-Eau Claire, USA
Tabona Shoko, University of Zimbabwe, Zimbabwe

Ashgate's *Vitality of Indigenous Religions* series offers an exciting new cluster of research monographs, drawing together volumes from leading international scholars across a wide range of disciplinary perspectives. Indigenous religions are vital and empowering for many thousands of indigenous peoples globally, and dialogue with, and consideration of, these diverse religious life-ways promises to challenge and refine the methodologies of a number of academic disciplines, whilst greatly enhancing understandings of the world.

This series explores the development of contemporary indigenous religions from traditional, ancestral precursors, but the characteristic contribution of the series is its focus on their living and current manifestations. Devoted to the contemporary expression, experience and understanding of particular indigenous peoples and their religions, books address key issues which include: the sacredness of land, exile from lands, diasporic survival and diversification, the indigenization of Christianity and other missionary religions, sacred language, and re-vitalization movements. Proving of particular value to academics, graduates, postgraduates and higher level undergraduate readers worldwide, this series holds obvious attraction to scholars of Native American studies, Maori studies, African studies and offers invaluable contributions to religious studies, sociology, anthropology, geography and other related subject areas.

OTHER TITLES IN THE SERIES

Indigenous Diasporas and Dislocations
Edited by Graham Harvey and Charles D. Thompson Jr.
ISBN 0 7546 3906 1

Aboriginal Religions in Australia
An Anthology of Recent Writings
Edited by Max Charlesworth, Françoise Dussart, and Howard Morphy
ISBN 0 7546 5128 2

The Vitality of Karamojong Religion
Dying Tradition or Living Faith?
Ben Knighton
ISBN 0 7546 0383 0

Indigenous Peoples' Wisdom and Power

Affirming Our Knowledge Through Narratives

Edited by
JULIAN E. KUNNIE
University of Arizona, USA

NOMALUNGELO I. GODUKA
Central Michigan University, USA

ASHGATE

Published by
Ashgate Publishing Limited
Gower House
Croft Road
Aldershot
Hampshire GU11 3HR
England

Ashgate Publishing Company
Suite 420
101 Cherry Street
Burlington, VT 05401-4405
USA

Ashgate website: http://www.ashgate.com

British Library Cataloguing in Publication Data
Indigenous peoples' wisdom and power : affirming our knowledge through narratives.
– (Vitality of indigenous religions)
1.Indigenous peoples 2.Ethnicity 3.Minorities – Social conditions
I. Kunnie, Julian II. Goduka, Nomalungelo I.
306'.08

Library of Congress Cataloging-in-Publication Data
Indigenous peoples' wisdom and power : affirming our knowledge through narratives / edited by Julian Kunnie and Nomalungelo I. Goduka.
p. cm. – (Vitality of indigenous religions)
Includes bibliographical references and index.
ISBN 0-7546-1597-9 (alk. paper)
1. Ethnophilosophy. 2. Ethnoscience. 3. Indigenous peoples–Religion. 4. Indigenous peoples–Social life and customs. I. Kunnie, Julian II. Goduka, Nomalungelo I., 1958- III. Series.

GN468.I43 2004
304.8'001–dc22

2003059607

ISBN-13: 978-0-7546-1597-2
ISBN-10: 0-7546-1597-9

Printed and bound in Great Britain by MPG Books Ltd. Bodmin, Cornwall.

*Dedicated to the Indigenous matriots and patriots who fought
to preserve their cultures and peoples in the wake of genocide
following 500 years of Western Colonization*

Contents

Prologue – *Intshayelelo*

VUMANI!
SIYAVUMA!
VUMANI!
SIYAVUMA!
Hello to You ALL!

We bring you greetings from the ancestors, elders and cultural and spiritual healers, or *izangoma*, from our Indigenous villages and communities. We invite you to connect with the authors and the narratives presented in this anthology. These narratives were conceived around certain times, events and contexts, and we are sharing them with you to give you a glimpse into the lived experiences of each contributor and collective experiences they share with members of their communities. In this prologue, or *intshayelelo*, I will journey with you to connect you to the times and events surrounding the conception of these stories. Julian Kunnie, the primary editor, will present synopses of the narratives that gave birth and life to this volume. Following the prologue and synopses, we will bring you each contributor's story, presented in their own voice and words. To begin with, I will invoke the ancestors and introduce myself.

Consistent with the spirit of this anthology, we, the co-editors and authors of this volume, are code-switching where appropriate in order to legitimize Indigenous languages and affirm culturally and spiritually centered wisdoms embraced by Indigenous peoples, as well as to validate ourselves as Indigenous storytellers. These are cultural and spiritual wisdoms that constitute the foundations of our being. Long before we spoke and read the foreign word and were assimilated and enculturated into European traditions and cultures through the school system and the church, we were imbued with these wisdoms. The elders, midwives, spiritual and cultural healers and members of our extended families in our villages, spoke and sang to us in Indigenous languages, and healed us with *umhlonyane nomthombothi* – indigenous herbs. In her chapter on Traditional Chinese Medicine (TCM), Roxana Ng remembers that "growing up in [what was] the British Colony of Hong Kong...special concoctions were prepared to alleviate symptoms of colds" and that "Knowledge of TCM is part of my cultural heritage...a healing system indigenous to my culture," she added.

Everyday we joined our parents, uncles and aunts in the field or around the homestead working, singing, dancing and eating together in harmony. Everything we did, the songs we sang, the food we ate, the herbal teas we drank affirmed our being Indigenous. In the evenings, children gathered around *iziko* – the fireplace to listen to *iintsomi* – Indigenous mythology and stories about Indigenous heroines and heroes. Where did that greater part of our being Indigenous go? We hope that projects such as this anthology provide a way to remember and capture what seems to be slipping away from our beings.

As is customary in Indigenous communities when one embarks on a spiritual journey, I will follow the protocol of invoking our ancestors and those of the contributors. I will also call upon *oo-khoko* – the elders from our villages and communities to provide us with the healing powers and humbling wisdoms to guide us as we remember the past, engage with the present, and predict a future built on inclusive paradigms and ways of knowing. In the process of paving the way for the contributors to tell these "cultural truths" as these truths were told to them, I am also calling upon their ancestors to support and sustain our contributors with spiritual wisdoms so they can have a clear heart and mind to capture and narrate these knowledges the best way they know how. During my brief visits to the various continents, countries, and villages to engage in conversations and listen to stories as they were told to me, I made every effort, in the early hours of the day or after sunset to jog, walk, and wander for spiritual revival, and to connect with the ancestors of each contributor.

As I invoke our ancestors, I will follow the lead of the cultural/spiritual healers – *izangoma*, who begin the process of healing – *bengxengxeza besithi* – by invoking the ancestors saying "*ezizinto asizenzeli, ezizinto zagqitywa zizinyanya...Ezinyaniso ayizozethu, ezinyaniso zifunwa sisizukulwana.*" English is inadequate to capture the essence of the spiritually centered wisdoms of these Indigenous people. A closer translation might be "our accomplishments are not of our own doings, they were told to us by the ancestors and the elders"... These cultural truths were passed on to us, and we have a calling to pass them on to the children of our children. We do this to keep Indigenous wisdoms and ways of knowing, healing, learning, and interpreting the cosmos alive within and among us and preserved and protected for posterity.

Having invoked the ancestors, let me say who I am. I will do this by positioning myself within the spiritual and cultural contexts, which is the accepted and appropriate procedure for the *ama-Xhosa* of South Africa, the group to which I belong, before presenting themselves and discussing the issues at hand. In the process of finding one's cultural and ethnic identity, *ama-Xhosa* do not ask "Who are you, what is your address, and phone number?" These are contemporary and foreign methods of identification serving a different purpose. Instead the Xhosa questions about identity are the following:

Uyintombi kabani – Who are you a daughter of?
Iphi inkaba yakho – Where was your umbilical cord buried?
Ngokwesiduko Ningamani – What are your panegyric legends?

Responses to these questions provide a holistic identification grounding the individual in spiritual and cultural contexts. These contexts form deep roots for Indigenous peoples that do not only connect us to one another in our villages and communities, but also to the land. Land for us is not a source of sustenance only, it also serves as a cultural and spiritual bond connecting us with our ancestors, and to the greater whole, Mother Earth. For Indigenous peoples, land cannot be owned, bought, or sold. She does not belong to us, we belong to her. We are born out of this land; we spend our lives on this land as her guests; and after death we go back to that same land. After the baby is born, *ama-Xhosa* bury the placenta and the umbilical cord in the ground very close to the homestead. The burial of the umbilical cord ensures the continual connectedness between the children and land. From the land originates their identity, art, history, and a foundation of *ubuntu*, or humaness. Land connects children with their past, as the home of their ancestors and their unborn sisters and brothers; with the present, as provider of the material and spiritual needs; and with the future, as the legacy they hold in trust for their children and the children of their children. Although Indigenous peoples around the world vary widely in their customs, traditions, rituals, languages, and so on, land is considered by all as the center of the universe, a parent, a giver of life, the core of our cultures, rituals, and traditions. However, given that Indigenous peoples are not a monolithic group, there are bound to be variations in how we ask and respond to questions about cultural, spiritual, and ethnic identity. For me, as an Indigenous Xhosa woman, my response to questions of ethnic identity would be as follows:

I am the daughter of *ndiyintombi ka-Tata u-Qhudeni, no-Mama u-Bhelekazi*.
My umbilical cord is buried in my village, *inkaba yam ikwa-Manxeba, e-Heshele*,
   in the Eastern Cape in South Africa.
According to our panegyric legends, *ngokwesiduko singaba-Thembu, oo-Ngoza,*
   oo-Qhudeni, oo-Mpafane!
Sitsho thina singama-Xhosa-Poqo, ase-Mbo xa sizithutha.

These are poetic and artistic expressions, albeit a frugal use of words to trace one's genealogy by the vintage Xhosa, *ama-Xhosa-Poqo*. But these responses reflect the cultural, spiritual and ethnic ties that connect me to the land, thus with my ancestors and my unborn sisters and brothers. They also show the significance of oral tradition not only encompasses storytelling, but also traditional ways of tracing one's ethnic identity. Somadoda Fikeni in this anthology elaborates on Xhosa panegyric legends and other oral traditions. Any Xhosa with the same legends can easily connect with me, is likely to know my genealogy, and can even help me discover my other relatives.

The United Nations proclaimed 1993 to be *International Year of the World's Indigenous Peoples*, giving Indigenous Peoples a platform to voice the pain of exclusion, dispossession, marginalization and genocide. At the opening ceremony in New York, leaders of Indigenous peoples spoke from the podium of the General Assembly for the first time in the history of the United Nations. Rigoberta Menchu Tum, a Mayan activist and winner of the 1992 Nobel Peace Prize, was appointed the UN's Goodwill Ambassador for the Year. The following year, 1994, the United Nations General Assembly declared 1995–2004 the *International Decade of the World's Indigenous Peoples*. Since then, there have been numerous Indigenous conferences and forums at the local and international level, and a plethora of publications addressing issues of land, spirituality, health, education, employment, development, identity, human rights, and self-determination.

In addition to these efforts, the International Indigenous Working Group operating under the auspices of the United Nations continues to meet in Geneva every year in July–August, and the first session of the Permanent Forum on Indigenous Issues was held in New York in April 2002 with the mandate to discuss economic and social development, education and culture, the environment, health and human rights. It has been through Indigenous conferences and meetings with a similar mandate over the last ten years that this anthology was conceived. Specifically, Julian Kunnie and I prepared the ground for planting the seed for this anthology following the 1998 conference "Developing Indigenous Knowledge and Cultural Systems," in Harare, Zimbabwe. Subsequent Indigenous conferences and meetings also helped us identify contributors, refine the title and themes covered in this volume, as well as find a publisher in Ashgate. Thus, the current volume is a small step by the editors and authors to join other Indigenous storytellers and writers who have committed time and effort to legitimize, affirm and disseminate Indigenous wisdoms and ways of knowing to help Indigenous youth, the children of their children to regain their voice, ethnic identity and their position for posterity on Mother Earth.

Indigenous philosophies and worldviews are the themes of this anthology, including ways of healing; *izibongo* or panegyric legends; human rights; development; identity; oral tradition; Indigenous spirituality and religion; agriculture and architecture. The elders, grassroots organizers and Indigenous scholars contributing to this anthology are revitalizing the power of storytelling, and in particular, stories that relate to the histories of Indigenous peoples. Although the final product of this anthology is in the literary or written tradition, most of the work that went into it was preceded by an oral tradition, that is the story of each individual. After Julian Kunnie and I decided to embark on this project, we developed the guidelines, and in most cases I brought these guidelines to contributors in their home countries. We sought contributions from elders, individuals working at grassroots levels, as well as Indigenous scholars. We made a conscious effort to solicit authors from each continent to give a global and balanced view of who Indigenous peoples are, and what they share in common despite their diverse languages, locations and cultures. Procuring an equal number of contributors from each continent was our greatest challenge, and in some cases, we secured only one contributor from a continent. To those individuals whose submissions did not make it into this volume, we express our profound apologies and hope that their contributions will make it into our next volume.

The guidelines specified that contributors did not have to adhere to the rigors of "scientific" and so-called objective research methods rooted in the European or Western traditions. Rather, contributors were encouraged to tell their stories from the heart, thus, engage in the process of deconstructing and decolonizing Eurocentric methodologies. Such work is grounded in Indigenous ways of knowing that challenge modernist assumptions that there are 'regimes of truth,' which most often reproduce and replicate systems of power that mutually sustain and maintain them. Indigenous approaches also challenge the notion that there are 'master narratives' that provide one way or even a certain method for writing and telling stories. Since the philosophical foundations of Western education are steeped in the European tradition and culture, Indigenous wisdoms and ways of knowing have been ignored and devalued in education the world over. To Indigenous peoples, Eurocentric methodologies and scholars have appropriated our cultural and spiritual wisdoms and misrepresented our stories. It is thus an accepted truism among Indigenous scholars that the system of education is a double-edged sword. While it has attempted to remove our identity, we are forced to utilize its tools and languages to dismantle colonial identities and images that conceal and distort our stories and voices.

The stories contained in this volume challenge these assumptions. Authors are "speaking" in their own voices and the voices with whom they share the same pain and vision. They "speak" in their languages where appropriate in order to validate their cultures as legitimate and authentic. As Pat Torres, one author in this volume puts it, "...[our stories and voices] cannot be justified by reference to anything external to our cultures, be explained to anyone, be compared or authenticated against the standard of Western science..." These authors claim the right for their stories to be told by them, deep from the heart so that feelings and repressed thoughts and memories come to the surface. In some cases these are feelings of joy that bring back good memories connecting individuals to their communities and villages. These are memories of how knowledge-building occurred within these communities. In other cases, these are feelings of sadness, loss, and a yearning to reclaim one's story and identity.

Some of this volume is from conversations at conferences and various UN meetings for Indigenous peoples. Others took place at the contributors' homesteads. My meeting and conversation with the Maori elder, Rangimarie Turuki Pere, occurred in her homestead in Waikaremoana in Gisborne, New Zealand. Before we sat down for the traditional evening meal which all members of the family (including myself, as she called me 'daughter' the moment she set eyes on me) had prepared, elder Pere invited me to the *Marae*, to welcome me "in a Maori tradition". She provides a full account of the *Marae* in her story. However, let me briefly tell you what she told me about the *Marae*. "It is one of the few places where the cultural identity, spiritual values and philosophy of the Maori people are reaffirmed. The *Marae* is sacred to the living, and is a memorial to the ancestors. For this the *Marae* must be entered in a reverent manner," she added. Entering the *Marae* and listening to the history behind it, gave me a feeling that cannot be put into words.

Following that visit, I proceeded to Nibutani, in Hokkaido, Japan, to meet with Kayano Shigeru, an Ainu elder and Koichi Kaizawa, a farmer. Both have been heavily involved with the preservation of the Ainu language and culture. At both homes I joined members of their families as they around the fireplace to roast corn and salmon and engage in stimulating conversations about the Ainu people, their history and culture. Details of their stories are in this volume.

In Sweden, the conversation with Asa Verde took place at the Saami Summer Festival in Ankarede in the northen part of Ostersund. I was also honored to be invited to her wedding which was taking place during the festival. At this occasion,

I not only met members of her family, but Saami people from Norway, Finland, and parts of Russia. I learned much more about the Saami culture and tradition from conversations with these scholars. Joining the Saami in their cultural dance and song, tasting their delicious meals, and engaging in conversations with Asa as well as other Saami, was one of the experiences that will remain etched in my heart for a very long time. The highlight of my visit was when Nora Larsson, secretary at the Gaaltjie Cultural Institute, invited me to attend the ear-marking of the reindeer calves on the mountain. This is one of the most spiritual and reverent traditions embraced by the Saami. Nora made it very clear to me that she was offering me this opportunity because I was a special guest at the Institute. However, she warned me not to bring a digital or video camera because of the secrecy of this ceremony. "It is sad that some Europeans attend these ceremonies and insist on taking pictures despite the strong opposition from the elders. Such behavior would be similar to one of us insisting on going into their bedrooms and taking pictures," she said.

At Flinders University in Adelaide, Australia while on a two-week visiting professorship, Julian Kunnie and I met with Lester-Irabinna Rigney. During that visit, we were able to go to Alice Springs in the central part of Australia and saw with our own eyes the abject poverty and inhumane living conditions of the Aboriginal people. We also visited Ayers Rock, in *Uluru-Kata Tjuta* National Park in Central Australia. This rock is one of the most secret and reverent places for the Aborigines. Here too, we sadly witnessed some Europeans and foreigners climb to the top of the rock despite vehement opposition from the elders, and even after being informed that many have lost their lives from such acts of desecration.

What we would like for readers to take away from our meetings and conversations with our contributors is their willingness to share their painful experiences within systems of domination and exclusion, and also the pride they all share in who they are as Indigenous peoples, and the hope they hold in a future where inclusion is the norm rather than an exception. In accordance with Indigenous ways of embarking on Indigenous research (what Linda Smith, the Maori scholar names "*Kuapapa* Maori Research"), a cultural and spiritual bond was established with each prospective author before they were invited to contribute. In addition, these initial meetings were to discuss with each prospective contributor the approach to be followed in telling and writing their story. This would be to put the focus on the storyteller/author placing him or her in the center, and to connect the project to Indigenous philosophies and worldviews and principles. It can thus be said that this anthology is to a large extent a truly collective effort rooted in the spirit of Indigenous research and oral tradition that is presented in the written form. This is the type of research Lester Irabanna-Rigney, in this volume, calls "Indigenist research," research that focuses on the lived historical experiences and struggles of Indigenous peoples. These are some of the efforts that Indigenous scholars and members of organizations that work at the grassroots level are making to join others in efforts to revitalize Indigenous ways of knowing and interpreting the cosmos.

Based on the value we place on oral tradition as a source of "data collection," this volume seeks to capture the traditional flavor and the atmosphere of tale-telling that adds authenticity to the stories. The stories and conversations presented in this anthology mirror the stories and voices of each contributor and are also a testimony of the inner yearning for storytelling that is part of being Indigenous. These stories and voices are expressions of the inhumanity in the history of Indigenous peoples and the arrogance of modernization that seeks to undermine and devalue other than Western cultural truths and ways of knowing. These are stories of wounded cultural and spiritual healers struggling against many odds to remember the past, engage with the present and formulate a better life for posterity. These voices invoke the democratic ideal of the right for Indigenous people to exist, search for their "truth" and tell and write their stories without conforming to the rigors of Western colonial methodologies. These voices also serve as conduits for venting out the pain, anger, frustration, and sometimes resentment that has resulted from being made invisible, silent and marginal. These authors are thus engaging in what Amadiume (1997) calls *nzagwalu*, an *Igbo* expression, for answering back when one has suffered many years of insult. Yet these stories and voices are also vehicles for healing, searching, teaching, learning and celebrating life and existence, as well as instruments to reclaim a part of our lives, that is, of being Indigenous.

This book signifies a struggle to rebuild the self-worth and self-esteem that Indigenous peoples lost through the dispossession of their land, the destruction of their spirituality and faith and ethnic identities tied to their land. Thus, while the renaissance continues in the political arena, the power and the significance of telling *our* stories increases in importance in the academy and in Indigenous communities. Such efforts, however, are made difficult by our own training so steeped in a Eurocentric and male-defined tradition that legitimizes and perpetuates the colonial mentality and way of telling or writing stories. In addition to the limitations imposed by this Euro-centered education, oral story telling is underrated and devalued because of the importance placed on reading and writing. Reading and writing, as well as the use of the imposed foreign languages of the colonizer, have diminished our ability to think creatively, culturally, and spiritually, while the printed word has constrained the minds and imaginations of Indigenous peoples whose thinking and speaking are grounded in the oral tradition.

Our storytelling began to be disempowered and dismembered the day the stranger began recording our stories by writing them down. From that day on, the stories started to change, they became a passive collection of words and phrases, sentences and paragraphs, pages of misinterpreted coding, derivative imagery, superficial characters and shallow portrayals. Indigenous cultural truths, historical teachings, spiritual depth, and *iintsomi* (or oral narrative) as methods of passing on and receiving knowledges and ancient wisdoms were undermined by the educated colonizer from the "civilized world," who viewed these ancient wisdoms as superstitious garbage that have no place in his "civilized world." The colonized peoples were often aware of these disparities and nullifying or interposing tendencies of colonial scholars. At times they simply gave the colonizer the versions of realities that they wanted to hear. Even worse, the colonized "non-white" "non-European," as the colonizer labeled the Indigenous in relation to the "master's" identity, were often reduced to justifying their own experiences in terms of the "master's" dominant culture. There can be no greater assault on a person's dignity than to be named in relation to what one is not, to have to justify one's existence, or apologize for who and what one is.

In a very few cases in these early writings by the colonizers is there any sense of the great and glorious history of Indigenous peoples. Rarely did the educated stranger write about Indigenous peoples' way of life as one with any positive virtues, nor was credit given for our ability to survive and adapt to the extreme conditions that the colonizers imposed on us. We were merely savages, set adrift on voyages of accidental discoveries. But taking into account the fact that Columbus thought he was in the East Indies when he "discovered" America, having actually plotted his course with the navigational aids of the day, and going to his deathbed unrepentant about the error he had made, Columbus still enjoys a hero's status, unparalleled among Western explorers in the Western world. The Indigenous peoples of Turtle Island (Native Americans) became "Indians" by default. To this day, history textbooks authors refuse to acknowledge the obvious monumental error that Columbus got lost in the Americas, and did not reach the shores of India. Such is the arrogance of the "discovery" myth, which renamed the entire group of people to justify European/ colonial "success," rather than acknowledge the tragedy of such exploits. This singular experience of Christopher Columbus is a powerful metaphor for countless Indigenous encounters with colonial powers.

This historical event also illustrates how a Western myth is perpetuated to give power and supremacy to the "planned and decisive discoveries" of the white man, and to recognize his superior knowledge in seafaring and navigation. Imperialists are very aware of the power of our stories to our cause, hence the shameless appropriation of our stories, and the co-optation of our imagery and symbols. European and Western scholars continue to inundate us with their stories in the written word, with books, including the Bible, and lending greater power to the written word, so that ironically, Indigenous peoples come to depend on their accounts to legitimize their historical accounts. It is doubly ironic that these scholars do not subscribe to the same written religious or legal principles that they insist Indigenous peoples follow. Similarly, colonial anthropologists have also placed themselves in positions of power that allow them to claim a right to have access to Indigenous sacred spaces and sites. These scholars are aware that their approach serves to channel us into levels of inferiority and weakness that devour the strength and eventually break the power of our stories and voices so grounded in oral tradition. Storytelling was and is always an important function in Indigenous communities. As we work our way through the multilayered, multifaceted storylines of Indigenous philosophies and world views; Indigenous ways of healing, teaching, learning and conducting research; issues about *izibongo* or panegyric legends; human rights; development, identity, oral tradition and history, Indigenous spirituality and religion, agriculture and architecture to name a few themes, we are always made aware of the spiritual and emotional well-being of Indigenous peoples. We are also made aware of the creativity, the beauty, the abundance of ideas, the depth of soul, the extended mental capacity, and the all-encompassing spirituality and richness of our cultures embedded in our stories.

During my visits with the elders Rangimarie Pere in New Zealand, and Kayano Shigeru in Nibutani, Hokkaido, Japan, they were pleased that the emphasis of the anthology was on oral storytelling, even though the final product would be in the written word. Although they have both written books and short stories, they spoke in one voice and lamented the loss of story and folktales in the so-called modern schools. "Deep in my heart I know that the loss of oral tradition in the lives of Maori youth and adults has robbed us of one of the foundations of our indigenous cultures," Pere said. At a different time and on a different continent, elder Shigeru commented on the value of storytelling in the Ainu culture. "It is using the positive powers of words, imagination, acting out, mime and embellishment to create an atmosphere for both the storyteller and the listeners to be engaged spiritually, emotionally and mentally. However, this is not to advocate for the importance of oral tradition over the written word. It is to remind the younger generation not to forget the Ainu ways of teaching and learning which are grounded in storytelling.

At the end of it all, we return to that compelling process with which this spiritual journey began. This suggests that Indigenous scholars, members of organizations at the grassroots level and other community members need to engage in a process to decolonize our minds and imaginations, revitalize our subconscious thinking and *indigenize* the format by which we tell and write our stories. This means going back to telling legends and narratives that are rooted in oral tradition, spirituality and other Indigenous ways of knowing. It sounds daunting, but that is precisely what contributors to this anthology have done! It has been a humbling and healing experience.

To our contributors, we say, *Siyenkosi kakhulu*, Thank you very much. To our readers, we say, may this humble project help you grow in the process of understanding us --- the Indigenous Peoples. We hope that you will use some of this information to broaden your horizons. We welcome your comments.

Camagu! Makube Chosi!
Kube Hele! Kube Njalo!
Ndiyema Kule Nginqi!
So be it!

Nomalungelo Goduka

Acknowledgements

Among all Indigenous traditions of peoples of the world is the cardinal principle of collective individuality. We want to first pay tribute to our Creator, *Umvelinqang*i in the Nguni tradition, and to the ancestors of African and all Indigenous peoples for the spirit which empowered us to persist in writing, rewriting and editing hundreds of pages of materials. This volume was made possible through the concerted synthetic efforts of various Indigenous peoples all over the globe and the editors owe invaluable debts to all authors in this volume who worked tirelessly to produce these evocative texts.

We want to acknowledge important people in this arduous task, particularly the various programs, committees, and colleagues from Central Michigan University for the financial support that enabled Lungie to travel to different parts of the world to meet and converse with numerous individuals, many of whom became contributors to this volume: Dr Phyllis Heath from the Department of Human Environmental Studies for her unrelenting support throughout; Mama Phyllis Jordan, one of the living Xhosa gurus, who read different drafts of the prologue and shared her wisdom with us; and students Melissa Brown and Tanya Wemple at CMU for reading and typing different drafts of this anthology.

Thanks also go to Dr Keibo Oiwa, teacher, writer, and translator at Meiji Gaskuin University in Yokohama, Japan, and his student Megu'u Ogata who served as Lungie's translators and friends throughout her visit to Tokyo and Hokkaido. Keibo arranged for all the meetings with Etsuko Aoki and Kiyoko Kitahara in Tokyo and with Kayano Shigeru and Koichi Kaizawa in Nibutana, Hokkaido; to Pat Dudgeon and Darlene Oxenham at the Centre for Aboriginal Studies at Curtin University in Perth, Western Australia, for hosting Lungie during her visit, and for introducing her to Pat Torres, one of the contributors to this volume; to Lester-Irabinna Rigney at Flinders University in Adelaide, Australia, for hosting both Julian and Lungie during our visit there in summer 1999 and to Lester for his contribution to this volume; to Dr Linda Tuhwai Smith, Director of the International Research Institute for Maori and Indigenous Education at the University of Auckland, in Auckland, New Zealand, for making Lungie's visit to the Institute possible to meet with faculty and students who work on Indigenous issues; to Dr Lee Anne Wilson who was then a visiting professor at the Polytechnicon in Wanganui, New Zealand, who made arrangements for Lungie to meet with elder Dr Rangimarie Turuki (Rose) Pere in Waikaremoana in Gisborne, and to Dr Pere who is one of the contributors to this volume; to Magdalena Broman, Director of the Working Group of Indigenous Minorities in Southern Africa (WIMSA), Windhoek, Namibia for arranging the meeting with Kxao Moses Oma and Axel Thoma, contributors to this anthology; to Dr Peter Gitu, visiting professor at the University of Arizona and from the University of Nairobi in Kenya for making arrangements for Lungie's meeting with Naomi Kipuri, one of the contributors in this anthology; to Ingwar Ahren, Director at the Gaaltjie Cultural Institute in Ostersund, Sweden for hosting Lungie at the Institute and to Nora Wasara Larson for serving as the translator at the ceremony for the earmarking of the reindeer calves; to Asa Verde for inviting Lungie to the Saami Summer Festival and her wedding in Ankarede and for contributing to this volume; and to Ellacarin Blind, a graduate student in the Department of Saami Studies at Umea University for making arrangements to visit Greta Huuva, Director at Ajtte Museum in Jokkmokk.

Special words of gratitude need to be extended to the Goduka family in South Africa and to Goduka immediate family in Mount Pleasant, Michigan, in particular Tando, Zipo, Makhonza and Akhona for their spiritual and emotional support.

To you all, we express our profound thanks, *"Sithi Ningadinwa Nangamso!"*

Julian would like to thank the University of Arizona's Africana Studies Department of the College of Humanities, specifically Dean Chuck Tatum, and the International Affairs office for support of his international travel in Africa and Australia and freelance editor Rose Byrne, as well as the Kunnie families in Arizona and Azania who need special mention, notably Kim, Mandla, and Sibusiso Kunnie.

Finally, we would be remiss if we neglected to acknowledge our indebtedness to Graham Harvey and Sarah Lloyd at Ashgate Publishing for their patience and support through the entire duration of this book project. We hope it was well worth the wait and the effort.

Julian Kunnie and Nomalungelo Goduka

Synopsis

In accordance with the principle of paying tribute to our elders, we ask for permission to speak from our elders. We also want to accord primordial voice to the oldest of Indigenous peoples, who declare: "We are Still Here!" Among Indigenous peoples of the world, the San people of Southern Africa and the Aboriginal people of Australia both trace their ancestry to a period 40,000 years ago. We thus want to initiate our volume by starting from the very beginning.

Kxao Moses, Oma, Axel Thoma and Elfriede Gaeses are activist representatives of the San nation who describe in clear detail the struggle against genocide and dispossession in Namibia, Botswana, and South Africa, against the derogatory designation of "Bushmen" ascribed to them by the Eurocentric world, and for self-determination and survival in a harsh and hostile environment. They illuminate issues of land struggles, cultural conflicts and formal education, economic survival, and the avenue of tourism and its effects. The situation of the San nation has reached such desperate proportions that they have been forced to resort to a dependence on tourism as a way of generating revenues for economic sustenance. There is a tacit recognition on the part of these authors that tourism signifies a double-edged sword: it generates income but leaves the door open for cultural objectification, exploitation, and commodification by the agents of Western imperialism. Ultimately, Kxao Moses ǂOma, Axel Thoma and Elfriede Gaeses express the hope that they will be able to establish a viable socio-economic way of life that is in harmony with the best tenets of their historical culture, that they will be left alone by imperialist hegemony and have their confiscated ancestral lands returned and be accorded the right of self-determination for the future. They insist that their Indigenous knowledge has empowered the San people to survive for scores of millennia, and they would like the world to both respect and recognize this historical truth.

Among the Aboriginal people of Australia, there is a similar yearning for self-determination and demand for materialization of the rights of survival and nationhood amidst genocidal policies of European colonialism. Pat Torres, from the *Yawurungany* tradition of Western Australia, recounts the powerful roots of her tradition. Named *Mamanyjun* at birth by her parents for a red berry that grows along the coastal bushlands in northern Western Australia in the area known as Quondong, north of Broome, Western Australia, this strong woman appreciates her culture as an Indigenous woman. She underscores the continued relevance of the *mamanyjun* berry, which was very important to the diet and social systems of ancestral relations and is still so for Yawuru people today, and notes the intricate and intimate relationship of animals, plants, and human beings to each other and to the sacred web of life. The Aboriginal world is permeated with spiritual beings who have always communicated with those people living, and this tradition must be preserved for future generations of Aboriginal people, *Mamanyjun* concludes.

Lester-Irabinna Rigney is an Indigenous Narrungga Australian who argues for an Indigenist research methodology when it comes to research on Indigenous people. Irabinna Rigney provides a very instructive critique of Western European approaches in research, which have most often promoted white supremacy while objectifying and primitivizing Indigenous people. He asserts that all knowledge is culturally and historically specific and never universally generalizable as Western European epistemologies have falsely posed. He challenges the hegemonic character of Western constructions of knowledge and insists that Indigenous people need to be at the heart of Indigenist research, that knowledge about Indigenous people must be informed by Indigenous people themselves, and that it must be emancipating in function as opposed to replicating the colonial status quo. He calls for a politicized ground of research that is actively involved in the decolonization project. Indigenist research, according to Irabinna Rigney, is geared toward serving the needs of Indigenous people and must be primarily informed by Indigenous people as opposed to demeaning of the knowledge systems of Indigenous people. He demands a respect and recognition of the autonomous validity and potency of Indigenous knowledge systems, arguing that Indigenous approaches and paradigms be employed when engaging in research on Indigenous people, where their interests, experiences, and aspirations are at the center of all such research efforts.

From the Turtle Island context, Laara Fitznor poignantly illustrates the struggles of living in colonial Canada as a Cree woman of multi-ethnic identity, because of the imposition of European colonial definitions of identity of Indigenous people in Canada, such as "Metis" status Indigenous people. Laara Fitznor describes in moving detail the personal tragedies that she and her family have experienced in negotiating their survival in the Cree-Euro-Canadian world and the manner that her Indigenous Cree tradition and heritage continues to thrive amidst this painful continuous assault on Cree people, particularly those of mixed heritage. Fitznor explains that she was raised in a traditional Cree community and environment, spiritually grounded in the power of Mother Earth, and engaging in traditional ceremonies around fishing and harvesting which were the principle means of livelihood for Cree people. These traditions were foundational in anchoring Fitznor in her Cree identity and assisted her in resisting colonial impositions in terms of her own identity and that of her community. The wisdom of the elders as described in Laara Fitznor's chapter remind us of the incredible power of Indigenous peoples' resilience and perseverance in a context of colonialism and genocide.

Jennifer Nez Denetdale is a member of the Dineh nation (also known as the Navajo) of the American Southwest. She elaborates on the struggle to define and describe her community's history and experience from a Dineh viewpoint, challenging the normative Eurocentric depictions of Dineh in history books and anthropological texts. She insists that the roots of Dineh culture, derived from thousands of years in the Southwest as an independent nation, were disrupted and invaded by Spanish and then Anglo colonial cultures. She recounts the painful memories of *Asdsaa*

Tá'ógí, otherwise known as Juanita, the wife of Manuelito, the Dineh leader who led the resistance movement against the European colonial armies until the Treaty of Hidalgo Guadalupe was signed in 1848. By reconstructing the experiences of *Asdsąą Tá'ógí* through recollection of oral narratives and photographs, the author here is able to shed light on the dynamic matrilineal traditions of the Dineh nation, unmasking the layers of Eurocentric patriarchal depictions that usually make Dineh women invisible. The decisive role that elders play in this persevering Indigenous tradition in the southwestern region of Turtle Island is underscored in Jennifer Nez Denetdale's chapter.

Roxana Ng writes about "Exploring Healing and the Body Through Chinese Medicine," from the perspective of an Indigenous Chinese-descended Canadian educator and psychological counselor. Realizing that she had been victimized by the Western European so-called Puritan work ethic following an illness, she awakens to the potency of her own ancestral traditions that recognize the complement of both body and mind in the healing process, in contradistinction to Western approaches that elevate the mind to the negation of the body, and vice versa. Ng describes in clear detail the complexity of *Qi Gong*, an adjunct practice of Chinese medicine, and how she took up Tai Ji Juan and yoga as part of a regular exercise regime, as part of the inclusion of Chinese medicine in the therapeutic and healing process. Her interesting chapter outlines the various steps of breathing and meditation in the healing process. Like the Taoist principles of the harmonization of the *ying* and the *yang*, traditional Chinese medicine articulates the delicate but essential balance between the *Qi* (the energy flow) and the body. Roxana Ng's seriousness in the healing process has revolutionized the manner that she teaches her students and engages in therapy sessions, underscoring the interwoven interconnectedness of mind, body, and breath. She asks her students to incorporate their body experiences into the healing process, urging them to engage in an intense self-reflexivity that affirms each component while struggling to maintain all three in harmonic balance with each other. She concludes her chapter by celebrating the re-discovery of the spiritual power of the body and the fact of her reconstruction of the "I-body" relationship, a discovery that she readily and happily shares with her students. For Ng, this form of Indigenous knowing and being has not only liberated her from the pain of past physical ailments, but also transformed her into a more centered and stronger person, a concrete practical application of the power of Indigenous wisdom.

From the South American context, Miryam Espinosa-Dulanpo pens an engaging chapter on the power of Indigenous Muchik Wisdom. Lamenting the fact of having to write in a colonial language and struggling as a Mestiza for the preservation of the Muchik tradition, Espinosa-Dulanpo offers an engaging fictional story about the Tellervo, a luscious tree that functions as the pivot of an Indigenous community and whose existence is threatened by the invasion of colonial predators bent on extracting the "dark heavy liquid" from deep below the earth's surface. The anecdote furnishes a satirical critique of the system of Western industrialism and "civilization," while constructively proposing a collective resistance that preserves the Tellervo tree and its relations with the community. Espinosa-Dulanpo's poetry provides much food for thought and is a penetrating reminder of the pain of Indigenous people in celebrating Indigenous Muchik culture while all the time resisting forms of dehumanization, particularly against women.

Dianne Stewart's contribution to this volume is quite distinctive. She highlights the dynamism of African-derived religions in Jamaica, specifically the practice of *Kumina* in eastern Jamaica. *Kumina* signifies the collective memory of African people in Jamaica, invoking the power of the ancestors and that of *Nzambi*, the Creator, as carried from the BaKongo heritage during the crucible of slavery in the 18th century. *Kumina* refers to the practice of ceremonies performed at events of birth, rites of initiation, during healing, and death, Stewart explains. *Kumina* instills a sense of revitalization among adherents and reinvigorates its practitioners, particularly empowering those who are afflicted by personal woes or social marginalization. *Kumina*, according to Stewart, exhibits the potency of Indigenous African spirituality and reflects the creativity of Indigenous wisdom traditions that enable Africans whose forebears were enslaved and brutalized by the scourge of the whip and the violence of the lash, to remember their valiant ancestors' courage and to thrive in a modern society that continues to scorn the aesthetics of Indigenous African religio-culture and dismiss it as "primitive."

Moving to the Pacific, the instructive anecdotal rendition by Rangimarie Turuki Pere on the complexity of Maori wisdom, substantiates the contention that Indigenous people, contrary to hegemonic Eurocentric views, are far from simplistic. Turuki Pere is an Indigenous Maori woman who is proud of her heritage and culture and shares intricate stories from her tradition about which most non-Maori people have little clue. Her chapter delves into the sophisticated value system of Maori culture, and how she learned from growing up alongside four generations. Maori concepts, like other Indigenous concepts, are often extremely difficult to translate precisely into English parlance because of cosmological differences and cultural nuances. *Hinengaro*, for instance, is the Maori word for the source of thoughts and emotions and the manner that one perceives reality, hardly encapsulated in a single English word. Turuki Pere describes in fine detail the various cardinal principles of Maori wisdom such as *Aroha*, the principle of divine love, and recounts the numerous institutions of worship, ceremony, counsel, eating, and community such as the *Marae*, the complex meeting house. Turuki-Pere also provides fascinating accounts of Maori cosmos stories that feature the plethora of divinities extant in the religious world of the Maori and how these divinities relate to human beings and the rest of the natural world, all organically linked in an inescapable web of harmony and reciprocity. It is evident from Rangimarie Turuki Pere's chapter that the process of healing within Maori culture, for example, is extremely complex, being pursued on multiple planes and across several generations, encompassing all spheres of personal and social existence, and connected to the vast spirit world beyond that of the terrestrial sphere. Turuki Pere closes with the prayer to *Aio*, the supreme being of divinity, who furnishes stability and wholeness, light and darkness, restoration and regeneration to all of creation and whose power is central in Maori ceremony and practice.

Chapter 10 introduces the Indigenous peoples in Asia, with an enlightening look at life among the Ainu of Japan. Through several narrators from the Ainu community in this chapter, Etsuko Aoki, Kiyoko Kitahara, elder Kayano, Kayano Shigeru, Koichi Kaizawa, Yuriko and Masamitsu Takiguchi, the power of Indigenous Ainu ancestral wisdom resonates powerfully throughout the narrative. Etsuko Aoki recounts her family history of hardship, many of her parents' generation having been forced to work as day laborers for Japanese industries, resulting in a form of internalized oppression in which Ainu people ultimately suffered self-hate and self-deprecation. In Etsuko's case, her brother, Sakai, was imprisoned for his involvement in the Ainu resistance movement and his life eventually was taken, supposedly in a drowning "accident" in a local canal. All of the elements of colonized life apply to the Ainu of Japan: chronic underpayment for labor, police harassment, unjust imprisonment, and refusal by the dominant society to recognize the legitimacy of Ainu culture. Kiyoko Kitahara describes how she struggled to preserve the Ainu language despite the denial of its legitimacy by the Japanese government. She fought to teach her son the Ainu tradition, practicing entrance ceremonies for instance. Elder Kayano, also a noted author, who narrates stories of folk wisdom such as "Why the Black Hawk Owl is Ugly," talks about the origins of the Ainu people and declares that Ainu culture is alive and well, persistent in preserving ancestral ways, tending the trees and the forests, and living in harmony with the natural world. Koichi Kaizawa notes that his father was one of the Ainu legends who fought to preserve the Saru River and the surrounding Nibutani lands. He shares glowingly the dynamic ceremonies such as the *chip-sanke* festival in the neighbouring museum, used to launch boats in the water each year in defiance of the dominant Japanese policy of cultural assimilation. It was Koichi Kaizawa's father who persevered in opposing the construction of the Nibutani dam which would flood Ainu lands. Masamitsu Takiguchi is a deaf Ainu sculptor, working with wood, whose life centers around carving and the spiritual power of wood. Takiguchi asserts that wood is never "dead" but filled with spiritual lessons for all, signifying an important element of Indigenous Ainu wisdom.

In Chapter 11, Pramod Parajuli describes the perspectives of Indigenous communities in Jharkhand, India, known in local parlance as *Adivasis*. Parajuli, an activist with the Social Movements Learning Project in Jharkhand, explores the subject of complex and multi-layered identities among the *Adivasis* of this part of the world, illuminating struggles for self-determination and ecological survival. The question of self-governance for such Indigenous peoples is primordial, particularly in the wake of Western European industrialization and modernization that has fractured ecological systems, decimated forests, and flooded lands through dam construction in these communities. Parajuli argues that the *Adivasis* have had historical institutions and practices of self-governance for generations prior to Western models, and proposes "ecological ethnicities" as a way of re-defining ethnic and cultural identity of *Adivasis*, so that issues like historical attachment to ancestral lands and harmonious co-existence with diverse ecological and geographical phenomena can be addressed. The ultimate objective then is to preserve the historical cultures of *Adivasis* and ensure that they thrive in a hostile and hegemonic world of mechanization and commodification.

Chapter 12 furnishes a glimpse of the generally unknown history, culture, and cosmology of the Indigenous Saami people of Sweden and Norway. As writer Asa Virdi Kroik notes in his description of the village of Vuornese in southern Lapland, it "is a rich cultural place with a clear continuity of the Saami's life in the region today." Kroik describes the power of Indigenous ancestral narratives that bespeaks a culture of religious harmony with the dear Mother Earth and all of creation. She narrates the bear ceremony, a long-time practice of the Saami that signifies their closeness to the world of four-leggeds, to the point that all vocations, including hunting, are viewed as sacred pursuits. So too, Kroik notes the existence of the cairns in the mountains of Klimpfjll and Biasjˆn, Dajmanjapp and Ingermanland, reminding the Saami of their far-reaching ancestral presence in these parts of Scandinavia. Rock art paintings found in the hills of Ingermanland confirm a complex history of cultural dynamism that the Saami are struggling to re-discover and re-claim. Asa Virdi Kroik laments the fact that so many of the Saami ancestral bones, instruments, and belongings, have been excavated and stolen by the museums of Western science, and insists that they need to be returned immediately to the Saami people, as such excavation represents cultural desecration. The ancestral spirits represent the spirit of those who have passed on to the spirit world, and not the "dead," as in European traditions, she argues, and hence the need to have various belongings of those who are buried travel with them in the journey to the other side. The buried drum and reindeer sacrifice serve as axiological reminders of the spiritual value attached to the drum, since the Saami feared that Europeans would destroy this vital religio-cultural symbol among their people. The oral tradition of the Saami people is still very alive, Kroik explains, and needs to be preserved in an age of imposed European cultural values.

Finally, the book goes full circle, returning to the African continent. Vimbai Chivaura in Chapter 13 makes a strong pitch for the assertion of Indigenous African values in the post-colonial context of Zimbabwe and contends that the wellspring of ancestral wisdom of the Shona and Ndebele traditions of Zimbabwe possess much from which Africans can draw for attaining political, economic, and social independence. He is critical of the Euro-philiac culture of Africans in Zimbabwe who often tend to emulate European value systems and denigrate their own in the development project. Chivaura elaborates on the sophistication and solidity of African knowledge systems which have humanistic ethics at their heart and harmony with the natural world as their focus, unlike the conflictual and capitalistic paradigm of development fostered by Eurocentric philosophical systems. He also notes that African wisdom is trans-temporal and function as survival strategies in harsh environments of oppression and exploitation because they are geared toward maintaining the foundational balance between the spiritual and material realms, the personal and the collective, and the economic and the social realms of society. Africa's Indigenous wisdom resources thus offer much through its countless proverbs, maxims, and folk-stories to establish a mode of development and national liberation of the continent that caters to the social, economic, and technological needs of her people, and Africans need to extricate themselves from an unhealthy epistemological dependence on the West, Chivaura concludes.

Somadoda Fikeni renders a powerful chapter on the complexity and gravity of the Indigenous *Izibongo* tradition among the Xhosa-speaking people of South Africa. He cogently critiques how European translations failed to comprehend the foundational role of *Izibongo* in Nguni societies, mistakenly reducing them to pyra-legends, and proceeds to illustrate in delineated detail the all-encompassing significance of *Izibongo* within the Xhosa culture and society, including critical areas of naming, personal identity and clan affiliation, the concept of *ubuntu*, birth, childhood and initiation, marriage and family, and their foundational role in the political life of the community, particularly with regard to leadership. Fikeni argues that the *Izibongo* tradition wields enough power to assume a formidable role in entrenching the concept and practice of *ubuntu* in reconstructing post-apartheid South Africa following almost four centuries of colonial degradation and conquest of African lands and peoples.

Kenyan author Noami Kipuri, with the Arid Lands Resource Management office in Kenya, provides an important perspective on the concerns of Indigenous peoples by defining and expanding the concept of "Indigenous" with specific reference to the Maasai people of Kenya. She observes importantly that the concept of "Indigenous" in Africa "has not been useful in the identification of poor vulnerable communities, since most Africans are Indigenous to Africa in the sense of having their origins in the continent..." and argues that the notion of "Indigenous" has in fact been used to further humiliate and subjugate African people who resist Western European cultural, economic, and social systems. Kipuri's chapter makes some excellent points on the manner in which Indigenous peoples continue to be the primary victims of modern Western-imposed political and economic systems in Africa. This is exemplified by the marginalization and alienation of Indigenous peoples like the Maasai and the Samburu from traditional ancestral land bases and herd grazing areas under colonial definitions of national borders, and the carving out of game parks and reserves from Indigenous peoples' homelands. Moreover, Indigenous peoples have their national rights consistently violated because of the widespread perception that Indigenous peoples are "backward" and not fully "civilized." This is compounded by the continued failure of the Kenyan government to consult with Indigenous peoples on issues affecting their land and livelihood, whereby groups like the Maasai are denied the right of access to elements foundational to their cultures such as lands that contain medicinal plants, fuel, wood, water, and animal products. Indigenous people are the only people who demonstrate cultural distinctiveness, yet their distinctiveness is systematically exploited for economic gain in the form of tourism, cultural shows, and "exotic" attractions for outsiders; and Indigenous peoples are systematically locked out of political representation and marginalized by policies that refuse to recognize the distinctive needs of Indigenous peoples in areas of political representation and advocacy, formal education, and social organization. The fraudulent nature of the Westminister form of democracy in places like Kenya, where politics has been reduced to a contest of individuals and opposition tendencies, are geared merely to replace certain individuals with others, leaving the undemocratic status quo intact, and further ensuring the removal of Indigenous peoples from the Eurocentric, neo-colonial African political ethos. Kipuri closes her chapter with a clarion call to more effective organizing and networking among all Indigenous peoples around the world, so that Indigenous peoples' survival and interest are ensured for future generations, which ultimately effects all of humanity and life on the Mother Earth.

Julian Kunnie provides closure to the anthology by discussing a critical issue particularly in the wake of the devastating effects of globalization which, we argue, is a euphemism or ideological veneer for re-colonization of the colored peoples of the world by the West. Kunnie demonstrates how all Indigenous traditions possess philosophical and analytical frameworks to foster cultures that cherish and protect human rights, not only in their individual communities, but in other societies of the world. He provides the historical backdrop of human rights preservation among various Indigenous cultures and subsequently suggests the concrete implications of Indigenous philosophies for human rights discourses, with particular regard to women, children, workers, the poor, and the environment, so desperately needed in a world dominated so heavily by Western European cultural and economic systems.

Julian Kunnie

Ancient Indigenous Cultures

Chapter 1

Indigenous San Knowledge and Survival Struggles

Kxao Moses ǂOma and Axel Thoma

Introduction

The San people are the oldest peoples of Southern Africa, tracing their history back some forty thousand years and numbering about 100 000 today. We resent being classified in European anthropology and pejoratively viewed as 'Bushmen' by most white people. We are among the earliest cultures of Africa and are proud of this far-reaching heritage. Our closeness to the natural world and our Creator ought not be construed as 'backward' and 'primitive' as so much of the Western world characterizes us. We are human beings like any other, yet we are distinctive in that we have lived on Mother Earth as people longer than most others.

We were dominated by other Indigenous African groups who moved south primarily from eastern Africa during the migrations prior to the medieval era of the first millennium CE, and were subsequently colonized by the Europeans who forced their way northwards from the Cape in southern Africa in the 1600s. These land-hungry pastoralist groups dispossessed the San of their land base and consequently their natural resources. Even under the independent governments of Namibia and Botswana this dispossession continues through so-called integration and resettlement processes.

It is estimated that only 10 per cent of the present San population still have access to their former natural resources, and only 3 per cent are currently allowed to manage their natural resources and exercise their traditional hunting rights. This land and resource loss has had an extensively negative impact on the San, particularly in terms of limiting their prospects for living according to their age-old cultures.

In this chapter, we will discuss obstacles to San survival, issues of land, economy and employment, and illuminate the issue of tourism as an avenue of economic support in the wake of the threatened genocide of our people.

Culture and Economy

The San consider their cultural practices to constitute the backbone of a healthy and socially intact community. The disruptions to an Indigenous culture caused by the injustice of land and resource dispossession are such that the affected community is unable to uphold its traditional consensual decision-making processes. For ages the San people had practiced democracy through the vehicle of community consensus, so that decisions that did not have the general approval of the membership of the community were never implemented. Today colonization has taken a devastating toll on our political and social institutions. However, the memory of a once strong and unified community awakens and rejuvenates the longing for the revival and reconstruction of culture and identity.

The recent introduction of tourism-based undertakings among San communities, forced onto us and other colonized Indigenous peoples by our economic deprivation, has made the San aware that their culture is a valuable social and economic asset. However we are fully aware that those communities which emphasize the income-generating potential of their culture risk the further demise of their culture if they perform cultural practices exclusively for the sake of tourists rather than also for the well-being of their communities.

One of the communities involved in running the Omatako Valley Rest Camp in Botswana appeared to have ceased the practice of its healing traditions, but after a neighboring community performed for visitors to the camp, this community seems to have regained its awareness of the social value of practices such as the healing trance dances. The San group that volunteered to dance for tourists at the camp came from an adjacent village where tradition still plays a significant role in community life. A decision was reached that the traditional dances would in the future serve the dual purpose of entertaining tourists and resolving societal differences. The trance dance in particular provides a means of healing and simultaneously enhancing the spiritual life of a San community.

Although some San youth still refuse to openly admit that their cultural practices have social value, they are prepared to learn more about such traditional skills as the ability to identify animal tracks, the knowledge of edible bush foods and the use of medicinal plants because they have recognized that these skills enable them to generate income.

Since the impact of colonization produced a genocide that annihilated millions of San people, we are compelled to pursue all strategies that would equip us to survive this holocaust. It thus behooves us to transform an activity like tourism to our optimal advantage so long as our culture is not denigrated and prostituted, which does occur among other colonized peoples, like for example the Indigenous people of Hawaii. Ironically, although tourism is a Western phenomenon it has fostered the cultural revival of San communities, especially among San youth who seem to have lost interest in their heritage. For one, it elevates the position of elderly community members as the teachers of San traditions. It remains to be seen whether other San communities involved in tourism will experience the same positive cultural impact as that experienced by the community at the Omatako Valley Rest Camp.

Indigenous San Values and Tourism

The governments of the southern African region have all decided to promote tourism in the region. This decision means that many San communities are confronted by the tourism industry whether they accept it or not. However, it is equally important for the economic vulnerability of San people not to be exploited and for us not to be uncritical of the manner that tourism is conducted in our communities.

Governments, private enterprise and development workers claim that the San should be allowed to make their own decisions regarding their participation in the tourism industry. Yet, is this sincere and real? As things stand, the reality for the majority of San communities means not having the necessary power to manage our own natural resources, nor even rights of access to these resources. In other words, reality for many San means a life of extreme poverty and marginalization, and communities in this situation may feel forced to participate in tourism activities because these activities constitute the only available source of income.

The decision on whether or not to participate in the tourism industry may be hampered by the San's lack of information about and experience of the impact of tourism on their community life. Nongovernmental organizations (NGOs) such as Working Group of Indigenous Minorities in Southern Africa (WIMSA) have been requested by various San communities to provide the information we need, assistance in obtaining legal advice, and training on tourism-related topics.

The traditional skills still practiced by the San pertain to game hunting and identifying and tracking wild animals, gathering and preparing bush foods, producing crafts, identifying and applying medicinal plants, and healing individuals and communities through traditional dances. Middle-aged and elderly San community members have a vast knowledge of these skills, yet these are not viewed as 'professional' knowledge in the eyes of the dominant society at large. This may be due to the fact that these skills are taught to the young on a trial-and-error basis or through a learning-by-doing approach, but not in an institution following a set curriculum. Only time will tell whether tourism will help the larger society recognize and promote the San's skills as an acknowledged profession, or whether these skills will continue to be relegated to the realms of 'myth.'

Hunting is traditionally the domain of men. The hunting skills of the San comprise, among other things, the management of natural resources including game, knowing where game browse according to seasonal changes and tracking them accordingly, as well as producing poisoned arrows with which to hunt. The skills of a San hunter are so profoundly sharp that he is able to interpret from an animal's tracks whether that animal is male or female, young or old, weak or strong. The San hunter is also able to determine the time at which the animal passed a certain place, whether or not it searched for water or a particular food, whether there were other animals of the same kind accompanying it and whether or not it was followed by a predator.

Unlike in most Western societies, there is a complementary division of labor between women and men in San society. Women and children are chiefly in charge of gathering bush foods. They too have a highly sensitized and specialized knowledge of these foods, including the harvest time of particular varieties, sustainable harvesting systems and cultivation methods to support higher yields. Women especially have distinctive botanical knowledge vital for the sustenance of the community. The gatherers often act as informants for the hunters with respect to game present in a vicinity. Women and children in particular know how to interpret game tracks.

The preparation of certain bush foods also requires specific skills. These foods have to be made easily digestible and any poison they may contain must be removed. This knowledge possessed by San women could be invaluable to nutritionists and researchers of nutrition if they recognized and respected the scientific basis of our knowledge.

San women, men and children are all involved in the production of arts and crafts. The wide range of crafts produced includes jewelry, tools and household items. Craft production requires a thorough knowledge of the materials used, such as ostrich eggshells, leather, wood, dried fruits and tree bark. It also requires an artistic talent for design.

Traditional San doctors possess a vast knowledge of medicinal plants. They understand the intricate manner that such plants need to be prepared for medicinal purposes and the complex application process required for treating a range of diseases. As part of the healing process, dances of the San are performed in the treating of diseases. These dances are performed under the guidance of a healer who has special powers. The dances are performed not only to cure individual illnesses but also community ills, underscoring the inextricable interwoven character of personal health and community well-being. The community sees itself as an extension of the individual, and individuals view themselves as inseparable and indivisible from the community. Individuality is strictly organically and collectively defined. No individual can be independently successful without benefiting the community at large, unlike the privatized individualism of Western societies where singular individuality is valued and prized.

If tourists are to appreciate the uniqueness of the San's skills it is vital that they be sensitive, open minded, well informed, devoid of Eurocentric biases and distortions and interested in specific areas of our culture. It can be assumed that the ordinary tourist romanticizes the perceived 'primitiveness' of the San's skills without recognizing the underlying knowledge of the practitioners. Only those tourists who have rejected the Eurocentric depictions and descriptions of Africans and other Indigenous peoples and who eschew racial arrogance and are prepared to learn from another culture will be able to recognize and promote the San's skills as having professional value.

Constraints Facing San Peoples

Most San communities face the socio-economic problems similar to other colonized Indigenous peoples such as the Aboriginal people of Australia. These include insecurity of land tenure, loss of culture and identity, lack of education and adequate health care, the pain of alcoholism wrought by colonial culture and a high unemployment rate.

• *Land*

In many conferences the San have stressed that land is life for us. Without land we are nothing. We cannot maintain the integrity of our historical and cultural identity without being able to live in harmony with and on our ancestral lands. Land is the 'water of life' for us, as with all Indigenous peoples. Land signifies the place where our ancestors are buried and is thus sacred, providing us with all the necessary ingredients for life. Cutting us from the land is severing us from our spiritual axis in Mother Earth. Like other Indigenous peoples who have been dispossessed of their lands by European colonialism, San communities throughout southern Africa have been deprived of their ancestral land. We are the most land-deprived community in this part of the world, with many government policies decrying our use of the land as 'primitive' and economically unproductive, essentially viewing our residence and utilization of the land as wasteful. The result has been constant relocation and dislocation of our people from our traditional land domain.

The Namibian government has been trying to evict the Kxoe community from their ancestral land in western Caprivi, and WIMSA, the NGO Working Group of Indigenous Minorities in Southern Africa, has helped the Kxoe obtain legal advice to prevent this. Acting on behalf of the Kxoe leaders, the Legal Assistance Centre in Windhoek took the case to the Namibian High Court in the late 1990s, but the Court has yet to announce its decision.

In Botswana almost all San have been moved out of the Central Kalahari Game Reserve. A number of them agreed to move because the Botswana government promised them cattle and a good infrastructure in their new settlements. Those San who remained in the reserve later felt forced to move out when the Botswana Ministry of Local Government announced that all services would be stopped for residents of the reserve.

A group of San in South Africa is claiming part of the Kalahari Gemsbok National Park as their ancestral land. The South African government's Department of Land Affairs supports this claim, but the National Parks Board and the neighboring Mier people do not.

• *Culture and identity*

Without land and natural resources the San are unable to maintain their culture and identity. If, for example, neighboring non-San groups drive too many cattle onto San land, the bush-food supply will decrease and an essential part of San culture – the gathering of bush food and medical plants – will not continue.

In a bid to stop such threats to our culture we have requested WIMSA to coordinate a regional oral history project with the help of the Kuru Development Trust in Botswana and the South African San Institute. The members of the WIMSA board of trustees will determine the practicalities of this project at future meetings. However, the importance of the San themselves being the implementers of this project has been stressed to all parties involved.

• **Education**

It has become apparent that the governments of South Africa, Botswana and Namibia have each responded to the San's educational and linguistic needs in distinctly different ways. The post-apartheid South African authorities acknowledge the existence of Indigenous populations in that country and guarantee them certain rights, such as the promotion of their languages.

The government of Botswana prefers, as do the governments of Zambia and Zimbabwe, not to explicitly recognize the particular needs of their Indigenous populations, and in Botswana it appears that the San's rights have been curtailed and ignored rather than supported by the government. However, the Second National Commission on Education in Botswana recommended renaming the National Setswana Language Council as the Botswana Languages Council, thereby providing the opportunity for minority groups to voice their aspirations.

Namibia's Ministry of Basic Education and Culture (MBEC) has actively advocated the San's educational and linguistic needs and rights, particularly through the Intersectoral Task Force Committee on Educationally Marginalized Children which the ministry established in early 1996. The task force has been assisting educational programs serving San communities, and it supported the First Secondary School San Learners' Conference held in Windhoek in 1996. During the First Regional Conference on Development Programs for Africa's San Populations held in Windhoek in 1992 and on numerous occasions thereafter the San of the region, as a united body, stressed their concerns regarding education and language.

One important concern is that San children have limited access to schooling. The San in Botswana and Namibia are aware that the ministries responsible for education in these countries have placed the construction of new schools in rural areas high on their lists of priorities, but in fact a large number of San children in both countries must still walk very long distances to reach the nearest school. As a result the students arrive at school exhausted or their attendance at school is highly irregular, especially during the winter.

The alternative here is being accommodated in a school hostel, but this option is not much appreciated by the San, especially young children who miss their familiar home environment, largely because a school hostel does not facilitate any freedom of choice and does not provide the emotional security that the extended clan's home environment provides. San people, like most Indigenous peoples, are collectively defined and a gregarious people. Their family units are closely knit, unlike those of European family structures. A great number of San children must endure the prejudice of their classmates and teachers who manifest their prejudice by ridiculing, bullying, discriminating against, and verbally and physically abusing San children. This hostility towards the San reinforces their sense of alienation from the larger society.

At most schools in southern Africa the San children constitute a small minority, thus they often feel dominated by children from other more aggressive ethnic groups. Almost all teachers of classes with San children belong to other ethnic groups, and they too have internalized the prevailing regional prejudice against the San culture. Consequently, many teachers lack an understanding of and sensitivity towards the cultural norms, values and beliefs of San students.

The curricula in most southern Africa schools generally do not acknowledge the unique traditions and cultures of the San either, with the exception of social studies, which in certain countries of the region refers to the San in very general terms when describing the ethnic groups of those countries. The lack of culturally appropriate curricula contributes significantly to the San's loss of cultural identity and self-esteem.

Another major concern of the San is the language instruction at government schools, which in Namibia and Botswana is either English, Afrikaans, or Setswana. San representatives have repeatedly requested mother-tongue education at least at the primary school level. This would enable students to grasp primary concepts in all their subjects and to express themselves clearly in the classroom, which would substantially enhance their education. To teach San children effectively in their mother tongue, teachers, and preferably San teachers, should be taught to read and write in a San language. Learning and teaching materials should be developed through the collaboration of educators, linguists, and most importantly, members of the community. The development of a standardized orthography of San languages has long been a deep concern of San delegates to WIMSA meetings, and this possibility is being seriously investigated.

Another concern of San leaders is the overall high dropout rate among the San, particularly among San girls 16 or 17 years old who are often forced by circumstance to leave school before completing their education. The high dropout rate of San pupils of both sexes can be ascribed to all the factors cited above which contribute to the students' academic failure or social insecurity or both. The significantly higher dropout rate among teenage girls can largely be ascribed to pregnancy and early marriage. Many a San husband refuses to allow his wife to continue with her schooling.

The majority of San parents cannot afford to pay school fees and purchase school uniforms for their children, and as a result their 'popularity' with school principals is diminished. In Namibia, although it is unlawful to refuse a child admission to school, many school principals do so on the grounds that the child does not have a uniform and cannot afford to pay school fees.

The San of southern Africa hope to see their communities provided with schools closer to where they live, their children taught in their mother tongue, teachers sensitized to San culture, culturally appropriate curricula, teenage mothers allowed to continue their schooling, and school expenses made affordable for all. It is an eye-opening exercise to compare the San's educational hopes to the current reality of the schools San students attend and the education policies in South Africa, Botswana and Namibia.

Difficulties commonly experienced by San children and their parents in terms of contemporary practices involve corporal punishment, teacher-centered approaches and a passive learning process. This reality is contrary to the San's child-rearing philosophy, which emphasizes that children should live with almost no restrictions and be naturally exposed to all facets of the daily lives of the adults around them, and learn by doing and by listening to traditional stories told around the fireside at night. The current school reality is also inconsistent with the educational reform policies developed by the relevant ministries in South Africa, Botswana and Namibia, which focus on, inter alia, child-centered approaches, active learning processes and the pupils' life experiences.

Teachers and development workers often complain about the lack of parental involvement in school matters and the regularity of a child's attendance at school. The reluctance of parents to become involved may be ascribed to the high number of adults, particularly mothers, who did not attend school themselves and who thus regard institutional learning as an alien concept. There are also parents whose memories of their school days are despoiled by negative experiences and who therefore wish to avoid any further involvement with a school. Many of the older generation are opposed to formal schooling out of a painful awareness of the increasing devaluation of traditional skills and beliefs and of the declining respect paid by young formally educated San to the views of their elders.

To enable an evaluation of whether and how the San have been able to influence their own educational development, the outlines below will focus on the current state of affairs in South Africa, Botswana and Namibia. Though there are common issues obtaining in each country, there are also significant differences.

San Schools in South Africa

Since 1991 the majority of the San in South Africa, that is 4 000 !Xu and Kxoe, have lived in a tent town at Schmidtsdrift near Kimberly. Although the children have access to schooling because there is a school situated in the town area, their irregularity of attendance increases during winter. The pupils are taught in Afrikaans rather than their mother tongue, and according to the standard Northern Cape Education Department curriculum. Individual teachers try to incorporate the pupils' life experiences into the learning process but the majority of Afrikaans-speaking teachers needs to be sensitized to the San's culture. The Schmidtsdrift school is a primary and secondary school, thus it accommodates students from grades 1 to 12. Dropout rates have recently increased, as some of the youth have elected to leave school to work on nearby farms for a cash income.[1] Poverty is a major factor in the phenomenally high dropout rates of the San, a condition further exploited by

---

1   Nyati-Ramahobo, L., 'Language in Education and the Quality of Life in Botswana', in *Poverty and Plenty, the Botswana Experience: The Quality of Life in Botswana.* Proceedings of The Botswana Society Symposium, 15–18 October 1997, The Botswana Society, Gaborone, p. 252.

white farmers who pay starvation wages for San children and youth labor. Although parents constitute the majority of the school governing body's members, their actual participation in regular school affairs is very low. However, three community members are employed by the Education Department as preschool facilitators, and six school-leavers who completed grade 12 work part-time as adult education facilitators.

As soon as the communities have settled in their town under construction, Platfontein, the representatives of the Schmidtsdrift !Xu and Kxoe community organizations and their project coordinator aim to address specific concerns. These concerns include for example, the need for teaching conflict resolution and traditional skills to the communities, the need to enhance the young generation's appreciation of the San culture and identity, and the need to develop a !Xu and Kxoe orthography and thereafter teaching and learning materials.

There are members of the =Khomani community living near the Kalahari Gemsbok National Park in the small town of Welkom. The government school at Welkom is attended by eight San students, who are reportedly not happy there because the medium of instruction is Afrikaans and the teaching is culturally inappropriate.

A small group of =Khomani community members resides at Kagga Kamma, a game ranch. For the past three years they have been negotiating with the assistance of a human rights lawyer for a fair joint-venture agreement with the ranch owner. Currently the private school at Kagga Kamma is closed because the ranch owner does not regard it as a priority need and is unwilling to support the San community by paying the teacher's salary. When the school was operating the Montessori-trained teacher applied a curriculum and methodology that attempted to meet the needs of the San children.

The new Constitution of the Republic of South Africa adopted in May 1996 guarantees principal educational and language rights. Under the heading 'Languages,' Article 6(2) states:

> Recognizing the historically diminished use and status of the Indigenous languages of our people, the state must take practical and positive measure to elevate the status and advance the use of these languages.

Article 6(5) states:

> A Pan South African Language Board established by national legislation must –
> (a) promote, and create conditions for, the development and use of –
>   (ii) the Khoi, Nama and San languages ...

The South African San Institute (SASI), a support and service organization to WIMSA, submitted reports on behalf of the San and Khoi communities in South Africa to the Pan South African Language Board, which referred to the concerns and recommendations of those communities. It remains to be seen if the Language Board and the Department of Arts, Culture, Science and Technology will take concrete action to pave the way for the implementation of the San's recommendations.

San Schools in Botswana

The majority of the San communities of Botswana live in scattered settlements in the Ghanzi, Kgalagadi and North West Districts. The San children attend government schools in which the medium of instruction is Setswana, the national language, and/or English, the official language of the country. The fact that the children are expected to understand, for example, mathematical concepts as taught in a foreign language and to express themselves in a foreign language undermines their academic performance. The general disapproval of San culture expressed in various ways by teachers and classmates is another factor contributing to the low self-esteem that San pupils have and consequently, in many cases, to their dropping out of school. The lack of parental support for their children's education and the reasons for this lack mirror the South African and Namibian situations.

At the pre-primary school level, the Bokamosa Training Program of the Kuru Development Trust has attained considerable achievements in terms of mother tongue education, parental involvement and culturally appropriate curricula. Training sessions for pre-primary schoolteachers and parents are conducted regularly in the villages and additional workshops for primary and pre-primary schoolteachers have been conducted at the Kuru Training Centre. The Naro Literacy Program, also run by Kuru personnel, has developed primers, storybooks and brochures relating to contemporary problems such as alcohol abuse, and it publishes the monthly newsletter *Naro Nxara*.

With regard to the official language policy for education, the First National Commission on Education of 1977:

> ... seemed to view mother tongue education for Setswana as a right and a resource which could foster national unity ... However, it did not make any recommendation on the use of minority languages in education. The Second National Commission on Education in 1993 reduced the number of years for Setswana as medium of instruction from four years to one.[2]

The commission made specific recommendations regarding mother-tongue education only for the pre-primary school level. Clearly, the systemic bias against the San by Setswana speakers is a major factor in the continued sense of self-deprecation on the part of San learners.

As already noted, the Commission recommended renaming the National Setswana Language Council as the Botswana Languages Council, thereby broadening the council's scope for developing a comprehensive language policy. Through a compromise between educators and linguists, a task force on the establishment of the Botswana Languages Council was appointed in March 1997. The task force worked in an advisory capacity to the Ministry of Education until August 1997. According to the task force's recommendations:

---

2 Personal Communication from Hennie Swarts, coordinator of the !Xu and Kxoe Project.

There are plans to accord all minority languages official recognition, to ensure that each one of them is used as a medium of instruction in elementary education, and taught as a subject when demand warrants ... Hopefully these plans will not be shelved for too long, but rather implemented soon.[3]

San Schools in Namibia

The majority of Namibia's San communities live in the north and east of the country. In the northern regions of Omusati, Ohangwena and Oshikoto the San live widely scattered in family homesteads of other ethnic groups, and in the eastern Omaheke region they work on commercial and communal livestock farms. Most of the 2 100 San pupils attending school in August 1994 visited one of 13 government-registered schools and eight government-aided schools.[4] For the first three years of schooling, the medium of instruction in these schools is either English, Afrikaans and/or one of the Indigenous languages. High school dropout rates, lack of parental support for formal education and cultural inappropriateness of the standard curricula are common features of the education system in Namibia.

The Nyae Nyae Farmers' Co-operative, with the assistance of the Ministry of Basic Education and Culture (MBEC), external donors and professionals from abroad established the Village Schools Project (VSP) in October 1991. The original philosophy of the VSP focused on the use of Ju/'hoan as the medium of instruction, the training of teachers from the Ju/'hoan communities, the teachers' attainment of the student teacher's official accreditation (which recognizes their traditional knowledge and comparatively low formal educational achievements) and the development of culturally relevant curricula and Ju/'hoan curricular materials reflecting the overall context of the integrated development program implemented in the Nyae Nyae area. Pupils currently in grades 1 to 3 are taught in their mother tongue in one class at five schools. Two student teachers still receiving in-service training run each school. Five student teachers have participated in the VSP for four and a half years and now have enough formal education to allow them to enroll for the Instructional Skills Certificate. It is hoped that one of the student teachers will soon have acquired the formal qualifications necessary for an appointment as principal of these five small schools.

Three San community-owned schools have recently been established with the assistance of WIMSA and concerned individuals. The Sonneblom/Donkerbos school and the Epako San preschool have attracted children of three to ten years old, although it was originally envisaged that these schools would cater to children under the age of six. The children are taught in their mother tongue and teaching aids are presently being developed with locally available materials. As is common during the

---

3   Visser, H. 'Language and Cultural Empowerment of the Khoesan People,' public lecture at the University of Botswana, 6 March 1998, Gaborone, pp. 1, 2.

4   Education Management Information System Division (EMIS), 'Marginalisation in Education: The Case of Bushman-Speaking People', *EMIS Bulletin No. 3*, Ministry of Basic Education and Culture Windhoek (1995), pp. 2–3.

inception period of such a project, the community as the responsible body still has to improve the running of the school and ensure the regular presence of the teachers.

The =Oenie Community School comprises three components: pre-primary education, student teachers' training and adult education classes. The student teachers communicate with the children in both !Xoo, their mother tongue, and Afrikaans. Adult education classes are conducted on three afternoons per week. The curriculum covers, as requested by the interested community members, basic reading and writing in Afrikaans and communicative English.

The MBEC formulated a language policy on mother tongue education for the first three primary school grades. The policy was developed on the following principles:

> All national languages are equal regardless of the number of speakers or the level of development of a particular language. All language policies must regard language as a medium of cultural transmission. For pedagogical reasons it is ideal for children to study through their own language during the early years of schooling when basic skills of reading, writing and concept formation are developed.[5]

In 1991 the MBEC officially recognized the Ju/'hoan orthography developed by the late Patrick Dickens, and by the end of 1993 the ministry's National Literacy Program published a Ju/'hoan adult literacy primer. In early 1997 a survey on the Namibian San languages was carried out which should serve as a basis for research on the possibility of producing teaching and learning materials for marginalized children. The San have repeatedly requested that their children be taught in their mother tongue. This request has not always been honored since there are several different San languages and only Ju/'hoan is recognized by Botswana and Namibia. In Namibia the Ministry of Basic Education and Culture (MBEC) allows children to be taught in their mother tongue for the first three years of schooling, but San teaching aids for the primary school level have only been produced in the Ju/'hoan language because this is the only San language whose writing is officially recognized.

An Intersectoral Task Force Committee on Educationally Marginalized Children (ITFCEMC), of which WIMSA is a member, was established by the MBEC in 1996. Following is an extract from a recent WIMSA report referring to the ITFCEMC's activities:

> In general terms, the ITFCEMC aims to raise awareness and advocate on the plight of these children, particularly within the MBEC and among school personnel countrywide. The ITFCEMC's terms of reference relate to improving accessibility to schooling for these children, assisting in finding solutions to their problems and fulfilling their needs, investigating complaints of abuse of these children, and developing national policy guidelines on educationally marginalized children in Namibia for presentation to the Cabinet.[6]

---

5   Ministry of Education and Culture, 'Toward Education for All: A Development Brief for Education, Culture and Training', Windhoek (1993), p. 65.

6   Working Group of Indigenous Minorities in Southern Africa, *WIMSA Report on Activities, April 1997 to March 1998*, Windhoek (1998), p. 6.

The final draft of the National Policy Options for Educationally Marginalized Children has recently been distributed to interested parties for discussion and as a basis for further consultations.

The ITFCEMC initiated the First Secondary School San Learners' Conference held in Windhoek in 1997. Representatives from various San communities had the opportunity to talk to government officials and held many discussions amongst themselves. Namibian San leaders were also invited to serve as role models for the students. The conference was a great success. The WIMSA activity report cited above had the following to say about the conference:

> The group discussions and the San learners' evaluation revealed that the students regarded the conference as a significant event, which provided them with the opportunity to obtain important information, become aware of the fact that a high number of San learners share the same constraints, identify strategies to solve some of their educational problems, deliberate on both the learners' and teachers' attitudes, gain more confidence, compare the various San languages and request new school facilities. In general, the conference was considered by all parties involved as a remarkable achievement. Currently the ITFCEMC is discussing with all stakeholders whether a Second San Learners' Conference should be organized.[7]

The MBEC's Intersectoral Task Force on Educationally Marginalized Children performs an important role in Namibia. The children served by this task force are mainly San and Ovahimba. As WIMSA trainees we participated in task force meetings along with the WIMSA coordinator and facilitated at meetings. The task force attempted to solve problems and share information, and it helped to write a 'National Policy Paper on Educationally Marginalized Children.'

It is evident from a detailed expose of the formal educational systems in South Africa, Botswana and Namibia that most San have a broad traditional knowledge but a limited formal education as defined by European peoples. Many San children drop out of school early because their teachers who are non-San do not understand their culture. Teachers and other children discriminate against them because they view San people as 'backward' and 'primitive.' Since marriage customs are radically different from those of Europeans, many San marry at an early age and subsequently drop out of school. Some children do not go to school at all because their parents cannot afford to pay school fees and buy a school uniform. UNICEF in Namibia has allocated funds to WIMSA to address this problem by way of a film on the value of education. The film will be shown to San communities in the hope that it will convince parents and children of the benefits of a formal education. It will also be shown to educational policy makers, teachers and trainee teachers to raise awareness of the special needs of San children. Yet the purpose of formal European education may not comply with the needs of the San community. Hence, many San people rightly wonder about where such formal education would lead and how it would be

---

7   Working Group of Indigenous Minorities in Southern Africa, *WIMSA Report on Activities, April 1997 to March 1998*, Windhoek (1998), p. 8.

relevant to their lives as San people. Much of the educational system is geared toward producing graduates for functioning in the dominant Setswana or Eurocentric society in Botswana, and does not address the particularity of San cultural and economic needs. This is a very serious problem area that requires widescale consultation with San elders and sensitivity to the needs of the community.

•   *Employment*

Most San are unemployed because they do not have the technical skills necessary for functioning in a commercialized capitalist market society. Those who are employed work on communal or commercial farms or produce crafts to sell to tourists. Their income is very low, and in fact the San are known to be the poorest of the poor in all the countries of southern Africa. However, a number of San communities have made plans for generating income. WIMSA has advised them on these plans as requested.

The !Kung in northeastern Namibia, for example, have set up the Omatako Valley Rest Camp for tourists to the area. The camp workers are paid for their services from the fees charged to visitors utilizing the camp.

Another San income-generating project is being run in a small settlement called Vergenoeg in the east of Namibia. Here, WIMSA and the Centre for Research-Information-Action for Development in Africa (CRIAA) assist the San and Nama population to harvest, in a sustainable way, the medical plant known as devil's claw. In former years the project workers sold the dried plant to neighboring Hereros for one to three Namibian dollars per kilogram. But now that they have been fully trained to organize the harvesting, they earn up to twelve Namibian dollars per kilogram of dried devil's claw. The capitalist economy ensures the economic impoverishment of the San community because the measure of value is in the form of the dollar and possession of the maximum number of dollars, of which most San people have very little.

San Survival amidst Western Modernization and Commodification

Many San communities have made the decision to generate income from tourism because it appears to be the principal strategy for economic survival, but it has become evident that certain culture-related constraints hamper the smooth accomplishment of their goals in this regard.

In the case of the Omatako Valley Rest Camp, the goal of the five San communities involved was to generate income by setting up a campsite and selling crafts and basic groceries in two separate shops. Almost all adult members of the five communities participated in constructing the campsite during the project's inception phase. With the first income from the campsite it became apparent that an unrealistic cash payment was expected by each of the relevant community members. To ensure the continuation of the project, an executive committee was set up to deal with such problems. But the hierarchical structure of this committee defied the traditional consensus-based structures of the San. As a result a number of community members rejected decisions made by the committee and demanded compensation for their input into the campsite, which they had originally offered free of charge.

In the subsequent phase of the project, when San were appointed by the committee to positions such as campsite manager, shopkeeper, tourist guide, translator or watchman, those appointed were seen by others as the 'haves,' while all those not holding positions saw themselves as the 'have-nots,' despite their having ample opportunity to derive an income through selling their crafts. The individuals whose jobs require them to handle money have been accused of fraud. The attempts of the executive committee to explain matters of finance fell on 'deaf ears' because so many community members lack the literacy and math skills and assumed even before any explanation was attempted that they would not understand it. In a traditionally egalitarian society such as the San's, it is difficult to cope with a gap between 'haves' and 'have-nots,' and the gap between formally and traditionally educated community members. The Eurocentric capitalist economic system that compensates some people at higher rates than others, producing income and wealth disparities, is alien to San culture and extremely difficult to comprehend and accept. Ironically, Western 'civilization' has fostered deeper socio-economic conflict among peoples of the world because of its obsession with progress and preoccupation with monetary accumulation and material possession, while the same civilization has disparaged Indigenous cultures for being 'uncivilized' because of cultural and economic practices that engender equality and reciprocity.

Nevertheless, from a development perspective, conflicts emerging in a community project such as the Omatako Valley Rest Camp do generally serve to strengthen the community. It should be noted that despite the conflicts that have emerged around traditional dancing, the dances have been incorporated as an additional activity in this project, and community members from several villages in the area have joined the project and continued to render this service to tourists at the camp.

Conclusion

In summary, San communities regard tourism as an option for generating income and thus as a possible route towards attaining some level of self-reliance. Communities already involved in tourism have become aware of the possible disruption of their cultural values created by the perceived benefits of tourism-related activities. However, they also believe that sensitive and unprejudiced tourists could help them in promoting their traditional skills as constituting a recognized profession and thereby dismantling the prevailing 'Bushman myth' regarding these skills. At this stage there seems to be no definitive answer to the question of whether tourism supports or destroys San culture.

It is imperative that the world supports the cause of Indigenous San cultural survival, political self-determination, and economic and social independence, in ways that harmonize with San culture. The San people need to be left alone, have their confiscated lands returned to them, and be mutually respected and recognized like all other 'civilized' peoples. Our wisdom traditions and scientific practices are rooted in Indigenous ways of seeing the world that have been around for scores of millennia and in fact have functioned to preserve the precious resources of Mother Earth and the natural world, and must be valued and not exploited, for they have helped our people survive in a world of intense cruelty, war and violence against human beings and the rest of the natural world. The San people are here to stay, and will remain for generations to come!

Chapter 2

Nila.Ngany – Possessing/Belonging to Knowledge: Indigenous Knowledge Systems in Yawuru Aboriginal Australia

Pat Mamanyjun Torres

Introduction

> Ngaji gurrijin? Janala gaja? Yangki juyu mabu? Ngayu mabu.
> Ngayu nilawarl Pat Torres, ngayu nilawarl Mamanyjun. Ngayu ngarrangu jarndu, Yawurungany, Nyul-Nyulngany, Jabirr-Jabirrngany.

Hello, everyone! How are you feeling? How are you getting on? Are you feeling well? I am good! My name is Pat Torres and my Indigenous name is Mamanyjun. Mamanyjun is a name for a red berry that grows along the coastal bushlands in Northern Western Australia in the area known as Quondong, north of Broome, Western Australia. The mamanyjun berry was very important to the diet and social systems for the women and their families of the Yawuru, Jabirrjabirr, Nyul-nyul, Bard, and Jawi peoples of the Dampierland Peninsular region of Western Australia. This berry was gathered in the bindjin, or bark and wooden containers, by the saltwater women during the middle of barrgana, 'southeast wind time' or cold weather season, which occurs around about June to August in the Kimberly region of Western Australia. The fruit resembles a jaffa lolly: it is red on the outside with a hard outer crust. Its taste was sweetened by cooking handfuls of it in the dying coals of the fire for a few minutes before the fruit was cooled down and then eaten.

The small inner black seeds were thrown widely onto the outer edges of the family camping areas. They were often scattered into the bushlands along the sand dunes and coastal fringes where families hunted and gathered within their clan communities. This casting of the seeds and the management of the land and its mayi or food resources enabled new plants to grow in the next rainy season, thereby providing food for the following seasons.

I am named after this important bushtucker that is high in vitamin C, carbohydrates, and protein. The mamanyjun fruit is symbolic for me as an Indigenous Australian woman of today. Just as the early mothers of the northwestern areas of this country gathered the mamanyjun fruit, today I am gathering my thoughts, heating it in the embers of investigation, cooling it down in our discussions and distributing the fruits of my labor in my search for the acquisition of new forms of knowledge within Indigenous Australian contexts. I believe that this process is fundamental for developing our identities as Indigenous Australian women, for the sharing and nurturing of our knowledge and for enabling more Indigenous women and their families to have greater power and control over their own lives and choices for the future.

Oral History and Aboriginal Women's Knowledge

My nurturing and caring role as a woman, a mother, and as a member of an extended Indigenous family has also created a great hunger which needs to be satisfied, that is, to establish our areas of knowledge so that they are relevant to the needs of our communities. I have attempted to do this by recording traditional women's areas of knowledge and responsibilities that are part of the maintenance and preservation of Indigenous Australian cultures. I only participate in those areas that are mine by right of familial relationships.

I have been able to make some changes within my own communities through the widespread production of culturally appropriate and relevant publications about and for Indigenous Australians, through Magabala Books, an Indigenous publishing company, and through my work as a cultural diplomat in international festivals and cultural celebrations of Indigenous peoples and their cultures. I have been committed to these kinds of national and overseas public celebrations of Indigenous Australian cultural activity. I view these activities as important: first, it means that my children and others grow up with strong, positive images about themselves as Indigenous Australians, and second, it implies that others outside of my cultural space get to understand some aspects of the diversity and richness of Indigenous Australian cultures.

My perspective as a ngarrangu jarndu, an Indigenous Australian woman, has been carefully formed by a close relationship with my extended matrilineal families – ties to land, people and country and our ancestral knowledge of language, culture, history, and spirituality. This has cultural and historical roots in the Broome and Peninsular region of Northern Western Australia. One thing I know for certain through the teachings by my Yawuru, Jabirrjabirr, Nyikina, and Bard Elders is that the Bugarri-garra, or Dreaming stories, are integral to our identity as Indigenous peoples.

I know that these oral histories reach across this continent into many diverse cultural communities. I know that women need to know these teachings from the women's side of knowledge and to learn about our religious beliefs of the giant ancestral women called the Gurdidi Ngurnu (to name just one among the many that exist in our oral histories) or the Three Sisters. They traveled this land at a time when this earth was still being formed and through their activities have made the landforms of the country we know today as Australia. These three ancestral women are our 'early mothers' of this country and the stories of their journeys link us to our traditional past. Knowledge of their activities and their special places ground us strongly in our historical past, our present and our future. We are taught in the land of my great-grandmother and great-grandfather, within Jugun-Julbayi Yawuru country, where the Gurdidi Ngunu created the freshwater springs and water holes along the coast, the saltwater clay pans, and certain species of seed-trees during Bugarri-garra.

As mature women today with children and cultural responsibilities, my female cousins and I now realize that it was the regular ritualized celebrations of the journeys by the early Indigenous women of this country that kept this country fertile and rich in its resources. Our cultural connections to the land and to women's specific areas of knowledge must be maintained as they were celebrated in my great-grandmother's generation.

The Indigenous Australian Women's Context – A ngarrangu jarndu or Black Women's Perspective

I am an Indigenous Australian woman from the Yawuru people, the Nyul-Nyul people, and the Jabirrjabirr people of the West Kimberley area of Western Australia. My mother's mother is from the Julbayi clan from Yawuru, my mother's mother's father is Jugun from Broome, Western Australia, and my mother's father's mother is Jabirrjabirr/Nyul-Nyul from Sandy Point, near Beagle Bay, Western Australia. My Yawuru skin name is Banaga and my children are all Garimba, just like my mother.[1]

My straight-one or husband's skin is Burungu, and my father's skin is Barrjarri. All the groups that I am related to belong to the 'saltwater culture' or gularraburu, also spelled goolarabooloo, which translates approximately to 'the place in the west' or 'place in the westerly direction.'

The language you have previously read and listened to was in the Yawuru language, the language of my great-grandmother. It was taught to me by my jamuny or grand-aunt, Doris Edgar, from Broome, Western Australia, who is first cousin to my grandmother, Irene 'Waddirr' Torres. We belong to the Yawurungany. The Yawurungany are the original people from around the Broome region. Our people occupied lands north of Broome around Willie Creek, east towards Nygina and Jirrgarli country, in the Derby shire and south of Broome down to Janyjagurdany, which is near Thangoo Station, north of Bidyadanga or La Grange community in Western Australia. Today there is a debate, particularly among white Australians, about whether Jugun is a separate group to Yawuru; however, in my family's oral history we were told that Jugun was 'Big Yawuru' and all other groups were 'Little Yawuru' and when elders spoke about the language, they always said that Jugun was 'heavy' Yawuru and the Julbayi dialect spoken by many surviving Yawuru elders,

---

1   'Skin name' among Aboriginal peoples of Australia refers to Indigenous names as opposed to the widescale practice of either imposed or 'adopted' European names.

belong to the 'light' Yawuru. My great, great-grandmother, called Miwarl, was my great-grandfather, Karim Drummond's, mother. My great, great-grandmother was born in Jugun country but gave birth to my great-grandfather in Julbayi country and my great-grandmother, Mary Therese or 'Polly' Drummond, was born near Echo Beach and the Gujarra Wangu, or two hills called Barn and Church Hill south of Broome, W.A. in Julbayi clan country.

We too had extensive clans and clan communities just like the Yolngu people of Arnhemland in the Northern Territories of Australia. However, due to the accessibility and location of the place, the influences of many factors on Broome's history and development, and the effects of European colonization, drastic changes have occurred in our diverse cultures and we were forced to make huge adaptations in the area. Today the cultural context of Indigenous people varies according to the degree of their grounding in cultures that were in existence prior to colonization. This situation I describe is also true of other people who have encountered colonization.

You have come to this particular space in time, within this context, already exposed to an enormous amount of information which has been stored within your minds as the future storehouse of knowledge to which you will need to gain access in the near future. These storehouses of knowledge will guide your attitudes, values and behaviors in any future human interaction with people from a range of cultural diversities. How you use this information will be up to you. I hope that you use it for positive and proactive outcomes that seek to empower yourself and others and not to disempower creation.

I would like to share with you some insight into my perception of knowledge and provide an Indigenous woman's perspective on the way in which I have participated in building such an Indigenous knowledge system. By examining my own process of knowledge building and what I perceive as the reality of how that knowledge is produced and validated within Indigenous cultural contexts, I hope I can contribute to your own.

The Interwovenness of Place, Ancestors, and Knowledge Among Aboriginal People

The location of place that I mentioned earlier is decisive for understanding our culture. Living beside the sea and its coastal environment meant that the majority of the time in our lives has been spent doing things that involve the sea and its environs. When you examine the ancestral stories that the Yawuru and other coastal groups have knowledge about, you notice countless stories of ancestral beings doing things that have had an impact on the physical formations of the land including river systems and rock formations, including their color, shape, and size. Their creative activity determined within the Bugarrigarra (many dreams) what animal and plant species can be found today in the area or what existed prior to British colonization. The activity of these ancestral beings not only explained the importance and sacredness of sites, objects, and the existence of skin systems, cultural practices, and rules for behaving, but also required that the people within these diverse cultural groups celebrated their ways of knowing and coming-to-knowing through ritualized activity that included dance, music, song, art, body decorations, and site decorations, just to name a few. This ritualized activity was complex and many-layered in its meanings and metaphors, and access was orchestrated by the elders, initiates, their kin and families, and those who were to become part of the initiated. This human activity served to sustain and perpetuate our societies within an ecologically sustainable environment, until colonial invasion and the enforcement of another society's ways of doing and thinking.

This invasion dispossessed and disempowered the Indigenous Australian people and our knowledge-building processes, and this dispossession and theft of our land affected the continuity of our land ethic. These forces altered our ways of doing. In its greed for land, the colonizing society systematically devised ways to discredit our people and our knowledge systems. This historical imposition of Western European ways of doing, thinking and acting created a situation where knowledge-building within Indigenous Australian contexts was disrupted and links were forcibly broken through government policies and its institutions. Only recently (within the last thirty to forty years) have Indigenous people felt empowered to articulate their differences, been supported by others to bring their experiences to the public forum, and felt comfortable about demanding that Indigenous perspectives be recognized, acknowledged and validated within white mainstream society without fear of being incarcerated in prisons or other institutions.

Intellectualizing about Indigenous knowledge systems brings our knowledge into the public arena, and the time is ripe for the airing of this knowledge as social scientists and others become concerned that Western European science has not furnished the answers to many human problems or delivered on numerous promised benefits for humankind. Indigenous societies attract Western scientists' attention because of our (Indigenous peoples') knowledge system, beckoning intellectuals to search through the 'mysteries' for another way. These discourses open the way for us to contribute our perspectives. This is now the new way for Indigenous people to build our knowledge and to have it validated and acknowledged in the lexicon of 'cultural differences' that have been embedded into Australian society today. Many Indigenous people may feel that Indigenous knowledge systems need neither be justified by reference to anything external to our societies and need not explain itself to anyone, nor be compared to or contrasted with the standards of Western European science. Yet until Indigenous scholars participate in the knowledge-building that occurs in white mainstream educational institutions, we will always be the objects of study in the 'them v. us' dichotomy of difference, and we will remain disempowered and be the fringe-dwellers once again, letting others become the 'experts' on our cultural domains.

Let me go back now to how knowledge-building occurred for me in the Yawuru context. I remember from 'small time' when I was a child of about three years old and beyond, living with my mother's mother, Irene Helena 'Wadarr' Torres (nee Drummond). I had the greatest respect and interest for the stories of the 'old people,' those people who were not necessarily old in age but were connected to the 'old ways' that existed before colonization. I remember being drawn to the middle-aged women and those elder women who lived in the tin shanties just behind our house in the area called Gujarragun, now known as Short Street, and the site of the picture gardens called the 'Sun Pictures' within 'Chinatown' or the central business district of Broome.

I remember vividly the warmth of the 'old people' who were known to me as mimi, jalbi or jamuny, all Yawuru terms for grandparent or great-grandparent. I remember those great aunts and grandmothers with wonderfully large full breasts that hung down onto their laps. I remember their welcoming hugs as they pulled me to them and sat me comfortably down on their wide expansive laps. I remember their beautiful Black faces framed with dark wavy hair, and the shining smiles of these women who held me close to their hearts and shared with me the stories of gumbun, the mangrove people, wirangu wakala or wirangu jarndu, the devil woman or red dress woman, dumbu, the giant devil dog, ngarri, the devil-man, and countless other stories of spirits, good, bad, ugly, and beautiful.

I remember the stories told to me by my mother's mother's mother, jalbi, Polly Drummond, a woman of tall stature, olive-brown complexion, and shocking white hair cropped in pageboy style. She was a respected matriarch and known locally by some people as widujangala for her wide hips and legs. This wonderfully strong-willed woman, who worked as a maid for the local white families, told me stories about the frog-mouth owls that lived in the Cork-trees, and about how the owls were the spirits of dead people coming to capture others to take them back to the land of the dead. She told us of the little black dog that grew and grew so tall, glaring its shining blood-red niminy (eyes) and bloody jalany (tongue), all dripping with garra or saliva and how it grew to a menacing height towering above the treetops. She told of the presence of ngarri, bad spirits, and how you could tell it was nearby by the smell of rotting flesh that surrounded its being. She told of how these spirits would seek out people who had done wrong to others and torment them. She warned us not to go out into the streets and to put our hands over our ears whenever we heard the high-pitched howling of the dogs at night, warning us that bad spirits or jalangngurru, 'pay-back' men, were outside searching for their victims. She talked in Yawuru, Garajeri, Malay, and Australian English, 'Broome-style.'

As the women in my family were Yawuru and the teaching of knowledge was done by the mothers, grandmothers, aunties, elder sisters and female cousins, this meant a strong matriarchal influence on the knowledge building in my childhood. With the early death of my jalbi, my great-grandmother when I was ten years old, my mother's mother and all her sisters and extended female kin continued the teachings of our culture.

My mimi, my mother's mother and her sisters, taught me about the meaning and realities of being Yawuru. They told of the significance of seeing single black crows too close to our house, and that this signalled death or bad news of close family or friends. They told of the danger of finding ganada the painted lizard or jabara the bearded lizard under the steps of the houses with their stomachs slit and sewn up with rocks in their bellies. This was a sign that someone was being sung to death and sickness for past wrongs. A jalangngurru man would have to be found to right the wrong and protect the people in the house. These are just some of the details that were taught in the knowledge-building of my childhood days.

This extensive array of knowledge that was linked to land, people, the cosmos, and our spirituality, was taught to us on a daily basis by our kinfolk and reinforced on our land whenever we passed sites of significance or animals, plants and people with which we were interrelated. Each season meant new experiences linked to new knowledge-building and our increasing age gave us access to increased levels of complexity of knowledge. Ritualized ceremonial activities were followed by my family while they were still being practiced in the Broome region. I remember being taken by my mimi to one of the last Yawuru ceremonies on the edge of the Dampier Creek floodplains near Rinjamarn Burru, not far from Garnin, and its effect of instilling great respect in me for our Indigenous cultures and my experiencing its amazing psychic energies to dream and receive visions.

I remember being told by my elders during my childhood days that the first people to live in the area now called Broome were the Jugun and other Yawuru people. They shared some places near where the Sun Pictures Theatre is standing today and right up along the coast to the Foreshore Beach or Manalagun, as it was known before European contact. The area near the Sun Pictures Theatre in Chinatown, Broome was originally called Gujarragun by the Yawuru people. It meant the place of the two, referring to the Two Men, ancestral men who walked the country. In the women's side of our oral histories, an ancestral woman lies buried beneath this site. Her spirit can still be experienced in this area late at night when everything is quiet. My mother has a special spiritual relationship to this site.

In my childhood days we learned from our female relatives that the first Jugun and other Yawuru people lived and used the areas along the coast, its nearby floodplains and the bush. Their areas included:

- Manalagun near Foreshore Beach,
- Winjilngan or Kennedy Hill,
- Rubibi or Streeters Jetty landing,
- Gujarragun or Sun Pictures Theatre site,
- Burrgugun or Hunters' Camp previously known as Morgan's Camp,
- Jugagun and Garnin near Fishermen's Bend,
- Warnyalirrmirr, Lirrigun, Garndilibagun, Bingkaja, Bugawamba, Barrangangngaba, Murraginygun, Mankalagun, Yiwalangu-nyudan, Ngurlungku, and further south to many other places down to Janyjagurdany and Yardugara near Tjangu or Thangoo Station, south of Broome.

The Yawuru people knew our land well, and the land from Yardugara near Janyjagurdany or Tjangu, known locally as Thangoo Station up to the town-site of Broome: all have Yawuru and Jugun names. These names were known to all the old people and are still being taught and handed down to our children and grandchildren.

The Yawuru people lived a hunting and gathering way of life, close to our land and within our clan countries, only meeting up with neighboring families and clans for ceremony or seasonal celebrations. For thousands of years we lived off the land and looked after our land. It is believed that in return our land looked after us. The Jugun and Yawuru people of the past, our old people, had their traditional hunting and gathering areas, their traditional places for getting water, and their traditional places for cultural business. The Jugun and Yawuru people's hunting and gathering way of life went on in the same way following the seasons of the law and the land until the white invading colonizers affected the regular access to sites and ritualized activities.

Today among our people there are those who live just like gadiyas or white people, and those who live a more traditional way of life, close to the land and in harmony with its rhythm and seasons. Even though many of us are forced to live like and under white people, we still think of ourselves as Jugun and Yawuru and we are still part of the Jugun-Yawuru 'saltwater' culture and way of life. The Jugun-Julbayi Yawuru people of today are still doing what our old people have done in the past. We hunt and gather our bush and seafoods, and prepare our medicines within the Jugun-Yawuru boundaries. We still use our traditional hunting and gathering places almost every weekend. Some of our families still camp out for days on end, to living off the land and receiving nourishment from the land. We go to these places every week and every season. We believe that this helps us to care for the land and to teach our children about their culture and birthrights.

From the age of ten to fourteen years, I lived with my bibi, Theresa Warrarr Barker, my mother, in Derby, Western Australia, who reinforced all the knowledge handed down to me by my mimi and jalbi, and introduced me to my extended kin from Bard, Nygina, Walmajeri, and Bunaba. Here my education into other 'salt-water' and martuwarra or river and 'fresh-water cultures' began. This knowledge was once again taught on the land and its stories were retold beside the fireplace, on the riverbanks, or in the creek beds, as we rested or prepared and gathered food for our families. Our dreams, visions and experiences were shared with one another around family fires. Stories of the importance of ancestral beings and constellations were retold while we rested out in the open countryside, on the ground and on our swags under the veil of walabarragaj, the stars, and the light of girradiny, the moon.

From the age of fifteen to twenty-six years, I left my community to further my studies at a Catholic private school and to attend tertiary education at Curtin University and the University of Western Australia, where I received an intensive Western-European-derived education and obtained a Bachelor of Arts degree and a Graduate Diploma of Education in Primary Education. In the tertiary program I was confronted with a vast array of knowledge including Western European perceptions of Indigenous people in the areas of linguistics, psychology, sociology, and anthropology. This kind of education brought me into contact with knowledge systems that were different from my own and though at times it was contradictory to my own belief systems, it helped me realize that I was different from them because of my culture and my worldview. This acknowledgement and self-identification into the concept of Aboriginality and the outside pressures that acted negatively on my indigenousness, served to reinforce my links to Indigenous knowledge and gave me a thirst for more that I could hand down to my children in the future. Thus began my own personal search into the detailed stories of Bugarrigarra and the ancestral journeys of the creator-beings of my Yawuru heritage. My education and knowledge-building had come full-circle, returning to its source, and back to my land and my kin groups and the worldviews that they taught and in which they believed, despite its unacceptability in the wider society.

This knowledge was vital to reclaiming my identity and reaffirming my reality as an Indigenous person. After years of research and study into the stories, their recordings into various children's stories, the poems and songs, videos, cassettes, storytelling sessions, and workshops in Australia and abroad, and the eventual revival of language programs and revitalization of cultural business, I once again remained grounded on Yawuru soil. I have further advanced my knowledge of Indigenous knowledge systems through the initiation of my brother in the 'old way' and my mother's link to women's law and my part in some of these ceremonies. I bring these experiences to my community development educative role and this knowledge-building determines how I act within the Indigenous Australian contexts I choose to work in, and the Western European-derived contexts I choose to participate in.

My participation as an Indigenous Australian person in the education process, which is sometimes in Indigenous contexts and sometimes in Western European-derived contexts, is today intellectually validated and acknowledged. I feel that my contributions to building new forms of cultural knowledge arise from my personal experiences that can be shared with others, and for building knowledge footprints that can be followed, built on, and further consolidated. How this knowledge-building occurs varies from culture to culture in its complexities. Its meanings depend on context and its realities are determined by our worldview.

Conclusion

I hope that my own explanation of knowledge-building and identification as an Indigenous person of Yawuru, Nyul-Nyul, and Jabirrjabirr heritage will assist you in understanding how knowledge-building occurs. Your further research into this topic will consolidate the reality of cultural differences and give you further insights into the process of knowledge-building.

As an Aboriginal woman in Australia, I know that the only way for us to reemerge as a strong and liberated people is to recapture and reclaim our ancestral traditions that span forty thousand years. The white man's presence in Australia is just over two hundred years old. Yet he claims to be owner of the country and the world. We cannot allow this invasion by colonization to be the last word among Indigenous peoples. We must re-tell our stories and proudly assert our ancestral traditions that were practiced for millennia until the white men came in the name of 'civilization.' We have always been a spiritual people closely interwoven with the land and the sea. We understood and practiced ways that respected the sacredness of creation. These ways helped our people thrive in the beautiful world that the Creator gave to us. We must never abandon these ways for the exploitative ways introduced by white culture. We must keep to the sacred path observed by our ancestors. We must rediscover the immeasurable value of our wisdom traditions that are still relevant for our lives and for the future.

May your story, your learning journey, your path to knowledge-building and coming-to-know be positive, appreciative of difference and self-empowering without disempowering others.

EXAMPLES OF INDIGENOUS KNOWLEDGE SYSTEMS

1. An Individuals' Learning Circle where knowledge building occurs

BALANGANS=Ancestral spirits who come to you in dreams or visions
MIRDANYA=ELDERS
WALABILING=Maternal learning circle including mother and child/daughter

E		E
L		L
D		D
E		E
R		R
S		S

NGAYU=Self/me/I
RAYI=inner spirit
LIYAN=inner feeling/intuition

B	WALABILING-NGURRU=	B
A	Family	A
L		L
A		A
N		N
G		G
A	MIRDANYA=ELDERS	A
N		N

BALANGANS=Ancestral spirits who come to you in dreams or visions
(Based on YAWURU MODEL using Yawuru words)

2. Female-specific learning circle where knowledge building occurs

mirdanya=elders
mimi-ni-jalbi=mothers mothers with mothers mothers mothers
(grandmothers with great-grandmothers)

M	darlu=inlaws	M
I	(includes Yagu=husband; yirlmada=husband's sister)	I
M	ngunu-ni-jalwal=	M
I	sister with cousin	I
N	ngunu-ni-babali=	N
I	sister with brother	I
J		J
A		A
L	with many mothers	L
B		B
I	jalygurr-ni-bibi=	I
	baby with/by mother	

marnja-barri bibi=with many mothers
ngunu-ni-babali=sister with brother
ngunu-ni-babali=sister with brother
ngunu-ni-jalwal=sister with cousin
darlu*=inlaws (includes Yagu*=husband/female inlaws)
mimi-ni-jalbi=mothers mothers with mothers mothers mothers
(grandmothers with great-grandmothers)

3. Male-specific learning circle where knowledge building occurs

mirdanya=elders
mimi-ni-jalbi=mothers mothers with mothers mothers mothers
(grand-mothers with great grandmothers)

M	darlu*=inlaws	M
I	(includes gabarli*=wife & male-inlaw)	I
M		M
I	gaga=mothers brother(s)	I
N	babala-ni-ngunu=	N
I	brother with sister	I

J   J
A   marnja-barri bibi=   A
L   with many mothers   L
B   B
I   jalygurr-ni-bibi=   I
                           baby with/by mother

                           marnja-barri bibi=
                           with many mothers

                           babala-ni-ngunu=
                           brother with sister

                      gaga=mothers brother(s)

                           babala-ni-jalwal=
                           brother with cousin

                           darlu*=inlaws
                  (includes gabarli*=wife & male inlaws)

                           mimi-ni-jalbi=
              mothers mothers with mothers mothers mothers
                  (grandmothers with great-grandmothers)

4. JALNGA=Kinship/Marriage system (seen from female Banaga viewpoint only)

BANAGA   marries   BURUNGU
(ngayu=me)   (yagu=husband)

GARIMBA   marries   BARRJARRI
(bibi=mother; wuba=children)   (gugu=father; darlu=inlaws)

Banaga woman marries Burungu husband, children are Garimba same like mothers'
mother, they call m.m=mimi; m.f.=jamuny
f.m.=jamuny; f.f.=mimi

Banaga man marries Burungu wife, children are Barrjarri same like mothers' mother,
they call
m.m.=mimi; m.f.=jamuny
f.m.=jamuny; f.f.=mimi
All children of sisters call each other brother and sisters

All children of brothers call each other brothers and sisters

Children of brothers and sisters call each other jalwal and can marry though they are considered first-cousins in Western ways

5. Moieties-binary systems of relationships

(i)   BARD=One Arm Point People
      (seen from the Jarnd perspective)
      Innar   Jarnd*
      (others)   (self/family)

(ii) WALMAJERI/MANGALA=Western Desert People
      Gidirr   Wiyar

(iii) YOLNGU=Arnhemland People
      Dhuwa   Yirritja

Chapter 3

Indigenist Research and Aboriginal Australia

Lester-Irabinna Rigney

Issues of ownership of knowledge in Aboriginal and Torres Strait Islander research can only be resolved when the power of decision making and self-determination is held by Aboriginal and Torres Strait Islander peoples, communities and/or organizations.[1]

Introduction

Increasing numbers of Indigenous Australians[2] and First Nations peoples around the globe are now undertaking higher degrees involving research at universities. But this has not always been the case. Until recently, Indigenous Australians did not have equal opportunity and access to a university education. Indigenous Australian involvement in research has been at the imposition of Western non-Indigenous researchers' agendas and their universities. Throughout history, Indigenous peoples have been the objects of research and never the initiator, manager or co-investigator of research. Similarly, knowledge productions about Indigenous worldviews and realties have always been obscured by the 'cultural' and 'race' bias of the non-Indigenous interpreter. Research practices by, on and with Indigenous Australians have seen a transformation in the past fifty years. A recent conference in Australia revealed a radical change in knowledge production taking place in the southern South Pacific. The rise of Indigenous research by Indigenous Australian scholars has brought new ways of knowing the past and the call for protection of such knowledge for the benefit of Indigenous peoples themselves. Moreover, Indigenous Australian

---

1 Brady, W. 'Beam me up Scotty, communicating across world views on knowledge, principles and procedures for the conduct of Aboriginal and Torres Strait Islander research', in *National Aboriginal and Torres Strait Islander Higher Education Conference Proceeding*. December, ed. C. White, University of Southern Queensland, Toowoomba, Australia (1992), pp. 104–115.

2 I acknowledge that there is no neutral term that encompasses the entire diversity of Australian Aboriginal or Torres Strait Islander peoples. I acknowledge the diversity in languages and cultures within the Aboriginal and Torres Strait Islander populations. Therefore, to be inclusive of both, the term Indigenous Australians in this paper refers to peoples who identify themselves as being Australian Aboriginal or Torres Strait Islander.

views of research are exploring new forms of theoretical and methodological issues through what has become known as the Indigenous Research Reform Agenda.[3] The purpose of this chapter concerns two main questions: What are the views of Indigenous Australians on research reform? What are the underlying principles fundamental to such reform?

Research: Indigenous Australian Views

I attended the fifth annual Indigenous Researchers Forum at the Australian Institute of Aboriginal and Torres Strait Islander Studies (AIATSIS)[4] held in October 2003. As in this forum, I recall how excited I was to attend the 1999 inaugural Indigenous Researchers Forum hosted then by the Umulliko Indigenous Centre, University of Newcastle.[5] This conference was the first of its kind in Australian history. Such a conference would have been unthinkable twenty years earlier, unthinkable in the sense that it was not until 1966 that Kumantjayi Perkins[6] became the first Aboriginal Australian to graduate from a university.[7] According to Colin Bourke, the first Indigenous scholar to become dean of a faculty, 'Indigenous Australians rarely, if ever, participated in universities in the first 175 years of European settlement in Australia.'[8] Indeed, the emergence of the Indigenous Researchers Forum specifically correlates to the emergence of the Indigenous Australian scholar, and both are recent historical phenomena.[9]

---

3   CRCATH. *Indigenous Research Reform Agenda: Rethinking research methodologies*, CRCATH, Casuarina, Northern Territory (2002).

4   See AIATSIS Website for IRF program http://www.aiatsis.gov.au/rsrch/conferences/ irf2003/index.htm (Accessed 6-11-03).

5   The inaugural Indigenous Researchers Forum of Indigenous academics, Indigenous researchers, and Indigenous postgraduates was the first gathering of its kind in Australia to focus primarily on research. It was organized by *Umulliko* Indigenous Higher Education and Research Centre at the University of Newcastle. Forum proceedings on web: http//www.ion. unisa.edu.au/umulliko/ (Accessed 27-8-03).

6   As is my Narungga custom I use the appropriate name of Kumantjayi here to pay cultural respect to Charles Perkins and his Arrernte Nation. This Arrernte name is assigned to those who have passed away.

7   See the following work for further details of Perkins: Bin-Sallik, M.A. *Aboriginal Tertiary Education in Australia: How well is it serving the needs of Aborigines?* Aboriginal Studies Key Centre, University of South Australia, Adelaide, Third Edition (1996).

8   Bourke, C. 'Aboriginal Autonomy in Higher Education,' in *The National Aboriginal Higher Education Conference, Conference proceeding final report*, Fremantle Western Australia, (11 July 1994), p. 1.

9   The historical emergence of Indigenous Australian scholars can be found in Bin-Sallik, M.A. *Aboriginal Tertiary Education in Australia: How well is it serving the needs of Aborigines?* Aboriginal Studies Key Centre, University of South Australia, Adelaide, Third Edition (1996).

The Indigenous Researchers Forums bring together Indigenous community historians, scholars, researchers, and post-graduate students to rigorously engage in the critique of academic research and the knowledge production process. It also promotes an opportunity to engage in cultural traditions of Indigenous knowledge while sharing experiences and ideas to retain Indigenous authority and ownership. Another prime objective is the promotion of an Indigenous body of knowledge and intelligentsia for addressing our status as colonized peoples. Such a forum has become a hub for the new think tank emerging for contemporary critical Indigenous scholarship.

The 2003 Forum discussions highlighted that contemporary Indigenous Australian intellectualism has drawn on a long history of social and political activism for self-determination. Many speakers openly acknowledge and celebrate past achievements of early Indigenous activists and scholars whose struggle opened the doors to university study for others. The debt owed is enormous, but one many acknowledge. The Indigenous Researchers Forums are used as a site of engagement where Indigenous researchers gather to share experiences and to chart an Indigenous theoretical and political future amongst ourselves. Here we engage in robust scholarly criticism of our own writings and those of non-Indigenous scholars, while also investigating the role of the Indigenous intellectual in an Indigenous Australian future.

The creation of the Indigenous Researchers Forum has been a significant historical moment for Indigenous research in the South Pacific. Prominent researchers in attendance include those from Aotearoa (New Zealand), Pacific Islands and Indigenous Australians from rural and remote locations. Its impact has caused a quiet methodological revolution in research where Indigenous Australian intellectualism seeks methodological reform.

The opening address at the 2003 Forum was presented by acting Chairperson Lionel Quartermaine of the Australian Aboriginal and Torres Strait Islander Commission (ATSIC). His paper titled *"Indigenous Research: What's It About?"* contained interesting insights for public policy that affect Indigenous lives and its connection to research.[10] A key element of his paper was the need for Indigenous agencies and individuals to forge partnerships with governments, business, and peak bodies including universities and researchers to advance the policy agenda. Quartermaine was clear that researchers can and must help Indigenous communities and individuals to maintain control over their cultural knowledge. Equally, researchers can assist Indigenous peoples reach their full potential by improved social outcomes. However, Quartermaine premised his comments on the notion that "history has shown a poor relationship existed between Indigenous peoples, researchers, universities, governments and policy makers." [11]

---

10 The address can be located at http://www.atsic.gov.au/News_Room/speeches_transcripts/default.asp?id=2926 (Accessed 6/11/03)

11 http://www.atsic.gov.au/News_Room/speeches_transcripts/default.asp?id=2926 (Accessed 6/11/03).

Historically, the tensions and dilemmas between researchers and Indigenous peoples included issues of representation, power, and control. These factors were exemplified in a body of knowledge about Indigenous peoples in what non-Indigenous authors Walton and Christie called 'Aboriginalism,'[12] defined as

The story about Aborigines told by whites using only white people's imaginations. Aboriginal voices do not contribute to this story, so in Aboriginalism, the Aborigines always become what the white man imagines them to be.[13]

To overcome "Aboriginalism" Walton and Christie suggest that "Aboriginal peoples develop a counter-discourse to such narrowly written texts that ignore Aboriginal voice and agency."[14]

Australia has a strong intellectual tradition of "Aboriginalism" that until the 1960s was the main discourse upheld in numerous academic disciplines.[15] Quartermaine's address offered insights into problematic issues that an Indigenous counterdiscourse agenda must target for reform, including:[16]

- Research that is framed by the researcher's priorities and interests rather than the needs of Indigenous communities;
- The reduction of Indigenous ownership of Indigenous knowledge and intellectual property;
- The lack of ongoing consultation, negotiation, and involvement of Indigenous communities in the design, facilitation, and publication of research;
- Inappropriate research methodologies and ethical research processes;
- The need for effective, appropriate and culturally sensitive research in relation to ethics and protocols.

The development of an Indigenous counterdiscourse to "Aboriginalism" was a clear subtext to the 2003 Indigenous Researchers Forum. Other prominent Indigenous Australian scholars presenting papers included Tracey Bunda, Eve Fesl, Marcia Langton, Len Collard, Mick Dodson, Sally Morgan, Jilpia Jones, and John Lester. Dialogue between speakers and participants addressed many research issues

---

12 This poor relationship is highlighted in Lippmann, L. *Generations of Resistance*, Longman Cheshire, Melbourne (1994).

13 Walton, C. and Christie, M. 'Aboriginal literature and critical pedagogies', *Ngoonjook*. 10 (1994), p. 82.

14 Ibid., pp. 81–82.

15 Attwood, B. 'Introduction', in *Power, Knowledge and Aborigines, Journal of Australian Studies*, eds B. Attwood and J. Arnold, La Trobe University Press, Bundoora, Victoria (1992), pp. i–xvi. Cowlishaw, G. 'Colour, culture and the Aboriginalist', in *Man: Journal of the Royal Anthropological Institute*, Vol. 22 (1987), pp. 221–37. Muecke, S. *Textual spaces: Aboriginality and Cultural Studies*, New South Wales University Press, Kensington (1994).

16 http://www.atsic.gov.au/News_Room/speeches_transcripts/default.asp?id=2926 (Accessed 6/11/03).

needed for reform. These generalizations centered on the production, reproduction, legitimization and dissemination of knowledge about Indigenous peoples and the role of universities and funding institutions that support research. Indeed, many of these discussions at the forum mirror the key points of research reform identified by the Cooperative Research Centre for Aboriginal and Tropical Health.[17] The CRCATH is a leading national research organization that advocates transformation in health knowledge production through what it describes as the "Indigenous Research Reform Agenda" (IRRA). Issues for reform include:

- Involvement of Indigenous communities in the design, execution, and evaluation of research;
- Defining a coordinating role for Indigenous community-controlled organizations associated with the research;
- Ongoing consultation and negotiation with Indigenous organizations throughout the life of a research project;
- Mechanisms for ongoing surveillance of research projects by Indigenous partner organizations;
- Process to determine research priorities and benefit to the Indigenous communities involved;
- Transformation of research practices from 'investigator-driven' to an adoption of a needs-based approach to research;
- Determination of ethical processes for the conduct of research;
- Linkage between research and community development and social change;
- Training of Indigenous researchers;
- Adoption of effective mechanisms for the dissemination and transfer of research findings.[18]

Similarly, another leading national research organization, the Australian Institute for Aboriginal and Torres Strait Islander Studies has addressed some of the above issues by developing nationally accepted guidelines for ethical standards and practices in Indigenous research. These guidelines maintain Indigenous authority and ownership of their knowledges through partnerships and reciprocity via agreements with researchers.

Clearly Indigenous Australian scholars and leading government research organizations recognize that complexities and contradictions continue within knowledge production processes and the institutional management of such research. In this chapter, I have no intention of casting my net as widely for solutions as my Indigenous colleagues have, but to emphasize that the task of research reform is as wide and as varied as its dilemmas. Methodological reform has clearly become a

---

17 http://www.atsic.gov.au/News_Room/speeches_transcripts/default.asp?id=2926 (Accessed 6/11/03).

18 AIATSIS, 'Guidelines for ethical research in Indigenous issues,' AIATSIS, Canberra, ACT (2002), pp. 6–37.

central issue in Australia, yet the issues of methodological reform are not new to the debate of Indigenous knowledge and their representation.

In the 1980s, Indigenous scholars Ros Langford[19] and Marcia Langton,[20] among others, were instrumental in announcing to the academy of research that Indigenous identities and cultures can only be partially understood from within inherited Western scientific research traditions. In addition, such writings demonstrated how 'Aboriginalism' promoted 'othering', homogenization, and reductionism of Indigenous cultures. Static and fixed constructs of 'Aboriginality' fundamental to 'Aboriginalism' are totally rejected by the newly emergent intellectual criticism known in Australia as Indigenism.

Influencing Developments on Indigenism

Over the past thirty years, a highly productive discourse has emerged that has witnessed Indigenous scholars in Australia and the Pacific challenge research and its applications to more progressive kinds of knowledge seeking methods that privilege the diversity of Indigenous experiences.[21] As I have argued elsewhere, I have used the term Indigenism to describe and define this body of knowledge and its discourse.[22] Later in this chapter I move to build on this work to define Indigenism more comprehensively. For now, what I mean by this term is a distinct Indigenous Australian academic body of knowledge that seeks to disrupt the socially constructed identity of the 'archetypal Aborigine', as a controlled and oppressed being, that informed the emergence of a distinct yet diverse Indigenist Research epistemological and ontological agenda.

There are clearly many historical, social and political factors that have led to the emergence of Indigenism in Australia. It is beyond the scope of this chapter to explore such factors in depth. However, it is important to note that classic scholarly works of anticolonialism have provided valuable theoretical approaches to the contemporary Indigenous Australian Intellectual Movement[23] in its interrogation of dominant

---

19 Langford, R. 'Our heritage, your playground.' *Australian Archaeology*, Vol. 16 (1983), pp. 1–10.

20 Langton, M. 'Looking at Aboriginal women and power: fundamental misunderstandings in the literature and new insights', ANZAAS, papers presented at ANZAAS Festival of Science, Clayton, Monash University (1985).

21 Arbon, Veronica 'Collaborative Research' in *National Aboriginal and Torres Strait Islander Higher Education Conference Proceedings*, December, ed. C. White, University of Southern Queensland, Toowoomba, Australia (1992), pp. 99–103.

22 Rigney, Lester-Irabinna. 'A First perspective of Indigenous Australian participation in science: Framing Indigenous research towards Indigenous Australian Intellectual sovereignty', in *Kaurna Higher Education Journal*, issue 7 (August 2001), pp. 1–13.

23 What I mean here by the 'Contemporary Indigenous Australian Intellectual Movement' is the emergence of the Indigenous academically trained scholar whose writing specifically focused on research reform for Indigenous Australian emancipation.

research tendencies that assume central positions of 'power' and 'truth'.[24] Moreover, the debates in Aotearoa (New Zealand), the United States and Canada by First Nations peoples, scholars of color, and non-Indigenous people have also influenced methodological reform developed by Indigenous peoples in the Pacific.[25]

Australian Indigenism has also capitalized on new and flexible ways to conduct research. In other words, while research and its methodologies have always been in a state of transition, intellectual space was created for Indigenism in Australia, as the academy of science responded to particular research concerns from the disciplines of feminism, postcolonialism and postmodernism. Essentially, over the last two decades the theoretical problems outlined in the social sciences through feminism, postcolonialism and postmodernism have brought about an 'undisciplining' of the disciplines in science. This has seen traditional disciplines destabilized to allow space for emerging theories of social discourse. Denzin and Lincoln term this process the 'blurring of distinct disciplinary boundaries' between social sciences and humanities.[26] Accompanying this transformation is the development of new qualitative research practices. Denzin and Lincoln highlight that the 'post-positivist period of science in the early 1990s saw a variety of new interpretive and qualitative research designs being developed'.[27] The academy's acceptance of multiple methodologies in qualitative research and the acknowledgment of the 'crisis of representation' in research fostered the right conditions to nurture Australian Indigenism. Clearly, these shifts in research approaches and the increased numbers of Indigenous postgraduates since the 1980s have enabled an active environment for contemporary Indigenous Australian scholarly criticism.

---

24 This classic scholarly work includes: Collins, P.H. *Black feminist thought, knowledge, consciousness, and the politics of empowerment*, New York, Routledge (1991). Deloria, V. *Custer Died For Your Sins*, Macmillan, New York (1969). Deloria, V. *Red Earth, white lies: Native Americans and the myth of scientific fact*, Scribner, New York (1995). Fanon, F. *Wretch of the Earth*, trans. C Markmann, Penguin Books, London (1967). Foucault, M. *The Archaeology of Knowledge*, trans. A. Sheridan Smith, Tavistock Publications, London (1972). Hall, S. 'The West and the Rest: Discourse and Power', in *Formation of Modernity*, eds S. Hall and B. Gieben, Polity Press in association with Open University Press, Cambridge (1990), pp. 275–331. hooks, b. *Ain't I a Woman: Black Women and Feminism*, Pluto, New York (1982). Ngugi Wa Thiongo. *De-colonising the Mind: The politics of language in African Literature*, James Currey, London (1994). Said, E. *Orientalism*, Penguin Books, London (1995). Spivak, G.C. 'Can the Subaltern Speak?' in *Marxism and the Interpretation of Culture*, eds C. Nelson and L. Grossberg, Macmillian, London (1988), pp. 271–313. Young, R. *White Mythologies: Writing History and the West*, Routledge, London (1990).

25 Archibald, Jo-Ann. '"Editorial": Researching with Mutual Respec't', in *Canadian Journal of Native Education*, Vol. 20. No. 2 (1993), pp. 189–192.

26 Denzin, N. and Lincoln, Y. 'Introduction: Entering the Field of Qualitative Research', in *Handbook of Qualitative Research*, eds N. Denzin and Y. Lincoln, Sage Publications, London (1994), p. 2.

27 Ibid.

Indigenism

In Australia, Indigenism has sought to conceptualize methodological reform using a variety of approaches that advocate a research compatibility with Indigenous realities, interests and aspirations. For the purposes of this chapter I seek to highlight two approaches by Indigenous scholars.

In his criticism of anthropological representation of the 'other', Torres Strait Islander scholar Martin Nakata has developed Indigenous Standpoint theory. Nakata seeks to 'develop an intellectual standpoint from which Indigenous scholars can read and understand the Western system of knowledge'.[28] For him, the dilemma facing Indigenous scholars is 'how the position of Indigenous peoples is understood both by others and by themselves as they view their position through the knowledge of others'.[29] His pursuit and advice to Indigenous tertiary students is 'that in order to understand our own position better, and to ultimately act to improve it, we must first immerse ourselves in and understand the very systems of thoughts and ideas and knowledges that have been instrumental in producing our position'.[30] He concludes that 'students are tutored to view and understand the position of Indigenous peoples through the same system of thinking, logic and rationality that have historically not served Indigenous interests at all'.[31] Nakata has therefore focused his attention on the need for new reading positions through research methodologies as a basis for decolonizing ourselves:

> Colonial discourses and their narratives are now so dense that it is very hard to make out whether one speaks from within them, or whether one can speak outside of them, or whether one can speak at all without them.[32]

The issue, as rightly pointed out by Nakata: How does the 'Indigenous scholar speak back to the knowledges that have been formed around what is perceived to be the Indigenous position in the western order of things.'[33]

Nakata's reading position seeks to inform the Indigenous student and scholar of the way knowledge construction and legitimation works, how it represents and misrepresents, and provides strategies to negotiate when reading the text. For Nakata, his advice to the Indigenous scholar as a way forward is directed at methodological reform.

---

28 Nakata, Martin 'Anthropological texts and Indigenous Standpoints,' in *Australian Aboriginal Studies*, Australian Institute of Aboriginal and Torres Strait Islander Studies (1998b), p. 4

29 Ibid.

30 Ibid.

31 Ibid.

32 Nakata, Martin. 'Plenary notes' to the Fifth International Literacy and Educational Research Network (LERN) Conference', October 1–4, Alice Springs, Northern Territory, Australia (1997), p. 63.

33 Nakata, Martin. 'Anthropological texts and Indigenous Standpoints,' p. 4

We all need to develop strategies that will assist us to read these knowledges, as others read them, but in full cognisance of their relation to our history, our current position and us. We need to do this within an intellectual framework and we need to do this in a way that will speak to those knowledges, that will speak within the discourse, but will extend the discourse to include what has been hitherto submerged, our understanding of them and how they give expression to relations of power.[34]

Indigenous Standpoint theory as articulated by Nakata is timely to furthering the process of methodological reform toward understanding the way power is embedded in knowledge production within the texts of the colonial and postcolonial. This is a likely genesis for Indigenous scholars to adapt old methodologies or invent new ones for their own interests.

Like Nakata's call for methodological reform, Australia has recently witnessed feminist reform through the emergence of Indigenous Woman's Standpoint Theory. In her book titled *Talkin' up to the White Women: Indigenous Women and Feminism*, Indigenous scholar Aileen Moreton-Robinson outlines her definition of this methodology and how it differs from dominant feminism. Her definition of Indigenous woman's standpoint theory is worthy of lengthy mention:

An Indigenous woman's standpoint is informed by the social worlds imbued with meaning grounded in knowledges of different realities from those of white women…they include sharing an inalienable connection to land; a legacy of dispossession, racism and sexism; resisting and replacing disparaging images of ourselves with self defined images; continuing our activism as mothers, sisters, aunts, daughters, grandmothers and community leaders, as well as negotiating sexual politics across and within cultures. Such a standpoint does not deny the diversity of Indigenous women's experiences. Indigenous women will have different concrete experiences that shape our relations to core themes.[35]

Moreton-Robinson methodologies seek to make visible 'whiteness in power relations between white feminists and Indigenous women through examining their self-representation and representations of others.'[36] Feminist texts are interrogated to disclose orthodoxies around notions of 'sisterhood' and to 'challenge the right of white anthropologists to speak on behalf of all Indigenous women.'[37]

Methodological reform for Moreton-Robinson centers on the need to move beyond research epistemes that center the privileges, experiences and values of the middle-class white woman. She draws upon 'postcolonial critique of epistemological foundationalism to argue that all knowledge is situated and therefore partial.'[38] The solution for Moreton-Robinson[39] is methodological intersubjectivity – the need

---

34 Ibid.

35 Moreton-Robinson, A. *'Talkin' up to the White Women: Indigenous Women and Feminism*, University of Queensland Press, Australia (2000), p. xvi.

36 Ibid., p. xxi.

37 Ibid., p. xvi.

38 Ibid., p. xxii.

39 Ibid., pp. 179–186.

to get beyond self-hegemonic privilege to examine realities from a multitude of differing perspectives. In other words, for non-Indigenous women to move beyond the conditions of their own privilege and therefore their own hegemony, they must begin to understand their position, as well as those of Indigenous women through Indigenous realities and experiences. Moreton-Robinson's works expose how non-Indigenous researchers in feminism tend to assume that appropriate research questions are framed around social difficulties and 'problems' in the Indigenous community, rather than how Indigenous peoples are treated socially and institutionally through the concept of 'Whiteness' by non-Indigenous society. Moreton-Robinson promotes a conversation with feminism and Whiteness in order to move beyond research methodologies that subjugate, vulgarize and marginalize the 'problems', expectations and aspirations of Indigenous women. In doing so Moreton-Robinson seeks to broaden the use of current methodologies that reproduce partial knowledges of Indigenous women, toward a productive search for methodological reform.

The ongoing challenge for Australian Indigenous scholars is rethinking research methodologies toward the development of reflexive practices which investigate and represent Indigenous worldviews. The clear potential of such challenge is to take seriously the need for methodological reform in order to strengthen knowledge production methods toward privileging Indigenous voices throughout the entire research process. While this means that Indigenism privileges the diversity of Aboriginal ontological and epistemological frameworks, it does not necessarily mean radically different theoretical and/or methodological research methods. What is distinctive about Indigenism is the Indigenist scholar speaking back to research epistemes that have contributed to the social construction of Indigenous Australians as oppressed. As outlined in the works of Nakata and Moreton-Robinson, Indigenism has no one singular method for research transformation and/or praxis. In other words there is no one essentialized Indigenist research epistemology and ontology. Rather there is a clear commitment to recognize the diversity of Indigenous ontology among Indigenous Australians while bringing reform to the process of knowledge production itself, according to the discourses of preference, engaged and employed by Indigenous scholars.

Having examined some of the theoretical issues within Indigenism, it is important to briefly explore some key principles within Indigenist research. Below I begin to identify three interrelated principles of Indigenist research to bring context to its definition. In identifying the foundations of these principles as Indigenist, I need to clarify what I mean, and what I do not mean, by this concept.

Toward a Definition of Indigenism: Three Key Principles

There are a number of significant dimensions to Indigenist research that set it apart from traditional research. In addressing these, I understand Indigenous research to be informed by three fundamental and interrelated principles:

- Involvement in resistance as the emancipatory imperative in Indigenist research
- Political integrity of Indigenist research
- Giving privilege to Indigenous voices in Indigenist research

Resistance as the Emancipatory imperative in Indigenist Research

Indigenist research seeks to chart our own political and social agendas for liberation from the colonial domination of research and society. I have written elsewhere on the emancipatory imperative in Indigenist research.[40] My thoughts on this principle include:

> Indigenist research is research undertaken as part of the struggle of Indigenous Australians for recognition of the right of self-determination and de-colonisation. It is research that engages with the issues, which have arisen out of the long history of colonisation, occupation, and oppression of Indigenous Australians, which began in earnest with the invasion of Australia by Europeans in 1788. It is research that deals with the history of physical, cultural and emotional genocide. It is also research that engages with the story of the survival and the celebration of resistance struggles of Indigenous Australians to racist oppression. It is research that seeks to uncover and protest the continuing forms of oppression that confronts Indigenous Australians. Moreover, it is research which attempts to support the personal, community, educational, cultural, and political struggles of Indigenous Australians to carve out a way of being for ourselves in Australia in which there is healing from the past oppressions and cultural freedom in the future.[41]

The functions of Indigenism encompass intellectual criticism that is embedded in Indigenous Australian experiences, and that is influenced by the intellectual work of Indigenous scholars to transform Indigenous Australian oppression. My definition here understands that while Indigenism is highly politicized it is not premised on a total rejection of English language or the culture of the dominant. Nor are orthodox research paradigms and methodologies repudiated for 'Indigenous only' knowledge production methods. Let me be clear that Indigenism should not be simplified or misunderstood as an argument for ontological or 'methodological separatism'. At the heart of Indigenist Australian intellectualism is the exploration of theoretical frameworks that encourage the possibilities of intellectual, political, social and economic emancipation. In this sense Indigenism is neither atheoretical nor anti-intellectual. Indigenism seeks the building of a robust Indigenist intelligentsia for the revision of ethics, meta-theories, research epistemes and methodologies to move beyond dichotomies such as object/subject, rational/irrational and white/black.

---

40 Rigney, Lester-Irabinna, 'Internationalisation of an Indigenous Anti-Colonial Cultural Critique of Research Methodologies. A Guide to Indigenist Research Methodology and its principles,' in _WICAZO SA review: Journal of Native American Studies_, Fall, Vol. 14, No. 2 (1999), pp. 116–117.

41 Ibid.

Such research challenges and actively resists the racialization of Indigenous social, cultural/ideological, and attitudinal and behavior formations. Indigenist research rejects the oppressively dehumanizing characterization of Indigenous peoples as oppressed 'victims' in need of charity. Indigenist research arises out of Indigenous social experiences, which celebrate the courage and determination of Indigenous people to survive. Therefore, Indigenist research acknowledges Indigenous peoples as resisters to racialization not victims of it. This approach challenges the power and control that traditional research methodologies exerts and directs attention toward ones that are compatible with Indigenous worldviews.

Political Integrity in Indigenist Research

Indigenist research is research that upholds the political integrity of Indigenous peoples as sovereign First Nations Australians. By political integrity I mean Indigenous ontological and epistemological views about the world that directly translate to Indigenous philosophies, languages, cultural and spiritual values and beliefs. To preserve this political integrity Indigenist research is research undertaken by Indigenous communities themselves who determine their own research priorities and agendas. In doing so Indigenism embraces the need for Indigenous communities to build their own capacity mechanisms to realize the benefits of research. Indigenism acknowledges that history has left Indigenous Australians with deep concerns and suspicion of research. These anxieties, if allowed to reproduce, threaten the work of researchers who seek to engage with Indigenous communities. I would argue that Indigenous autonomy and control over Indigenous knowledges, languages and cultures are fundamental to Indigenist research and that such anxieties about these matters must be resolved if Indigenous communities are to trust research.

Indigenist research is also research conducted by those who identify themselves as Indigenists. Within these writings I acknowledge that there is no unanimous view that exists among Indigenous Australian scholars on the definition, borders and/ or boundaries of Indigenist research. Nor is there a unanimous view on method, methodology and epistemes in conducting research with Indigenous peoples. It is my belief that what is central to Indigenist Research is that Indigenous Australian ideals, values and philosophies are core to the research agenda even if there is difference about what constitutes such values and ideals. However, Indigenist researchers are united in the belief that it is inappropriate for research contributions to Indigenous social movements to come solely from non-Indigenous Australians. Non-Indigenous Australians have until this point essentially monopolized research on Indigenous Australians and this paradigm must be forcefully arrested. Indigenism seeks to privilege the Indigenous researcher if for no other reason than because of our exclusion historically from the entire traditional research enterprise.

Is there a role for non-Indigenous researchers in Indigenist research? Power relations have always exerted a decisive impact on the research relationship of the viewed and the viewer. Therefore, I agree with prominent Indigenous Australian academic Wendy Brady in her analysis of power of who has the right to speak, investigate or research Indigenous issues. She clarifies this position thus:

> This is not about denying critiques, but it is about the right of Aboriginal and Torres Strait Islander people to engage in discourse about setting parameters on how engagement with non-Indigenous researchers is determined. It is also about Aboriginal and Torres Strait Islander people taking away the power of 'experts' to define us as the 'other' and placing Aboriginal and Torres Strait Islander research in a so-called objective framework which displaces us as people and we become alienated from our own knowledge base.[42]

Indigenist research and indeed the social movements of Indigenous Australians are indebted to the research contributions of non-Indigenous Australians. However, many non-Indigenous researchers have built their academic careers on being 'experts' in all things Indigenous, essentially reproducing them as opposed to according the right of Indigenous peoples to speak for themselves and engage in self-reflection in research. Given the colonial nature of 'Aboriginalism' research and the skewed distribution of power between Indigenous and non-Indigenous people in Australia, it becomes the role of non-Indigenous researchers and universities in fact to support the work of Indigenous communities and their researchers to create avenues to facilitate such support.

Indigenist research challenges neocolonial dominance of research based on traditional relationships of researchers and 'subjects' that benefit the researcher interests. It would be misleading to overgeneralize about Indigenist research as a total solution to hegemonic research practices. This is neither expected nor possible. However, the inclusions of Indigenist ideas for methodological reform are functions that promote the redistribution of power. This is a critical feature of Indigenist research. Indeed, such dialogue gives power to authentic voices and authorities not only to research texts but also to the processes themselves. Maintaining Indigenous political integrity throughout the whole research process is vital to self-determination and is a fundamental ingredient of this approach. Mutual respect and power sharing in methodological negotiation and collaboration is essential.

Privileging Indigenous Voices in Research

'Indigenist research is research which gives voice to the voiceless.'[43] Given the history of exploitation and prejudice, it is particularly appropriate that it is Indigenous Australians who determine their own research agenda to make public the voice and experience of their communities in their own way. This is not to suggest that

---

42 Brady, W. 'Beam me up Scotty, communicating across world views on knowledge, principles and procedures for the conduct of Aboriginal and Torres Strait Islander research', in *National Aboriginal and Torres Strait Islander Higher Education Conference Proceeding*. December, ed. C. White, University of Southern Queensland, Toowoomba, Australia (1992), p. 106.

43 Rigney, Lester-Irabinna (1999).

Indigenous researchers are free from bias in their research about Indigenous issues, but that Indigenous researchers working with their communities can determine their own research needs. In saying this, I am also not suggesting that there is cultural homogeneity among Indigenous Australians. Like Indigenous communities on other continents, there is cultural heterogeneity and diversity. Nor am I suggesting that there are no cultural barriers between or intercommunal hostilities within Indigenous communities in Australia. Like all colonized contexts, tensions exist in and between Indigenous peoples. Put simply, 'there are no automatic or natural rapport between Indigenous Australians.'[44] Neither am I suggesting that the minds of Indigenous researchers are free of the propensity for acting out in colonial hegemonic ways as a result of colonialist psychic and cultural internalization.

Indigenous Australians, however, do tend to be more aware and respectful of each other's cultural traditions. Similarly, in some cases, Indigenous researchers are accountable to not only their institutions but also to their communities. It is certainly politically more appropriate that Indigenous Australians be given the option to speak through Indigenous researchers.

Indigenism in its advocacy for methodological reform does not attempt to be free of discourses outside the Indigenous experience; rather it attempts to modify old methodologies and develop new ones for Indigenous intellectuals to write and speak about each other, and about the role our work must play in the development of a neocolonial-free future. It rejects the notion that research on Indigenous people is for the sake of knowledge itself.

I name this research approach *Indigenist*. I am an Indigenous Australian deeply, passionately, and actively committed to and involved in the struggles of my people. The research that I do I see as part of that involvement and therefore must be overtly political. For that I make no apologies. Indigenist research is research which focuses on the lived, historical experiences, ideas, traditions, dreams, interests, aspirations and struggles of Indigenous Australians. I desire that Indigenist research contribute to methodological reform for social justice.

Conclusion

This chapter sought to acknowledge a number of developing views Indigenous Australians have in relation to methodological reform. These include the concerns that the Indigenous Australian has about research into our Indigenous lives. These concerns focus on the power and control in research upheld through methodologies.

Increasingly the dominance of Western-orientated discourse is being challenged by proactive Indigenist research approaches. Recently, Indigenous peoples have embraced higher education and scientific research as tools for social and economic mobility. These approaches are embedded in Indigenous Australian philosophies and

---

44 Ibid.

principles informed by Indigenous knowledges, languages and cultures. Indigenist research approaches are based on a growing consensus that research involving Indigenous knowledges and peoples needs to be conducted in culturally appropriate ways that fit the cultural preferences, practices and aspirations of Indigenous peoples.

In developing the Indigenous Research Reform Agenda, Indigenism is calling for a new engagement with Indigenous Australians to bring research methodologies and practices in line with the priorities of Indigenous peoples. The development of this critical framework for identifying and addressing the barriers in research symbolically demonstrates that Indigenous scholars and their communities are not overwhelmed by these problems nor are we short of solutions. For me, an exciting aspect of Indigenism in Australia is that our success does not rest on whether there is uniformity on the problems nor their solutions, but that a commitment is made to robust debate on reforming the culture of research for social change.

Acknowledgements

Writing is a demanding activity that imposes a responsibility to recognize those who make this act possible. To my family, Tikari, Tarniwarra and Kurraki. It is for you my pen writes with precision. To the members, Elders and community leaders of the Narungga, Kaurna and Ngarrindjeri Nations. I hope my words here do justice to your wisdom. It is the sharing of your knowledge and your trust in me, for which I am truly humble. Similarly, I could not write one word without recognition of the committed struggle of my fellow Indigenous activists and academic colleagues who came before me. For this I thank you for your struggle. To the current generation of Indigenous leaders and scholars. I hope my writings here assist our relentless intellectual pursuit of academic excellence. For to strive for academic excellence is to serve the struggle for liberation from colonialism.

References

Asante, M.K. *The Afrocentricity Idea*, Philadelphia: Temple University Press (1987).

Bishop, R. *Collaborative Research Stories: Whakawhanaungatanga*, Dunmore Press, Palmerston North, New Zealand (1996).

Foley, D. *An alternative research approach: Indigenous standpoint theory.* Paper presented at the Australian Studies Conference, Flinders University, Adelaide, Australia (July 2002).

Martin, K. 'Ways of knowing, being and doing: A theoretical framework and methods for Indigenous and Indigenist re-search', in *Voicing Dissent*, eds K. McWilliam, P. Stephenson and G. Thompson, University of Queensland Press, Australia (2003), pp. 203–257.

Nakata, Martin. 'But what does it mean?' in *Ngoonjook, Journal of Australian Indigenous Issues*, (December 1998a), pp. 19–28, Bachelor College, Northern Territory.

Rigney, Lester-Irabinna. 'Indigenous education, languages and treaty: The redefinition of a new relationship with Australia', in *Treaty: Let's get it right*, eds ATSIC & AIATSIS, AIASTSIS, Canberra, ACT (2003).

_____ 'Indigenous Education and treaty: Building Indigenous management capacity', in *Balayi: Culture, Law and Colonialism*, Vol. 4 (2002a), pp. 73–82

_____ 'Foreword', in *Alas for the pelicans: Flinders, Baudin and Beyond*, eds A. Chittleborough, G. Dooley, B. Glover and R. Hosking. Wakefield Press, Adelaide, Australia (2002b).

_____ 'Research with respect: Supervising Aboriginal and Torres Strait Islander Students', in *Assisting Research Students From Non-Traditional Background*, eds J. Sillitoe, G. Crosling, J. Webb and S. Vance, HERDSA, Victoria (2002c), pp. 8–19.

_____ 'Internationalisation of An Indigenous Anti-Colonial Cultural Critique of Research Methodologies. A Guide to Indigenist Research Methodology and its principles', in *HERDSA Annual International conference proceedings; Research and development in Higher Education: Advancing International Perspectives*, Vol. 20 (1997a), pp. 629–636: Reprinted with permission in *WICAZO SA review: Journal of Native American Studies*, Fall, Vol. 14, No. 2 (1999), pp. 109–122.

_____ *Racism and physical education: A critical Indigenist analysis of the Senate Standing Committee's Report on Physical and Sport Education*, unpublished Master Thesis, University of South Australia, Adelaide (1997b).

_____ *Tools for an Indigenist methodology, A Narungga perspective*, paper presented at The World Indigenous Peoples Education Conference, Albuquerque, New Mexico (15–23 June 1996).

_____ Indigenous Australians: Addressing racism in Education, in *Dulwich Centre Newsletter*, No. 2–3 (1995), pp. 5–15.

Scheurich, J. and Young, M. 'Coloring Epistemologies: Are Our Research Epistemologies Racially Based?' *Educational Researcher*, Vol. 26, No. 4 (1997), pp. 4–16

Smith, G.H. *Tane-Nui-a-Rangi's Legacy: Propping up the sky: Kaupapa Maori as resistance and intervention*, Paper presented at the New Zealand Association for research in education/Australian Association for research in education joint conference, Deakin University, Australia (1992a).

_____ 'Research issues related to Maori Education', in *The Issue of Research and Maori (Monograph no 9)*, Department of Education, University of Auckland, New Zealand (1992b).

_____ *Research issues related to Maori education*, paper presented to NZARE, Special Interest Conference, Massey University, reprinted in 1992, *The Issue of Research and Maori*, Research unit for Maori education, University of Auckland (1990).

Smith, L.T. *Decolonising Methodologies: Research and Indigenous peoples*, Zed books, University of Otago Press, Dunedin, New Zealand (1999).

_____ 'Te Rapunaite ao Marama: Maori perspective on research in education', in Morss, J.R. and Linzey, T.J., eds, *The Politics of Human Learning, Human Development and Education Research*, Dunedin, University of Otago Press (1991).

Stanfield, J.H. 'Ethnic modelling in qualitative research', in N. Denzin and Y. Lincoln, eds, *Handbook of Qualitative Inquiry*, Newbury Park, CA: Sage (1994), pp. 175–188.

_____ 'Epistemological considerations', in J.H. Stanfield II and R.M. Dennis, eds, *Race and Ethnicity in Research Methods*, Newbury Park, CA: Sage (1993a), pp. 16–36.

_____ 'The ethnocentric basis of social science knowledge production', in *Review of Research in Education*, 12 (1985), pp. 387–415.

Te Hennepe, S. 'Issues of Respect: Reflections of First Nations Students' experiences in Post-secondary Anthropology Classrooms, *Canadian Journal of Native Education*, Vol. 20. No. 2 (1993), pp. 199–201.

Turtle Island (North America)

Chapter 4

The Power of Indigenous Knowledge: Naming and Identity and Colonization in Canada

Laara Fitznor

I acknowledge and give thanks to the Creator for all of life and all the gifts we have received to sustain the healing, wisdom, and strength in mind, body and spirit. I acknowledge and give thanks to the Creator for this opportunity to create, to give, to share, and to live in a healthy way. I follow the lead of elders and traditional teachers who when they start a teaching begin by saying: 'This was told to me, this is what was given to me, I was asked to pass this on, I acknowledge the many teachers I have had and I thank them for these teachings that I share with you'[1]

Introduction

'I've often wondered how you do it. You seem to live with such ease in two worlds.' A colleague and sister in Aboriginal education said these words to me when we were talking about the capacity we, as Aboriginal peoples, need to have to be able to live in 'two worlds,' that is, the mainstream world and the Aboriginal world. This is one of the obvious legacies resulting from European intrusion on Aboriginal lands and peoples: living in multiworlds. The response to my friend reflected my lifelong experiences, knowledge acquisition and learning to come to a place where I could understand and live effectively in the two worlds, and a third to be explained later. Though I am conscious of the fact that I live in and am influenced by two worlds I am aware that path has not always been easy.

I value and wish to celebrate my heritage as an Aboriginal and Cree woman to the fullest potential of our philosophies and perspectives in spite of the odds against living in this manner. I have learned that '[A]sserting Aboriginal philosophies is a daily struggle because of the differences between our two worlds and because the "white world" has the status of legitimacy in North American society.'[2]

---

1   Fitznor, Laara, 'The Circle of Life: Affirming Aboriginal Philosophies in Every Day Living'. In Dawn McCance (ed.) *Life Ethics in World Religions*. Scholars Press. Atlanta, Georgia (1998), p. 23.

2   Ibid.

My colleague and I discussed themes that reflected clear family and cultural identification and familiarity with our Aboriginal heritage, among other things. I related the kind of understandings and knowledge I have gained about the complex issues related to our multiple locations of 'Aboriginal statuses,' a legacy of European colonialism and subsequent imposition of Eurocentric labeling of our peoples' names, cultures, religions, languages, policies, and practices. I experienced a Western-influenced Eurocentric educational background, countered by the intentional educational focus on Aboriginal rights, issues, perspectives, and understandings throughout my personal, social, vocational, and academic life.

As my friend and I talked, I shared thoughts which I believe have served as guiding principles in my life. I acknowledged people like the many Aboriginal cultural/spiritual teachers and elders who have made an impact on my thinking, teaching, and learning. I also acknowledged many non-Indigenous people who were colleagues, friends, and supporters, even those who gave me reason to struggle against the oppression of the inequities in the mainstream white world. I acknowledged the educational processes of becoming aware with each learning situation that served either to deepen my thinking or challenge my own limited paradigms about life in general and about our location as Aboriginal peoples in Canada, and as Indigenous peoples across Mother Earth.

I recognized early on in my youth that having an Aboriginal identity in white-dominant Canada was not to be an easy one. I found myself in situations where I was continually and inadvertently working to correct misconceptions and inaccuracies about Indigenous peoples. I needed to assert myself as an Indigenous person, to promote and to stand up for what we Aboriginal peoples believe in, for our rights and for our worldviews. There have been far too many situations in which I was spurred to counter misconceptions, prejudices, stereotypes, racism, and sexism about Aboriginal peoples. There were many times that I was asked questions that reflected stereotyped notions of how I should be or act in situations. I've been asked 'How do you cope?' or 'How come you are not angry?' after I have told about my encounters with oppressive, racist, and sexist incidents. Interestingly, people from the dominant culture have their own perceptions of how we as an 'oppressed' people should behave. Yet ironically when we do erupt in outbursts of passion or anger, we are told that we have a 'chip on our shoulder' and we 'should get past the anger.'

As an Aboriginal person today, the complexities that I can live out and navigate quite effectively are evident to me, but not without some level of anxiety about the many struggles and difficulties that confront many of us Indigenous peoples today. I would argue that these struggles and complexities are prevalent in the lives of many Aboriginal people. Yes, my friends, I have learned to negotiate living in two worlds, sometimes more. I have learned to understand where the worlds overlap, diverge, or converge after years of trying to understand our Aboriginal-European Canadian context. There were times I wondered about this love-hate relationship that some white people seem to have toward us. I believe that one of my tasks is to understand and counter this conflict as I work to celebrate our heritage. Actually, after giving some thought to what it is like to live in these worlds and after listening to elders speaking about our situations, I realize that we live in three worlds: the Eurocentric imposed world, the Aboriginal world and the world in between where there is some overlap or integration ... that space that is sometimes fraught with misunderstandings and conflict but has the potential for understanding and cross-cultural bridging.

Certainly, the struggles and complexities we live out as Aboriginal peoples implicated in multiworlds against a Western Eurocentric dominance is like a complex dance that requires constant attention to its choreography. There is this recognition, a 'knowing' that the usual equilibrium has been spun out of its center and there is that constant struggling for balance for meaningful connections and wholeness. I recently read a novel by Tomson Highway, who is in Cree relational terms my brother, a Cree colleague, skilled storyteller and author of a novel entitled *Kiss of the Fur Queen*. It is the story of two young Cree brothers who were wrested away to Indian residential schools and suffered disruptions and attacks on their language, their innocence as children, their culture, self-esteem and dignity because of assimilative and racist policies and practices. To their horror they also suffered sexual abuse at the hands of priests, the residential schools' so-called caregivers. The novel also speaks to the experiences of navigating in two worlds and the constant struggles and reminders that they are not really free *to be* in either world. Tomson uses his Cree knowledge against Western European perspectives by interspersing Cree concepts and words into the novel that make for an interesting read. I suggest that this 'blending' of two perspectives is the space in between the two worlds ... one of the three worlds I mentioned earlier.

In this chapter, I share some stories about my understanding regarding the position of Aboriginal peoples within Canadian society (read: filtered through the legacies of the Indian Act of Canada). I then connect some stories of my family and aspects of my life that reflect the bigger picture of Aboriginal peoples in Canada. My intention is to share some of my earlier experiences about my Cree identity since I believe that upbringing influences my life today. I argue that there is the constant struggle of living in diverse situations: challenging stereotypes, racism, and prejudices by the dominant Eurocentric culture; educating biased and uninformed non-Aboriginal people about us; and educating Aboriginal people who have lost all positive connection to their ancestral heritage.

Aboriginal Peoples in Canada: Tricked, Cheated, Confused, Humiliated and Divided by Colonizing-Eurocentric Policies

My heart is sorry all the time; it cries every day. All the Indian country feels sad.[3]

If there was a crime ... It was more your crime than ours ... You abolished our governments, annihilated our laws, suppressed our authorities, took away our lands, turned us out of our houses, denied us the rights of men (sic), made us outcasts and outlaws in our own land,

---

3   Big John, Skokomish-1850s, in *From the Heart: Voices of the American Indian*, Lee Miller (ed.), 1996, 330.

plunging us at the same time into an abyss of moral degradation which was hurling our people to swift destruction.[4]

These quotes speak so jarringly and sadly of a time of sadness and fear of continual Eurocentric encroachment upon our lands, languages, cultures and peoples both in Canada and the United States. Now, five hundred years later, while we still have the same concerns, we are also now more confident that we are regaining a sense of who we are as peoples and we are asserting our rights, perspectives, cultures and languages in a climate somewhat more open to diversity. Finally, too, there is the recognition of the distinct place we as Aboriginal peoples hold in Canadian society, different from immigrant groups. I refer to us, as Aboriginal peoples of Canada, to frame some of the same issues we encounter and confront while highlighting our needs and aspirations. It is important to clarify that while I speak of Aboriginal peoples, the term may strike one as a seemingly identical group of people. I need to stress that we comprise much diversity in our communities:

> There are over one million Aboriginal People in Canada; over 2000 Aboriginal communities…[across]…every province and territory. Aboriginal People live in cities; they live in primarily white rural settings; they live in mostly Aboriginal settings like First Nation's communities but ones primarily controlled by white governments and bureaucracy; they live in mixed White, Metis, and status Indian communities. All of this makes full functioning of Aboriginal philosophies and practices difficult to achieve. We need to be aware of the complexity of the Western centric dominance and have an appreciation for the fact that there are many struggles involved in focusing energies and scarce resources to challenge stereotypes and problematic social conditions ….[5]

I cannot emphasize enough that I believe these social conditions have resulted from the history of Canadian oppressive, sexist, and racist policies and practices that have been directed at Aboriginal peoples. Breaking free from these patterns of dominance and control has been a constant struggle for Aboriginal peoples.

I would like to draw attention to two interrelated issues: the confusing policy of the Indian Act of Canada, and how the paternalistic, racist, and sexist Canadian governmental policies have affected my own family. This process highlights the historical and political background on the terminology, or naming, of Aboriginal peoples: First Nations (Indians), Metis peoples and nonstatus Indians in Canada as these groups relate to the Indian Act. I will show how these are the primary Aboriginal 'classifications' to which my family and cultural group belong. It also sets the context within another European legacy of imposing hierarchical classes on Aboriginal peoples that did not exist prior to European colonial contact.[6]

The Highlights of the 1994 Report of the Royal Commission on Aboriginal Peoples noted that treaties were originally intended as nation-to-nation agreements

---

4   Stand Watie, Cherokee-1850s in *From the Heart: Voices of the American Indian*, Lee Miller (ed.), 1996, 344.

5   Fitznor, 1999, 24–25.

6   (DIAND) Department of Indian Affairs and Northern Development, 1999, viii.

to *share* the land and its resources. Unfortunately, over time relationships changed when policies were introduced with intentions to subjugate and control the lives of Aboriginal peoples:

Treaties were replaced with policies intended to: remove Aboriginal Peoples from their homelands ... suppress Aboriginal Nations and their governments...undermine Aboriginal cultures ... [and] ... stifle Aboriginal identity.[7]

One of these policies, the Indian Act legislated in 1876, '... consolidated and expanded previous Indian legislation'[8] and determined who were 'Indians' in Canada. I submit that 'Indians' in reality are binding 'wards' of the government. Additionally, I would contend that the assimilative intent of the Indian Act limited the number of people who could be considered 'Indians.' These relationships therefore limited any financial or protectorate responsibilities governments had that were tied to treaties. Thus, the fewer 'Indians' that existed as per the Indian Act, the lesser the financial responsibility. Furthermore, I contend that Aboriginal self-determination has been compromised many times over because the intent of the Indian Act reflected exclusionary, expulsive, territory confining, patriarchal, racist, sexist, and assimilative goals.

It is important to point out that the main intention of the Act was to get rid of our distinctiveness as First Peoples as we existed in our unique relationship with the land and our cultures, ways, spirituality and languages. Battiste,[9] an Aboriginal scholar who has challenged Eurocentric paradigms through her writing and research, states:

For a century or more, [the Department of Indian Affairs and Northern Development] DIAND attempted to destroy the diversity of Aboriginal world-views, cultures and languages...Through ill-conceived government policies and plans, Aboriginal youth were subjected to a combination of powerful but profoundly distracting forces of cognitive imperialism and colonization...The outcome was the gradual loss of these world-views, languages, and cultures and the creation of widespread social and psychological upheaval in Aboriginal communities.

It is an insult to our integrity as sovereign peoples that an alien government can impose classes of categories on our peoples. It says nothing about the cultural and linguistic diversity of Canada, but does say a lot about how the government of Canada views each group and defines how each people will relate to it. These 'classes' are visited in the next section.

---

7   Report of the Royal Commission on Aboriginal Peoples, 1994, 1.

8   Borrow, John and Rotman, Leonard, *Aboriginal Legal Issues: Cases, Materials and Commentary*. Butterworths, Toronto and Vancouver (1998), 615.

9   Battiste, 1999.

'Indians' According to the Canadian Indian Act

According to the Indian Act, Indians in Canada are those individuals who are registered as an 'Indian' with the government of Canada and as holding First Nation membership associated with Treaties and Reserves (First Nation's communities). During the early years of policy enactment, only men were considered 'Indians.' That 'man,' his wife and children followed his line as 'Indian' people. Only men were allowed to vote in local band elections. It is relevant to note neither Indian men nor women were allowed to vote in Canadian elections prior to 1960. Further, '... all "legal" Indians were wards of the government and were to be treated as minors without the full privileges of citizenship.' Many of my relatives were and are 'Indians' according to this act and many of them live in First Nation communities in northern Manitoba and northwestern Ontario. Both my paternal and maternal grandmothers lost their statuses as 'Indian' when they married my nonstatus Indian grandfathers. (My maternal grandfather was a nonstatus Indian while my paternal grandfather was a German immigrant to Canada.) Clearly then, 'Indian' is a legal definition describing one of the groups of the Aboriginal peoples of Canada.

When it came to access to formal education, the Indian Act proved more complex with the federal and provincial jurisdictions regarding state laws and responsibilities for 'Indians.' Youngblood Henderson indicates how complex the education process proved in exercising Aboriginal rights and education because of provincial and federal jurisdictions regarding various obligations to Canadian citizenry and Indians under the Canadian Constitution Act of 1867 and later the Indian Act of 1876:

> ... both Indians and lands reserved for Indians were exclusive matters of federal responsibility ... whereas schooling and education was a matter of provincial responsibility ... [T]he federal government created 'Indians' as an exclusive constitutional class of people in the provinces which confederated, and 'Indians and lands for Indians' were transferred to federal jurisdiction, separate from provincial authority.[10]

This assertion explains somewhat the complications that arise when attempting to promote Aboriginal education across the provinces when each province has the jurisdiction for education. Furthermore, because of the Indian Act, residential schools were implemented with the intention to educate and 'civilize' Aboriginal peoples along with other '...[P]olicies, combined with missionary efforts to civilize and convert Indigenous people.'[11] Unfortunately for us, on the whole these efforts '... tore wide holes in Aboriginal cultures, autonomy and feelings of self-worth'[12] that we are now mending and healing. O'Meara (1996) related this same sentiment of how the worldview of her people, the Nawash Ojibway, 'was shaken by its very core by the assimilationist policies of the federal government.'[13] I argue here that

---

10 Henderson, Youngblood, 1995, 248.
11 RCAP, 9.
12 Ibid.
13 Ibid., 136.

although we have been quite shaken up from the impacts of these policies, the assimilative efforts failed to make us completely forsake our lands, languages, and cultures in favor of the imposed ones. We are emerging and regaining confidence in and asserting our traditions, our elders' knowledge, our stories, wisdom, cultures, languages and philosophies and in ways our elders from the past had prophesied!

The 'Metis' Aboriginal Peoples: Not Indians, Nor Nonstatus Fate

Another group of Aboriginal peoples were the Metis who were born out of the unions between, for the most part, the first colonial European men and Aboriginal women. The Metis were not considered Indian due first to the exclusion of their involvement in many of the treaties and secondly because of exclusionary and discriminative clauses in the Indian Act:

> The Canadian policy toward Metis people was dismissive. They were not 'Indian' and they were not legitimate 'European-type' settlers. The usual practice was to declare them 'squatters' and edge them off the land they were farming when preferred settlers moved in.[14]

The Metis forged political alliances and a collective identity that reflected both European and Aboriginal cultures as they struggled for recognition and for their own land and government. For example, in the case of the province of Manitoba, 'They were promised both in the Manitoba Act of 1870, but those promises were later denied … to this day, their claims for a secure land base and their own form of government have not been settled.'[15]

Over time, the Metis political groups expanded the original definition of their people, which originally referred to the offspring of colonial French and Indian intermarriages or from colonial English and Indian intermarriages. As immigrants from various parts of the world colonized and settled on our lands through Canadian colonial immigration patterns, they subsequently entered into relationships with Aboriginal people and had offspring from these unions. For the most part, the children and grandchildren from these unions were eventually recognized by the Metis organizations as Metis peoples. Those individuals unable to claim status as an Indian could do so under the Metis banner and did so then, and do so today. The assertion is that people self-identify and that they can provide evidence of Aboriginal ancestry. When the Metis Nation took up this issue in the 1980s it was a hotly contested one, but people identified quite strongly with their Aboriginal ancestry and recognized the influences from both cultures they inherited. Today the biological integration of our diverse peoples is greater than ever, where many Aboriginal peoples have interracial admixtures from people from various parts of

---

14 Highlights RECAP, 9.
15 Ibid.

the world who settled in Canada. In my family alone we have mixes with people from the following backgrounds: European, Asian, Afro-Caribbean, and African.

Although the term *Metis* has been associated primarily with mixed-blood peoples, those individuals who hold 'Indian' status can also be of mixed blood, which clearly makes it a political and social definition in addition to the recognition of Aboriginal ancestry. For example, prior to the 1985 amendment to the Indian Act (discussed later in this chapter), when an Indian man married a white woman the offspring from this union would have been mixed-blood. However, because the man has Indian status then the children are considered of Indian status and attention to the mixed ancestry is not singled out. Presumably, the child's identity as an Indian is 'protected' under the Indian Act. Yet when an Indian woman married a non-Indian the offspring were considered of mixed blood and therefore Metis.

It is important to note that there are yet numerous definitions that the Metis peoples have had imposed on them over time both in the US and Canada. It is distressing that Metis people have gone through so many different labels fraught with derogatory connotations imposed from both sides of their heritages. However, the scope of this chapter permits only a few definitions.

How did my family become classified as holding Metis status? There is often the confusion between understanding that there are differences between cultural, political and social definitions of people. When we were growing up in our small northern community we saw ourselves as Cree, a major cultural linguistic group in Canada and the United States. We did not think about the political, social or governmental classifications unless they emerged in conversations with status 'Indian' relatives who visited us, or in school when the teachers asked for Indian status numbers from students of Aboriginal ancestry. I recall that I used to wonder why the teacher needed to know that information during my school years. Now in my adult years of working as an educator and faced with gaining access to funds for program development, I learned that the school administrators submit documents to the provincial government who then forward them to the federal government for reimbursement. Presumably this was done to receive funding to offset the costs of the education of those of Indian status (read: 'Indians' are a federal responsibility yet education is a provincial responsibility). I contend that this was a sneaky (unethical?) practice where the intentions were not usually disclosed to the students or their parents. Furthermore, this is definitely an issue of offloading and jurisdiction. Today there are more equitable education and tuition agreements that have been negotiated between various First Nations and the Canadian government.

During the late 1960s and early 1970s the Metis political movement directed their efforts to recruit northern Manitoba nonstatus Indians and 'mixed bloods' to join their organization. At that time our family members who were nonstatus Indians and/or mixed-blood (Metis) would have been labeled half-breeds, a derogatory intended term applied to my father in his youth (earlier in this paper I wrote that my father was a child of a German father and Cree mother who was stripped of her status as an Indian). A political association, the Manitoba Metis Federation, organized chapters or local organizations in northern Manitoba communities where a core of nonstatus or Metis people lived. For example, many Metis and nonstatus Indians lived as 'squatters' on Crown land that bordered reserve (First Nation) communities. Individuals who identified themselves as Metis could join this political organization which addressed their political and social needs and aspirations. Many people joined this organization and because we were not status Indians, we would have been identified with being Metis Cree (the word Metis identifies mixed heritage and the word Cree identifies the cultural linguistic group). Even if people did not actually sign up for membership, the local Manitoba Metis Federation groups often took up issues that affected them in relation to housing, employment, and training. Therefore, according to the original definition of a Metis (mixed white/Indian heritage) and not having full Indian status, many of my family members were considered Metis.

'Nonstatus Indians' According to the Politics of Naming Aboriginal Groups

Another group, the nonstatus Indian peoples, have also had a precarious existence in Canadian society. Although they are of Aboriginal heritage (whether full bloods or not), they were not considered 'Indians' for a number of reasons, some of which included discriminatory clauses in the Indian Act, such as being uncounted for the treaty registration processes for band membership, and originally not being considered Metis according to the colonial Canadian definition of a Metis. It is also important to note that some Aboriginal communities did not cede their territories for treaties and therefore would have been considered nonstatus Indians. The Metis political organizations recognized the precarious state of nonstatus Indians early on in their organizing efforts and therefore included nonstatus Indians in their organizations for common struggles and assertion of rights. For example, I know of a story passed down from my father about the Indian men from his and his mother's home reserve who went and fought alongside other Metis and the Manitoba Metis leader Louis Riel in the Riel 'Rebellion' of 1885. When the Indian men attempted to return to their homes, the Indian Agent barred them from living on the reserve because they were considered 'traitors' for daring to stand up to the government. Their Indian status classification was stripped from their identity and they became 'squatters' on Crown land along with the Metis who also returned to their 'squatters' community.[16] Hence, the nonstatus Indians who were originally Indian as defined by the Indian Act but who lost their status through the oppressive, racist and sexist assimilative policies related to the Indian Act for all intents and purposes became as marginalized as the Metis people.

Furthermore, prior to the 1985 amendment of the Indian Act, there were other reasons an Indian was required to give up his or her status as an Indian and thus become a nonstatus Indian. Reasons Indian status could be removed included gaining any profession such as teaching or medicine; entering the military in the First World War; having been adopted out during the adoptions scoops of the 1950s, 1960s, and

---

16 Quinlan, D. and Reed, K., *Aboriginal Peoples: Building for the Future*. Oxford Canadian Challenges (1999), 44.

1970s; or buying private or Crown property. These actions were the result of another Indian Act, a related policy of enfranchisement to gain the 'right to vote,' as Indians were denied voting rights prior to 1960 when they were 'given' the right to vote in federal elections. Another interesting legacy where the term enfranchisement, a concept of liberation, meant '... giving up or losing Indian status since the only way an "Indian" person could gain the right to vote was if s/he gave up status ... [as Indian!]'[17] What a quandary it must have been for those individuals who were forced to move in these conflicting and convoluted directions. Even so, I suspect that many individuals would not have thought about the outcomes of their actions until they made moves to return to their home 'reserve' communities. At that point they would be informed that they are no longer 'Indian' and therefore could no longer reside with their families! These changes would also affect the descendants of the individuals who were forced to give up their status as Indians.

Another one of the more insidious forms of racism and sexism in the Indian Act, prior to its 1985 amendment, was the way it discriminated against Indian women, some of whom were my grandmothers and other female relatives. For example, Indian women lost their status as Indians if they married someone who was a non-Indian (whether the man was Metis, nonstatus Indian or European was not relevant). Yet if an Indian man married a non-Indian woman she became 'Indian' (whether she was Metis, nonstatus Indian or European was not relevant). Many non-Indian white women become Indians through this ludicrous ill-fated policy while many Indian women lost their status as Indians! Consider how this affects future generations: all the children born of the union between a status Indian husband and his biologically non-Aboriginal but status Indian wife were granted status as 'Indians.' However, if a status Indian woman married a nonstatus Indian man, as in the case of my Cree Indian status grandmother and non-Indian German grandfather, then all the children from this union fell under the category of nonstatus Indian or Metis. There have been cases where one set of cousins had Indian status and the other had nonstatus Indian designations. These distinctions have created many chaotic situations for many relatives. Furthermore, when the women were stripped of their Indian status they were usually barred from living in the community of their families! This has happened to both my grandmothers who married non-Indian men, one of them a nonstatus Indian man. Imagine the conundrum it caused to traditional familial and cultural ties, practices and obligations! In our case, it was difficult to maintain consistent and meaningful contacts with our on-reserve status Indian relatives. When we visited our Indian relatives during summer vacations, while our cousins accepted us we were often not accepted by some reserve Indian children because in their eyes we were 'white,' even though they knew we were related to the community.

Borrow and Rotman highlight this inequality. For many years, Indian women who married non-Indian men automatically lost their status under the Indian Act. If an Indian man married a non-Indian women, no such disability was incurred. The disparate impact of these provisions reflected the patrilineal assumptions that

---

17 Ibid.

underlie the Act. Once a woman lost her status she could no longer reside on the reserve, secure treaty promises and policy initiatives designed to assist Indians, or participate in the political and social life of the community. The effect of these provisions was to fracture extended families and exile women from their homes and culture. This legislation sent women from the reserves and undermined their influence and position within their communities. In the last few decades this negative change in gender relations created a drive to reconstruct Indian communities and restore the dignity and respect Indian women once enjoyed. The effort to reinstate this dignity was undertaken by some very courageous women who worked hard against the discrimination they faced.[18]

I argue that the parochial, patriarchal, sexist and racist policy, the Indian Act, reflected Canada's ideologies of the time. It certainly ignored the traditional matriarchies and philosophies of many Aboriginal groups. Still today we struggle against such ideologies. We owe many thanks and gratitude to the brave and courageous women who lost their Indian status because they married non-Indian men when they took the issue up in court and it reached the highest court in the land. Consequently, the Supreme Court of Canada ordered changes to the Indian Act in 1985, the Bill C-31 amendment.

Bill C-31: Indians in the Canadian Indian Act of 1985

A major change to the Indian Act legislated in 1985 was the Bill C-31 amendment. For the most part, this was a triumph for many Aboriginal people who felt they were without choice disconnected from their destiny as Aboriginal peoples and felt that their cultural, familial, social and political destiny could best be served under the status Indian classification. Therefore, any nonstatus Indian or Metis person who could provide evidence against a reinstatement criteria was eligible to apply for Indian status through the Bill C-31 amendment of the Indian Act. Although there was a change to the Indian Act many Aboriginal women still feel that it did not go far enough to protect future generations of female children. For example, there could potentially be one generation of nonstatus Indians or Metis who could regain Indian status but their children or following descendants would be reverted back to their earlier designated classification of nonstatus Indian or Metis. Marilyn Buffalo, President of the Aboriginal Women's Association of Canada stated that 'under Bill C-31, an individual who has just one Indian parent must marry a status Indian if the children are to inherit Indian status.'[19] For example, in my case I was reinstated as an Indian as a result of the Bill C-31 amendment to the Indian Act, and my daughter also regained Indian status; however, her children would not have Indian status unless the other parent was also Indian. Thus the discrimination and classification shifting continues under the Bill C-31 amendment.

---

18 Borrow and Rotman, 1998, 612.
19 *Edmonton Journal*, May 17, 1999.

Statistics show that the status Indian population increased quite dramatically after 1985 due to successful Indian status reinstatement applications. At the same time, many Metis organizations reported that decreased membership rates were a result of successful reinstatement from Metis and nonstatus Indian classifications to status Indian. It is clear then that the amendment of the Indian Act in 1985 created yet another classification of Indians within the Indian Act. Many 'Bill C-31 Indians' have had problems with accessing benefits associated with status Indians. Having Indian status does not automatically guarantee benefits associated with treaties. In fact, having Indian status without the Bill C-31 reinstatement does not guarantee benefits, as the individual could be an off-reserve status Indian. Most of the meager benefits associated with status Indians often are limited and confined to residency on reserves. Furthermore, many First Nations' band councils objected to the Bill C-31 reinstatement process citing concerns related to cultural and language losses and the distribution of resources like land, education funding and housing might be problematic.[20] *Buffalo* (The Edmonton Journal) noted that many First Nations communities have denied reinstatement to band membership in spite of the amendment to the Indian Act. The issue here is that the individual must apply to both the Department of Indian Affairs and the individual First Nation for membership. Not gaining acceptance in a First Nation membership simply means that the reinstated individual cannot access any benefits associated with band residency.

Confusing Labels and Classification Test Cultural Ties

It has taken generations to try to turn around the devastating results of these policies and it is up to us as Aboriginal peoples to take the path to healing and self-determination. Yes, though we are constitutionally recognized as original inhabitants of this land, as Aboriginal peoples we are divided into classifications. The unfortunate outcomes are many: we are stratified into a hierarchy that is 'resource' driven. Issues of who is a 'real' Indian can spark interesting discussions when we speak of Metis peoples, nonstatus Indians, Indians (and within this classification the Bill C-31 Indians) and Inuit peoples of Canada. This has created awkward relationships wherein two groups, the Metis and nonstatus Indians usually (though some Metis groups have been successful with their land claims) do not have a land base or a resource base as accorded to (status Indian) First Nations' groups.

Many misconceptions occur when it comes to cultural, linguistic, and family ties and expressions. Having 'status' as an Indian does not mean that individual is necessarily culturally connected to her or his language, family or spirituality as one might wrongly assume. Nevertheless, spiritual, cultural, family, political and personal expressions of Aboriginal identities are alive and well in spite of the status/ nonstatus issue. Aboriginal peoples cover the spectrum of being fully assimilated

---

20 Borrow and Rotman, Ibid.

into western Canadian society to fully immersed into Aboriginal society and many expressions of both in between.

Classifications clearly are a threat to collective cultural and Aboriginal identities. 'Who is a real Indian?' questions tend to arise when educators attempt to provide culturally relevant educational experiences. As I mentioned earlier in this paper, these Aboriginal classifications say nothing about the cultural and linguistic diversity of our peoples, it only speaks to the kind of relationship each has with the Canadian government.

There are interesting paradoxes that exist here from the making of Aboriginal classifications related to the Indian Act. Yes, the Metis, nonstatus Indian and status Indian (and Bill C-31 Indian) groups are all Aboriginal peoples. Yet consider the following: it is fact that many Metis people have more biological Aboriginal ancestry than do status Indian people. Some Indian people do not even have biological Aboriginal ancestry (read: case of white women who married Indian men prior to 1985, white children adopted by Indian families, and in the early days of treaty making some white men and women were counted as Indians in some communities). A few Indians have used their legal status category only to access benefits, not necessarily to sustain or express their full cultural, social and political affiliations. Their reasons are many, some of which related to negative identification with Aboriginal ancestry. Many nonstatus Indians and Metis are full-blood Aboriginal peoples as are status Indian people.

It is clear then that the 'quantum blood' of Aboriginal ancestry is not the primary factor of being an Indian. I submit that it is the connection to the hegemony of government policy making and the individual's Aboriginal historic fate of gender, residence at the time of treaty making, and individual choices to access mainstream property, education and professions for their vision of survival. For the government it was all in the name of assimilation. Clearly too, for the Aboriginal person, the connections to the Aboriginal Nation, family, culture, community and language is an important consideration. For Aboriginal people it is also concern related to the loss of recognition of being Aboriginal. It is easy to determine then that the Indian Act has created many social, personal, cultural, political and economic disruptions related to the oppressive laws of Canadian governmental processes. Notwithstanding the degree of cultural genocide we suffered, the government's past intent to assimilate us through the Indian Act and other policies that related to Aboriginal peoples were failed prospects indeed!

Sticks and Stones May Break My Bones, Names will Never Hurt Me??? Do Hurt!

'Sticks and stones may break my bones but names will never hurt me' is an old saying that bears false security that names do not hurt. If we were to listen to the many stories of our peoples, we would know from the tears they shed as they speak that names do hurt. I have been a teacher/facilitator of many circles where people have shared their innermost thoughts related to racism, sexism, cultural displacements, labeling and such atrocities where they have shared hurts and pains.

Furthermore, because of the nature of our relationship to the government, a number of other social classifications related to Aboriginal peoples do indeed exist, but I do not take them up here as they are beyond the scope of this paper. These labels are indeed a part of the Aboriginal fabric of identities that play into our lives as we live within the Canadian context. These labels include 'urban Indian,' 'off-reserve Indian,' 'on-reserve Indian' and other less flattering terms I will not mention. We have been wrung through so many descriptions, labels and names imposed on our peoples, as aptly stated by Deloria: 'For most of the five centuries whites have had unrestricted power to describe Indians in any way they chose.'[21]

Imposed categories and descriptions have, without doubt, created much confusion in our identifications as Aboriginal peoples. Canadians in general, too, tend to get confused, as many times the Canadian public does not know how to refer to us. There are numerous times in my classes on Aboriginal education and perspectives that I have been asked 'Well, what should we call people in these communities then?' I usually respond that people need to educate themselves about the historic patterns of Canadian policies related to Aboriginal peoples, as well as find out from Aboriginal perspectives what their needs and aspirations are. Get to know the people, and for the sake of good manners and respect find out from the people with whom they are connected. How presumptuous it was on the part of government officials to even define our peoples by names not originating from us or reflected in our own languages. As Aboriginal peoples we have defined ourselves in our own languages but rarely do our own cultural/linguistic names get into the public mind. I have encountered many reactions and responses to these classifications from well-meaning educators who assert that these classifications really mean nothing and we as Aboriginal peoples should not be so 'caught up' with this issue. I say that to propose that these classifications do not hurt people is to deny the colonizing and oppressive processes of assimilation and to deny the emotional and cultural pain that people experience from being shifted from one Aboriginal classification to another. I hope that my story in the next section will provide a glimpse into this conundrum.

Moving between 'White' and Cree Worlds

I place this next story in context of my life: of who I am and where and how I grew up to demonstrate the values I learned about living in our world as a young person and today. I focus on being a young person because this is primarily where I draw strength from certain understandings, values and experiences as I connect to the people around me and live today. I realize also that as time goes on I may change

---

21 Deloria, V., 'Comfortable Fictions and the Struggle for Turf: An Essay Review of *The Invented Indian: Cultural Fiction and Government Policies*'. In Devon A. Mihesuah (ed.) *Natives and Academics: Researching and Writing About American Indians*. University of Nebraska Press (1998), 66.

certain perceptions and perspectives about Aboriginal life in Canadian society as I am immersed in my learning and living. I share those aspects of my young life that I have reflected upon many times and realized that these experiences have sustained me as I quested for visions of Aboriginal expressions in my personal, educational and work experiences. For my readers, I focus on my Cree influences and my community of origin, my ancestral roots through my Cree family, some of my schooling and youth experiences which leads briefly into my adult life including where I am today. Before I do this I need to attempt to answer the question 'Who am I?' in relation to my multiple locations as an Aboriginal woman.

Who Am I?

I am a single mother of a 17-year-old daughter, daughter to kind and caring parents (although my father is now deceased), sister to 13 siblings, aunt to over 80 nieces and nephews (including grand nieces and nephews). In addition, I have a large extended family of aging aunts and uncles and middle-aged cousins with grown up children and grandchildren. I have been a granddaughter in a significant way in that as a young girl I was closely connected to my maternal Oji-Cree grandfather who imprinted many cultural and spiritual influences on my life. I mention my family members because of the tremendous energy and time it takes to maintain and sustain familial and cultural relations and obligations over and above the call of my academic work. I have come to recognize that working in a Western based, nuclear family oriented, individualistic and competitive profession, and coming from an extended family orientation where group/family cooperation and sharing of resources is the norm, has its own tensions. I realize as well that often discussions about family and cultural obligations are silenced against a Western centric academic milieu where the focus is to be successful in academic teaching, research and service activities as defined by institutional norms. I find there are very few times I can discuss with colleagues with whom I feel free to share the cross-cultural tensions and stresses related to the responsibilities of being a dedicated professional and a dedicated family and cultural member.

I am an Aboriginal woman, Nahéyow, Inninew, Cree, and I have been identified with the designated Aboriginal classifications of Metis and nonstatus. I was eligible to be a status Indian through the amendment to the Indian Act; once I got reinstated I became a Bill C-31 status Indian. I maintain that exposing these political/legal/cultural/linguistic descriptions of my Aboriginal identity are important to locate here to demonstrate the added complexities to my work as an Aboriginal educator.

As discussed earlier in this paper, it is evident that the Canadian government, through its colonialist historical and political processes, imposed classifications on my ancestors as policies were crafted primarily to suit the principles of Eurocentric paradigms. Even though we remain immersed in our Nahéyow heritage and culture, members from both sides of my family have lost their status as Indians in spite of the fact that our Aboriginal heritage/biology is greater than our European side. After researching my family history I found that the loss of Indian status in our situation was due to the discriminatory clauses related to Indian women, and to Indian men purchasing private property and possibly gaining a profession. The amendment of the Indian Act in 1985 enabled both my parents and many of my brothers, sisters, cousins, aunts and uncles to apply for and obtain reinstatement as 'status Indians.' For some, reinstatement as an 'Indian' has meant a strengthening of a sovereign recognition of Aboriginal identity where certain benefits intended for Indians can be accessed through resources to certain programs in education, culturally relevant training, cultural and spiritual places in First Nation communities. For some, reinstatement has meant regaining ancestral recognition and rights lost through the Indian Act. For example, my father was raised on a reserve (First Nation) with his Cree grandparents even though he was nonstatus: Indian reinstatement meant a rightful reconnection to his community without feeling like an outsider.

When I give talks at seminars or conferences, sometimes I purposely introduce myself as Inninew, Metis-Cree, nonstatus Indian, eligible to be status Indian through Bill C-31 just to demonstrate the confusion that can comes from ludicrous policies. Also, I do this to demonstrate the complexity of my identity as an Aboriginal educator and to illustrate how Canadian policy confronts and contradicts Aboriginal peoples' ways of life. The responses I generally get to this introduction range from surprised looks on people's faces to outright laughter from those who recognize the problem. The laughter is out of a shared recognition and a challenge to the situation in a farcical sort of way.

I write about my Cree heritage that grounds my Aboriginal cultural and language identity because this is the place where I started on my path as a human being. This is the place that comforts me the most in my quest for understanding life and living life to the fullest. It is important to mention that the cultural and language identification has always been strong for my family, and it is more important than whether we are classified as Metis, status Indian, or Bill C-31 Indian. The whole issue about classifications of Aboriginal peoples has emerged in the struggle for the recognition of our rights, land, distinct culture and self-determination as Aboriginal peoples in Canada. It is a necessary but confusing undertaking that needed to be challenged.

I was born two hundred miles away from my community in a Roman Catholic Eurocentric hospital with nuns who were nurses. I imagine my baby ears were exposed to either the English or French language as the nurses did their work, and I would have heard the Cree language as my mother spoke to me. After the few obligatory days in the hospital, my mother traveled back to our home in Wabowden, Manitoba, Canada, known in our Cree language as Meskanakahnik (my spelling).

Wabowden is not a reserve, but a small mixed white and Native community of 500 people. It is a community where Aboriginal peoples and whites came together to meet, gather, travel and eventually live following a Euro-settlement dominant pattern. The demographics have changed over time from 100 per cent Aboriginal (Cree) pre-European contact to about 80 per cent Aboriginal today. The town of Wabowden has its own Cree name of Meskanakahnik, translated into English it means 'a trail that has been made' or 'the pathway.' Traditionally Wabowden would have been a popular Aboriginal trading and traveling route and meeting place similar to the many modern roads that have been fashioned after Aboriginal traditional traveling and trading routes. Wabowden is accessible by small airplanes, roads, waterways through portaging, and railway, hence its Cree name. Wabowden is the town's 'official' name, derived from a Euro-Canadian man who was a station agent in the early days of the railway development in the 1930s. His name was actually W.A. Bowden and when mail was sent to the community via railway it was addressed 'in care of W.A. Bowden' listing the railway milepost. Eventually the name Wabowden took precedent over Meskanakahnik through the dominant and 'legitimate' Eurocentric settlement legacies. The older people of the community still refer to its original name of Meskanakahnik when they speak in our Cree language and share stories of long ago. When I make visits to my childhood memories through reflective processes, one of the things that fascinates me is how readily it seemed that the Eurocentric name of our community was accepted. But I believe in the hearts and minds of Cree speakers it remains Meskanakahnik. In my younger years I do remember people referring to this word. I found that I think about what they were saying and I realize, Oh, they are talking about Wabowden. Today I ask myself: Is this an indication that in my generation the Eurocentric dominance was internalized without question? It would seem so as I hear Wabowdenites using the word Wabowden with ease. I wonder how many people now know of the Cree name.

My early years in 'Wabowden' until I was six were grounded primarily in Cree surroundings: language, nature, traditional medicines and foods, people, economy and ways of being. Our daily existence was living primarily in the Cree language. Both my father and grandfather were trappers and fishermen first, but they also took on labor or construction jobs that were available to them in their day. We were still dependent on the land for much of our diet: for game, berries and other various foods. We relied on many traditional ways of harvesting and preparing and preserving our foods and preparing our clothes. When we harvested medicines for our health needs, we offered tobacco to Mother Earth to show gratitude for her gifts to our health. When we hunted game we shared what we got with relatives and other community members. Each child, male or female, learned how to hunt for small game, how to trap and procure food. There was a division of labor, but each boy and girl, man and woman, had to know all that was needed for living off the land and looking after each other. It wasn't so boldly stated – we just lived in this way. Also, because the first four of the fourteen siblings were girls, our parents involved us in both indoor and outdoor activities regardless of 'expected' gender roles. Life was challenging with its physical and emotional demands and discipline, but culturally and spiritually rewarding with good values grounded in Cree ways. Values like sharing, interconnectedness between relatives, land, plants, animal life, all was an unspoken understanding, as was the responsibility to our group and family members for sharing material and nonmaterial goods. I remember the many responsibilities we had as children in our family where we were expected to actively participate in the work. I remember doing the following work: I have helped set traps for food and furs; set fishing nets, cleaned fish and prepared it for shipping to places unknown;

chopped and hauled firewood; hauled water from the lake to our dwellings; helped my mother and aunts prepare hides for tanning; preserve and cook food; make clothes; tend our vegetable garden and look after the younger siblings, among many other chores. We learned many local and traditional and modern ways of making clothing, tanning hides, and preparing foods. We worked hard and seemingly long hours, we shared, we laughed a lot, we prayed, we loved the land and Mother Earth's bounties, and we appreciated and loved the beauty of the Northern skies, lakes, rivers and forests, and the plants and animals who kept us healthy. We were fully aware that this life was slowly being eroded as Eurocentric modern conveniences and economic changes pulled us into the modern realities and directions.

In spite of our work ethic and close-knit family circle, I did see the problems associated with alcohol in my community amongst extended family members and neighbors. I fear I may leave the reader with the impression that all was rosy in my growing up years. However, in spite of my immediate family trying our best to live our life in a good and self-sufficient way, living problems did exist. We were hungry during the in-between times of food abundance, and my father had concerns about the well-being of his large family then and for the future. My father also had his struggle with alcohol. Although he rarely brought it into our home, it did affect my mother who did not drink. She was displeased with him when he was out drinking because that meant he wasn't home with us. My father wasn't a heavy or frequent drinker, but he was very aware that his drinking was a distraction from his family responsibilities, so he quit when he was in his forties. Also, he stopped working away from home due to a heart ailment and diabetes. He had old World War Two injuries that also affected his physical condition. When he stopped working there was an interval of relying on social assistance until his war veteran's pension was processed. My mother continued to work as she always had from our home. She prepared baked goods that were sold door-to-door in our community. She also subsidized our income by selling her crafts. All in all our family believed in being self-sufficient and any outside income was subsidized by any gifts of Mother Earth, be it food or medicine.

Our house and property was at least a mile from the nearest house so when we did not have phones and we needed help, one of the children had to run to the community for help, day or night. Furthermore, I wish to be true to the reality of the Euro-settlement transition my community faced and the inevitable social problems that surfaced. I remember being confused and wondering about the partying and the violence that seemed to scream out from some of the homes as I was walking to school. I saw these same people involved in life-nurturing activities at various times, consequently, seeing the partying and violence was confusing to me. It was a contradiction to the way we lived. I recall that my maternal grandfather, who lived with us, forbade the presence of alcohol in our home; he knew how it was becoming a problem with our community. My grandfather opened each morning with a prayer and closed each night with a prayer, albeit in the Bible read in our Cree language. It was known that any of my extended family ought not try and bring parties to our house. They knew this was a household that worked hard and prayed a lot! I suggest here that the praying that went on was a practice that reflected peace, a nurturing place, sacredness, and devotion to a greater power. I don't recall many Bible stories but I do recall the sounds of our language and that was very comforting.

Upon reflection, I realized that because of the fast changes to our economy and ways of living that people were losing their confidence in what we were as Cree peoples. I learned that the community people were losing their traditional livelihoods and were having trouble finding other work to keep their families healthy. They faced racism when they applied for new forms of work that came into the community and surrounding areas like mining and logging. As time went on the social disruption became evident in our community in spite of those who tried to maintain a more traditional lifestyle or for those who continued to live out Cree values in a modern context of Euro-economic livelihoods.

I was aware then too that the attitudes toward 'Indians' in textbooks and the community were fraught with prejudice, stereotypes and racism. The social signification of 'Indian' was not positive, it implied all the negatives stereotypes of the day such as drunk or lazy; I used to wonder which 'Indians' were being referred to in textbooks because we perceived ourselves as Cree people. Even the cowboy-and-Indian movie portrayals did not make sense to us children who would laugh and play cowboys and Indians! What a sham, and a shame, it was to be fooled into playing out these games when we didn't even want to be the Indians! Did that mean too that we did not want to be Indians in real life? As I grew into my teenage years the identification with and distinctions between status Indians, nonstatus Indians, and Metis groups became more apparent. It also became unmistakable to me that the social signification of an 'Indian' was often intended to be negative. Also, this was the term that was used by the public in the generic sense to refer to all Aboriginal peoples regardless of cultural or linguistic differences. Talk about an eye opener! It became evident why my father made it clear to us that we were 'Indians' even though we didn't have 'status'; looking back now I know what he meant. He was referring to the generic use of the term. This was the way the public saw us – not as the cultural and linguistic Cree people that we were. Though my father would not have discerned it this way, I submit it was a personal political statement and a challenge to the notion that we as Aboriginal peoples have been shafted by circumstances of Euro-foundational legacies of government policies.

My father, who had experienced a lot of racism in his First Nation and neighboring white community because of his first-generation mixed heritage, prepared us for the racism and sexism that we would eventually experience. He reflected Cree traditions when he taught us that we should not think of ourselves as less or better than white Canadians – we were equal to everyone. He taught us to be proud of and celebrate our Cree heritage but to acknowledge that we have mixed ancestry too. He was certainly aware that it was the 'Indian' part of his and our heritage that would come under racist attacks. He taught us that the racism we would likely face was because we are 'Indians.' Of course this meant not the legal definition of 'Indians' according to the Indian Act, but that this was the way people would perceive us, as 'Indians' first (the 'othering' of our peoples as not white but Indian), not as Cree or Metis, or even as Canadians for that matter. So as 'Indians' we were always under suspicion in the stores and public places! This suspicion acted out as being followed and watched in stores is an experience familiar to many of my Aboriginal friends, particularly darker-skinned ones. I remember also that my father was reflective about our position as women in society. He told us that we would face acts of sexism because we were women. Although he did not actually use the words 'racism' or 'sexism' he certainly was able to relate the ways we would/might be perceived and treated. As I reflect upon my father's way of being I realize that I have always valued his words of wisdom. He was a strong natural philosopher who valued and celebrated his Cree heritage yet he acknowledged his German heritage out of respect to his father. He worked hard to keep his family fed, clothed and sheltered and loved. In 1993, he passed on at the age of 71.

My mother, on the other hand, who was raised in Wabowden and on traplines, was and still is a hard working woman living life to the fullest extent possible. She taught by example to be the best you can be through pride in who you are and what you do. She was and remains the main caregiver, the cultural teacher by example, the life skills teacher, the practical advisor, the tower of strength showing us how to work with what we had to live self-sufficiently. At the time of writing, my mom is 75, and in many ways she is still a traditional woman; she speaks our language with proficiency, she speaks English fluently. Furthermore, she still does the traditional bead and craft work with leather and hide on moccasins, jackets, and mukluks. Sometimes these goods are for our family members, or her little 'market' of customers interested in purchasing her work. When we can and those of us family members who are willing still go with her to gather medicines and herbs for our health or food needs. My mother is still exceptionally knowledgeable about the variety of roots, herbs and plants that function for medicinal purposes. It is important to note that the practice of gathering medicines is becoming less frequent as our community turns more to contemporary amenities. I fear that we are losing this critical activity which reflects many of our cultural ways, so every chance I get I include my 17-year-old daughter. Fortunately and gladly my daughter is a willing participant in these activities, as she seems to sense the urgency of the potential disruption of our ways. Also, she enjoys the company of her grandmother whom she does not see frequently because of her far distance from us.

Finally, my mother is the caregiver and comforter at many funerals for our relatives, as she is becoming the elder person within our extended family. Over the last few years as relatives and friends pass on, whether tragically or due to natural causes, my mother is the one the relatives turn to for comfort and understanding. As with many of our people, her leisure time activities are playing bingo and cards, another Euro-legacy of shifting the kinds of leisure activities in which community members could participate. I contend that leisure activities of this type are the intergenerational ramifications of outlawing our traditional activities where cultural dances, songs, games and leisure activities would have been evident. My guess is that the Anglican church we attended would have had rules against our Cree traditional dancing and singing beginning with my maternal great-great-grandfather's generation in the early

1800s. In spite of these displacements, my mother acknowledges our traditions in being who she is, and for this I thank her.

As I grew up in Wabowden, I believe that we understood and knew that others, white people, lived and dominated the businesses and professional positions. We saw this when we ventured to go 'downtown,' an example of European encroachment in our communities that led to systemic inequities. For the most part, racial segregation existed in that mostly white folks lived 'downtown' where the businesses and services were concentrated, while the majority of the Aboriginal people lived a good distance from downtown in an area called 'The Point.' Our family lived near 'The Point' where our closest neighbor was about half a mile away. So I literally grew up in the bush!

Most of the people who ran and occupied positions in the businesses, stores, nursing station, train station, missions, schools and such were non-Aboriginal, and a minority Aboriginal. Since the movement in the 1900s of Euro-Canadian settlers putting up businesses, taking positions in the medical, teaching and service aspects, the economic development of our community became more imposed with Western thought and Christian influences. European-foundational legacies affected yet another aspect of my family and community: that of imposing Christian ways. My family grew up with the influence of the Anglican Church. When I was a young girl there were two churches in our community vying for our dedication and 'souls': the Catholic and Anglican. I remember some of my extended family members were indoctrinated to the 'allegiance' of the Catholic Church. For us, however, the clinch was on us to attend the Anglican Church and my family participated in its maintenance without question.

I share another retrospective insight here: there were two sermons held each Sunday in the Anglican Church. One sermon was in English and was scheduled first in the morning while the second sermon was in Cree language in the latter part of the morning. My maternal Oji-Cree grandfather would deliver the sermons in our Cree language. I suggest that there would have been a segregation of white and Native people according to language and race here as well.

The experiences of my maternal Oji-Cree nonstatus Indian grandfather contextualizes the continual Eurocentric and Christian encroachment on our lives as Cree people. He was from the northwestern region of Ontario where Oji-Cree people live. He traveled from Ontario to Manitoba with a couple of relatives as a young man of about 24 years. He arrived in a northern Cree First Nation community where he met his future wife, my status Indian Cree grandmother. They were married in 1913 in her community, the Nelson House Cree Nation (a reserve). What an irony to have the marriage ceremony conducted on the very reserve community that could not legally allow my 'Cree-status-Indian then nonstatus Indian' grandmother to live in this community with my Oji-Cree nonstatus Indian grandfather after they were married. They moved to settle on Crown property about one hundred miles further south where my grandfather obtained trapline property through provincial trapping licensing processes of the day. My grandfather was a self-sufficient man who spoke both the Cree and Oji-Cree language proficiently. He understood and spoke very little English. The Oji-Cree language is a language that includes both Cree and Ojibway dialects integrated to make it one recognizable language. My grandfather also had Scottish ancestry where his own grandfather was from Scotland, who I estimate arrived in the northwestern region of Ontario around 1850. I am guessing that this Scottish ancestor married a local Oji-Cree woman ancestor and had children who would have been first-generation Scottish-Cree mixes, as early as the 1850s. From this union came my grandfather's father who in turn married back into the Cree community in which my grandfather was born. I once asked my mother if she knew why my grandfather decided to serve in the Anglican Church rather than fully participate in Aboriginal spirituality. She said he told her that he realized he had two choices, and in order to survive against Western intrusion he chose the Anglican Church as he could continue to speak his language. He however did *not* leave his traditional ways or language behind. He used tobacco as intended in its sacred significance when harvesting plants for our use. He did pray every day in our Cree language, which I believe served to maintain and sustain our traditional ways more than assimilation into Christianity would.

However, I do remember that after my grandfather passed away at 71 we did attend the morning sermons held in English. Our attendance diminished soon after that, for what reason I don't know. It could be too that my father influenced our decision to remain absent from the church activities. My father who did not come to the church with us and was openly critical about our attendance at the church informed us that in the 'old ways,' referring to the Cree ways, our people did not need to go to a church to worship. Although my father was respectful of my grandfather's choice to work in the Anglican Church he did not really support our attendance, but he did not stop us from going either. The opportunity to worship was everywhere in nature he told us, God was in nature – not in the church. It is only in my adult years that I have begun to critically reflect on my upbringing and my father's comments about our Cree worldviews or philosophies about spirituality.

I got accustomed to this regular routine in our lives of going to church on Sundays although I never really understood the full significance of what a church was. Now I cringe because I know it was an instrument of Eurocentric values and Christian dominance and assimilation. I just dutifully followed my grandfather because he and I were close. When I eventually left my community to go to a mixed white and Aboriginal residential school at the age of 15, I rarely set foot in any church. I do not feel that it speaks to my spirit the way it did in my community when *ni mosoom* (my grandfather) conducted the sermons in Cree. I was 10 years old when he passed on and that is probably the last time I would have heard sermons in our Cree language. When I think back, I realize I lost interest in attending any church services other the odd wedding conducted in Western ways. Even though my family and I would have attended these activities, I have always felt detached from these events as I always felt they alienated who we really were as Cree people. Now when I venture into a church it seems strange to me to hear the sermons being conducted in English. I feel disconnected as if I do not belong in this type of setting. This is not to say that I am passing negative judgment on these church attendees. I just do not feel comfortable in a church because I know it is not my way – just an imposed belief, an act of oppression that temporarily displaced my original Cree ways that I am now reclaiming. Now I certainly do pray in English and Cree, drawing from Aboriginal philosophies and perspectives. So I guess I can say that I have moved from hearing and saying prayers in Cree and English, drawing from the Christian Bible to the comfort of saying prayers in English and Cree, and drawing from Aboriginal spirituality, an interesting path indeed.

The two-language 'sermoning' was not the only systemic hegemony of colonization. As children, when we attended Sunday school the language of instruction was English, the imposed philosophy was Christianity. I find it interesting that this is yet another aspect of my life I hadn't really thought about until I revisited my childhood memories and reflected on the Eurocentric influences on my life. What an insight! What a feeling of being tricked into thinking that Christianity was the norm for my people! Although I know that we used tobacco as an offering and gave thanks to the Creator for the medicines we gathered for our health, shelter and food needs, I never thought to question that this was a practice not in tune with Christianity. My memory of attending Sunday school was my being quiet and not very participatory other than being there. However, one of the other memories I have about Sunday school and other church-run activities, aside from the sermons conducted in our Cree language, was the refusal of the missionaries to allow us to speak in our own language as we were immersed in our activities. In other words, there was an *English language only* rule! The missionaries punished what they considered language 'infractions' by withholding rewards, dismissing us from various activities and competitive events, or scolding us in front of our friends and relatives. I do remember getting scolded and punished for speaking Cree, which seems to contradict my stating that I was quiet. Perhaps I just felt silenced. I still remember these incidents, which might seem insignificant to others but to us, Cree-speaking friends and relatives, they were real and alienating experiences.

In retrospect, this is another Eurocentric legacy: denying the right to our Indigenous language. Furthermore, an oppressive paradox existed with these church activities: in the morning sermon my grandfather would deliver his talk in the Cree language and that was perfectly fine for the missionaries who were also present. However, in the afternoon the Cree language was forbidden in the Sunday school programs! It is disconcerting to realize that this colonizing actually went on right under our noses! I suppose that the missionaries reasoned that this was the only way to get people into church, to convert and 'Christianize' the older by 'allowing' them to speak their language: trickery in disguise? I maintain that it was easier to control us young people by imposing the English-only rule because the church teachers were English speakers and our parents would not have been present in the Sunday school. Even if they were present I wonder if they would have realized was happening and spoken against these acts. I highly doubt it as I reflect back; our people were kind to outsiders and I believe that they feared the church because it reflected the authority of the government that replaced our self-determination. I imagine that there were still many memories that reminded them that our people have been jailed and murdered in their recent past just for being who they were, practicing our ways of dance, song and worship!

School and Education: Eurocentric Meandering

When I entered school in first grade I was almost seven. I entered what was to be a very Eurocentric system that denied positive discussions or discourses about Aboriginal peoples in our society. In truth, I do not remember any books or classes that would have included any Aboriginal content that was accurate, positive, or critical to Western paradigms throughout my school years. I attended school in my community from the early beginnings of a one-room schoolhouse to classes of four rooms that meant some doubling of classes.

My memory of schooling is the following: I enjoyed reading and learning. I was a studious pupil. I, along with other Aboriginal students experienced negative treatment from some of the teachers who did not hide their prejudices. We walked at least two miles to get to school in the fall and winter. All my teachers were white women or men. When we did study about Aboriginal peoples it was often very brief content with stereotyped and inaccurate information. I along with my relatives and friends encountered acts of racism. I share one here that always stands out in my memory: when I was in second grade, I was once caught chewing gum, something that was forbidden in class. My teacher proceeded to do the unthinkable: she made me stand in front of the class in our one-room schoolhouse and ordered me to stick the gum on the bridge of my nose. That part was not so bad as this was common practice if one was caught chewing gum! She then got a scarf and tied it around my head like a bandana. She then took a ruler and stuck it behind my head in the bandana so that it would stand straight up to imitate a feather (read Indian stereotype: feathers and bands around their heads). The image she created was that of what she considered a 'stupid Indian.' So imagine that I am standing in front of the class with the gum on my nose, the bandana around my head and the ruler stuck up in the bandana behind my head. She made me stand in front of the class costumed up like that. I recall that when she turned to write stuff on the board that I looked at the students who were looking at me with looks of bewilderment. I remember wondering what I should do as I was standing there feeling hot and embarrassed and wanting to cry. I did not cry because I did not want her to know that she got to me! I decided to do something to defy the situation and show that she was not going to get the best of me: I pretended to do a dance, a stereotypical 'Indian war hoop' to portray dancing around with this ridiculous contraption on my head and nose. The students howled with laughter when they saw me. The teacher turned around to see what was happening, but before she could see what I was doing I was standing stiff as a board again looking very serious. The students would not tell her what made them laugh – they protected me. I repeated this action a couple more times just to defy her and I was never caught, nor did the students snitch on me. I look back on this incident and realize that at grade two, I *was* defiant toward injustices because I recognized that was what was happening. Today I realize that the teacher committed an outright act of racism, cultural stereotyping and public humiliation. I remember that this teacher did not like me and there were other times that she would try to embarrass me. She also treated other Native students much rougher than the white students who got away with a lot of mischief. I often wonder if she didn't like me because learning came easy to me and I did the work with ease, and that was going against her stereotyped notion of 'stupid Indians.' I wonder about this because she also ripped up an exam paper in front of my face and accused me of cheating when I came into the classroom late and began to take the usual books out for reading. Imagine, in second grade I was struggling with my teacher. When it came to exam time and after her ripping up my exam I refused to go back to school for the rest of the exams – needless to say she failed me! So I had to repeat grade two. Thank goodness my second grade experience was with a different teacher who really loved us kids and it was evident that she loved the community by the way she treated us. My second year in grade two was a breeze with almost 100 per cent of my work. Looking back, I certainly did not need to repeat that grade! Whenever I tell this story to students in my professional years of teaching they are astounded that things like that could happen. I usually relate that our cousins and relatives who attended Indian residential schools experienced greater atrocities in their school years. The pain of relating these experiences lessens as I try to forgive and move forward in healing old wounds.

The remaining years of my elementary education do not stand out other than the fact that I worked hard and excelled in my studies. I did come across some great teachers but the fact remains that I have little recollection of having learned about Aboriginal content and perspectives that were affirming. I just remember feeling angry and defiant when we would read stereotyped and inaccurate perspectives about us. I do recall feeling affirmed when my father would tell me that the information in the texts was not at all reflective of who we were as Aboriginal and Cree people. I could still hear my father saying 'Be proud of your Cree heritage.'

I entered ninth grade, high school, when I was fifteen. I had to leave my home community to attend a newly formed collegiate that came with a dormitory. An old army base was converted to accommodate a school and residence primarily for Metis, nonstatus Indian students and other rural white farm kids that had to leave their community for high school but could not afford to go to school in the cities. This school was interracially mixed, as was the dormitory. My memories of this school are that I did not enjoy dormitory living, as I lived in fear of what might happen. I kept recalling the negative experiences many of my status Indian cousins related when they passed through our community as they went to their respective Indian residential schools. Nothing happened like that of the horror stories of Indian residential schools. However, I do remember that the education I received was very Eurocentric and boring. I recall that the stereotyping about Aboriginal peoples continued and it was difficult to do anything constructive about it because we just did not know what to do. I stayed quiet, went to school, and socialized with my cousins for the next two years. I went to another high school in a mining community for my grade eleven. I saw only two other Native students in this high school and there I endured many racial slurs and being excluded from social and personal networks because I was Native. I did not finish my grade eleven; instead I left school to go to work.

Finding Spaces to Assert Indigenous Perspectives

I worked at a number of different jobs – as a receptionist, home advisor and employment counselor before I decided that it was time to attempt education again. When I worked at these positions, it was always with Aboriginal peoples in mind. I worked at asserting an Aboriginal focus in my work, readings, and personal and social networking because I realized that we needed to work at improving our quality of life without forsaking who we are as Aboriginal peoples. Years later, I returned to another educational institution, the university, as a mature student where I continued my quest to maintain an Aboriginal focus in my studies, research papers, activism work, service work and personal and social growth in traditional circles and teachings. When I entered graduate school I continued to work in asserting Aboriginal perspectives, gaining more knowledge, more experiences, working with more elders and traditional and cultural teachers to deepen my understanding of the issues, needs and aspirations of our peoples. I have worked in universities since 1982 and my academic positions were such that I could and did my work grounded in Aboriginal epistemologies. For the most part, although working in institutions has been a challenge in trying to shift and break through the stereotypes, racism and sexism, I have found it to be a very rewarding experience. I feel fortunate to be able to build my scholarship grounded within Aboriginal and Indigenous epistemologies, perspectives, philosophies and expressions in spite of the Eurocentric tendencies of academia.

It has been through the medium of education and academic scholarship that I am able to articulate the intricacies of our Aboriginal identities, which have been measured up to suit colonialist domination in Canadian history. The many labels that we are given remain invisible to the eye, unfortunately so are the cultural and linguistic names we would wish to use. I know that we would wish to be known as Nahéyow, Anishnawbe, Haudenosonee, Mic Maq and so on to include the cultural linguistic diversity in Aboriginal country. However, the public still primarily thinks of us as stereotyped 'Indians,' a social construction. Meanwhile the government authorities still see us as categorized entities of status Indians, nonstatus Indians, Metis, Inuit, off-reserve status Indians, Bill C-31 Indians and so forth. By doing this, I contend that the government continues to define and control its relationships to us because this limits the types and level of redressment strategies they might be required to pursue.

Conclusion

In closing, let me say that as I wrote this paper I was aware that I wanted to honor and draw from principles of oral literacy as I wrote and spoke these words. I work with the understanding and appreciation that committing words to print does not always honor the integrity of oral traditions. I understand as well that in our print and research-driven scholarly academic lives citing references and other works are important. I have tried to do this here. As I close, I bring my mind to the many Indigenous groups that have been affected by colonization policies and practices. I believe that there must be hope to continue living life to its fullest within our Indigenous aspirations while we continue to make our life in the many worlds that are now a part of our life. I offer *Ke nuna'skomitin* – I thank you, to the Creator for another opportunity to acknowledge Mother Earth and the struggles, needs and aspirations of all her inhabitants.

References

Ray, Arthur, *I Have Lived Here Since The World Began: An Illustrated History of Canada's Native People* (1996), p. 203.

Young, Mary, *Anishnabe Voice: The Cost of Education in a Non-Aboriginal World (A Narrative Inquiry)*. Unpublished Thesis. University of Manitoba (1997).

Chapter 5

Remembering Our Grandmothers: Navajo Women and the Power of Oral Tradition

Jennifer Nez Denetdale

Introduction

The multiple efforts to bring Native perspectives into the historical record have proven fruitful. Scholars of color have endeavored to deconstruct Western scholarship that purports to tell our stories and our histories as well as work to create our own Indigenous research, research protocols, and methodologies. As a Navajo woman and a scholar, I am committed to presenting Navajo perspectives of the past. This chapter describes my own search for information on a Navajo woman who is known in the historical record primarily as Juanita, the wife of the great leader and war chief of the Navajos, *Hastiin Ch'il Hajin* or Manuelito. Manuelito is one of the *Diné* leaders who led the resistance against American invasion of *Diné bekéyah* in the nineteenth century.

An Indigenous Woman's Perspective on Navajo History

While Manuelito remains an important historical figure and a cultural hero in Navajo history, his wife, like so many women in American history and world history, has been relegated to the shadowy confines of a home, made invisible within the parameters of recorded history. Very little about Juanita can be gleaned from historical accounts. However, oral interviews with Juanita's descendants, her maternal great-grandchildren, shed some light on Juanita and the centrality of women in Navajo society. These narratives demonstrate how Navajo versions of the past contradict Western versions, how oral traditions illuminate the centrality of Navajo women in Navajo society, and how archival materials such as photographs find their way back to Indigenous communities, thereby providing an impetus and a rich source for renewed storytelling.

To demonstrate the contrast between Navajo histories written by non-Navajos and oral traditions that circulate in Navajo communities, I begin with one of the watersheds in Navajo history, the American war against the Navajos in 1863 and the subsequent incarceration of Navajos in a prison camp from 1864 to 1868. For many years, Navajos were reluctant to speak of the American war against them that led to the Long Walk (the forced march to the prison camp) and then imprisonment. It is a trauma that remains etched in the collective Navajo memory, and until fairly recently, it was largely white historians who wrote of this nightmare. Non-Navajo versions emphasize both the military actions that led to Navajo surrender and the role of Manuelito in the final defeat of the Navajos.

Hastiin Ch'il Hajin or Manuelito (as he was named by the Mexicans) is recognized as the Navajo leader who openly challenged American claims to *Diné bekéyah* in 1858.[1] When war broke out in 1863, Navajos initially resisted the American invasion, but eventually were forced to acquiesce owing to the sheer magnitude of violence and ferocity of American weaponry, as was typical of colonial-Indigenous encounters in war. However, it was not until Manuelito voluntarily surrendered in 1866 that the Americans considered the Navajos to be wholly defeated.[2] In 1868, along with other Navajos, Manuelito returned with his family back to their former residence. As headman, he played a role in Navajo affairs until his death in 1894. His role in Navajo history is well documented by historians. Today Manuelito is a Navajo cultural hero and his image can be seen in different forms all across the Navajo Nation. For example, in the 1980s the Navajo Nation established a Chief Manuelito scholarship to recognize high-achieving Navajo college-bound students. The scholarship memorializes Manuelito's commitment to provide American education for Navajo children so that we could effectively fight to retain our land and tradition.

In contrast, the oral narratives that I have collected mark as significant the Navajos' return from *Hwéeldi*, the prison camp, and emphasize the reestablishment of life in *Diné bekéyah*, which had been turned into a reservation following the Treaty of 1868. Navajos became one of the few Indigenous peoples who managed to rebuild their population and retain their cultural beliefs and practices in the face of oppressive living conditions that also characterized other reservations across the United States.[3] While Manuelito looms large in the collective national Navajo memory, his wife Juanita is a significant figure in clan stories, which begin with the return to *Diné bekéyah*. Stressing the return to the homelands and the efforts to reestablish *hózhó–* balance and harmony, oral traditions make clear that Navajo women were crucial to the survival and continuity of Navajo life and culture. Clan stories relate how women were part of the reestablishment of social organization where matrilineality established identity and lineage and where land-use patterns were dictated by matrilocality. Significantly, women reclaimed their former positions

---

1   Lawrence D. Sundberg, *Dinétah: An Early History of the Navajo People*. Santa Fe: Sunstone Press, 1995.

2   Frank McNitt, *Navajo Wars: Campaigns, Slave Raids, and Reprisals*. Albuquerque: University of New Mexico Press, 1990, 319.

3   Richard White, *The Roots of Dependency: Subsistence, Environment, and Social Change Among the Choctaws, Pawnees, and Navajos*. Lincoln: University of Nebraska Press, 1983.

of grandmothers, mothers, and daughters, positions used to assert a measure of authority and autonomy.

Reclaiming Indigenous Oral Tradition

Linda Tuhiwai Smith notes that Indigenous peoples often view research with suspicion and disdain because it is linked to Euro-American imperialism and colonialism.[4] For Indigenous peoples, Euro-American researchers have appropriated our material culture and misrepresented our past and present. Yet, as Indigenous scholars trained in Western academic institutions, we are still compelled to employ Western scholastic approaches if we are to dismantle entrenched and distorted images that conceal the realities of our lives and obscure important issues. As a Navajo woman who has spent a great part of her life in the United States academy, I draw upon my personal and academic experiences to offer a Navajo perspective on the past. My educational experiences are similar to those of many other Indigenous peoples: I was not introduced to the written histories of Indigenous peoples, including my own Navajo past, until I was a university undergraduate. However, because I am fortunate to live in a culture that adheres to and practices its traditional beliefs, my research and writing reflect my commitment to illuminate Navajo life and culture, particularly concerning women's roles. My use of oral traditions and archival documents such as written accounts and photographs reflect my background and my education.

Juanita and Manuelito are my maternal great-great-great grandparents. My matrilineal clan, the *Tl'ógi*, trace their lineage to Juanita. My grandparents, the elders whom I interviewed, are Juanita's maternal great-grandchildren. They are descended from Juanita's two daughters. While there are several grandparents whom I interviewed for this chapter, I utilize interviews from Mike Allison Sr. and Faye Yazzie. Both are descended from Juanita and Manuelito's younger daughter and live near Tohatchi, New Mexico, on lands that Juanita's daughter left for them. At the time of my interview, Mike was ninety-nine years old, and his sister, Faye, was eighty-four. After several generations, we *Tl'ógi* continue to remember our grandmothers. Our elders tell us that we should not forget our grandmothers, Juanita and her daughters.

Today, oral traditions in the form of autobiography, biography, and creation narratives associated with ritual and ceremony circulate within matrilineal clans as they have for generations.[5] One form of narratives circulates within Juanita's

---

4   Linda Tuhiwai Smith, *Decolonizing Methodologies: Research and Indigenous Peoples*. New York: Zed Books, Ltd., 1999, 1.

5   Angela Cavender Wilson, Wahpatonwan Dakota historian, notes that conventional definitions of oral traditions and oral histories tend to separate them while she views oral traditions as being enmeshed in the experiences and told as part of oral histories, i.e. life stories and personal recollections. See Angela Cavender Wilson, 'Grandmother to Granddaughter: Generations of Oral History in a Dakota Family,' *American Indian Quarterly* 20:1 (Winter 1996): 7–13.

matrilineal clan, the *Tł'ógi* of Tohatchi, New Mexico, as it has for generations. These stories include one of how Juanita and her family reestablished their homes in *Diné bekéyah*, particularly after the death of Manuelito in 1894. Similar narratives within other Navajo clans also serve to create and recreate a Navajo sense of community, as they do for Manuelito and Juanita's descendants.

Navajo oral tradition has largely been studied as a topic separate from that of history. In the nineteenth century, oral traditions became the domain of anthropological inquiry, a critical component of the 'salvage ethnography' that was designed to preserve the frozen Navajo past, presumed to be dying and expected to become extinct in the twentieth century. Oral traditions have also been studied for their literary value. These approaches present an ahistorical vision of Navajo society that posits distinct and separate spheres of traditional/modern, sacred/profane, and prehistory/history, among others. Narratives passed down by Navajos through their matrilineal and matrilocal clan kinship belie these dichotomies and, in fact, elucidate their connectedness. Story and history cannot be separated here because storytelling is a valid form of historical production.

Recently, oral traditions have been examined to illuminate Indigenous peoples' perspectives on the past.[6] If we view oral traditions and history as cultural constructions embedded in social processes, we discover that the meaning of the past differs across cultures and raises questions about the authority we continue to give to documentary evidence.[7] As Julie Cruikshank points out:

> All societies have characteristic narrative structures that help members construct and maintain knowledge of the world. The exercise here is less one of straightening out the facts than of identifying how distinct cognitive models generate different kinds of social analysis, leading to different interpretations of events, one of which gets included in official history, the other relegated to collective memory.[8]

As I conducted interviews with Navajo elders, I became aware that these narratives were markedly similar in structure to the traditional creation narratives. They also feature similar motifs and themes. Cruikshank notes that cultures have characteristic narrative structures that are embedded in a framework for understanding the past.

---

6   Julie Cruikshank, 'Images of Society in Klondike Gold Rush Narratives: Skookum Jim and the Discovery of Gold,' *Ethnohistory* 39 (Winter 1992): 20–41; Jonathan D. Hill, ed., *Rethinking History and Myth: Indigenous South American Perspectives on the Past*. Urbana: University of Illinois Press, 1988; Enrique Florescano, *Memory, Myth, and Time in Mexico: From the Aztecs to Independence*. Translated by Albert G. Bork with the assistance of Kathryn R. Bork, Austin: University of Texas Press, 1994; and Peter Nabokov, 'Native View of History' in *The Cambridge History of the Native Peoples of the Americas*, Volume 1, Part 1 edited by Bruce G. Trigger and Wilcomb E. Washburn. New York: Cambridge University Press, 1996, 1–59.

7   Julie Cruikshank, 'Discovery of Gold on the Klondike: Perspectives from Oral Tradition' *in Reading Beyond Words: Contexts for Native History*, eds. Jennifer S.H. Brown and Elizabeth Vibert. Toronto: Broadview Press, 1998, 434.

8   Ibid., 435, 436.

Other scholars such as Enrique Florescano describe these qualities of history and 'mythical' frameworks.[9] For example, he notes that the qualities associated with oral tradition include an emphasis on primordial origins and a cyclical concept of time. There is a sense that the most important time occurred in the past when the foundations of the cosmos and human life were formed: the aim of storytelling is thus to preserve and revitalize what was created in primordial times. Finally, the qualities of the actors are emphasized and include relationships between humans and animals. Ancestral memory and the form it takes as oral tradition provides one of the most powerful resources that Indigenous peoples have for asserting Indigenous status.[10] In contrast, Eurocentric modes of history as a framework for understanding and talking about the past emphasize the idea that time is linear and humans are always progressing and improving. Humans are presented as primary actors and their actions are the major events. As Cruikshank asserts, history has often been used to legitimize Western European expansion at the expense of Indigenous societies and extermination of Indigenous peoples.[11]

Drawing upon oral interviews with Navajo elders and archival materials such as documents and photographs and placing them in an historical framework that emphasizes the structure of the oral tradition, a portrait emerges that demonstrates how Navajos frame their understanding of the past and present. This vision of the past illuminates the centrality of women in Navajo society. While Navajo society has been influenced and shaped by Euro-American cultural beliefs and practices, we still value clan relationships, which define who we are and tell us about our responsibilities as Navajos. Finally, taking nineteenth- and early twentieth-century photographs from archives back to Navajo families has resulted in the telling of stories that reaffirms the teachings of our grandmothers and grandfathers.

Images of Navajos

The discourse on Navajos by several generations of anthropologists, historians, traders, writers, travelers, and photographers reinforces stereotypical images of Navajos as late arrivals into the Southwest and merely cultural borrowers. Because the people known today as Navajos kept their distance from the succession of colonizers such as the Spaniards and Mexicans in the colonial Southwest, very little is known about early Navajo life and culture. Rather, what is most visible about Navajos, like the adoption and/or incorporation of nearby Pueblo cultural elements such as religious beliefs and ceremonial practices and agriculture, and the incorporation of the horse brought by the Spaniards, has come to signify 'Navajo.' Further, Navajos are primarily depicted as aggressive and warlike. A republished history of the Navajos regurgitates those images and characteristics still used to define 'Navajo':

---

9   Florescano, *Memory, Myth, and Time in Mexico*, 100–183.
10 Ibid.
11 Cruikshank, 'Images of Society in Klondike Gold Rush Narratives,' 20–167.

It is generally supposed that in very early times the Navajos were wild, reckless, roaming Indians without any definite or limited territory they called their home...The Navajo is thought to have been a general outlaw, roaming at will wherever his fancy or love for adventure might lead him, seeking at all times what or whom he might devour. He continually wages war upon the more peaceful and sedentary Pueblos and gradually gathered to himself the lawless and outcasts of other tribes with whom he frequently came in contact. These in time he assimilated, almost completely changing his character, until to-day, after being subjugated, tamed and disciplined by United States soldiers, we find him peace-loving and industrious, pursuing the quiet industries of agriculture and stock-raising.[12]

While this particular excerpt seems to exaggerate the characteristics attributed to Navajos, it also indicates the process by which Navajos were to be integrated into American society, the process being a natural movement toward 'civilized' society. These stereotypes of Navajos as nomadic and aggressive have very real consequences. For example, they have resulted in one of the largest relocations of Indigenous peoples in North America. Under a 1974 federal mandate, approximately ten thousand Navajos were forced to relocate off their ancestral lands because these lands had been awarded to the Hopis. During the court hearings that determined the rightful ownership of these lands, Navajo were portrayed in the stereotypes of aggressive and warlike cultural borrowers who had invaded the peaceful Hopis' lands.[13] The ruling by American courts that Navajos must move off lands awarded to Hopis has wrought devastation on Navajos and its effect is only now becoming visible. As James Faris observes, '...the Navajo are one of the Indigenous peoples of this continent whose own histories contrast most dramatically with the European-American histories of them.'[14]

If Navajos are understood within Western frameworks that contradict their own perspectives of who they are and what their past means, then Navajo women are doubly obscured from view. Defined by Euro-American definitions of gender roles, American Indian women have been cast into the dichotomy of princess/squaw drudge.[15] However, as Carol Douglas Sparks argues, historically, Americans had difficulty categorizing Navajo women as they seemed to fit neither the princess nor squaw drudge images used to define Indian women.[16] Further, non-Indian categories

---

12 Oscar H. Lipps, *A Little History of the Navajos*. Cedar Rapids, Iowa: The Torch Press, 1909; reprint, Albuquerque: Avanyu Publishing Co., 1989, 34.

13 David M. Brugge, *The Navajo-Hopi Land Dispute: An American Tragedy*. Albuquerque: University of New Mexico Press, 1994.

14 James C. Faris, 'Photographing the Navajo: Scanning Abuse,' *American Indian Culture and Research Journal* 20:3 (1996): 67.

15 Rayna Green, 'The Pocahontas Perplex: The Image of Indian Women in American Culture' *in Native American Voices: A Reader*, ed. Susan Lobo and Steve Talbot. New York: Longman, 1998, 182–192.

16 Carol Douglas Sparks, 'The Land Incarnate: Navajo Women and the Dialogue of Colonialism, 1821–1870' in *Negotiators of Change: Historical Perspectives on Native American Women*, ed. Nancy Shoemaker. New York: Routledge, 1995, 135–156.

have reduced Navajo women to victims of patriarchy who are slowly reasserting their rightful places of authority. Finally, because Navajo society is matrilineal, non-Indians find it difficult to characterize female-male relationships in any way other than as relationships where men are confused about their proper roles and have even been emasculated as a result of women's strong roles.[17] In contrast, stories of Juanita illuminate the centrality of women in Navajo society. As mothers, wives, daughters and sisters, Navajo women claim a place of autonomy and authority in their society.

Navajo Perspectives of the World and of History

To understand Navajo perceptions of the world and how the creation narratives act as a framework for understanding and talking about the past and present, it is important to be familiar with these narratives. The foundation of the Navajo world begins with the concept of *Sa'ahnaaghaíí bik'eh hózóón nishłóo naasháa doo* (The word *hózhó* means the same as this phrase). Many Navajo Studies scholars have attempted to translate the meaning of this phrase. Navajo writer and poet Rex Lee Jim provides my favorite translation: 'May I be Everlasting and Beautiful Living.'[18] He suggests that it essentially means '… this declaration of a healthy and wealthy lifestyle'… refers to 'the beauty of life realized through the application of teachings that work.'[19] These teachings of which Jim speaks are embedded in the creation narratives. A central concept is that life is a journey in search of harmony and balance. Importantly, the Holy People – the contingent of deities who created the world and human beings – include female deities such as Changing Woman and White Shell Woman, signifying gender complementarity in creation. Finally, the elders are especially thought to be wise and worthy because they have traveled the road of life and reached *Sá* or Old Age. As Jim notes, 'Reaching *Sá* is a lifelong goal for the individual, and an everlasting goal for a people.'[20]

In contrast to Western portrayals of our past, we, the *Diné*, point to a specific place in *Diné bekéyah*, in present-day northeastern New Mexico, from which we emerged from the lower worlds to the present one. Journeying through the lower worlds, we searched for *hózhó* or balance and order. Along the way, the local inhabitants treated us hospitably. However, because of our disrespect to our hosts, we were ordered to leave these various worlds. It is in the fifth and present world that we begin to learn how to live in a fruitful manner. In the fifth world, the Holy People created the *Diné*

---

17 See for example, Gary Witherspoon, *Navajo Kinship and Marriage*. Chicago: University of Chicago Press, 1975, and Dorothy C. Leighton, 'As I Knew Them: Navajo Women in 1940,' *American Indian Quarterly* 6 (Spring/Summer 1982): 34–51.

18 Rex Lee Jim, 'A Moment In My Life' *in Here First: Autobiographical Essays By Native American Writers*, ed. Arnold Krupat and Brian Swann. New York: Modern Library, 2000, 232.

19 Ibid.

20 Ibid. 233.

in their image. The boundaries of *Dinétah,* our homeland, were established with soils brought from the fourth world. Today our homelands are still defined by the four sacred mountains. The creation narratives also explain how we acquired sheep and skills such as weaving from the Holy People.

The inclusion of females in the contingent of Holy People reflects the prominent place that women have in Navajo society. Changing Woman is perhaps one of the best loved and certainly the most benevolent of the deities. Ethelou Yazzie tells this version of Changing Woman's birth:

> One morning at dawn, First Man and First Woman saw a dark cloud over *Ch'óol'í'í* (Governador Knob). Later they heard a baby cry. When they looked to see where the crying was coming from, they realized that it came from within the cloud that covered the top of *Ch'óol'í'í.* First Man searched and found a baby girl. She was born of darkness and the dawn was her father. First Man and First Woman brought her up under the direction of the Holy People. They fed her on sun-ray pollen, pollen from the clouds, pollen from the plants and the dew of flowers. This baby became *Asdzáá Nádleehé* (Changing Woman), one of the most loved of Navajo Holy People.[21]

Changing Woman is a major figure in the creation narratives. When she reached puberty, a ceremony called the *Kinaaldá* was given to recognize her ability to procreate. Today, Navajo girls who come into puberty are given the same ceremony.

One story that is important to understanding the stories of Juanita and her daughters is the one of Changing Woman and how she created the first Navajo clans. Changing Woman gave birth to Monster Slayer and Born for Water (who came to be warriors of the Navajo people), whose father was Sun. After a time, the Sun and his sons convinced Changing Woman to live on the Western Ocean. Some of the *Diné* went with her, but then became lonely and went home to *Dinétah.* According to Yazzie:

> Changing Woman thought that there should be more people, so she created more of them (humans) by rubbing the skin from her breast, from her back and from under both arms. In this way she created the first four clans. Changing Woman rubbed the skin from her breast and formed people who became the *Kiyaa'aanii* clan. From the skin rubbed from her back the *Honágháahnii* clan was formed. From the skin under her right arm the *Tó'dích'íi'nii* clan was created, and from the skin under her left arm the *Hastł'ishnii* clan was made.[22]

The creation narratives continue to be a template by which Navajos measure values. The narratives remind us of good and proper behavior towards the earth, animals, and other human beings. In these stories, women are active agents. They speak their minds and make decisions that will benefit them and their children. They are responsible for the creation of humans and of clans. As mothers, they are all

---

21 Ethelou Yazzie, ed., *Navajo History*. Chinle, AZ: Navajo Curriculum Center, Rough Rock Demonstration School, 1971.

22 Ibid., 74. The English names for the four original clans are: Towering House, One Walks Around You, Bitter Water, and Mud People.

beneficent. A comparison of the creation narratives and the stories about Juanita bears similarities. In short, an examination of Juanita's characteristics and traits reflects those of Changing Woman.

In my search to learn about Juanita, I discovered that she and her daughters played a significant role in the survival and continuity of their families and clan members. Oral interviews with the descendants of Juanita and Manuelito refocus the meaning of the 'Navajo wars' from traumatic years of imprisonment and loss to those where Navajos endeavored to recover their families and communities. Rooted in creation stories, the stories of our ancestors, our grandmothers and grandfathers, testify to the bravery, courage, and resilience of our ancestors.

Narratives about Juanita or *Asdzáá Tł'ógi*

One of the things that I learned during my search to illuminate Juanita's life was that she had been known among her Navajo people as *Asdzáá Tł'ógi. Asdzáá Tł'ógi* can be translated as Lady Weaver. Her name suggests that she was a weaver and that she had kin ties to Zia Pueblo (*Tł'ógi* refers to the Zia people who today live in northwestern New Mexico). Born around 1845, *Asdzáá Tł'ógi* witnessed many of the transformations occurring in Navajo society. Non-Indian accounts suggest that *Asdzáá Tł'ógi* was a Mexican slave whom Manuelito married. Historians have relied upon Indian agent John Bowman's report, in which it states that he had confronted Manuelito and ordered him to free his slaves. Bowman notes that Manuelito declared that he had no slaves, but rather had family members who were free to go where they pleased. Juanita is not explicitly named as one of Manuelito's slaves.

In contrast to historians' reports, Navajo oral accounts name Juanita as a Navajo woman. Perhaps the answer to her identity lies in the nature of cross-cultural relationships where identities were constructed differently than the way they are constructed in the present. Historically, Navajos incorporated people from other cultures into their society. After the Spanish reconquest in 1692, many Pueblo refugees fled to their Navajo allies. Female refugees intermarried with Navajo men and bore children who became the basis for clans such as Jemez. In the colonial Southwest slave raiding was rampant and Navajos took slaves as well as mourned and raged at the loss of their own members to New Mexican and Indian raiders who preyed upon them.[23] Captives who found themselves in Navajo society often carved out a place of relative security. One of the best known captives, Jesus Arviso, was taken captive in Sonora by the Apache nation and then sold to Navajos. Arviso came to be an important member of Navajo society where he served as an interpreter between Navajos and the Euro-Americans.[24] The incorporation of Indian and Hispanic people

---

23 Brugge, *Navajos in the Catholic Church Records*; James F. Brooks, 'This Evil Extends Especially to the Feminine Sex': Captivity and Identity in New Mexico, 1700–1856, in *Unequal Sisters: A Multicultural Reader in U.S. Women's History*. New York: Routledge, 2000, 20–38.

24 Brooks, *This Evil Extends Especially to the Feminine Sex*, 171–175.

into Navajo society, including those taken as slaves, continued even into the late nineteenth century. The ways in which Navajos incorporated and extended kinship to non-Navajos are reflected in the stories of *Asdzáá Tł'ógi.*

The great-grandchildren of *Asdzáá Tł'ógi* begin their stories with the Navajo return from *Hwéeldi,* the prison camp, to *Diné bekéyah* in 1868. The narratives mirror the creation stories where Navajos began their journey because of chaos and a desire to establish balance and harmony. Just as the people journeyed through various worlds in search of *hózhó, Asdzáá Tł'ógi* and her kin left years of chaos at the prison camp to reestablish their lives. The great-grandchildren's version of their ancestors' return to *Diné bekéyah* stress the *Tł'ógi's* role to reestablish *hózhó.* As Mike Allison Sr. recalls, his grandmother was of the *Tó'dik'ozhi* clan, and upon release she and her kin traveled back to *Diné bekéyah.* Along their journey, exhausted and hungry, they decided to stop at Zia (*Tł'ógi*) Pueblo where they had friends. As Allison remembers:

> I don't know the origins of the clan ... They just said the *Tł'ógi* came. They journeyed. They came from Salt Water (*Tó'dik'ozhi*). I don't know where that place is, *Tó'dik'ozhi.* My grandmother, the one I told you about, she had a donkey. This was her story. She said, "You will be Salt Water." So we are Salt Water. I don't know where they had traveled (return route from Ft. Sumner). They had run out of food. Part of the group stopped at the Pueblos. The group that was known as Salt Water split up and one part kept going. I don't know how many of them were hungry and they slowed down. They said, "Let's drink some coffee from the *Kiis'áani* (Pueblos). Let us eat there." And they went in that direction. They were fed by the *Kiis'áani.* The *Kiis'áani* shared their food with them. The *Kiis'áani* that the Salt Water had come to, were the *Tł'ógi.* They ate from the *Tł'ógi* and were given bread to take. As they were leaving, they were told, "You will be *Tł'ógi.* You will be our relatives. Now you are *Tł'ógi,* not Salt Water. Not Salt Water. Now go."

> And the group journeyed on to meet their relatives. So when they met, one group was called *Tł'ógi* and the others were Salt Water. That's how they came together. My grandmother said, "The *Kiis'áanis* named us that, *Tł'ógi.* They named us first as *Tł'ógi.* The real *Tł'ógi* are the Zia Pueblos. They said, 'We will be your relatives.'" So we have relatives at Zia.[25]

From that day on, the descendants of *Asdzáá Tł'ógi* through her two daughters, who were part of the contingent, identify themselves as *Tł'ógi* or Zia clan.

Allison's story about his grandmothers' journey from *Hwéeldi* illuminates the nature of Navajo social organization, where women are in a distinctive position for they alone convey the kinship ties essential to tribal existence.[26] Navajos, as do other

---

25 Mike Allison, Sr., Interview by author, Tape recording, Tohatchi, New Mexico, 10 October 1996.

26 Theda Perdue provides discussion on how a world ordered along kinship lines operated in her study of gender and Cherokee social organization. See Theda Perdue, *Cherokee Women: Gender and Culture Change, 1700–1835.* Lincoln: University of Nebraska Press, 1998.

Indigenous peoples, understand relationships in terms of kinship. Thus, in order to communicate effectively with other clans as well as across cultures, it was imperative to establish kin relationships that Navajos understood; women were crucial for establishing these relationships. *Asdzáá Tł'ógi* accepts the *Tł'ógi's* invitation that she 'become' *Tł'ógi* to cement their kin relationships. Allison also notes that his grandmother was indeed Navajo and her clan was related to the *Tó'dích'íinii* (Bitter Water), one of the original clans. Finally, by quoting his grandmother, saying, 'She said' the story is given credence as *Asdzáá Tł'ógi* speaks to us from the past.

Today, it is my observation that many of us from the younger generations have forgotten these old kinship ties between Indigenous peoples, between Navajos and the neighboring Pueblo peoples. The portrayal of historical relationships between Navajos and Apaches with Pueblo peoples as mostly contentious has resulted in the loss of kin ties that we once had with each other. We need to recover these historical kinship ties.

That *Asdzáá Tł'ógi* is remembered through her matrilineal descendants and named as the creator of the *Tł'ógi* clan demonstrates the significance assigned to the power of reproduction. *Asdzáá Tł'ógi's* attributes include the ability to create a clan and the qualities of generosity and benevolence. These same qualities reflect those for which Changing Woman is known. While *Asdzáá Tł'ógi's* descendants had to reflect for some time before remembering her name, they did recount her and her two daughters' – their grandmothers' – characteristics. Kind and generous, the grandmothers provided for their children and grandchildren and left land upon which their descendants continue to live.

History makes note of Manuelito and his family's return to *Diné bekéyah* in 1868. So too do the stories of their descendants. Manuelito remained an important leader and land issues preoccupied him to the end of his life. Stories about *Asdzáá Tł'ógi* and *Hastiin Ch'il Hajin* indicate that women were just as concerned. Although women controlled land use and dictated its allocation among clan members, no studies delineate the nature of women and land use. In 1874, *Asdzáá Tł'ógi* was the only woman in a delegation of Navajos who traveled to Washington, D.C. to meet with the President of the United States. *Asdzáá Tł'ógi* accompanied her husband Manuelito, who had insisted on personally speaking to President Ulysses Grant. Although historians dismiss the Navajos' motives for going to Washington, D.C. as frivolous and merely an excuse for adventure, Navajos did believe that talking directly to the President was one of their rights.[27] Written accounts, including newspapers from this period, do not note *Asdzáá Tł'ógi's* presence. However, because of the time period and the accompanying Indian agent's interest in creating a national market for Navajo textiles, I contend that he intended to take advantage of her presence to promote Navajo arts and crafts to the American public.

The great-grandchildren remember their grandmother's trip to Washington, D.C. *Asdzáá Tł'ógi* accompanied her husband, Manuelito, because he considered her

---

27 See for example, Herman J. Viola, *Diplomats in Buckskins: A History of Indian Delegations in Washington, DC.* Bluffton, S.C.: Rivilo Books, 1995, 39, 40.

to be an excellent orator who had the ability to persuade people. As Faye Yazzie, a descendant, tells it, 'Her husband, Manuelito, wanted his wife Juanita to go on the trip because she spoke well and maybe she could persuade the President to let the Navajos keep their lands. Manuelito said the President's back was "stiff" and perhaps Juanita's words could "soften" (persuade) him.'[28] In Navajo society, even today, to be able to speak well and persuade through oratory is a sign of intelligence. Notably, even women are thought to be capable of rationality.

Some of the most poignant stories about *Asdzáá Tl'ógi* reveal her place as mother and wife. As mothers and wives, Navajo women claim authority and autonomy. The centrality of women's roles in reasserting and preserving traditional beliefs and practices is demonstrated in the stories about *Asdzáá Tl'ógi's* journey to Washington D.C. While the United States government sought to strip Navajos of their very identity, women strove to retain Navajo beliefs and traditions. One way they sought to retain Navajo traditions was by imbuing traditional foods with its former significance. During the wars, Navajos were defeated because their food sources had been destroyed. Faced with starvation, they turned themselves in at the American forts at the end of 1863.[29] The incarcerated Navajos were forced to rely on Euro-American rations such as white flour, beans and coffee. Ignorant about the preparation of these foods and unused to their taste, hundreds of Navajos died from diarrhea and dysentery. Food is connected to power. By destroying Navajos' food sources and then substituting their own kinds of foods, the Euro-Americans attempted to assimilate Navajos. Although Navajos have accepted many of these foods as staple, they continue to plant their cornfields and raise sheep as they have for generations.

As Navajos reestablished their lives by replanting their cornfields and rebuilding their livestock herds, they also endowed traditional foods with their former meanings. Faye Yazzie recalls her great-grandmother's journey to Washington, D.C. Traveling from mid-November 1874 to 1 February 1875 through a number of cities that included Denver and St. Louis, the Navajo delegation must have been struck by the strangeness of the American cities. Once in Washington, D.C., because they were Indians, they were forced to sleep in a hotel basement where mattresses were thrown on the floor.[30] When I asked grandmother Faye about our grandmother's journey, she shared this story with me:

> Our grandmother took with her Navajo foods. When the men became homesick and hungry, she brought forth Navajo food: jerkied meat, parched corn, and a paste made

---

28 Faye Yazzie, interview by author, tape recording, Tohatchi, New Mexico, 10 September 1993.

29 Broderick H. Johnson with Ruth Roessel, ed., *Navajo Stories of the Long Walk Period*. Tsaile, AZ: Navajo Community College Press, 1973.

30 Viola, *Diplomats in Buckskin*, 127.

from ground pinons mixed with ground parched corn. She took these foods in bags with her. Periodically, she doled it out to the men who were grateful.[31]

To ease the men's loneliness, *Asdzáá Tł'ógi* dispensed the traditional foods she had brought along in careful portions. Eating is more than a biological activity; it is a vibrant cultural activity as well.[32] As the Navajo delegation traveled for months, they experienced loneliness, homesickness and a growing distaste for strange foods. In sharing familiar foods with the homesick and hungry men, *Asdzáá Tł'ógi* assumes a central and vital place in Navajo society. As bell hooks declares, homes are places where we 'strive to be subjects, not objects, where we could be affirmed in our minds and hearts despite poverty, hardship, and deprivation, where we could restore to ourselves the dignity denied us on the outside in the public world.'[33] The act of remembering is a conscious gesture to honor the efforts of women like Juanita who endeavored to provide for their own.

After the death of her husband in 1894, *Asdzáá Tł'ógi* moved with her two daughters to the lands of their husbands' clan (the husbands were brothers) near present-day Tohatchi, New Mexico. There *Asdzáá Tł'ógi* spent the remainder of her life with her extended family, caring for grandchildren and livestock. She was a common sight around the Tohatchi community as she herded sheep. Historians write that Manuelito was an early advocate of American education for Navajo children but reconsidered its value after two of his sons died of diseases at Carlisle School. His melancholy over the deaths of his sons led to his increased alcoholism.[34] In contrast, *Tł'ógi* clan stories indicate that *Asdzáá Tł'ógi* and her older daughter continued to relay their husband's and father's messages of an American education for Navajo children. They helped Tohatchi school enroll Navajo children. Manuelito has been portrayed as ineffectual at the end of his life, reminiscent of the noble savage who had become demoralized and debauched as a result of exposure to White civilization.[35] On the other hand, *Tł'ógi* clan stories reaffirm his call for education for Navajo

---

31 Faye Yazzie, interview by author, Tape recording, Tohatchi, New Mexico, 10 September 1993.

32 Sidney W. Mintz, *Tasting Food, Tasting Freedom: Excursions into Eating, Culture, and the Past*. Boston: Beacon Press, 1996, 48, 49.

33 bell hooks, *Yearning: Race, Gender, and Cultural Politics*. Boston: South End Press, 1990, 42.

34 Virginia Hoffman and Broderick H. Johnson, *Navajo Biographies*. Rough Rock: Navajo Curriculum Center, 1970.

35 Hoffman and Johnson, *Navajo Biographies,* and Frank Waters, *Brave Are My People: Indian Heroes Not Forgotten*. Santa Fe: Clear Light Publishers, 1993. For my analysis of these biographies of Manuelito as yet another set of constructions about noble and debauched savages, I rely on the following studies: Richard Slotkin, *Regeneration Through Violence: The Mythology of the American Frontier, 1600–1860*. Middletown, Ct: Wesleyan University Press, 1978; Brian Dippie, *The Vanishing American: White Attitudes and U.S. Indian Policy*. Middletown, Ct: Wesleyan University Press, 1982; and Robert F. Berkhoffer, *The White Man's Indian: Images of the American Indian From Columbus to the Present*. New York: Vintage Books, 1979.

children; his message continued to be conveyed through his family members, his wife and daughter. As grandmother Faye says of *Asdzáá Tł'ógi's* older daughter:

> No one followed in her footsteps. They say that she was an orator. They would tell her to speak to people. She would get on her knees, rise on her knees, and her arms moved about as she talked. She would tell them about her father and what he envisioned ... She did not have difficulty with speaking.[36]

The stories remind us that our ancestors' qualities should be emulated. On several occasions, my grandmother's oratorical skills have been pointed out to me, perhaps in hopes that I might cultivate those particular skills, for it is thought that our ancestors' qualities are transmitted to the coming generations. These stories are also a reminder that our behavior must be exemplary, for we will be models for the coming generations.

Those afternoons of sitting in living rooms and listening to my grandparents' stories will remain with me. The stories were punctuated with interruptions, sighs, laughter, pauses, and we often reflected quietly while images of our grandmothers appeared in our mind's eye. Our grandmother *Asdzáá Tł'ógi* moves across the landscape with the sheep and goats. As she and her grandchildren herd the sheep, she tells them stories of her life and the Long Walk. She tells them of Washington, D.C. *Asdzáá Tł'ógi* died around 1910. During a sheep dip, *Asdzáá Tł'ógi* ate some corn stew that had spoiled. She lay deathly ill at a place called Red Willow with a grandchild cradled in her arms. She slipped into unconsciousness while her kin desperately tried to awaken her by repeatedly shooting a rifle outside the shelter. Even at the sunset of her life, *Asdzáá Tł'ógi* remained a mother. It is an image in keeping with the place that Navajo women continue to claim: to be a mother means to play a central role in Navajo society.

While my search in the archives for information on *Asdzáá Tł'ógi* yielded few written accounts, I did discover a cache of photographs, many not previously published. These photographs, taken at different stages of her life, depict *Asdzáá Tł'ógi* as a young woman in her twenties at the end of the Bosque Redondo captivity, as a mature woman in her late thirties or early forties, and as a grandmother in the early twentieth century. Some of these photographs depict *Asdzáá Tł'ógi* with her two daughters and several do not identify her or her family.

The endeavor to recover the Native American past includes reexamining portrayals of Native Americans in photographs, particularly those from the nineteenth and early twentieth centuries. Photographs have been used to suggest the familiar stereotypes that Native Americans are remnants of a dying civilization or noble savages symbolic of a pristine past.[37] However, recent works have begun to

---

36 Faye Yazzie, 21 October 1997.

37 See for example, Christopher M. Lyman, *The Vanishing Race and Other Illusions: Photographs of Indians by Edward S. Curtis*. Washington, DC: Smithsonian Press, 1982; and Patricia C. Albers and William R. James, 'Travel Photography: A Methodological Approach,' *Annals of Tourism Research* 15 (1988): 134–158. For Native American responses

illuminate Native American responses to these same photographs. As Lucy Lippard demonstrates, there is still much to be said about these photographs, particularly from a Native American perspective.[38]

Significantly, as historical documents such as photographs find their way into Native societies, they function as catalysts by promoting and re-creating a sense of community, particularly the meaning of clan kinship ties. These photographs are visual evidence of the incredible courage and resilience of our ancestors, our grandmothers and grandfathers. Upon viewing a photograph of grandmothers, *Asdzáá Tł'ógi's* great-grandson Isaac Allison, who was in his nineties in the late 1990s, said with emotion:

> Last night I was thinking about our past, the walk to *Hwéeldi*. It is just like I am seeing my grandmother again.

His love and respect for his grandmothers was evident in his voice. The photographs call up memories of the past, a past in which *Asdzáá Tł'ógi* and her daughters played central roles in the survival of Navajo families and community.

Reflections on Constructions of the Navajo Past

Re-examinations of history and oral traditions as different ways of viewing the past, of differing historical consciousness, have raised questions about the legitimacy of Western/Euro-American histories to represent the Native past, particularly in this case the Navajo past. Revisionist historians such as Patricia Limerick and Richard White have pointed out that Western/Euro-American history has positioned the West as the place where democracy was created and where individuals achieved autonomy, a prototypical Eurocentric view.[39] As Julie Cruikshank notes in her examination of how Euro-American histories and Native oral traditions construct notions of society differently, Euro-Americans desired to 'affirm the advantages of an emerging social order in which individualism was a value widely shared …'[40] Navajo histories, written by non-Navajos, reflect Euro-American notions about the meaning of the past as well.

As I have indicated earlier, the war against the Navajos and their subsequent imprisonment at Fort Sumner from 1863 to 1868 is a watershed in Navajo history.

---

to photographs, see *The American Indian Culture and Research Journal* 20:3 (1996). For specifically Navajos and photography, see James Faris, 'Photographing the Navajo: Scanning the Abuse,' *American Indian Culture and Research Journal* 20 (1996): 65–81, and *Navajo and Photography: A Critical History of the Representation of an American People.*

38 Lucy R. Lippard, ed. *Partial Recall: With Essays on Photographs of Native North Americans.* New York: The New Press, 1992.

39 Richard White, '*It's Your Misfortune and None of My Own': A New History of the American West.* Norman: University of Oklahoma Press, 1991, and Patricia Limerick, *The Legacy of Conquest: The Unbroken Past of the American West.* New York: Norton, 1987.

40 Cruikshank, 'Images of Society,' 33.

Navajo histories interpret these events within Euro-American categories of the meaning of the past. Specifically, history is seen as the movement toward a national Navajo sense of identity. Second, history is interpreted as the emergence of a Navajo national government based on Euro-American democratic principles where both Navajo and white men played major roles in the reestablishment of Navajo life and culture. Hence, in histories and in biographies, Manuelito, who was one of the major resisters to Euro-American invasions, is represented as an advocate of assimilation, including the necessity of a Euro-American education for Navajo children, during the early reservation era. Finally, as historian R. David Edmunds has noted, Indian histories, relying on written documents including military records, focused on the interactions between white military leaders and Indian leaders.[41] This sort of focus rendered Native women's roles invisible.

In contrast, Navajo stories like those about *Asdzáá Tł'ógi* demonstrate that Navajo women played central roles in the reestablishment of life in *Diné bekéyah* after 1868. Oral traditions serve as vehicles relaying beliefs and values to the next generation. Importantly, creation narratives, which feature female deities, provide the grounding by which Navajo women continue to assert their traditional places as mothers and daughters in Navajo society. Further, stories about women like *Asdzáá Tł'ógi* demonstrate that women draw upon their roles as grandmothers, mothers, and daughters to claim a measure of authority and autonomy traditionally accorded to them.

While clan stories may illuminate the Navajo past, even more significantly they indicate that clan kinship responsibilities continue to be important to the survival and persistence of Navajo life and culture. As Angela Wilson notes about oral histories that are part of her family, 'The stories handed down from grandmother to granddaughter are rooted in a deep sense of kinship responsibility, a responsibility that relays a culture, an identity, and a sense of belonging essential to my life.'[42] Just as oral traditions are important for the Dakota, the stories of our Navajo ancestors renew our spirits and our faith in the strength of the old ways. Rex Lee Jim observes in this regard:

> ...I have concluded that those who have died of old age must have done something right to reach old age. For Navajos, death of old age means dying at the age of 102. My question is "What did this person do to live for so many years?" So today when an elder says, "Let me give you a word of advice about life," I sit up and listen with all I've got.[43]

---

41 R. David Edmunds, ed., *American Indian Leaders: Studies in Diversity*. Lincoln: University of Nebraska Press, 1980, ix.

42 Wilson, *Grandmother to Granddaughter*, 514.

43 Jim, *A Moment in My Life*, 232.

Conclusion

Our history is similar to those of other Indigenous peoples. Waves of conquerors wrested away significant portions of our lands. European colonizers sought to impose their political, cultural, religious, and economic institutions upon our way of life. In contrast to many other Indigenous peoples, we Navajos have retained much of our own cultural traditions. One way of understanding this process is by examining the ways in which oral traditions serve as windows to the past, explaining how the past informs the present. Historically, Navajo women have held positions of authority and autonomy in their society. Even as Euro-American institutions sought to undermine their positions through domestication, Navajo women continue to play central roles in their society. The narratives of *Asdzáá Tł'ógi* and her daughters are testimony not only to the vitality of the oral tradition, but demonstrate how oral traditions serve as vehicles to transmit and recall the past and to connect it to the present.

Chapter 6

Exploring Healing and the Body Through Indigenous Chinese Medicine

Roxana Ng

Introduction

This chapter presents my introduction of Chinese Medicine into a graduate course in an education faculty as a way of disrupting the mind/body divide foundational to Western liberal and critical education. I begin with my own experience as an antiracist, materialist, and feminist scholar who has been trained and steeped in the Western scholarly tradition. I am now convinced that Western European, or at least Euro-American liberal education did not only colonize our minds, it has also made it impossible for Western, North American-trained academics, regardless of their race, gender, class and other social positioning to confront the reality and limits of their embodied experiences. I came to this realization during episodes of illness, which coincidentally but not accidentally began when I began my doctoral study in 1978. In my continual attempt to grapple with my health and to strive toward balance as an academic and an activist I finally realized, not only through my intellect but through my physical and emotional malaise (that is, through recognizing how I embodied my struggles) that what did many other women and me in was the deep-seated bifurcation of the intellect (frequently considered to be equivalent to the mind) and the body-spirit.

In this chapter, although I attempt to present the philosophy and theories of Chinese Medicine accurately, I must state that I am not a clinician. My interest in Chinese Medicine is firstly theoretical and secondly pedagogical; that is, I use it in my teaching as a contrasting system to explore different ways of constructing knowledge. I am not claiming in any way that Chinese Medicine is a superior healing system, or recommending that readers should adopt it as part of their personal health regime. Indeed, since Chinese Medicine originated in a patriarchal and feudal society – in ancient China – I would assume that its clinical practice if not its theoretical foundation was laden with sexist assumptions about the female body. However since I did not set out to interrogate this aspect of Chinese Medicine I have not analyzed its theoretical foundation and clinical practice in light of its sexist subtext.[1]

---

1   An interesting and nuanced discussion of the how male physicians understood women's health in late imperial China can be found in F. Bray, 'A deathly disorder: Understanding

I will first describe my personal healing journey that led me to Chinese Medicine, and through it to reclaiming part of my cultural roots. Out of this experience I raise questions about the body and illness as an epistemological site: what would knowledge construction look like and what would it be capable of if we began with ourselves as embodied subjects? I then describe the course I teach and how I incorporate Chinese Medicine and its adjunct practice, *Qi Gong*, into the course. Since this collection is concerned with traditional systems of knowledge, I give a fairly lengthy discussion of the philosophical basis of Chinese Medicine and how it conceptualizes the body. In the spirit of this book, I end by describing how we may use Indigenous knowledge in a Western context to reclaim forms of knowledge developed prior to colonization, and to challenge Western scientific thinking and learning that privileges rationalization over emotions, experience and embodied ways of knowing.

The Body and Illness as an Epistemological Site

My healing journey, which led to my integration of Chinese Medicine and other healing systems into my scholarly and professional life, began when I started my doctoral program in 1978 after an intense period of activism. One of my main goals in returning to school was to develop 'immigrant women' as a legitimate field of scholarly inquiry and a feminist sociology that would speak to women's experience.[2]

In the ensuing years I threw myself relentlessly into my academic work while participating in organizing immigrant women, firstly in Toronto where I studied, then across the country as my academic jobs (many on a sessional basis) took me to Saskatoon, Kingston, Fredericton, and eventually back to Toronto. I began to develop physical symptoms of stress, at first manifested as frequent colds and flu, skin rash and stomach cramps that came and went and culminated in several health crises such as pancreatitis in the mid-1980s and chronic fatigue in the late 1980s.

These conditions were serious in that I felt so ill at times that I could not work. However they were never specific or acute enough to warrant biomedical interventions. In fact, a fundamental weakness with biomedicine is its inability to successfully treat chronic nonspecific, as well as degenerative, diseases. Since most of my ailments were unresponsive to biomedical treatments I began to

---

women's health in late imperial China' in D. Bates, ed., *Knowledge and the Scholarly Tradition*. Cambridge: Cambridge University Press, 1995, 235–250.

2   This intellectual and political journey began when I worked with other feminists to establish the Vancouver Women's Research Centre (WRC), which we envisioned to be a place outside of the academy that would contribute to the development of feminist theories and research arising out of women's concerns in the everyday world. Dorothy Smith was a central figure at WRC at the time. I was so impressed by the feminist methodology she was developing that I left Vancouver in 1978 to study with her at the Ontario Institute for Studies in Education (OISE).

explore alternative healing systems around 1980, at first mainly bodywork such as chiropractic, massage and shiatsu and then homeopathy, with good results relative to my encounters with biomedicine.[3]

In my heart, gut and mind, I knew that much of my ill health was the direct result of both my academic work and my activism in the feminist movement, as I joined other women of color in anti-racism activities directed at the women's movement and at other hierarchical structures, including the university, that marginalize and exclude us. It is not easy to be an Indigenous person, a woman and an immigrant living in a society that upholds white male supremacy. As a nation colonized by Europeans, notably the English and the French, we live with the legacy of colonialism in Canada which began with the subordination and genocide of the Aboriginal people. This subordination is extended to other groups that are seen to be different (physically, linguistically, culturally, ideologically), and hence inferior. As we move up the power hierarchy, this inferiorization of the 'other' becomes much more entrenched and difficult to disrupt. As part of the institutional structure created historically to preserve the privilege of certain classes of men, the academy is no exception in entrenching white male privilege, values and knowledge constructed based on European men's experience of the world. The fact that white women and some people of color have made inroads into this bastion of patriarchal power does not mean that they belong to these Eurocentric institutions. Indeed, there is now a burgeoning literature that exposes the barriers that we encounter in the university, be they teachers or students, both because our presence challenges the once homogeneous makeup of the university, and because we challenge the process of knowledge production based on white, male, and elitist assumptions.[4]

The exercise and maintenance of power takes multiple and complicated forms. Elsewhere I have identified three major power axes in the university: that between the classroom and the larger academic institution; that between the teacher and the students; and that among the students.[5] Thus although a faculty has formal authority as a representative of the university, this authority can be challenged by students in the classroom. For example, a woman of color who is a faculty member may be challenged more than her (white) male colleagues because she is relatively powerless in the larger society. Faculty whose teaching does not conform to the expected convention in terms of content, style, and so forth is challenged more. Sexism, racism, class privilege, ability and so on are operative in interactions among students as well.

---

3 Chiropractic and homeopathy were and are part of Western medicine, but with the rise and predominance of biomedicine, especially in North America, they were pushed out of the mainstream.

4 See, for example, S. de Castell and M. Bryson, eds, *Radical interventions: Identity, Politics, and Differences in Educational Praxis*. Albany: State University of New York Press, 1997; L. Roman and L. Eyre, eds, *Dangerous Territories: Struggles for Difference and Equality in Education*. New York: Routledge, 1997.

5 R. Ng, 'A woman out of control: Deconstructing sexism and racism in the university' *Canadian Journal of Education*, 18(3): 139–205.

What is important to point out is that power is never enacted as mere intellectual encounters. All intellectual encounters are exercised through confrontations of bodies, which are differently inscribed. Power play is enacted and absorbed by people physically as they assert or challenge authority, and therefore the marks of such confrontations are stored in the body. Each time I stand in front of a classroom I embody the historical sexualization and racialization of an Asian female (who is thought to be docile, subservient and sexually compliant) even as my class privilege, formal authority and qualification ameliorate some of the effects of this signification. My presence is a moment in the crystallization of the historical and contemporary contestation of ideas and practices that are constantly changing. That is, my physical presence in the academy in turn challenges the sexist and racist construction of the archetype and stereotype of an Asian female.[6] It is indeed the encounters of bodies, not only of intellects, that give dynamism to the process of teaching and learning. As we engage in critical teaching and bring our activism to the university and our classrooms, this dynamism is what excites us at the same time that it makes us sick when we go against the grain.

And yet despite feminist scholarship's insistence that 'the personal is political' we have no language to speak of how we embody our political and intellectual struggles. While we wage these struggles in our professional and public lives, when we get sick we see and treat it as our personal and private problem that is unspeakable publicly. This bifurcation points to how fundamentally we have been influenced by Cartesian thinking, which posits a separation between the body and the mind,[7] and the privileging of mental over manual labor.[8] Thus for almost fifteen years my professional and political work on the one hand, and my personal explorations on health and illness on the other, occurred in two separate and nonintersecting spheres; the success or ongoingness of the former depended on the latter, yet the latter remained submerged and hidden as my private preoccupation.

In 1991, I had the opportunity to teach a course on 'Health, Illness, and Knowledge of the Body: Education and Self-Learning Processes' (hereafter 'Health and the Body'); my colleague who initiated the course had moved into another field of study. This coincided with yet another health crisis in my life. This time, in addition to the therapies that I had integrated into my health regime I turned to and (re)discovered Chinese Medicine, as the other modalities offered temporary relief but produced little sustained effect. The only thing my biomedical physician could offer was a diagnosis of depression (much better than 'it's all in your head'), a lot of sympathy

---

6   I am using the term 'archetype' here in a common sense way to indicate that a stereotype is made out of an archetype. It is not to be confused with C. Jung's theorization of archetypal psychology.

7   See S.R. Bordo, *The Flight to Objectivity: Essays on Cartesianism and Culture.* Albany: State University of New York Press, 1987, especially Chapter 5.

8   K. Marx and F. Engels, *The German Ideology.* New York: International Publishers, 1970.

and advice for psychotherapy. But at last here was an opening for me to bring the two seemingly unconnected spheres of my life together.

I used the word (re)discovered above because, growing up in the British colony of Hong Kong, Chinese Medicine was not completely alien to me. Although my paternal grandmother was a Western-trained physician who rejected Chinese Medicine, seeing it as inferior, and my father believed in the superiority of Western science, we were 'smuggled' herbal teas and soups in certain seasons as part of our regular dietary regime. We also described our internal bodily states in terms of climatic conditions such as hot, cold, and dampness. For example, in the summer we drank tea made from white chrysanthemum flowers to 'clear heat' from the body. Special concoctions were prepared to alleviate symptoms of colds and flu. This knowledge was passed on and maintained in the family frequently through women; in my childhood household it was my mother and a maid who administered these concoctions to us when my grandmother was absent, to avoid reprimand and disharmony in the family. These examples show that knowledge of Chinese Medicine is part of my cultural heritage, even if I was unaware at the time of the fact that it is a systematic healing system indigenous to my culture, because biomedicine was and is the dominant medical system in the colony.

In the ensuing months, as I went through an intensive regime of Chinese medical treatments consisting primarily of herbal therapy, acupuncture, and later on exercises such as *T'ai Chi Ch'uen* (or *Tai Ji Juan*) and *Qi Gong* (or *Chi Kung*, depending on the system of romanization used) with dramatic results, I also began to read about the philosophical and theoretical foundation of Chinese Medicine.[9] In this healing process I recovered a lot of the so-called folk knowledge that I acquired growing up in Asia, but which had been buried in my consciousness as I immersed myself in the Western educational system. Through feminism and antiracism, I discovered the colonizing effects of Eurocentric 'male-stream' thoughts.[10] I now discovered through my body, as my health improved over the next several years, the extent to which they have shaped the bifurcation of my consciousness. This journey, which is continuing, has led to a profound psychic, philosophical and political shift that ultimately reshaped the way I work, teach, relate to others: in short, it transformed my life. By returning to my cultural roots, albeit with an antiracist, feminist spin, I found a way toward a more balanced life, one that enables me to integrate my mind, body and spirit (or soul, which is not distinct from the spirit in Chinese thought), as well as my professional and personal life.

---

9   I also kept a daily health log that detailed changes in my body as I took the herbs and received acupuncture treatments (and sometimes these changes were dramatic). Later, with the encouragement of my psychotherapist, I incorporated emotional and psychic changes in the log.

10   M. O'Brien, *The Politics of Reproduction*. London and New York: Routledge & Kegan Paul, 1981.

Health and Body as a Pedagogical and Alternate Epistemological Site[11]

'Health, Healing and Knowledge of the Body' is designed to disrupt Western academic knowledge that privileges intellectual and critical thinking over other forms of knowledge construction. I do this in three ways: using course materials (readings, video and audio materials) aimed at raising questions about prevailing assumptions in biomedicine and exposing students to other healing systems; incorporating *Qi Gong*, a form of Chinese meditative and breathing exercises, into the class; and using a reading notebook and health journal as key ingredients in the self-learning process.

The course has evolved over the years and has gone through numerous revisions. It began as a course that juxtaposed biomedicine and other alternative healing systems with an emphasis on Indigenous Chinese Medicine. As I gained more comfort and confidence with Chinese Medicine and *Qi Gong,* I moved away from a cursory exploration of other healing systems, which I call 'the boutique approach,'[12] to focus more on Chinese Medicine in order to avoid superficiality. The course is now concerned with embodied learning and embodiment using Chinese Medicine and other conceptions of the body (from biomedicine, phenomenology and sociology to name a few of the disciplines and perspectives we explore) as a basis for our collective exploration.[13] Over the years this course has gone through various permutations as my own interest and knowledge in the area develops.

My own study of Chinese Medicine, as well as research and writing on the subject is also body-centered. I acquired my knowledge not only through intellectual learning by reading books on the subject, but through embodied learning by consulting with health professionals who specialize in different treatment modalities of Chinese Medicine.[14] In each consultation I asked the practitioners to give me reference materials and to explain the theory underpinning their treatments. In the case of

---

11 Since the writing of this paper in 2001, I have changed department (from Sociology and Equity Studies to Adult Education) and am no longer teaching the course mentioned in this chapter. The contents described here are now integrated into two of the courses I teach. However for the purpose of this publication I have decided to use the present tense to preserve the immediacy of the writing.

12 See R. Ng, 'Toward an embodied pedagogy: Exploring health and the body through Chinese Medicine' in G. Dei, B. Hall and D. Goldin-Rosenberg eds, *Indigenous Knowledges: Multiple Readings of Our World.* Toronto: University of Toronto Press, 2000, 168–183.

13 In the fall of 2000, borrowing from this course, I also developed a specialist course entitled, 'Toward an Integrative Approach to Health Education,' for a group of M.Ed. students who are physicians in a program for health professionals. Next year, this course will have a new name: 'Embodied Learning and Qi Gong' that identifies the central concern of the course in a clearer way.

14 I take this opportunity to thank Marie Graff, RMT, CST; David Bray, CMD; Kevin Heckendorn, CST; Mark Kremko, CST (deceased) for generously sharing their knowledge with me and for supporting my journey toward health and balance over the years. I want to pay a particular tribute to Mark, whose premature death in the fall of 2003 is a huge loss to those he has helped as a shiatsu therapist.

acupuncture and *shiatsu,* a form of 'pressure point' massage developed in Japan based on Chinese meridian theory, for example, I asked the practitioner/therapist which acupuncture points and meridians he was working on and why. Over time, together with studying, I came to know the fourteen major meridians that traverse through the body not only as an abstract concept but also as 'entities' that can be experienced *in* the body. I learned about the functions and efficacy of the herbs that made up the prescriptions by questioning my Chinese herbal doctor and people who work in the herbal stores. I learned about the principles of cupping and when it is used as a treatment method (vis-à-vis acupuncture for instance). Through referral by these practitioners I attended lectures and workshops on Chinese Medicine. There is usually an experiential component in these workshops. For example, Chinese medical theory and *Qi Gong* exercises were integral to a weekend workshop I attended on 'women's health' offered for both professionals and lay people. I took up *Tai Ji Juan* as a practice over ten years ago, and soon after incorporated *Qi Gong* as part of my health and exercise regime, paying special attention to how I activate *Qi,* a central Chinese concept in health and healing, in my body. In addition to weekly lessons in *Qi Gong,* as time permits I attend workshops and retreats offered. In this way my own learning is also experiential and embodied, paralleling what I advocate in 'Health and the Body.' Indeed all of the components of Chinese Medicine that I incorporate into my teaching are an integral part of my daily life. I begin the day with yoga and *Qi Gong* exercises, practice *Qi Gong* and *Tai Ji Juan* as much as I can in addition to other forms of exercises, and consult with a Chinese medical doctor and *shiatsu* therapist regularly to maintain my health and well-being as well as to deepen the knowledge I have acquired.

In this chapter I will not describe the course in detail, although I will mention elements of it that pertain to my discussion on Chinese Medicine as a traditional knowledge system and issues of embodied learning derived from Chinese Medicine. I will focus on the philosophy and principles of Chinese Medicine and its adjunct practice of *Qi Gong* to illustrate how we may challenge Western knowledge construction and reconceptualize scholarship using insights and practices derived from this ancient healing system.

Chinese Medicine as an Alternate System of Knowledge[15]

Chinese Medicine is a rational healing system developed and refined in China over 5000 years ago. Since it was developed in an ancient period when there was a lack of advanced technologies (such as the sophisticated and complicated machines and instruments employed by biomedicine today) to assist in the detection of diseases, its

---

15 The rationale for selecting Chinese Medicine as a focus for this course and my overall approach to the course has been discussed elsewhere. See R. Ng, 'Toward an embodied pedagogy: Exploring health and the body through Chinese Medicine' in G. Dei, B. Hall and D. Goldin-Rosenberg eds, *Indigenous Knowledges: Multiple Readings of Our World.* Toronto: University of Toronto Press, 2000, 168–183.

evolution and refinement was based largely on human touch and senses. Observation, touching, especially taking the pulse, questioning and observation constitute the core of the diagnostic procedures of Chinese Medicine to this day. When I call it a rational system I mean that Chinese Medicine is a systematic medicine whose logic, diagnostic procedures and treatment modalities are internally coherent and consistent, albeit radically different from Western notions of diseases and treatments. Don Bates[16] includes Chinese Medicine as a scholarly tradition, among others, because the knowledge that constitutes the core of Chinese Medicine is based on written texts that are studied, debated and revised over the years. While this was a predominant form of medicine practiced in China, Chinese Medicine went through a period of decline during the nineteenth century.[17] It is now more widely known as 'Traditional Chinese Medicine,' or TCM.

Ironically, TCM is a relatively recent term that refers to a *style* of medicine that emerged after the communist revolution in 1949, according to some TCM scholars and practitioners.[18] Prior to this time, although many of the healing practices have a common philosophical origin, one based in Taoism, the modalities used varied according to local customs, plant life (in the case of herbology) and climatic conditions, to name only a few variants. It is perhaps its variability that Chinese medicine, like many other forms of Indigenous medicines, never gained the visibility and prominence as biomedicine did in the West.[19] The precise dating of TCM is debatable. Although this style of medicine can be traced back to the late

---

16 D. Bates, ed., *Knowledge and the Scholarly Medical Traditions*. Cambridge: Cambridge University Press, 1995.

17 Paul Unschuld outlines two reasons for the decline of Chinese medicine: first, toward the end of the nineteenth century China suffered many defeats in confrontations with Western powers, to the extent that all traditional knowledge and ways of doing things became suspect by many educated Chinese; and second, Western medicine was not an entirely alien body of knowledge to the Chinese and thus with the rise of Western power it was accepted as superior. See P. Unschuld, 'Episteomological issues and changing legitimation: Traditional Chinese Medicine in the twentieth century' in C. Leslie and A. Young, eds, *Paths to Asian Medical Knowledge*. Berkeley: University of California Press, 44–61. This speaks to the colonization and hegemony of Western thought I mentioned at the beginning of this chapter.

18 B. Flaws, Before Completion: Essays on the Practice of TCM. Boulder: Blue Poppy Press, 1992.

19 One central force, too complex to describe here in detail but nevertheless significant, that led to the disappearance of many traditional healing systems is the expansion of Western, notably British, imperialism in Asia. So, for example, when Britain colonized India, medical schools of traditional healing systems such as Ayurveda were closed down, and Ayurveda as a legitimate healing system went underground. It wasn't until recently that these medical systems were revived in India. See T. Kaptchuk and M. Croucher, *The Healing Arts: A journey through the Faces of Medicine*. London: British Broadcasting Corporation, 1986. In China, the disappearance of Indigenous forms of medicine from the public sphere coincided with the invasion of colonial powers (Britain, France, Germany) in the eighteenth century. But I am unable to find sources that posit a direct relationship between the two. This deserves further research.

Han Dynasty, some scholars say that it was created around 1953, while others argue that its conscious beginning occurred around the time of the Cultural Revolution.[20] In any case, TCM refers to a standardized style of medicine that is codified by means of common terminologies and a common language (such as the labeling of herbs and names of acupuncture points). The purpose is to establish a common system of communication and education among practitioners across the diverse regions of China, and to enable transferability of treatments in patient care as China established itself as a modern nation state. This move transformed Chinese medicine from different regional styles to a national standard style. In the process, those elements that were considered 'unscientific' and superstitious, such as astrology and geomancy, were eliminated from the mainstream of TCM. In modern China, TCM is composed of five aspects or branches: physical medicine (such as *tui na* massage), acupuncture, herbology, diet and exercise (such as *Qi Gong*).[21]

TCM is based on the central Taoist principle of unity of opposites yin and yang. According to Chinese creation myth the universe was an undifferentiated whole in the beginning. Out of this emerged yin-yang: the world in its infinite forms.[22] In both Taoism and TCM, yin-yang is a symbolic representation of universal process (including health in the latter case) that portrays a changing rather than static process.[23] Kaptchuk puts it succinctly thus:

Yin-Yang theory is well illustrated by the traditional Chinese Taoist symbol. The circle representing the whole is divided into *Yin* (black) and *Yang* (white).

The small circles of opposite shading illustrate that within the *Yin* there is *Yang* and vice versa. The dynamic curve dividing them indicates that *Yin* and *Yang* are continuously merging. Thus *Yin* and *Yang* create each other, control each other, and transform into each other.[24]

The important thing to understand is that the two opposite states are not mutually exclusive or independent of each other. They are mutually dependent and they change into each other.[25] Therefore extreme yang becomes yin and vice versa. Health is

---

20 B. Flaws, *Before Completion: Essays on the Practice of TCM*. Boulder: Blue Poppy Press, 1992.

21 I owe a great debt of gratitude to my TCM doctor, first *Tai Chi Ch'uen* teacher, and friend, David Bray, for sharing with me his knowledge of Chinese Medicine, and to check the accuracy of the information presented here.

22 H. Beinfield and E. Korngold, *Between Heaven and Earth: A Guide to Chinese Medicine*. New York: Ballentine Books, 1991, 50–51.

23 T. Kaptchuk, *The Web that Has No Weaver: Understanding Chinese Medicine*. Lincolnwood, Chicago: Contemporary Books, 2000; G. Maciocia, *The Foundations of Chinese Medicine*. Edinburgh & London: Churchill Livingstone, 1989.

24 T. Kaptchuk, *The Web that Has No Weaver: Understanding Chinese Medicine*. Lincolnwood, Chicago: Contemporary Books, 2000, 23.

25 G. Maciocia, *The Foundations of Chinese Medicine*. Edinburgh and London: Churchill Livingstone, 1989, 2–6.

seen to be the balance of yin-yang aspects of the body and disease is the imbalance between these aspects. This is a form of dialectical thinking radically different from the causal linear thinking and logic of biomedicine and positivist science. The body in TCM is seen to be a dynamic interaction of yin and yang: it is constantly changing and fluctuating.

Proceeding from this fundamental understanding of the nature of yin-yang and health as balance, TCM views illness not so much in terms of discrete diseases but in terms of patterns of disharmony.[26] Thus TCM goes on to outline eight guiding principles for determining these patterns of disharmony.[27] Again these are not mutually exclusive but can coexist in a person.

A major difference between biomedicine and TCM theory is the way in which the body is conceptualized. The Chinese body has no Western anatomical correspondence. For example, Chinese medical theory does not have the concept of a nervous system yet it can treat neurological disorders. It does not perceive an endocrine system yet it is capable of correcting what allopathy calls endocrine disorders.[28] Although TCM language makes reference to what the West recognizes as organs such as lungs, liver, stomach and so on, these are not conceptualized as discrete physical structures and entities located in specific areas within the body. Rather the term 'organs' is used to identify the functions associated with them. Furthermore, TCM does not make a distinction between physical functions and the emotional and spiritual dimensions governed by the 'organ' in question. Furthermore, it does not only describe an organ in terms of its physiological processes and functions but also in terms of its orbit (sphere of influence).

For example, in TCM the spleen is the primary organ of digestion. It extracts the nutrients from food digested by the stomach and transforms them into what will become 'Qi' and 'Blood'.[29] A way of expressing this is that the spleen is responsible

---

26 Here I make a distinction between illness and disease following Kaptchuk's definition: "...illness is the state of a patient, beyond discomfort, but defined in the patient's terms. Disease is an objective condition, independent of the patient's judgment, which many medical models often assume to be the whole of illness" (T. Kaptchuk and M. Croucher, *The Healing Arts*. London: British Broadcasting Corporation, 1986, 9).

27 G. Maciocia, *The Foundations of Chinese Medicine*. Edinburgh & London: Churchill Livingstone, 1989, Chapter 18; H. Beinfield and E. Korngold, *Between Heaven and Earth; A Guide to Chinese Medicine*. New York: Ballentine Books, 1991, 77–80.

28 T. Kaptchuk, *The Web that Has No Weaver: Understanding Chinese Medicine*. Lincolnwood, Chicago: Contemporary Books, 2000, Introduction.

29 Note here that the Blood in TCM theory is both similar to and different from the Western notion of blood, the red liquid, which is perceived to be the red fluid that circulates throughout our bodies in arteries and veins. Although it is true that the Chinese Blood is a liquid that circulates through the body, where it is said to circulate is conceptualized differently. Again, the physical pathways are less important than its *functions*. The major function of Blood is to nourish, maintain, and moisten the body. TCM also distinguishes different kinds of blood (see T. Kaptchuk, *The Web that Has No Weaver: Understanding Chinese Medicine*. Lincolnwood, Chicago: Contemporary Books, 2000; G. Maciocia, *The Foundations of Chinese Medicine*.

for making blood, whereas the liver is responsible for storing and spreading blood. As such the spleen is responsible for transformation, transmutation and transportation and these functions apply to physical as well as mental and emotional processes. At the somatic level, 'weakness' in the spleen means that food cannot be transformed properly into nutrients that nourish the body.[30] At the emotional and psychospiritual level, a weak spleen affects our awareness of possibilities and disables us from transforming possibilities into appropriate courses of action, leading to worry and confusion. Ultimately it affects our trustworthiness and dependability.[31] This example shows that Chinese medical theory encompasses, rather than segments, physical, mental, emotional and spiritual dimensions of human existence.[32]

The body, then, is conceptualized not so much in terms of distinct parts and components as in terms of energetics or energy flow (Qi). Qi, a fundamental concept in TCM and Chinese thinking, although frequently translated as 'energy' or 'vital energy' it has no precise conceptual correspondence in the West.[33] Qi is what animates life.[34] Thus while there is Qi there is life; when there is no Qi life ceases. It is both material and immaterial.[35] Qi is present in the universe in the air we breathe and in the breaths we take. It is the quality we share with all things thus connecting the macrocosm with the microcosm. Qi flows in the body along lines of energy flow

---

Edinburgh and London: Churchill Livingstone, 1989). For example, the concept of 'stagnant blood,' which can arise from blood stagnation in the body or result from injury, is foreign to the West.

30 This is a Western characterization. In TCM terms, the two major disruptions pertaining to the spleen are dampness and deficiency, which produce different problems in the transformation and transmutation process too complicated to explain here. But this example indicates clearly the conceptual differences between East and West.

31 This insight is derived from a seminar in Toronto given by Ted Kaptchuk entitled 'Ladders of the soul and Oriental medicine: The East Asian perspective on psycho-spiritual issues in therapy' (November 17, 1996).

32 The term 'Spirit' should not be equated with the Western notion of spirituality or the notion of the Holy Spirit in Judaism and Christianity. Although some of the discussion concerning Spirit may appear 'religious' in the Western sense, its understanding and application in Chinese Medicine is very specific. According to Ted Kaptchuk in *The Web that Has No Weaver* (Lincolnwood, Chicago: Contemporary Books, 2000), the Spirit in Chinese Medicine can be divided into five smaller spirits, each one of which is responsible for a particular virtue. However instead of a religious connotation, the discussion of Spirit and virtue 'is about capacities and responsibilities inherent in the human condition that are recognizable across cultures' (p. 59). He further states, 'The focus is how Chinese medicine, as a "secular healing art," has traditionally sought to conceptualize and integrate the nonphysical aspects of a person's life into its discussion of illness and health' (p. 59).

33 T. Kaptchuk, *The Web that Has No Weaver: Understanding Chinese Medicine*. Lincolnwood, Chicago: Contemporary Books, 2000.

34 H. Beinfield and E. Korngold, *Between Heaven and Earth: A Guide to Chinese Medicine*. New York: Ballentine Books, 1991, 30.

35 G. Maciocia, *The Foundations of Chinese Medicine*. Edinburgh & London: Churchill Livingstone, 1989, 35–37.

called meridians or organ networks.[36] Another way of conceptualizing disease is that it arises when Qi is not flowing smoothly, leading to blockage and stagnation which if persistent will lead to disease (pathological changes in the body). Thus an important part of the healing process is to unblock and facilitate the free flowing of Qi. Different treatment modalities (massage, acupuncture, and herbology) are aimed at promoting the smooth flow of Qi and rebalancing disharmony.

Instead of discussing the structure and argument of the materials (like in other courses I offer), the emphasis in 'Health and the Body' is on how the readings alter the participants' original thinking (or not). Reflection is a key element of the course. Participants, including myself, are to constantly reflect upon how the experience in the course (in terms of readings, lectures, discussions, films, audiotapes, physical exercises and so on) alters the way they think about health and the body – *their* body.

Qi Gong

Together with these notions of health and the body, the Chinese have developed exercise forms called *Qi Gong*. These exercises have been around for at least 2000 years. Again it is impossible to provide a comprehensive description of what Qi Gong entails in this limited space. Briefly, they are exercises aimed at regulating the breath, the mind and the body simultaneously. There are literally thousands of forms of Qi Gong, from sitting postures similar to what the West recognizes as meditation to Tai Ji Juan, which at its most advanced is a form of martial art aimed at honing the body-mind to respond to external attack without force. Indeed, Qi Gong is a recommended exercise form in TCM and is taught widely as a healing art in China.[37]

Practitioners of Qi Gong believe that by disciplining, activating and regulating the normally automatic, involuntary way of breathing, they are able to regulate and alter other functions of the body such as heartbeat, blood flow, and other physical and emotional functions. Thus Qi Gong is not simply a physical exercise. Nancy Zi, a professional vocal soloist who studies Qi Gong to enhance her singing in classical Western opera, puts it concisely:

> The practice of *chi kung* ... encompasses the ancient Chinese understanding of disciplined breathing as a means of acquiring total control over body and mind. It gives us physiological and psychological balance and the balance of *yin* and *yang* ....[38]

Thus, Qi Gong is based on the same principles as TCM; they are complementary. In 'Health and the Body,' in addition to exploring an alternate conception of the body

---

36 H. Beinfield and E. Korngold, *Between Heaven and Earth: A Guide to Chinese Medicine*. New York: Ballentine Books, 1991.

37 See 'The Mystery of *Chi*,' the first in a six-part television series of 'Healing and the Mind' narrated by Bill Moyer in Bill Moyer, *Healing and the Mind*. New York: Doubleday, 1993.

38 Nancy Zi, *The Art of Breathing*. New York: Bantam Books, 1986, 3.

through readings on TCM (that is, through the intellect) and to complement these readings, therefore, I conduct Qi Gong exercises as a way of integrating the body-mind, not only in theory but in practice.

'Health and the Body' begins with gentle stretching and breathing. The purpose is to direct attention to the parts of the body that are normally ignored in carrying out intellectual activities (such as reading and discussion). I then ask students to assume the basic Qi Gong posture, which can be done by standing or sitting. In this basic posture, the practitioner stands (or sits) with feet parallel, shoulder-width apart (that is, the feet are aligned vertically with the hip and the inside of the shoulder joints). The spine of the practitioner should be straight 'like a string of pearls,' that is, the practitioner should stand in such a way that the spinal column is straight with each vertebrae loosely connected from the tailbone to the top of the head so that the spinal column resembles a string of pearls. Finally, the Dan T'ien, an energy center approximately two inches (or four fingers) below the navel, should be aligned laterally with an acupuncture point in the lower back called the Ming Men. This is done by bending the knees slightly, thereby straightening the lower back. This posture is said to maximize the flow of *Qi* in the body.

While standing (or sitting) with the right body alignment, students are asked to move their arms until they feel a new or different sensation. This gives them an experiential sense of what I mean by Qi, and how we can direct the flow of Qi by intention (for example making the hands warm). Based on my own experience, I know that usually most people, if not everyone, feel something when they attain the right body alignment. They are asked to share their experiences. Apart from serving as a checkpoint for me, I want to explore the diversity and uniqueness of the experiences and to emphasize that there isn't a right or wrong experience. Experience simply *is*. And this should be honored and respected both individually and collectively. Here is an entry recorded in one of the students' journals:

> We moved our arms, as if holding a big balloon, until we found the position that was conducive to E[nergy] flow. My arms didn't make it far from my sides and I could feel a tingling sensation between my arms & body. There was a strange feeling of a magnetic field that kept my arms from moving further out & preventing them from falling back towards my body. We kept that position for a while and allowed the *chi* to flow and warm our arms, hands. [student journal, 23 Sept. 1996]

In addition to the exercises themselves, I also explain the Chinese view of the body in terms of meridian theory (which is explored through readings later on in the course), and the rationale for the exercise. For instance, to complement the readings on the Five Element Theory of TCM, I teach a set of Qi Gong exercises called the Five Seasons Exercise, which corresponds to the major meridians of Lung (autumn), Kidney (winter), Liver (spring), Heart (summer), and Spleen (late summer).[39] The exercise begins with autumn.

---

39 The Chinese calendar is divided into five seasons, with two summer seasons (early and late summer), and not four seasons as in the European calendar.

Attaining the basic standing posture, the practitioner begins the autumn exercise by raising both arms to just below the shoulders as if she is holding a ball in front of her body while breathing in. The palms of her hands should be facing her breasts. When her hands reach this position, she turns over her palms to face outward. With the out breath, she moves her hands and arms outward laterally until they are beside her body, with palms facing backward. This movement stretches the Lung meridian, which begins at a point where the clavicle and the arm meet, and runs down both arms to the outside of the thumb. She turns over the palms to face heaven when breathing in again, taking in heavenly energy. With the next out-breath, she moves her arms toward each other until they are shoulder-width apart with palms facing up. While breathing in, she rounds the arms as if she is holding a ball between her hands as in the starting movement. She turns over her palms to face the earth. When she exhales, she lowers both hands and arms slowly until they rest beside the body.

The movements of the autumn exercise are aimed at rhythmically stretching and contracting the Lung meridian (that is, the line of energy flow that influences the function of the lung). This is because the lung is the body's first line of defense against the external environment. Autumn signals the end of the summer and the movement into winter, when we are more susceptible to invasion by cold leading to colds and flu. Strengthening the lung helps to reduce our chances of succumbing to these maladies.

Two important points about Qi Gong is that most if not all the movements are performed gently and gracefully, as if every joint in the body is a well-oiled hinge. The mind of the practitioner should be 'on the breath' and the breath should be 'on the mind' (that is, with concentration and intention). In the Five Seasons Exercise set, as in other exercises, visualization is an important part of the exercise as the practitioner moves through the set. Thus, Qi Gong is a form of moving meditation that calms the mind and regulates the breath at the same time. By actually performing the exercises rather than merely describing them, the students get an experiential rather than intellectual sense of the philosophy and practice of Qi Gong. As I explain the meridians that are affected with each exercise, they obtain an *embodied* knowledge of meridians and energy flow central to Chinese medical theory. This contrasts radically from the dominant mode of learning in Western liberal and critical education, which is preoccupied with learning 'through the head,' what I call intellectual learning. Indeed, one student in the fall term decided to stay in the course in spite of its unorthodoxy precisely because I pointed this out in my introduction to the class. She wrote in her note to me when I asked students why they wanted to take the class and what they expected to get out of it:

> I was deeply moved by your example of traditional learning being from the neck up and also by your accounts of trying to alter the rigid structure of learning (certain size, room, etc.). [student note, September 2001]

Throughout the segment of the course on TCM, I talk about acupuncture as a treatment modality in TCM, the anatomical location of selected acupuncture points and their functions, and show students how to find these points on their bodies in relation to the Qi Gong exercises. Through this kind of experiential learning students obtain a different view of the body and are encouraged to acknowledge and value their physical and emotional experiences in addition to their intellectual experience. As well, they are asked to use their experiences in the exercises to reflect on the readings and discussions in an attempt to close the body/mind divide.

Reading Notebook and Health Journal

To facilitate and systematize the reflective process, two tools are used. First, the participants are required to keep a reading notebook, which serves as a record of the readings, lectures and exercises. In it they are asked to use the following key words to guide the entries: (a) what I see/read/experience, (b) how I feel, and (c) what I think (Course Outline, Fall 1996). Second, the participants are asked to keep a health journal, which is a record of their physical and emotional health at least during the course. I ask that journal entries be made minimally on a weekly basis and preferably daily if students have a specific purpose in mind (for example, if someone wishes to use them to trace her menstruation cycle). Students can use either tool to record their experiences of the Qi Gong exercises and other thoughts arising out of/related to the course.

I encourage students to develop a format for recording their observations that is most appropriate for their purpose. Over the years, I read with interest the systems students develop to map their own health. One student used a series of codes that she developed to describe how she felt over her menstrual cycle and recorded the codes daily on a monthly calendar. Another student developed a series of symbols of faces (from smiling to downturn mouth) and colored stars (red equals energetic; silver equals feeling tired) in relation to her daily entries. At the end of each week and month she added up these symbols as a quick measure of how balanced her life had been. This journal with faces and stars was fun to read and I surmised was fun to do as well. As a general rule, I do not read the journals unless a student wants me to; however I glance through them at the end of the course to make sure that they are done.[40]

I encourage students to use the materials recorded in the notebook and health journal as 'data' for their term papers, especially if they wish to integrate their experiences into their scholarly inquiry or to explore writing as embodied subjects. For example, one student used the term paper to work through her experience of being sexually abused by her father and how she reclaimed her body as a result of

---

40 I changed the assignments for the course slightly in the fall term of 2000, combining the reading notebook and the health journal, and asking the students to write a one-page summary of the readings and their experiences of *Qi Gong* to share in class. However, the result was not satisfactory and students were unclear about the distinction between the notebook and the summary, so I will not use this format again.

Qi Gong; the paper was subsequently published[41] and is now part of the reading materials for the course. In fact I now specifically include a topic entitled 'Learning to write as embodied subjects' in the course content and use pieces of social scientific writing to legitimize this form of writing and how such an account can be written not merely as a self-absorbed autobiography.[42]

Another example of how students use their experiences as data in their writing is Diana Gustafson, whose reflections on the course, written initially as her term paper, have become published papers. Her reporting of connecting body and mind recorded in her journal is worth quoting at length, because it displays the interconnection between experience and learning that is grounded in the body:

> I felt my feet rooted to the floor. I sensed the movement of my limbs located in relation to the space I occupied. I sensed the tension and relaxation of my muscles as a physical experience of my tissues. I felt the flow of breath that was at one moment a part of me, inside my lungs, and at the next moment, a part of the air that surrounded me. I experienced these things with my body, that physical part of my self. There were times when I was so involved in the physicality of the experience that my surroundings faded from my vision. I was aware of the professor's verbal instructions and my efforts to translate those instructions into coordinated physical movement. I was aware of concentrating on the cycle of my breathing. I knew these and other things from the cognitive part of my being. At times it was as if I were an outside observer watching the experience of my body. My mind, my body, and my breath were connected yet separate entities engaged in *qigong*. It was like a revelation that day I was able to articulate a sense of body - my body from those oppositional and interdependent positions. Through repetition of body movement which replicates the cycles of breath I was echoing the rhythms of life and nature...

Qi Gong training was embodied exploration of the invisible process of constructing.

Discussion

Looking back, I owe how I teach now to my rather difficult teaching and activist career in the academy for the last twenty or so years.[43]

---

41 S. Transken, *Reclaiming Body Territory*. Ottawa: Canadian Research Institute for the Advancement of Women, 1995.

42 For example, M.A. Paget, 'Life mirrors work mirrors text mirrors life...' *Social Problems*, 37(2): 137–148; S. Wendell, 'Feminism, disability and transcendence of the body,' *Canadian Woman Studies*, 13(4): 116–122; S. Transken, *Reclaiming Body Territory*. Ottawa: Canadian Research Institute for the Advancement of Women, 1995.

43 D.L. Gustafson, 'Embodied learning about health and healing: Involving the body as content and pedagogy,' *Canadian Woman Studies,* 17(4): 52–55. In this chapter I have not included materials on student resistance and negative experiences in the course, since they are not central to the discussion here. For student resistance, see R. Ng, 'Teaching against the grain: Contradictions and possibilities' in R. Ng, J. Scane and P. Staton, eds, *Anti-racism, Feminism and Critical Approaches to Education*. Westport: Greenwood Publishers, 1995, 129–152.

Seen in this light, using Chinese Medicine and embodied learning presents an invaluable and promising opportunity for me to interrogate, with like-minded or at least curious students, Western knowledge construction. Despite the difficulties I faced over the years in teaching, including teaching 'Health and the Body,' and despite the discomfort the students experienced by taking the course, students do make shifts in their thinking and being. The following excerpts from student papers in the fall term of 2000 illustrate how some members of the class take up and extend the class contents (including the reading materials, exercises, and their own reflective journals) in their own thinking, and how the contents have led to a transformation of their own thinking, knowing and living. Although the quotes are rather lengthy, I have decided to include them here because they display the uniqueness and diversity of what embodiment as an epistemological and pedagogical strategy may yield:

> As I reflect on all of the insights I have made during "Healing and the Body" and my process of digging deeper, I am able to better understand the essence of embodied learning. I now identify embodied learning to be learning that synthesizes the knowledge and experiences of the mind, body, and spirit. When I cut myself off from the emotions that reside in my body and spirit, I cut myself off from embodied learning. When I do not listen to what my body is trying to tell my mind, I also short-circuit embodied learning. Rather, when I open myself up to any and all messages that my mind, body, and spirit are trying to communicate with, then I am truly embracing embodied learning.
>
> Now that my work for this course is coming to an end, I breathe a sigh of relief. It feels as though I was being led on a journey blindfolded, and have now reached its completion. The use of the first person in the narrative-based readings made me resonate with some thoughts and feelings that I would not have independently chosen to relate to. By the same token, I would not have delved into my psyche as I have done, if it were not for the more personalized nature of the material in the second half of the course. "Health and the Body" has enriched my OISE experience more than my M. Ed. Integrative Paper described. As Roxana commented to me on one of my first one-page summaries, this course is not necessarily about "feeling good." I now see how right she was, yet I do feel good about having gone through the experience of stretching beyond my comfort zones.[44]
>
> Exploring TCM has been a tool for personal change. Fundamental principles in Chinese thought provide guidance to living and flowing throughout our life. Furthermore, a search for truths in my life is an approach that I am trying to incorporate and in doing so I can be more open to the gifts that life can offer.[45]
>
> Participation in "Health, Healing and the Body" guided me through a self-learning process that opened doors to new ways of being and knowing. There are many ways of constructing the body and I am embodying the knowledge of my body as I meditate and practice *Qi Gong*. The Chinese philosophy of life provides a guide to living in this hectic, fragmented society, with health as a way of being. "Find your center and you are cured,"

---

44 Sally Issac, Integrative Paper, December 2000, p. 10. The majority of the grade for the course (40 per cent of the total grade in the fall 2000 session) was based on an integrative paper, where students are asked to write about the learning that has taken place, utilizing their notes in the reading notebook and the journal. Student permission for quotations were obtained when the chapter was written in 2001.

45 Natalie Wilson, Integrative Paper, December 2000, p. 11.

an individual in the video "The Mystery of *Chi*" claims. I have not found my center, but I have experienced peace and calm through meditation and *Qi Gong* practice that gives me a sense of control. I recognize that many of the things that I consider important are not because in the realm of all things, what do they matter. I am one part of the universe, complete within myself, made of clay, returning as clay, living the seasons of nature.

I am learning a sense of the "self," my body, and who I am. As Beinfield and Korngold write, "We want to live the life of our bodies and want our bodies to permit us to fully live our lives. Chinese medicine is a beginning" (Beinfield and Korngold, 1991, p. 386). Embodied learning is another source of knowledge, and as we experience life in our body, only we can find meaning in the experience and the knowledge of our body. TCM provides an alternate approach to life and health with the emphasis on the body as a "body-spirit".[46]

This essay illustrates how I have gone from not acknowledging or 'owning' my own body to beginning to attempt to reclaim my body. An internalization of an Orthodox Western medical tradition (allopathy) that values a mind/body binary coerced me to neglect my bodily sensations, unless they could be reduced by this system to a single 'cause' or illness. Introduction to TCM gave me the opportunity to conceive of an alternative construct of the relationship between the mind, body, and spirit. I began to reconstruct my relationship with my body, theoretically, once I was introduced to this novel health model. I recognized that my ignorance of my body's intellect might be a construction, something I could overcome. But how? The practice of embodied learning (standing meditation) answered that question; it enabled me to apply a different construction of mind and body. My resistance to these embodied exercises only made me further realize how entrenched I was in the allopathic model. Recent grievous events made me further resist these exercises because my coping strategies were interfering with my bodily recognition. A "five Seasons" embodied exercise allowed me to recognize the potential of these coordinated movements on my body, mind, and spirit. Together these practices and insights have allowed me to recognize my 'discourteous' relationship with my body and has allowed me to 'bond' with my body. For me, this reclamation has just begun and I am still working on holistically attending to my body's needs. The focus of my struggle continues and will probably modify in the future but I am willing to accept this ambiguity because it was steadfastness and a lack of options that encouraged me to originally construct my relationship with my body offensively.[47]

Conclusion

Needless to say, there are limits, drawbacks and exceptions to the increasingly overwhelming positive feedback I receive from students, and the transformative possibilities I witness in this mode of teaching and learning. Although I have not documented this systematically (because students who disliked the course either

---

46 Mary Patton, 'Embodied Knowledge: Application to Life and Work – Nursing Education,' Integrative Paper, December 2000, pp. 17–18.

47 Allison Glaser, 'Everlastingly Constructing and Reconstructing my Relationships with My Body: How I came to realize and reconstruct my relationship with my body and the world', Integrative Paper, December 2000, pp. 14–15.

withdrew or did not voice their discomfort and disagreements with me and other students during the course),[48] my impression is that much of the resistance concerns the students' difficulty in grasping materials and methods that are outside the forms and contents that students see as acceptable graduate level work. One notable exception to the experiences reported above is that of Teresa Macias,[49] who took the course in the fall of 1997 and withdrew after the first quarter of the course due both to the dynamics of that particular class, the course contents, and my method of delivering the course contents. As a self-identified third-world woman of color who felt extremely vulnerable in the context of what she called a Western-defined classroom, she found the Qi Gong exercises undoable because it exacerbated her feeling of vulnerability in a context dominated by white people and hegemonic discourse. More seriously, she raised questions about the possibility of cultural appropriation when Indigenous knowledge is taught in a Western classroom.[50]

Although my predominant experience, as well as most students' experience of the course differs from Teresa's, her discomfort and critique raises critical questions about how Indigenous forms of knowledge can and should be introduced into the academy in North America and other Western educational contexts. I do not have all the answers to the pros and cons of teaching Indigenous knowledge within a milieu dominated by Euro-American-centered ideology and practice. However Teresa's experience did teach me to interrogate my own motive for teaching 'Health and the Body' and to articulate my intent much more clearly and forcefully at the beginning of the course. I have learned to support students to raise questions and views contrary to mainstream ideas, and to provide a forum where sharply contrasting views can be tabled and debated while making my own position transparent. I try to encourage students to use resistance and discomfort as starting points of, rather than as barriers to, learning. I have incorporated emotions, in addition to the body, as the basis for knowing that integrates the notion of the body-mind-spirit unity espoused in Chinese Medicine. As I myself acquire more knowledge, skill and ease in this mode of knowing and learning, I believe that I am able to communicate what a pedagogy of embodiment may look and feel like to the students. Much of the work I quoted above in the 2000 session is an indication of the learning I have done myself.

---

48 I did discuss issues of resistance in an earlier paper. See R. Ng, 'Teaching against the grain: Contradictions and possibilities' in R. Ng, J. Scane and P. Staton, eds, *Anti-racism, Feminism and Critical Approaches to Education*. Westport: Greenwood Publishers, 1995, 129–152.

49 T. Macias, 'Learning in the occupied territories: Third World women, First World classrooms and the undertaking of indigenous knowledge.' M.Ed. Qualifying Research Paper, The Ontario Institute for Studies in Education, University of Toronto, November 1998.

50 After Teresa Macias withdrew from the course, I encouraged her to explore her sense of discomfort in the class, which became her term paper for her reading course that I directed. She subsequently expanded the paper for the course into the Qualifying Research Paper (QRP) for her M.Ed (see Endnote 49, above). The QRP is the final requirement for the M.Ed. Degree, which is a non-thesis degree at OISE.

When I teach this course again it will be retitled 'Embodied Learning and *Qi Gong*' to indicate unambiguously the intent and content of my evolving struggle in introducing Chinese Medicine into critical education in a North American context. Although teaching Indigenous knowledge in such a context is filled with risks and perils, it is also a way, albeit not the only way, of challenging Western hegemonic knowledge that holds promise in pushing the existing boundaries of what counts as knowledge in the academy.

South America

Chapter 7

Indigenous Muchik Wisdom At Work: The Tale of a Mestiza

Miryam Espinosa-Dulanpo

Introduction

It is always painful when one is forced to speak, communicate, or write in a language that represents the culture of colonizer. In this chapter I will describe the aesthetic quality of the Indigenous Muchik in the Andean region of South America, note the paradoxes of my social existence, and demonstrate how, not withstanding the attempt by colonization and capitalism to erase us from this land and our planet, we are still here! I will narrate the tale of *Tellervo*, valuable in our Muchik tradition and show how this tale has been empowering for our community. Finally, I will close with a poem dedicated to my beloved family members.

The Colonial Pain of an Indigenous Writer

There is so much pain while writing in a language that is not one's native tongue, but that pain is minimal compared to the unbearable fact of not having the option to write in one's native tongue. My Indigenous tongue was banned by the hegemonic forces that colonized my land. Its sounds and teachings were denied and over time, the language of the ancestors, the language in which Muchik traditions were immersed, was not spoken at large. Does it mean that the inheritance of the Muchik has been forgotten and the children of today have no ties to the *Apus* and the *Cochas* of the land?

A question with no answer if one expects sounds, but a plethora of responses if one is able to understand not only the sounds but the silent screams from every fiber in our souls. Participating in this effort is one of my screams. A silent hail that translated to English – one of those hegemonic languages – will not allow non-Muchik to go away without learning about me and the hegemonic powers that took away my sounds even before my grandparents' grandparents were born. Who am I? A nonspeaking Muchik with diluted blood, in Western terms (and a colonial obsession) a mixture of many ethnicities and worldviews – in which the powerful colonizers are included. Am I a *costeña*, a *norteña*, a woman who was born and grew up in one of the driest desert areas of the world, the northern Coast of Peru, or a Latina, Hispanic, *wetback* foreigner in the United States, or a professor in charge of a teaching program in a major US research university? It does not matter, I do not need to define myself as one or another. I am a *mestiza, muy orgullosa de su herencia*, a woman extremely proud of her heritage. My home is not in one particular place but in my heart, filled with *dunas* from the sandy, golden desert, with *playas* washed by dark blue-green cold ocean waters, and I live in the shadow of the best shelter anyone could dream of, the tall Andes, the eternal protectors, the *Apus*.

My tale begins with *Tellervo*'s story, which is a fictionalized account that could apply to a variety of cultural encounters. It functions as an explanation of moments in which different situations require different kinds of awareness because life as it was understood in each situation is no longer valid. It involves the realization that different sets of rules have been established, some of which could either aid an existing situation or be irrelevant. Either way, the individuals have to re-learn, re-create, and re-order their own to establish common ground for surviving. In an ideal democratic society, as in *Tellervo*, the process of learning leads to re-covering, re-creating, and re-inventing a safe environment in which trials and attempts are encouraged and failures are understood as part of the process.

The Tale of Tellervo

Once upon a time there was a tall, luscious, full-of-ripe-fruit tree named *Tellervo*. Her sole purpose was to stand upright protecting us, the children of *Pinky-Times*. Under her shadow, boys and girls came to have their morning snack, their afternoon nap, and their all-day laugh. *Tellervo* grew taller and more powerful each day, pushing her roots deep inside Mother Earth for her daily nourishment, the town sounds of peace and happiness. For Pinky-Times, nothing was more beautiful, peaceful and powerful than *Tellervo*, the tall, luscious, full-of-ripe-fruit tree. She was a safe haven from earthquakes, floods, droughts, sadness and loneliness. One just needed to come closer to feel the goodness coming from the tree – *Tellervo* gave out protection and peace.

One day a group of people, the *Progress-and-Change* folks, came to town with many strange loud things called digging machines. They were fast-pacers, eagerly digging the soil, stopping only when a geyser of dark heavy liquid came out from the Earth's insides. The *Progress-and-Change* folks were so thrilled with their achievement that they invited more people to join them. Amazingly, their pace grew faster and faster, building and digging, digging and building more vigorously each time. They put together large homes with many more rooms than people living in them. They gave us, in exchange for our land, little green papers with old men's pictures and numbers on them. They called it 'money.' They were funny, urging us to earn it because 'with money you can get anything you want.' We responded that we had everything in *Pinky-Times* and inquired as to why we needed such papers. The *Progress-and-Change* people looked like their machines, big, noisy and greasy. But we had enough space to share, so we let them stay and play.

Pinky-Times became a lot more noisy and a more densely populated community, adding one more geyser of dark and heavy liquid every so often, but still, there was enough space for everyone. Suddenly, without warning, things changed dramatically. Our *Tellervo* began to curl up all over, losing her leaves and shining greenness. She looked so sad and different! This had never happened before since she had always been strong and healthy. We didn't know what to do. So we sat around her. Our children came to sing and to dance for her, but we knew *Tellervo* couldn't get her nourishment. Her roots were debilitated from the dark heavy geysers surrounding her. "Use your money," the *Progress-and-Change* people told us. So we did. We put all the green papers around the tree and waited for the money to work, to use its power to give us back *Tellervo*, our tall, luscious, full-of-ripe-fruit tree. *Tellervo* was the only thing we wanted, so we waited. And waited. And waited even longer. She became a small dark coil, withering in the sun. A hundred years have passed and in *Pinky-Times* we are still waiting. How much longer do we need to wait? What else do we have to do to get *Tellervo* back?

The *Pinky-Times* people waited longer than anyone could remember ever having to wait. We waited and our waiting became sadness, loneliness and uncertainty. Our grandchildren had no shadowed place to play or nap. Worst of all, we *Pinky-Timers* were out in the empty fields when the floods and the earthquakes came. There was no safe haven for us. It took long, more than a hundred years to get ready, to understand that we needed to do something. We *Pinky-Timers* were not aware that new rules had been made. We didn't know this. Nor did we want to change anything since our lives were quite full. However, it moved our hearts, the *Pinky-Timers* town's heart, to see our friend, our protector almost gone. We wanted *Tellervo* back for ourselves, for our children and for the ones to come. This yearning for *Tellervo* made all the difference. *Pinky-Timers* started talking, calling, writing and discussing new ideas. It was surprising to find other *Pinky-Timers* and *Laughing-stars* and *Purple-bears* people. This time the strange visitors were different in their outlook. They came with glowing looks on their faces, full of songs and laughs. The town was bubbling with excitement and began to work with these new people. Together, we all tried different things, with some succeeding and some failing, but it felt right. *Pinky-timers* were not alone, were not waiting anymore. *Pinky-Timers* had become agents of their own lives. *Pinky-Timers, Laughing-starers* and *Purple-bearers* had a reason to go on: we all were looking for our friend, the tall-luscious-full-of-ripe-fruit tree, *Tellervo*.

Growing up was always paradoxical with more than one set of rules and traditions. I lived among Western European people, looking and acting like one while receiving loving care from brown women. I spoke only Spanish but understood the feelings, the sounds, and the smells of the Indigenous Ocean-desert. My weeks were spent in the Catholic all-girls boarding school while my summers and weekends were submerged in brown sand and earthy life.

My story is a tale that is not unique for many Indigenous people and repeats itself over and over again, when we are compelled to move away from the roots of our home and family environment to a new place which we re-create and still connect with our ancestral traditions like the Indigenous poet, Simon Ortiz. It is the tale of a creature that has inside of her more than one culture, more than one love, more than one language, more and more of the beauty of this world, while being rooted in her Indigenous heritage. It nourishes a life that is full of contradictions, interspersed with guilt, yet reflecting pride in being able to live as an Indigenous person, free to define her existence, resisting the hegemony of a Eurocentric world in the process.

Adorable WHITE BREAD playing with a WILD CAT, *mi mujercita*

Worlds colliding harmoniously yet passionately
working their way from a dark metal bench
inside the universal, inviting night
worlds of passion, desire, fears, and loves
from which kisses are oscillating orbits
driven by the powers of Venus and the Earth moon

Oh Jesus, I never knew my body could feel this way
neither were my bones such a delicacy
that made me stop, for a day and its night, my journey of solitude
warming my white bread skin with the passion of a wild cat, *mi mujercita*

Oh God, how can a person leave aside the guttural claims
of this corporeal body
how can I continue this journey of solitude when I learned
that the wilderness of peace is calling me
when I am craving only for your deflowering juices
that I have no more a single world to express my-your feelings
when we have already collided inside and my being is penetrated by the power
of love

Oh wild cat, centennial female, newborn child,
sweet mother, strange sister, *mi mujercita*
touching, caressing my body with every part of your being
painful pleasures, soft mating, copulating with nature,
and nameless forces
you have opened the doors of time and given me
the taste of the foreign soils

Oh sweet white bread, caressing me as soft water from the nearby stream
believing that fingers, tongues, legs and toes are one to enter me
possessing my infinite caves more than one, more than more
and then wake up into a world of rules, in a marked orbit
in which only the memories of your scent and heat
give me the stamina for my journey in solitude,
for choosing life.

Family Traditions and Everyday Life

Inside the Ocean, plankton made fish grow, then the fish jumped into the fishing nets to allow us to complete the circle of life. The Ocean brought enough moisture to develop a life-pasture for the *cabritos* – in our peaceful sand dunes guarded by the Andean walls. Growing up was a beautiful time with no consciousness of how much that beauty weighed on others. I was fortunate because I was surrounded by people who took care of me and showed me nothing but the comfortable side of life. It took me a long time to feel any urgency for change. It took me longer to see the injustice that happened outside the protected areas. It took me even longer to understand that Western meant 'modern' and 'best' and that our traditions were disposable. It took me much longer to find my voice to reclaim my heritage.

Grandpa's home

Our house is like a full Peruvian bus
        If one gets off, four get in!
Grandpa says
with a voice and laugh
that fill the hallways
Grandpa's home
has a door that never locks
like his heart
it is big enough to love and care for us all

Nuestra casa es como un microbus
si baja uno, suben cuatro.

No matter the country politics
or the martial law imposed last month
or money that is never enough
or all the jobs we need to hold

Grandpa's house is always filled
with the *hijos* and the *nietos*
the *sobrinos* and the *ahijados*
every love-one who has lost a part of life
in a country whose government
doesn't recognize our rights
nor its own rules
nor has any respect for the first people

It's almost a ceremony that repeats
itself each time that a *familia* arrives
from cries and desperation

to soft giggling
to full laughs on Sunday lunch
to sharing pride when leaving

Our house is like a Peruvian bus
If one gets off, four get in!

Boiling basil, tomatoes and carrots
fresh fish and potatoes
enough to feed twenty-five
it has to be Sunday
Sunday is the smell of tomatoes and basil
fresh fish and potatoes
all boiling hard getting ready for lunch.

Nuestra casa es como un microbus
si baja uno , suben cuatro.

It's our turn to be at Grandpa's
a bunch of children whose *Papi* just went to heaven
whose *Mamy* is too sad
she knows only to sit and cry
once in awhile she sips a little tea
from a cup that gets magic refills

At Grandpa's we get to laugh
and his hugs bring *Mami* back
sitting near us
listening to stories
before he gets all tucked-in
with a sweet kiss and
que duerman bien

Our house is like a Peruvian bus
If one gets off, four get in!

Cousins Genaro, Cristina, and Genarito just arrived
with a lot of crying
some suitcases and a huge *perol*
all of what they've saved from the *El Niño* storm
Genarito carries their saved treasure
a pan bigger than him
to cook the potatoes, he says

That is your room, the one with the blue canopy
Grandpa instructs

the miracle of our *familia* does it again
Cristina dares a timid smile
while entering her new little blue room
Potatoes boiling getting ready for lunch
this time we are more than twenty-five
a loud, happy, hopeful, crowd
squeezing for a place
Sundays have their own sounds and smell

'Our house is like a *microbus*
si baja uno, entran cuatro'
In my mind, I correct him
Our house is like a city-bus
None gets off and thirty stay!

Conclusion

Who am I? Really? It does not matter, I do not need to define myself as one or another, in those fixed categorical boxes created by European colonials for the purpose of controlling the vast majority of humanity. I am a *mestiza, muy orgullosa de su herencia*, a woman extremely proud of her heritage and the future to build....

The Caribbean

Chapter 8

Indigenous Wisdom at Work in Jamaica: The Power of *Kumina*

Dianne Stewart

Introduction

Africans who were brought to Jamaica from the sixteenth to the nineteenth centuries consistently demonstrated their deep attachment to African religiosity and culture to which European authorities (the planters, colonial government, and missionaries) responded with three basic strategies: trivialization, censorship, and secularization. Whether Christianization and civilization were sincere bases upon which Europeans instituted both forced and coerced labor in Jamaica and other colonies is of no significance in considering the outcome for Africans. The result was simply four centuries of gross exploitation under two circumstances of captivity and enslavement and indentureship. Although the twenty-six-year period of African immigration to Jamaica was brief when compared to three centuries of slavery, the socio-economic conditions in which indentured African laborers worked and lived were tantamount to those endured by enslaved Africans in Jamaica.[1] Yet socio-economic hardship, estrangement from family and homeland, and European subjugating practices did not prevent many of the Central Africans from remembering and reconstituting ancestral religious and cultural practices in what would become a new home to their descendants. Over the past one hundred and fifty years, this collection of practices has come to be called Kumina by the descendants of Central African indentured laborers in Jamaica.

The retention of African religious practices like the *Kumina* tradition in eastern Jamaica is a concrete expression of African resistance to European racism and anti-Africanness. In colonial Jamaica, African immigrants had virtually no control over the economy or social conventions. Moreover, with the proliferation of missionary activity across the island, there was significant social pressure to abandon African religious and cultural traditions in favor of any number of Christian traditions. The by-products of Christian civilization, formal education, social privilege, and economic stability, although scarcely and conditionally extended to Africans, were undoubtedly attractive features to some dispossessed Africans. Many Africans never relinquished the connections they had to their homelands

---

1 Kenneth Bilby and Bunseki Fu-Kiau, "Kumina: A Kongo-based Tradition in the New World," Cahiers du CEDAF 8:4 (1983).

via language, food, music, drumming, medicinal practices and religious rituals.

This chapter will illustrate graphically how today *Kumina* exists as a subversive testimony to the yearnings of African-Jamaicans for Africa and their willingness to remember their Kongo homeland, illuminate the wisdom of their African ancestors, and describe the African-Jamaican struggle to define itself as a movement for self-determination in a community that thrives notwithstanding the legacy of slavery, colonialism, and neocolonialism.

Kumina Notions of African Identity

Kumina is often described as an insular ancestral cult that places little if any significance upon analyzing and responding to social oppression. Maureen Warner Lewis suggests, for example, that the ancestral focus in Kumina is cultural and distinct from the kind of political consciousness embraced by other African-Jamaican religions such as Rastafari, Revival/Zion, and Myal.[2] My own research among Kuminaists in the parishes of St Thomas and St Catherine, however, has introduced me to a Jamaican worldview steeped in forms of African consciousness that I had only previously associated with Rastafari culture. Like the Rastafari, Kumina practitioners are self-identified Africans. However, Kuminaists conceive of their African identity exponentially. They are simultaneously ethnic 'Africans and Pan-Africanists.'[3] If we are to hear and understand what Kuminaists intend by their assertion of African identity, we must be willing to surrender or at least suspend postmodern critiques that render diasporic ethnocultural and racial identifications with Africa essentialist, romantic, and therefore inauthentic and contrived.

The African identity claims of people eight generations removed from ancestors who were born and buried on the continent of Africa disclose that Africanness has always signified something symbolic, intangible, and even inaccessible to many descendants of enslaved Africans in the Caribbean and the Americas. Yet it has also taken on a very specific meaning in the Caribbean and the Americas – one with which continental Africans must also identify – that is, Africanness, as an identity, is a consequence of the rise of the modern West. Europe's *Africanization* of distinct ethnic societies such as the Igbo, Yoruba, Fon, Ga, Asante, etc., was essential to the proliferation of racist ideological justifications for the Atlantic slave trade. Thus for many of the Igbo, Yoruba, Fon, Ga, Asante, etc., who became shipmates

---

2   Warner Lewis, "The Ancestral Factor in Jamaica's African Religions," in Kortright Davis and Elias F. Jones eds, *African Creative Expressions of the Divine* (Washington, DC: Howard University School of Divinity, 1991), 74.

3   In 1978, Bilby and Fu-Kiau documented a strong consciousness and assertion of BaKongo ethnic identity among Kumina practitioners. "Like their ancestors," they write: "many present-day 'Africans' in eastern Jamaica maintain the concept of tribal affiliation, if not an actual genealogical map behind it. Individuals may assert, for example that they are descended primarily from the Muyanji or Munchundi tribes." Bilby and Fu-Kiau, "Kumina: A Kongo-based Tradition in the New World," 11.

on slave vessels, African identity often replaced ethnic identity in contexts of exile from family, clan, civilization, and ancestral homeland. For a significant number of diasporic Africans, 'Africa' has been an all-encompassing symbol of the inaccessible ancestral homeland and the preservation or re-articulation of multiple African continental institutions and worldviews in spite of slavery, Western cultural dominance, and their devastating impact upon African diasporic cultures.[4]

For Kumina Africans, Africa – that intangible inaccessible something – is also awesome, and sacred, indeed something transcendent and deserving of reverence. And thus, in Kumina anthropology we find clues for understanding why Kumina Africans do not experience the kind of ambivalence many diasporic Africans (especially those persuaded by postmodern critiques of essentialism) experience regarding their African heritage. Kuminaists do not subscribe to a universal theological anthropology such as the Christian doctrines of creation, original sin, and universal redemption. They believe that each human being is essentially who she or he is due to the unique combination of her of his kanuba (spirit), deebu (blood), and beezie (flesh). The kanuba shapes the human personality and is patrilineally derived. The beezie, on the other hand, is matrilineally derived, and the deebu can be derived from either side. Some Kuminaists maintain strict taboos regarding these three components of their human makeup.

The *kanubu, deebu* and *beezie* signify the umbilical cord unifying the individual with his specific *nkuyu* (ancestors) and the larger community with the entire ancestral community.[5] The ancestors are those departed beings who achieve spiritual status as members of the Divine Community and as Nzambi's messengers in the invisible world domain.[6] They acquire power and use it to assist their living descendants in the visible world domain. *Kuminaists* are in constant communication with ancestors who validate and replenish their steadfast identification with Africa.

At the core of *Kumina* culture is a collective memory, grief, and indignation regarding African people's capture, exile, enslavement, and oppression under whites or 'the white supremacists' as one informant constantly remarked. *Kumina* practitioners identify their heritage in Jamaica with the period of African enslavement. In each community, there are several elders and leaders who can give accounts of ancestral journeys from 'Africa' to Jamaica, with specific details about the brutalities

---

4   See Anthony Appiah, *In My Father's House*, for a discussion of Europe's construction of Africa. While I agree with Appiah's critical assessment of the European construction of "Africa," he misperceives the problem of exile from "Africa" and African diasporic responses to that problem. Appiah does not give enough credit to the reasons *why* many people in today's African diaspora hold tenaciously to less than "factual" ideas about Africa, nor does he understand the *religious* meaning of the symbol "Africa" for Africans in the diaspora. Compare with V. Mudimbe, *The Idea of Africa* (Bloomington: Indiana University Press, 1994).

5   Joseph Moore, "Religion of Jamaican Negroes: A Study of Afro-Jamaican Acculturation" (Northwestern University, Dissertation Thesis, 1953), 115–17.

6   Nzambi is the BaKongo supreme divinity. Kuminaists sometimes salute Nzambi with the title King.

suffered on the slave ships and the hardships endured both during slavery and after emancipation. One such narrative was recounted by 'Uncle' P, [7] the 67-year-old grandson of a belated *Kumina* queen in Port Morant, St Thomas:

> I say the White man is wicked! He took our ancestors on the ship and made them suffer like never before. My grandmother was raped on the slave ship. They took her, a fourteen-year-old girl, and raped her! ... So the blood is mixed up because she got pregnant, and they never helped her one bit (the white people I mean). . . . We don't trust them because they are wicked, but you can't blame the child . . . it's not her fault her father was white. We Africans are all one people.[8]

One's immediate reaction to Uncle P's story might be suspicion, for when we do the math, it is highly improbable that his grandmother was born before the abolition of slavery in the British Caribbean, let alone before Britain's abolition of the slave trade in 1807. However, studies of the slave trade and the abolitionist movement in Britain provide insight into how and when the rape could have taken place.

The British navy rescued Africans from Portuguese-Brazilian and Spanish-Cuban slave ships throughout the 1860s. It is possible that Uncle P's grandmother was raped on a ship en route to Brazil or Cuba during the latter 1860s before the British navy arrested its crew and rescued the Africans from their impending captivity as slaves. She could have survived to pass down her story to her children and grandchildren or to other members of her community who helped to preserve the memory of her violation.

Ultimately, the rape narrative is the collective property of *Kumina* Africans, who are now bearers of their ancestral legacy in Jamaica. Uncle P's 'grandmother' is the archetypal victim of sexual exploitation – a dehumanizing rite of passage experienced by African females throughout the Middle Passage and slavery. The *Kumina* community today, apparently unaware of the unique sequence of events that led to their foreparents' arrival in Jamaica only *after* official emancipation, actually situate themselves within the broader collective history of African experience in pre-emancipation Jamaica and function then as retainers of national memory. For example, Edward Brathwaite cites another archetypal lynching story from a taped interview with one of the most celebrated and publicized *Kumina* queens, Ms. Imogene Kennedy. Kennedy described the lynching of African people on a cotton tree in Port Morant, St Thomas:

> is not dey-one came, is a whole heap-a-dem come 'ere in de slavery . . . because take for instant Morant Bay . . . when dey came here . . . you 'ave a cotton tree out dere . . . what de buil' a gas station now . . . dat dey *use to heng people* . . . an' your usban' leave an come . .

---

7   Initials are used to protect the identities of most informants. I only reveal the names of famous or well documented informants like Ms. Imogene Kennedy.

8   I have decided to translate long citations such as this one from Jamaican Creole into English because the original Creole parlance would be just as unintelligible to non-Jamaicans as German would be to an English-speaking person. "Uncle" P, Personal interview, Port Morant, St Thomas, Jamaica, 19 September 1996.

. after you . . . an' dey heng you; you husban' come to look fuh you . . . dey d'win de same . . . you children come out in de slavery time . . . but dose time it was still de African-dem . . . you understan . . .? Well dey hang dem out there, because at de las' time since I been here, an' when dey gwine to cut down dat cotton tree to buil' de gas station, it lick dung about four to five men . . . kill dem . . .[9]

In relating her version of countless African lynchings in Port Morant, Ms. Kennedy establishes that many Africans apart from her BaKongo ancestors came to Jamaica as slaves. Thus, her report of these brutal executions concerns Africans both within and outside of her personal ancestral lineage, reflecting an inclusive and Pan-Africanist understanding of African community.

At the time I collected information from *Kumina* adherents in 1996, I observed a spirit of Pan-African unity in the attitudes of *Kumina* Africans toward nonpracticing Jamaican Blacks. They uniformly embraced nonpractitioners as kinfolk and held that any person of African descent from any cultural or geographic location has a right to claim allegiance to the 'Bongo' ancestors and a space in the *Kumina*-practicing Bongo nation. When I pressed informants to explain exactly what they mean by referring to themselves and their ancestors as 'Bongo' they often responded that Bongo is the African place of national origin. One informant, a *Kumina* queen well respected by fellow practitioners for her upkeep of the culture, also described the ancestors as 'Kongo' and explained that 'Bongo' and 'Kongo' are interchangeable names for the specific African lineage claimed by the *Kumina* community. The *Kumina* community's extension of membership in the Bongo nation to Blacks in the wider society synchronizes its particular sense of ethnic affiliation and its universal Pan-African sense of affinity with all Jamaican Blacks.

The depth of African identity consciousness in *Kumina* culture can also be assessed in the practitioners' perceptions of whites. *Kumina* practitioners view whites as culturally and spiritually 'other.' 'White people can't hear the drum,' said one *Kumina* queen when I asked if they are allowed to join *Kumina* bands.[10] Another *Kumina* queen responded by asking of me 'How can white supremacists ask the Bongo ancestors for help?' Ms Kennedy stresses the importance of speaking the 'African language' in communicating with the ancestors and responded that 'Whites don't know the language or the rhythm of the dance. They can't talk to the ancestors.' *Kuminaists* are convinced that white supremacy is the dominant factor in African people's chronic suffering worldwide. They remain suspicious of whites and blatantly critical of white religio-cultural traditions. Even more telling of the anti-white ideological tendency in *Kumina* is the affirmative responses received when I asked those same informants if Indians and Chinese people are welcome to join *Kumina* bands (as Jamaica has a small Asian population). Ms. Kennedy responded

---

9 Edward Brathwaite, "The Spirit of African Survival in Jamaica," *Jamaica Journal,* Vol. 42 (1978), 47.

10 A Kumina group is referred to as a "bands." The term is used to describe a single group or many groups.

that Asians could participate if they desire because they are colored.[11]

The deep-seated African consciousness exhibited by *Kuminaists* is generated as well by the community's resistance to and contempt for white supremacy and white oppressors. Their distrust of whites is derived from the lessons taught by oral tradition. I take exception to Warner Lewis' characterization of *Kumina* as lacking in social consciousness when compared with Rastafari. I would argue that the memory of the violence and violation that their ancestors endured during the latter nineteenth century, when they were literally liberated from slave ships and accorded free status, has actually served to engender a type of pro-African consciousness among practitioners that Rastafari adherents would endorse. With each generation, recycled stories about their ancestors' exploitation and confinement on the plantations, despicable wages, and harassment and intimidation had to have reinforced the *Kumina* community's collective suspicion that the white person is an altogether different type of human being with a greater potential to harm Africans than to bring about any authentic liberation. One informant (with the initials B.H.) attempted to recount the dreadful conditions under which Central Africans were brought to Jamaica. Her vague account was slightly incoherent, difficult to follow, and virtually indecipherable until I discovered documentation that corroborated the pieces of her memory that remained intact. A portion of our dialogue is presented below:

BH: They would tell them to join the line or they wouldn't get help. They really didn't have a choice.

DS: What line?

BH: They had to join the force and fight the war for the white man or stay slave.

DS: Where did this happen?

BH: Back in Africa.[12]

Our conversation took place within a larger discussion about the British navy rescuing Africans from slave ships. I was trying to discern if contemporary *Kumina* practitioners have retained any oral traditions about the specific details of their ancestors' extended Middle Passage from Sierra Leone and St Helena to Jamaica under the indentured labor program. B.H. did not confirm or deny any of the information I shared with her about the conditions of her ancestors' passage to Jamaica during the post-emancipation period. She immediately began talking about Africans having to 'join the line.' B.H.'s story always intrigued me but I did not know how to contextualize it. I initially assumed that when she discussed 'the white man' she was possibly referring to the British naval officers. I had also presumed that when she said the exchange occurred in Africa, she meant Central Africa. My conjecture was that she could have been describing Central African encounters with colonial officials or missionaries in the region. I was to discover some months later that B.H.'s story

---

11 Imogene Kennedy, Personal interview, St Catherine, Jamaica, October 7, 1996.
12 Fieldnotes, October 23, 1996.

presented a fraction of the interaction that took place between recaptured Africans and British government representatives ('the white man') in Africa, as she stated, but not Central Africa, rather Sierra Leone. In her study of African immigration to Jamaica during the post-emancipation period, Monica Schuler notes:

By 1844 forced emigration of recently arrived recaptives from the Freetown Queen's Yard was an idea whose time had obviously come. In February the Colonial Secretary dispatched instructions to the Sierra Leone governor to offer recaptives the choice of immigrating to the West Indies or remaining in Sierra Leone without government assistance formerly offered. An older option, which had always existed for men – that of enlisting in the West India Regiments – remained. In reality the new dispensation read, "emigrate, enlist, or fend for yourself." The instructions made no exceptions for children.[13]

Schuler's research lends support to B.H.'s faded recollection and to the community's record of 'the white man's' ill treatment of recaptive Africans. B.H.'s account suggests that the 'older option' of military enlistment also noted by Schuler was not interpreted as a humane option by recaptive Africans. Schuler provides even further evidence for why this was so:

Newly liberated Africans had never before exhibited any interest in emigrating to the West Indies and were prone to take to the bush when emigration recruiters approached their villages. Recruiting in the Queen's Yard [Sierra Leone], therefore, was not simply a matter of inviting people to travel to the West Indies…The standard practice was to isolate new arrivals from all except West India Regiment and plantation recruiters, and in some cases recaptives were detained in the Queen's Yard for one to three months awaiting the arrival of an emigrant ship.[14]

Faced with the options of 'no help,' 'joining the line,' or immigration to the Caribbean, recaptive Africans were forced to accept emigration. They never chose it. They had endured the hardships of torture and unsanitary conditions on slave ships, and were rescued only to confront abandonment in still a foreign country (Sierra Leone), the extended Middle Passage to the Caribbean as indentured laborers or, for males, enlistment in the West India Regiments. It was unlikely that they would settle on boarding another ship under the direction of white men to labor yet in a country thousands of miles away. The oral traditions, songs and rituals of the *Kumina* culture in Jamaica suggest that the only ships recaptured Africans desired to board were those that would take them back to their original birthplaces. Those ships never materialized and so they found ways to resurrect traditions from home in their new settlements in Jamaica.

Kumina narratives disclose a collection of experiences that have been extensively shaped by the sea. Their inclusive sense of shared peoplehood with all Jamaicans of African descent is salient in individual and communal identity formation. However their sense of a shared situation of oppression with those in the Asian Jamaican minority who would participate in *Kumina* culture also points to an inclusive principle

---

13 Schuler, "Yerri, Yerri, Koongo," 74.
14 Ibid., 75.

in the community's assessment of social oppression and to an acknowledgment of their extended Middle Passage as a context for identity formation and group solidarity. According to Schuler, the Central Africans who settled in St Thomas displayed many levels of identification and group affiliations with all Africans, shipmates, all Central Africans in the parish of St Thomas, Central African sub-ethnic groups, and fellow villagers.[15] Ship records indicate that East Indians sailed to Jamaica as indentured laborers with Africans from depot stations in St Helena.[16] The shared shipmate experience of transportation to Jamaica and subsequent experiences of working side by side on the plantation estates apparently shaped the *Kumina* community's perception of their Asian neighbors and their acceptance of those who have expressed interest in *Kumina* practices and ceremonies.

Through stories like Uncle P's, Ms Kennedy's, and B.H.'s *Kumina* Africans acknowledge the historical struggles of their ancestors who withstood pervasive forms of violence in the African Jamaican experience. They feel existentially connected to the ancestral narratives in that they too encounter violence, censorship, and religio-cultural persecution in a Jamaican society that has absorbed the traditional Western Christian perception of African religions as pathological and uncivilized. More than anything else, *Kumina* ancestral narratives emphasize the indefinite quality of African suffering. For a community devoted to ancestral legacies, it is not surprising that the stories told reach back to the period of African enslavement, which is considered by many diasporic Africans to be the genesis of their collective oppression. And yet, the experiences of abuse during slavery recounted time and time again by griots like Uncle P, Ms. Kennedy, and B.H. may well be orally recorded accounts of the conditions to which African indentured laborers were subjected during their extended Middle Passage from Africa to Jamaica and thereafter as exploited laborers in a post-emancipation plantation economy.

The *Kumina* Tradition in Jamaica

There is a *Kumina* song that celebrates the achievements of a beloved *Kumina* dancer called Jenny. 'Tange Lange Jenny' describes the ancestors' warm and joyful reception of Jenny into their community. The story is told in reconstructed derivatives of BaKongo languages, as are a number of popular *Kumina* songs known as 'country' or 'African.' A second set of songs called 'bailo' is sung in Jamaican Creole. Some songs are petitions to *Nzambi*, the Creator, and to their ancestors for an abundant harvest and healthy cattle. Others pay homage to great ancestors and cultural heroes or heroines. Still others describe customary pastimes or rites of passage such as significant births, weddings, and burial ceremonies.[17]

The songs of *Kumina* help to transfer ancestral memory from one generation to

---

15 Ibid., 175.

16 Ibid., 78, 183.

17 From personal fieldnotes, November 5, 1996. Also see Joseph Moore, "Religion of Jamaican Negroes," 174–76.

the next. These songs are passed down during official ceremonies and in relaxed settings where children are able to practice the dances and drumbeats that accompany the songs. At official ceremonies children become acquainted with the ancestors who come when they are called. They are also taught to cultivate a relationship with those ancestors in accordance with the core rituals of the tradition. Some boys will develop into master drummers and percussionists. Some girls will be identified as potential *Kumina* queens. After many years of training they will assume posts as leaders of *Kumina* bands.

The *Kumina* 'bands' are comprised of adherents – drummers, dancers, and singers – who organize and take part in ceremonies and important activities. The term *Kumina* is the actual name of the ceremony whether for the purpose of ancestral commemoration, offering thanks, healing a client, celebrating a birth, or burying the deceased. The goal of each ceremony is to procure ancestral power and insight. The definitive indication of ancestral power and wisdom is spirit possession, the most intense of which carries the name *Myal* – the same name as an African-derived, eighteenth-century, Jamaican religious tradition. Ancestral presence allows for healing, the prevention of imbalance within the universe, and the resolution of personal and social problems.

When the ancestors manifest themselves, they possess human mediums and communicate with specialists in the tradition who speak their 'African' language and are experienced in negotiating their diverse personalities. Ritual food offerings and animal sacrifice are also an essential component of *Kumina* practice. Specialists undertake extensive preparations for ceremonies, which, along with their ritual duties, they categorize as work. Utilizing the elements – water, fire, earth, and wind – as well as other products of the natural environment, *Kuminaists* summon the ancestors and with their help work to restore health and vitality to their clients. With every ceremony they also reestablish their commitment to their Central African ancestral traditions.

As an African-based religion, *Kumina* is primarily characterized as 'primitive' and 'evil magic,' which many Jamaicans view as an embarrassing liability to their progress as a civilized society. The paucity of comprehensive scholarly research on *Kumina* and the relative isolation of *Kumina* from mainstream Jamaican culture render it a severely misunderstood tradition. Leonard Barrett (1970) identified *Kumina* with Akan culture, linguistically tracing the term to two Twi words: *Akom* (the state of being possessed) and *Ana* (relationship, or ancestor).[18] Barrett believed that the Maroons, who were mostly of Asante heritage, introduced *Kumina* to the wider Jamaican society during slavery. In *Soul Force*, he writes 'It is our intention here to show that *Myalism* was the legitimate survival of the traditional religion of Africa and that *myal* and the Jamaican *Cumina* religion therefore are one and the same phenomenon.'[19]

---

18 Leonard Barrett, *Soul-Force: African Heritage in Afro-American Religion* (New York: Anchor, 1974), 69.

19 Ibid., 68.

Relying on Melville Herskovits' research on Dahomean ancestral veneration, Orlando Patterson traces *Kumina* to a Dahomean origin and concludes that 'in addition to establishing the origins of the *cumina* cult in Jamaica . . . it is clear that *cumina* existed in Jamaica from at least as early as 1730, the date of [Charles] Leslie's book.'[20] Patterson bases his assessment on a white Jamaican historian's general description of African deities which appear to be Dahomean in origin. Patterson's interpretation, however, is unsatisfying. Although his later research establishes *Kumina's* BaKongo roots, his argument is unpersuasively supported by generic comparisons between *Kumina* and a Dahomean ceremony – comparisons that could be made between *Kumina* and any number of African religious traditions.

The misinterpretation of *Kumina* as a pre-emancipation West African tradition can be traced to one basic factor: the significance of *Myal* possession to *Kumina* adherents. Having established that *Myal* was a noted African-derived religious practice among enslaved Africans during the eighteenth century, scholars presume that *Kumina* is a current expression of eighteenth-century *Myal* religion. However, *Kumina's* regional appearance in eastern Jamaica is consistent with the importation patterns pertaining to Central African indentured laborers in the same region. *Kumina* oral tradition also includes references to geographical locations and traditions from the Central African region. The most convincing evidence of *Kumina's* BaKongo origin is the 'African' language. *Kumina* adherents have retained a significant vocabulary of BaKongo words. Bilby and Fu-Kiau collected lexicons from a number of *Kumina* bands, and found BaKongo cognates for nearly all of the words. Many of the *Kumina* 'country' songs are also unintelligible to native African Jamaicans because they are sung in a BaKongo-based language.[21]

How should the marriage between one of the oldest (*Myal*) and one of the youngest (*Kumina*) African-derived religions in Jamaica be understood? Importation records indicate that Africans came to Jamaica from several regions on the continent, especially West and Central Africa. It is possible that Central Africans established the *Myal* tradition in Jamaica during the slave period. It is also possible that *Myal* emerged as an amalgamated institution that integrated Pan-African beliefs and rituals into one synthesized religion. One thing is clear: Myal is astoundingly resilient. *Myal* has survived by attaching itself to host institutions that appear with novel times and experiences in Jamaican history.[22]

---

20 Orlando Patterson, *The Sociology of Slavery* (London: MacGibbon and Kee, 1967), 201.

21 I also collected lexicons and songs similar to the ones included in Bilby's and Fu-Kiau's article "A Kongo-based Tradition in the New World."

22 See Joseph Williams, *Voodoos and Obeahs: Phases of West India Witchcraft,* (New York: Dial Press, 1932); Barry Chevannes, *Rastafari and Other African-Caribbean World Views*, (The Hague, Netherlands: Institute of Social Studies/MacMillan, 1995), 8–9; and *Rastafari: Roots and Ideology* (Syracuse: Syracuse University Press, 1994), 18–19; and Monica Schuler, "Myalism and the African Tradition," in Margaret Crahan and Franklin Knight, eds, *Africa and the Caribbean: The Legacies of a Link,* (Baltimore: John Hopkins University Press, 1979), 65–77.

In the eighteenth century the '*Myal* dance' was apparently performed prior to and during the visitation of the ancestors or spirits. During a *Kumina* ceremony I attended in 1996 a young woman who went into *Myal* immediately reached for one of the sick clients for whom the *Kumina* was organized. Upon being touched, he fell unconscious to the ground and remained so for several hours while practitioners attended to his head and body. The client's healing included elaborate processions to ancestral burial grounds, while both the client and the healers were under the influence of ancestral spirits; he had to be carried in his unconscious state to each site. He did not regain consciousness until the climax of the ceremony had passed.[23] Such loss and revival of consciousness in the healing process was perhaps that component of *Myal* healing rituals during the period of enslavement that white observers often belittled as a feigned exhibition of death and resurrection. This was the ritual practice emphasized by the Jamaican historian William Gardner when he wrote of *Myal* in 1842:

Its first mode of development was as a branch of *Obeah* practice. The *Obeah* man introduced a dance called *Myal* dance, and formed a secret society, the members of which were to be made invulnerable, or if they died, life was to be restored. Belief in this miracle was secured by trick. A mixture was given in rum, of a character which presently induced sleep so profound, as by the uninitiated and alarmed, to be mistaken for death. After this had been administered to someone chosen for the purpose, the *Myal* dance began, and presently the victim staggered and fell, to all appearance dead. Mystic charms were then used; the body was rubbed with some infusion; and in process of time, the narcotic having lost its power, the subject of the experiment rose up as one restored to life.[24]

Another white resident of Jamaica, Matthew Lewis, also printed an account of an 1817 *Myal* ceremony that closely resembles Gardner's description above. Lewis however distinguished between the Obeah man who caused the death and the Myal man who, in the same ritual, restored the person to life.[25]

In the *Kumina* ceremony I attended, I spent the entire day with the bands. The sequence of events rendered it highly unlikely that the young man was given any substance to induce his state of unconsciousness or restored consciousness. What appears more likely is that this healing procedure, caused by ancestral manifestation (which *Kuminaists* identify as *Myal*), was incorporated into the tradition as a result

---

23 I was convinced of the authenticity of events as they unfolded, in part because the young man's mother had requested the Kumina to correct what appeared to be a psychological affliction upon her son. The young man cooperated but seemed unprepared for what was to happen. When one of the young women caught Myal, the young man began to laugh hysterically. Before I could say "Kumina" he had collapsed on the ground in an unconscious state. At first, I actually thought he was dead, but later learned that his collapse into unconsciousness was the work of the ancestors which was necessary for the healing process.

24 William J. Gardner, *History of Jamaica from its Discovery by Christopher Columbus to the Present Time* (London: Frank Cass, 1842), 192.

25 Matthew Lewis, *Journal of a West Indian Proprietor, kept during a Residence in the Island of Jamaica* (London: J. Murray, 1834), February 25, 1817 entry.

of its actual encounter with Jamaica's 'oldest' African-based religion – *Myal*.

Kumina's Contribution to Jamaica

Indentured African laborers were either promised outright or given the impression that they would be transported back to Africa upon completion of their terms of service. In actuality, only a handful of liberated Africans from Sierra Leone were able to obtain passage home. There are *Kumina* stories about indentured Africans who overcame their exile by simply flying back to Africa. They acquired the power to do this after abstaining from salt intake. Today *Kuminaists,* as do other African religious practitioners in the Caribbean, prepare ancestral food offerings without adding salt. Rastafari groups also maintain fairly rigid food taboos including restrictions against salt intake and the use of salt in the preparation of *ital* (natural) food.[26]

Although 'flying' narratives abound in *Kumina* lore, it is a lamentable consequence of history that Africans were prohibited from uncensored expression and preservation of their cultural heritages during slavery. The case of the Caribbean is especially grave when compared with North America. Unlike North American Africans, Caribbean Africans have no corpus of slave narratives, nor do they have on record any extensive survey of African testimonies about their experiences with enslavement.[27] One would expect that there is yet a wealth of credible information to tease out of history's annals about sociocultural formation among enslaved Africans. However, it might require interdisciplinary collaboration to arrive at creative methods for accessing and analyzing that information. This will certainly be the case for projects that aim at reconstructing well-grounded interpretations of African religions during the period of enslavement.

It might be the case that the *Kumina* community offers tremendous resources for confronting the problem of historical erasure with regard to the African experience in Jamaica. *Kumina* is a site of African historical consciousness where the experience of slavery and African oppression are viscerally remembered through cultural institutions and the natural terrain – the mountains where the Maroons and Bongo

---

26 Barry Chevannes, *Rastafari: Roots and Ideology*, 34–35. Chevannes convincingly argues that the persistence of the taboo against salt in the Kumina, Revival, and Rastafari religions is a symbol of African resistance to European culture.

27 In the United States, there is a significant corpus of testimonies from formerly enslaved Africans which were collected by interviewers working for two distinct agencies at different time periods. Interviewers employed by the American Freedmen's Inquiry Commission collected testimonies during and immediately following the Civil War; and interviewers employed by the Works Progress Administration conducted 2,194 interviews between 1936 and 1938. For a critical discussion of these collections, see the "Introduction," pp. xiii–xv of John Blassingame ed., *Slave Testimony: Two Centuries of Letters, Speeches, Interviews, and Autobiographies* (Baton Rouge, LA: Louisiana State University Press, 1977). Blassingame's entire book serves as one of the most comprehensive examples of "slave testimony" in North America. Also see B.A. Botkin, *Lay My Burden Down: A Folk History of Slavery* (Chicago: University of Chicago Press, 1968).

nation lived and took asylum; in the sanctuary of forests where healing power is stored in every plant, bush and tree; in the shallow streams that Africans crossed in flight from captivity; and at the grave sites and extant 'slave shacks' of the African ancestors.[28] *Kuminaists* retain local knowledge of both significant events and conventional traditions that characterize much of eastern Jamaica's history.

Kumina challenges the contrived selected memories Jamaicans have been conditioned to retain regarding the nation's socio-political and religious history, memories that would credit certain forms of Christianity rather than African-derived religions as the religious source of progress and upliftment among Blacks in their history on the island. *Kumina* culture belongs to the spirituality of Africa and the African diaspora, to those who can 'hear the drum.'

Kumina also signifies the potency and resilience of Indigenous ancestral wisdom. When the Africans were transported thousands of miles away from their homeland to forcibly work as slaves in lands of other Indigenous people stolen by white men, they did not surrender their souls, even though their bodies were brutalized under the terrible yoke of chattel slavery. They persevered in retaining their spiritual connection to Mother Africa, and though it may have appeared that the white slavemasters and plantation owners had total physical control over the enslaved Africans, deep inside was a grounded ancestral spiritual mooring which constantly reminded them of who they were and from whence they had come. In some sense, they were able to trick their oppressors into believing that they were totally subjugated by slavery; however, their visceral anchoring in the spirituality of their forebears and their response to the calls of the ancestors as reflected in Kumina demonstrates the power of Indigenous ancestral wisdom among Africans in Jamaica, which ultimately enabled them not only to physically survive amidst the greatest violence known to humankind – that of chattel slavery – but to thrive as a people informed and empowered by an inner power higher than that of the idols of white men.

Conclusion

The *Kumina* tradition persists today in spite of its marginalized and illegitimate status in Jamaican society. It remains an unfinished document about African people's struggle to surmount the horrors of slavery and its aftermath in Jamaica. Studies of this resilient tradition render subtle connections between African retentions, the slave trade, abolitionism, and what I have called the extended Middle Passage, transparent. First, with regard to African retentions, *Kumina*, a post-emancipation tradition, has reinforced and helped to preserve some of the oldest African-derived *Myal* practices in the island. This phenomenon in Jamaican religious history illuminates our understanding of religious repression and religious formation among African Jamaicans from slavery to the present.

---

28 I was personally escorted through these sacred places by Kuminaists during my research in St Thomas in 1996.

Second, when evaluated alongside historical documents, *Kumina* lore brings credibility to the subjugated narratives of indentured African laborers – to their individual and collective memories of captivity and compromised liberation. These records provide a crucial lens for examining Britain's anti-slave-trade agenda from the 1840s to the late 1860s. What can be gleaned from these records, both oral and official, exposes the paradoxical nature of Britain's recaptive African immigration program. What was construed as a humanitarian battle against the reprehensible traffic in human cargo was anything but humane to the Africans who were liberated from impounded vessels into the hands of British authorities. Liberating Africans from slave ships proved to be a lucrative enterprise for declining British West Indian colonies and a more profitable venture than Britain's original anti-slave-trade strategy of destroying slaveholding factories along the West coast of Africa.[29]

Finally, *Kumina* traditions offer insight into an indispensable dimension of post-emancipation identity formation among Africans in Jamaica. Hence, Rastafari is not the only nor the original site for the cultivation of self-conscious Pan-African ideals and convictions in Jamaica. My impression is that the *Kumina* tradition has indeed influenced Rastafari in more areas than those already noted by scholars, namely music and dietary taboos.[30] *Kumina* demonstrates that contemporary expressions of African-derived religions can also nurture Pan-Africanist values within their adherents while striving to preserve the specific continental African ethnic foundations of their traditions.

---

29 Schuler, "Yerri, Yerri, Koongo," 109–111.

30 Kenneth Bilby and Elliott Leib, "Kumina, the Howellite Church and the Emergence of Rastafarian Traditional Music in Jamaica," *Jamaica Journal* (19/3 1986), 22–28.

The Pacific

Chapter 9

A Celebration of Maori Sacred and Spiritual Wisdom

Rangimarie Turuki Pere

Introduction

Many in our Maori tradition view elders such as myself as the *Tohuna*, 'Keepers of the Secrets who know when and how to sow the seeds.' Women and men like me are born into families who have the key to the higher schools of learning on the upper twelve planes.

This chapter delves into the complex formation of ancestral connections for Maori people and the intricate value system we cherish. It illuminates our sacred sites and spaces, describes the complexity of social institutions that have survived the ferocity of colonization, and highlights the complex nature of Indigenous Maori spirituality, all interwoven to produce the marvel of Indigenous wisdom of which few people around the world are aware. One of the important elements in this chapter is the elucidation of the *Marae*, which is the central meeting of the community, the tangible institution that enables other cultures to meet with the Maori people on Maori terms. This story has much to offer the reader …

My Story

I have never been colonized and never been assimilated. I was raised by people whose values and teachings were deeply steeped in Maori traditional wisdom. Born in Ruatahuna nearly half a century ago, I was strongly influenced by my natural mother's kinship groups. I was transferred from my natural mother to my maternal grandparents soon after birth. I regarded my maternal grandmother as a mother. The word 'mother' has a wide range of meaning in the Maori culture, quite unlike the narrow biological sense of most Western/European cultures. For instance, in Maori kinship terminologies no distinction is made among the related women of one's parent's generation. One's aunt in English becomes one's mother. In Maori tradition individuals use *ëmatuai* (father) for all male relatives and *ëiwhaeai* (mother) for all female relatives in their parents' generation.

For the first seven years of my childhood, I lived with my maternal grandparents on an ancestral block of land called Ohiwa, approximately 20 kilometers southeast of Waikaremoana. Ohiwa is a 270-hectare block of land that was originally cultivated and settled by Ngati-Hika, a subnation of Kahungunu. Many sites, burial grounds and various artifacts remind me and my kin of its sometimes turbulent history, particularly since the Europeans invaded our land.

A brief account of my ancestry is also important to me as a Maori. It establishes rapport with readers. My maternal grandfather, Te Iriheke, was himself the son of a Kahungunu father by the name of Te Rangi and a Tuhoe-Potiki mother, Ngawini. My maternal grandmother, Mihomiho, was herself the daughter of an Englishman, Fenton Arundel Lambert, and a Tuhoe Potiki mother, Te Au. Some of these forebears lived and farmed on Ohiwa along with elders and other relatives. Many other people used Ohiwa as a meeting place and a place for stopping over when traveling through on horseback.

I worked and learnt alongside four generations and was never excluded from anything my grandparents were involved with, including attending celebrations, *tangihanga* (ceremonial mourning) and many other gatherings. Our children were embraced and warmly loved by the elders. I learnt through observation and participation. It was my grandparents' generation and older that influenced most of my learning in those early formative years. After my grandfather died in 1944, I joined another part of the family at Waikaremoana so that I could attend the Kokako Native School, but my grandmother, Mohimiho, continued to influence my life until her death ten years later.

I should also acknowledge Ngati Kahungunu, my natural father's ethnic group and in particular members of the following ëhapuí (sub-ethnic communities), Ngati Kika and Ngai Tahu-matua. Harry, my paternal grandfather who died in 1931, was the son of Bertram Lambert and Teia of Ngati Hika. Wiki, my paternal grandmother, who today lives in Wairoa, Hawkes Bay, is the daughter of Tu Kapuarangi and Ani. Regretfully, Wiki died in September 1983. Wiki, through one of the descent-lines of her mother, Ani, is linked up to Hauiti Tuatahi and Hine-te-ra of the Tairawhiti nations.

I will be drawing extensively on my own experience and on the knowledge that has been shared with me by Maori people and from my *ëwhanaungaí* (relations), and through consulting the work of other community researchers in some instances.

These ancient teachings have been secretly passed down through generations, waiting for the right time to be revealed. These teachings are symbolic stories of wisdom that originated in the Maori ancestral home of Hawaiki. They are finally being told through a monograph entitled *Ako – Concepts and Learning in the Maori Tradition* (1982) and in her book, *An i Te Wheke – A Celebration of Infinite Wisdom* (1995). It is the first time some of this knowledge has been written for general publication. These teachings of Hawaiki in traditional Maori terms have been protected, awaiting a time when the world would be ready. This ensured that people outside those selected individuals entrusted with the information could not tamper with what was originally intended with these texts. The teachings say that when the stars (*Turuki* and *Rehuna*) align it is time to share the ancient teachings of Hawaiki. I assumed the alignment wouldn't happen until the year 2000 but in actual fact they aligned themselves in 1990. I wrote that book because it is important to preserve this knowledge for our future Maori generations and even for non-Maori people.

An i Te Wheke is about love, peace, joy and truth in the universe and dates back over 12 000 years to ancient Hawaiki. Writing the book was one of the greatest challenges I faced because everything I discussed in my books and here I learned during my childhood and my adolescent years in the Maori language. My thinking is thus grounded in the Maori culture and tradition.

My books and this chapter are written in English because sadly there are many young people that cannot speak or understand the Maori language today. I see our language as economical and easy to understand for the outside world. However, to appreciate and completely understand the Maori language people must understand the mythology behind it.

Our Maori wisdom is based on our knowledge of asteric knowledge and learning. I talk about a world that divides, consumes and challenges. The planet Earth to me is hallowed or sacred ground, all of it, *Papatuanuku.* It amazes me that people try to put it in a box.

As someone who has been teacher trained in European institutions, with twenty-four years of teaching experience involving learners from all levels of schooling and including every position of responsibility within the teaching service, I have been exposed to some of the similarities and differences that exist between *Pakehatanga*, or Western institutions, and *Tuhoetanga-Tuhoe*, the Maori basic philosophy. In the former everything falls under some form of classification such as a department, a subject area or some framework that has clearly defined boundaries. Coordination between areas has to be deliberately provided for and arranged. In the latter, according to Maori basic philosophy, nothing exists in isolation or in clearly demarcated bounds. Instead, all things merge into each other and therefore need to be understood in relation to each other and within the context of the whole.

Resultantly, in Maori tradition learners are integral to the coordinating of developmental and integrated approaches used in primary schools. In both cases we see children deeply involved with their work and freely using their senses, feelings and intellect to encompass their world, working alongside adults who understand the experiences children have in specific curriculum areas, and being encouraged to discover new relational concepts and ideas, as opposed to static rote learning from textbooks.

Maori Philosophical Wisdom

Hinengaro is the Maori word for the source of thoughts and emotions. *Hinengaro* refers to the mental and emotional experiences that a person has in learning. Thinking, knowing, perceiving, remembering, recognizing, abstracting, and generalizing are processes that refer to the intellectual activities of the *hinengaro*. Emotional activities such as feeling, sensing, responding, and reacting are also processes of the hinengaro.

Matauranga is the Maori word for knowledge and understanding. The process the word refers to takes place wherever we find ourselves and through whatever we experience, covering the process of learning throughout the whole of life. The *matauranga* of a person is dependent on the state of their *hinengaro*. The challenge of sharing what I know within the academic context of another language and culture outside Maori experience is real. However the key word for me is sharing and trying to communicate in any way I can the feelings, the views, and the hopes that some of us have.

An oversimplification of the diversity of Maori institutions not only produces errors inherent in averages but disregards the dynamism of the Maori people themselves. Our lives and institutions were far from static and frozen in time and space before the arrival of the *Pakeha* (white people) and have continued to be dynamic since then. But it is convenient for the *Pakeha* to collectivize the Maori and restrict an understanding of the conflicts between us to their preconceived areas of explanation. This is characteristic of most Pakeha perceptions of Maori history, culture and society.

My own small contribution to resolving these difficulties is to share at least a part of my knowledge with you. I cannot share it all because these ancient wisdom traditions are not public matters; however the memories of childhood experiences coupled with my position as a *Tohuna* (elder) accords me the privilege to share with you what I was told by the elders and what I have lived by throughout my life.

Nga Koreo a nga matua tipuna... The source of the Maori worldview used in this chapter stems from *Tuhoe-Potiki* and *Kahungunu*. This is the knowledge I have of traditional institutions that have been transmitted to me by the women and men of my kinship groups. While much of the information I have received about my own descent-lines is personal and not for general publication, the time has come for this wisdom to be integrated into the school curriculum for the Maori learners and shared with all other learners around the world to know who we are and our understanding and interpretation of the universe.

Principles of the Maori Way

a) The Marae

Marae are places of refuge for our people and provide facilities to enable us to continue with our way of life within the total structure of our own terms and values. We need our *Marae* for a list of reasons:

That we may rise tall in oratory
That we may weep for our dead
That we may pray to god
That we may have our feasts
That we may house our guests
That we may have our meetings
That we may have our weddings
That we may have our reunions
That we may sing
That we may dance
And then know the richness of life
And the proud heritage that is truly ours.

The *Marae* is an institution from classical Maori society that has survived the impact of Western European colonization. It is central to the concept of *Maoritanga* and the Maori cultural identity. Maori oratory, language, values and social etiquette are given their fullest expression on the *Marae* at the *tangi* and *hui* (assemblies). The *Marae* is also a place where values and philosophy are reaffirmed. It is the only institution where the dignity of the *tangi* can be preserved and the ones who have passed from this life bid farewell to the living in the appropriate customary fashion. The *Marae* is sacred to the living and is a memorial to those who have passed on to the spirit world. For this reason the *Marae* must be entered in a reverent manner.

The *Marae* is socially integrative in the sense that it fosters identity, self-respect, pride and social control. The *Marae* is also integrative in that all people are welcome as guests. It is one institution where the *Pakeha* can meet the Maori on Maori terms and come to a better understanding of what it means to have a bicultural society.

The *Marae* consists of the following: *Maraenui-atea-o-Tumatauenga*, the sacred courtyard in front of the meeting house. *Tumatauenga* is the god of war. Going into the *Marae* means entering into a special discussion zone where issues are debated. All newcomers to the *Marae* must be greeted formally by the *tangata whenua* (hosts) whether in the warmth of a welcome, in the sadness of *a tangi* or even in verbal battle on mutual issues. It is the place where people formally come together on a specific occasion for a specific function. Different communities of the Maori nation have different procedures and formalities in interacting with the *Marae*.

b) The Meeting House

The *Marae* and the meeting house are complementary and together serve as the focal point for community sentiment. The meeting house is normally the major central building and, in the main, ornately carved. The meeting house has many names, including *tipuna whare*, *whare nui* and so on, and in nearly all cases it is not only named after an ancestor but it is structured to symbolically represent the ancestors. Thus the *tekoteko* (carved figure) on the rooftop in front represents the ancestor head, the *maihi* (carved angles from the head down towards the ground) represents the arms, *tahuhu* or *taahu* (the ridgepole down the center of the building) is the backbone, and the *heke* (rafters) reaching from the ridge pole to the carved figures around the *poupou* (walls) represents the ribs. The *poupou* are normally carved ancestors representing other tribes. *Poupou* then function as identifiers in a feeling of belonging. The uprights, normally holding up the *tahuhu*, represent the connection between *Rangi* the Sky Father and *Papa-tuanuku* the Earth Mother. While there are other interpretations, it follows appropriately that meeting houses are named after an ancestor. Entering the house is viewed as entering the bosom of an ancestor. The interaction between the people on the *Maraenui-atea-o-Tumatauenga* should be significantly different from the interaction that normally occurs inside the house. It is believed that inside the house *Rongo* the god of Peace reigns and it is in this atmosphere that people are expected to interact with one another.

c) The Whare Kai

As the name implies, this is the eating house, the place where the inner person is satisfied. The *Whare Kai* is a separate sphere and a differently based concept or belief. The concept of *tapu* prescribes where food can be eaten and not eaten and also where drinks can be drunk and not drunk. To the Maori, *noa* (food) is a common element and the opposite of *tapu*. Whereas the *tipuna whare* meeting house is *tapu* and food cannot be eaten there, the *whare kia* is free from *tapu*; the two are at opposite ends of the continuum.

d) Other Sacred Sites, Spaces, and Principles

Many *Marae* have churches situated nearby. This is significant in terms of the acknowledgment of the Creator as an ever-present Being in the daily lives of people on the *Marae*. Many *Marae* also have a *urupa* (gravesite) nearby, acknowledging the ancestors as the living dimension of life. An ancestor is commemorated within the building; respects are paid to those who have passed on to the *hono-i-wairua* (gathering place of spirits) within a *whaikorero* (formal speech making), reflecting the belief in the merging of life and passing on. The *te hunga ora* (people living) are the result of a combination of the *te hunga mate* (those who have passed on) and the *te hungs ora* (living). Reference to these concepts are very frequent is *whaikorero*.

i) Whakapapa

This principle has several meanings and interpretations. For the present purpose, its meaning points to the Maori name of the Earth, *Papatuanuku*, and the reciting of things in order, including genealogy.

Papatuanuku, the primeval earthly mother, and *Rangi-nui-etuiho-nei*, the primeval celestial father, spring from a series of forces that are both male and female. The union of the primeval parents as one deity is one of both a spiritual and physical nature. The primeval parents embrace and cling together as one deity for eons of time producing many children. *Papatuanuku* and *Rangi-nui-etuiho-nei* found great fulfillment in their union as one.

Papatuanuku and *Rangi-nui-etuiho-nei* held their many children close to them. The many children shared a whole host of innate capacities and traits among their number – some resembled their father with their celestial attributes, others resembled their mother. From these spirits humanity was descended according to Maori tradition.

Many of the children resented being so confined and restricted within the closeness and the darkness of the parental union. These vibrant children wanted independence and desired moving away from the union of their parents to explore and to make new discoveries. The *ikai-whakangiraî* (kindlers of fires or initiators) made their views known, which caused great unrest among the parent spirits. Some of the more adventurous children moved out through *Papatuanuku*'s saliva. The world outside was a world of light, with a different beauty, and once this information was given to those who were still within their parental union further debate took place, further unrest occurred.

All of the children of *Papatuanuk* and *Rangi-nui-etuiho-nei* were supernatural beings possessing strange powers. *Tane*, one of the illustrious sons, was known by many names because of the numerous feats he performed. But *Tane* is perhaps best known for transmitting the divine seed of life that emanated from *Io-matua-kore*, the supreme spiritual being, through seeking and finding the female element and also for thrusting *Rangi-nui-etuiho-nei* upwards with his feet, thus separating *Rangi-nui-etuiho-nei* from his beloved *Papatuanuk*. *Tane* forced his parents asunder so that they no longer embraced and clung together as one union. He also brought with that action family strife and quarrels. Some of the children remained on and within *Papatuanuk*, while others followed and remained attached to *Rangi-nui-etuiho-nei*. Both parents are the universe.

Tane, who was also known as the origin and personification of trees and birds, was regarded as the most important of *Papatuanuk* and *Rangi-nui-etuiho-nei's* children. Having begat the trees and the birds, *Tane* also sought *ite uhaî*, the female element that was within a woman. *Tane* questioned many supernatural beings about *ite uhaî* until finally two beings showed him a formation of earth within the bosom of *Papatuanuk*. This formation was the first woman, a formation that was known by several names, one of whom was *Hine*.

Tane inherited both spiritual and earthly characteristics from his primeval parents, but when he gazed on the womanly form he succumbed to his physical rather than his spiritual needs. With his first male attempt, Tane interfered with *Hine's* eyes and brought forth tears. He interfered with her ears and from them brought a discharge. The efforts he made around *Hine's* nostrils brought about mucus. *Tane* moved on to interfere with the mouth and from that he caused saliva to flow.

Determined to find *ite uhaî*, *Tane* continued to move downwards. As he moved around the armpits, *Hine* began to sweat. *Tane* made his next attempt in the pubic region. *Tane* felt a tremendous force from within *Hine*, a powerful force such as he had never experienced before. All that *Tane* had sought and hoped for he found with

Hine: together they brought forth humanity. According to this version of the origin of humanity the fruits of that union still exist. *iTanei* is the Maori word for man and *iwahinei* the word for woman. It has also been said that if *Tane* had not meddled the way he did with *Hine,* that physical death would never have assailed humanity.

One descent-line of the Maori, *Tuhoe Potiki*, contains the following names and clearly indicates the way in which *Tuhoe Potiki* includes the natural environment and the phenomena of the universe:

Rangi-nui-e-tu-iho-nei	=	*Papa-tuanuku*
Tane-te-waira	=	*Hine-waoriki*

The Maori line of the *iwhakapapai* has a system of social stratification that depends on seniority of descent among the many descent-lines of a previous couple. The *ituakanai* and *iteinai* are also terms used by members of the same sex. For example, a brother to a male is called either his *ituakanai* or his *iteinai* rather than *itunganei* (brother), a term used by females for brothers.

Traditionally every adult person is expected to know and be able to trace descent back to their ancestors, or back to at least the common ancestor after whom the person's group was named. The rights and claims that an individual could make to a particular group depended on their knowledge of that particular group.

The serious responsibility of passing on this knowledge is that of the senior-most persons of each *iwhanaui* (usually consisted of at least one *itipunai* with three or four generations of direct descendants and their spouses). Some *whanau* also includes captives from other nations who were employed as servants or slaves. These persons had no rights. *Whanau* also pertained to birth.

People from the *irangatirai* (people who could claim direct descent from the *tuakana* of each descent-line, or claim descent from the *tuakana* descent-line) class had a lot more information transmitted to them about the genealogies and the life experiences of ancestors within the descent-lines because they were involved with the higher schools of esoteric learning. Obviously a depth of knowledge about *whakapapa* and related issues gave an individual advantages within the group.

Due to the great importance placed on *whakapapa* and seniority in descent-lines, a person would usually identify more closely with the natural parent whose *whakapapa* and kinship group would receive the greatest advantage. Keeping regular contact and sharing in the activities and responsibilities of the kinship group(s) with whom one chose to identify were important. An industrious creative person who worked hard towards strengthening and uplifting the economic assets and the spirituality of their kinship group(s) was held in very high esteem. The descendants of such ancestors, who continue to uphold these traditions, are accorded the same respect and status.

In some *whakapapa* one parent can be a generation or more ahead of the other parent, not in age but in the number of steps from a common ancestor. The direct descendants need to know the *whakapapa* of all the descent-lines to take the advantage this entails.

For instance, children from a union between *Hinehou* (aged 25) and *Hemi* (aged 30) can, if they choose to, identify with their mother's line, with *Hinehou's* line. Some children prefer to identify with their father's line.

With regards to marriage, parents made the choice of mates and usually betrothed even children in their early infancy. However there are examples of male and female *rangatira* selecting their own partners, often with the blessing and support of the elders. Except for female *rangatira,* young people were allowed to indulge in sexual relationships before marriage providing it was done with discretion and did not interfere with their responsibilities to the community.

ii) Wairua

Literally translated, *iwairuaî* denotes *wai* (water) and *rue* (two), a word that can depict the name of Te Rangi and a Tuhoe-Potiki mother, Ngawini. My maternal grandmother, Mihomiho, was herself the daughter of an Englishman, Fenton Arundel Lambert, and a Tuhoe Potiki mother, Te Au. Some of these forebears lived and farmed on Ohiwa along with relations of *Io*, the supreme influence to only selected *rangatira*, and this reaffirms and enhances the position of influence such people held. People of lower social standing render their invocations to other *Atua.* The senior-most descent-line of the *rangatira* particularly, were seen as people possessing spiritual powers that could protect them from evil forces, threats, and warn them of impending danger not only from their own immediate world but from the outside. Some of these people were also regarded as prophets and had the gift of foretelling the future. There are certain individuals descended from these ancestors who have such gifts to this very day.

Hine-Matioro is an *Ariki* (firstborn male or female from an aristocratic union of great note. *Ariki-tamora* is male and *Ariki-tapairu* is female. The early European missionaries also adopted the term *Ariki* to denote Jesus Christ, the founder of the Christian religion. *Ariki* had many senior genealogical descent-lines converge on her, including *Ngati Kahungunu*, who was regarded as a divine person and was extremely sacred. People from outside her ethnic affiliations often went to her for both physical and spiritual protection and help. A repository of the highest forms of esoteric learning, *Hine Matioro* devoted much of her life to helping and relating to numerous people. Her grandson *Te Kani-a-Talirau* also became a famous Ariki during the last century.

The Maori recognized *iAtuaî* (spiritual beings with supernatural influences). Some of the *Atua* and personifications are common to all Indigenous areas and are often referred to in Maori folklore. However, each group, *hapu* and *habau*, also had their own exclusive forms of *Atua.* The term *Atua* was also applied to ancestral spirits, the spirits of stillborn babies, to primal forces or beings, natural phenomena, images and supernatural creatures.

Atua was the term that early European missionaries adopted to denote the supreme God of the Christian religion, because the Maori aristocracy continued to restrict the higher forms of learning to themselves, including the concept of *Io*. The concept of *iwairuaî* was used in everyday life situations and in formal Maori ceremonies.

There were both male and female spiritual spheres that were seen as carrying either identical or complementary roles. *Hine-te-iwaiwa* presided over childbirth as well as all the art forms involved in weaving. She was regarded as helpful and benevolent and as such had female babies dedicated to her. *Hine-te-iwaiwa* was associated with other personifications from both the land and the great ocean. One of these was *Rongo*. *Rongo*, as a recognized influence, promoted peace, hospitality, growth and benefits to humanity and was associated with *Hine-te-iwaiwa* within the meeting house where people gathered.

Other personifications who stood for peace and life-giving pursuits were *Haumia*, *Ioio-whenua*, and *Pu-te-hue*. *Haumia* was recognized as the origin and personified form of the common fern-root, and other forms of principle vegetable foods. He was seen as providing food for the descendants of *Rangi-nui-etuiho-nei* and *Papatuanuku*. *Pu-te-hue* was regarded as the origin of *ihueî* (ground), a female personification who flourishes through producing fine fruit for the physical salvation of humanity. Like her male counterparts she was seen as an influence that promoted peace, physical growth and development.

Tangaroa was spoken of as the essence, the origin, and the personification of the fruits of the ocean, although he is linked up with the land in some mythology. There are many legends relating to *Tangaroa* and his descendants. Creatures such as whales, sharks and octopi were not only sometimes described as pets by the Maori, but were often referred to as *iKai-tiakiî* (guardians or protectors) that exposed themselves to their benefactors in either the physical or spiritual sense.

Alongside *Tangaroa* was *Wainui*, a female personification who represented all the waters of the earth. Her role involved her with associates from both the land and the sea. To this very day there is not much from the realm of spirituality that pertains to water. *Tawhirimatea* was looked upon as the origin and personification of wind, all forms of moving air. His descendants are many and varied. Some people were believed to have the power to cause winds of varying degrees, or to lay them. *Ruaimoko* was also seen as the son who remained within the womb of his mother, *Papa*, where he made his presence felt in a variety of ways.

Maori mythology depicts the strengths, weaknesses, and complex characteristics of human beings by portraying them through perennial influences and *Atua* generally. *Tumatauenga* is regarded as the personification of war and everything that is associated with such a concept. Male babies were dedicated to both *Tumatauenga* and *Rongo* although their qualities and attributes differed considerably. The *marae-atea* (courtyard in front of the meeting house) within *Tuhoe Potiki* tradition is regarded as the domain of *Rongo* and *Hine-te-iwaiwa*.

Tane, who was mentioned in the *whakapapa* section, also had his name linked with incest in that he begot children from his own offspring. The feeling of shame comes into Maori mythology when *Hine-titama* realizes that *Tane* is also her father and grandfather. According to one version this trauma made *Hine-titama* run away from *Tane*, bearing deep feelings of remorse and shame to find revenge in the realms of the underworld. *Hine-titama* then became *Hine-nui-te-po* (*Hine* of the great night), the personification associated with the physical death of mortals.

The circumstances in which people found themselves affected their decision to influence, appease, invoke or commit themselves to the *Atua* who existed for them within their own beliefs. The people believed that *Atua* could help them procure benefits, overcome obstacles, achieve desired goals, avert disasters and destroy the enemies. There are many examples of incantations and different types of offerings or sacrifices made to various *Atua* by the Maori.

What in English may be expressed as the realm of spirituality is just as meaningful and important to the Maori as the physical realm, but their beliefs, values and traditions ensure that both realms are recognized, sustained and nurtured together as one. Whether a tribute to the divinities was made in the physical or spiritual form, the correct ceremonial procedure was of the utmost importance. The slightest error was regarded as an ill omen that brought with it some retribution. To the Maori a mistake was a definite *itohuî* (sign) that all was not well and that some disaster or tragedy would strike before long. The people who took the lead in spiritual matters had to be perfectionists and highly disciplined. There are still many Maori people today who are strongly influenced by their *itaha wairuaî* (spiritual side). Like many other Indigenous peoples the Maori believe that to disregard spiritual or ancestral ceremonial custom, or to conduct ceremonies without each ritual element performed, constitutes a serious religio-cultural violation that would cause untold harm to the community.

iii) The Reo

The term *ireoî* has several meanings. The emphasis here is on its meaning as a language and concentrated on aural and oral skills as means of communication. The language expresses the values, beliefs and ideology of people in a powerful way. Solid command of the language was critical to the experience of being Maori.

Some Europeans during the early period of colonizing the Maori nation learned how to speak Maori with fluency. However they never participated in the ethos, the living experience of what it means to be a part of and truly belong to an Indigenous Maori community with ancestral roots deep in the land.

The proverbs, legends, stories and history have hidden meanings and symbolic reference for those who understand the mythology of the clan group to whom they belong. Many legends, chants, historical accounts and proverbs have been interpreted and translated into English. This was a literal translation and woefully inadequate, with little or no understanding of the depth of information and knowledge of the cultural nuances implied in specific words. One word or phrase can convey a host of meanings depending on the context in which something is said, including the intonation that is used. *Whanau, hapu* refer to those Indigenous groups jealously guarding those things that were of special significance to them by using verbal expressions that could be interpreted in several ways and inaccessible to outsiders. For example, the following *whakatauaki* (proverbial saying) reads:

ìHe ao te rangi ka uhia a ma te huruhuru te manu ke rere aiî

This proverb means 'As clouds bedeck the heavens, so do feathers enable birds to fly.' It is of special significance and fully appreciated only by people who know the origin of the statement and the context in which it was first used. The proverb originated thus:

> When asked to recite a *ìtohiî* (ceremony before battle) over a war-party, *Tama-te-rengi,* a famous Ngati Kahungunu paramount chief, first made the above statement without having the correct attire for such a special occasion. His younger brother, *Makoro,* understanding his plight, took off his cloak and placed it around *Tama-te-rangiî's* shoulders. *Hinerangim, Tama-te-rangiî's* wife, was regarded by Makoro as a person unable to support and provide what was necessary for her high-ranking husband. *Makoro* did not hesitate to acknowledge his own wife, *Hinemuturangi,* who was able to provide the correct apparel for the special role that such *a tangi* ... or even in verbal battle. It is the place where people formally come together on a specific occasion for a specific function. Different communities of the Maori nation have different procedures and formalities in interacting with each other: 'waster of food, waster of property, waster of people consigned to death.' *ìHe iti na Tuhoe, kata te poî,* which means, 'Be it but a few from Tuhoe, they can still laugh at death.'

This proverb is heard in speeches and song to indicate identity, to remind one perhaps of a turbulent but colorful past or perhaps to inspire one to face up to challenges.

A tremendous amount of Tuhoe history relates to the above sayings and as such may only be of interest to Tuhoe people. Another proverb says: *ìToi te e* interaction between the people on the *Maraenui-atea-o-Tumatauenga* should be significantly different from the interaction that normally occurs inside the house. It is believed that inside the house *Rongo* the god of peace reigns and it is in the atlas of the Maori people.

The following diagram represents the practice of healing from the heart with love:

A (ah)°, The Divine Mother on my left, I (ee)°, the Divine Child, the Inner Being in the center of me, and O(or)°, the Divine father on my right, I send you my love, I feel your sacred reflection in the mirror of my heart.

The Mirror of My Heart
The Mirror of My Heart

Left   Center   Right
Left   Center   Right

A   I   O
Mother Divine Child Divine Father
Sacred River, Sacred Seed
    From the Central
    Sun, the Divine Spark

    In Tangata (Human Being)

    I° – Child (from the)
    Ra° – Central Sun, Divine Spark

    Ta° – Blue Print, DNA.; from the Godhead
    Nga° – Breath from the Godhead
    Ta° – Hologram of the Godhead

    iv) Aroha

The energy of Aotearoa (New Zealand) is Aroha, the presence and the breath of the Godhead, unconditional love. May our constant companion during this gathering be Aroha. Our mountains, our rivers, our lakes, our glaciers, our hot pools, our forest lands, everything that uplifts the oneness of all things also extend their greetings of *Aroha* to everyone who is present. A common form of greeting in Aotearoa is *ëkia oraí* in its ordinary meaning, and yet the depth of sacred meaning is awesome in that it also conveys the following energy and vibrations:

    K = Iao Ra
    K= Subtle vibration
    I = The Divine Child
    A = The Divine Mother
    O = The Divine Father
    Ra = The Central Sun, the Divine Spark

    Two-thirds of our communication in Maori is completely abstract, to the point that people who learn our language fluently may learn only about ordinary meaning but not sacred meanings. Our ancient wisdom is transmitted by the *ëTohunaí,* who are 'keepers of the secrets who know when and how to sow the seeds.' These types of people are born into families who have the key to the higher levels of learning on the upper twelve planes.

    Prior to 14 January 1990 when the alignment of *Turuki* (the North Star) and *Rehua* (the smallest star that can be seen by the naked eye in the Southern Cross) took place, I would not have been able to share much of what I have with anyone. The *Tohuna* have great discipline, and although there were many temptations to share the sacred teachings before the appropriate time our people managed to keep everything intact until the right time. What we basically shared with the Europeans before 1990 represents European versions of our traditions and teachings. This was the only way in which we could prevent the Europeans from interfering with our ancient paths of wisdom.

When the Europeans came to Aotearoa they spoke about the father and the son in their religious teachings. From the ancient Maori period to the present time we realize the importance of linking with the oneness of all things. When we are in perfect harmony we are in tune with Mother Earth and creation. We can indeed become the stars, the trees, the coral reefs, the dolphins, the sun, the moon and anything we need to become to help the process of healing, be it with people, with other living things, with our Earth Mother and with other planets and galaxies.

Spiritual healing always precedes physical healing, healing that may include massaging, herbal medicines, sound and vibration, water, *kumara* (sweet potato), or stone. What European cultures may refer to as disease or illness is referred to as 'being unclean' in the Maori tradition and in need of 'cleansing.'

Some people may experience the same type of cleansing several times over because they have not truly understood how they may have gone against the natural belief system with which they were born. They thus are in need of cleansing themselves spiritually. One has to live and abide by the natural laws. For example, our Maori people find the whole notion of cloning horrendous and soul destroying because it violates the spirit of each creature as endowed on that creature by the Creator. No individual spirit can be replicated by human beings. This is a serious breach because it makes humans the creator and disregards the divine mandate from the Creator to respect the creation. I myself am descended from the sacred seed and the sacred river, so are my children and grandchildren. We come from the Mother/ Father Source of life. To heal ourselves and others we need to celebrate our absolute uniqueness as individuals. There has never been anyone else exactly like me and I pray there never will be! *Taku mana, taku mana, mana motuhake!!!!*

We also recognize and accept other forms of healing that may be brought into our space from another culture. To us the most important part of healing is to feel and have faith in the power of unconditional love that comes from the Godhead. Right now I am traversing on spiritual planes above the earth, and I am aware that my physical body needs help to keep up with the frequency changes. Twelve light beings have come into my space to help me receive the balance that I need to be in harmony with the Earth Mother.

The potential of healing is in every person. The assumption is that every person is born with great wisdom and great power because she is the essence of the Godhead, *AIO*. European Christian missionaries came to the Maori in New Zealand quite convinced that they had to save the Maori from damnation. This attitude still exists in some circles. We also have other people including white spiritual healers trying to teach us how to adjust to the so-called New Age and how we need to cleanse our sacred places!!! It has not yet entered their heads that we Maori have been the Keepers of the South Pacific Rim of Fire for thousands of years, as decreed by our ancient forebears. We have never let the fires die out by hordes of darkness either, as suggested by the white 'saviors.' In fact the fires are burning brighter than ever in that some of us have always chosen to be Warriors for Peace, even against great odds. We even refer to gatherings that occurred over five billion years ago since the spirits we have are very ancient. Sometimes we refer to other cultures as our 'senior' brothers and sisters to be polite, but on a spiritual level no one is more senior or junior.

Another wonderful thing is that people basically heal themselves once they meditate on the power of the Spirit and put their minds to it, although other people can come in alongside to help them remember how to call on their own energy, and other energy flows that can help. Loving hands that massage or help heal in some other way are always a precious blessing and must always be appreciated and celebrated. Everything from my first communication with you in this chapter has been an absolute delight, a real bonus. I thank and honor you all! I pay tribute to you, your ancestors, all those who have passed on beyond the veil. May they be at peace. May we who continue to live on this plane also be united in peace. As is customary, I will sing you a song of peace. The ordinary meaning of *AIO* is peace, but within the realms of its sacred context we include love, joy and truth.

AROHANUI – Lot of love to you all, from Hawaiiki Tautau, the ancient name of New Zealand when she flourished and was recognized as the pulse of the ancient Hawaiiki, the largest continent in the world before most of it went under water 12 000 years ago. This Motherland included Australasia, the whole of the Pacific Basin. So be it!

Conclusion

This story reminds us of the power, the beauty, the resilience and the perseverance of Indigenous Maori wisdom, so precious yet devalued in a supposed modern and ostensibly civilized world. It recalls us all to the deep lineage that connects us to our ancestors and to the spirit world, which is the ultimate hope for all life on earth. This narrative underscores too that the path of Indigenous peoples is one of resistance, even as we all practice our sacred ceremonies and observe our traditional rites and beliefs, to the imposition of European colonial cultures that are foolishly still engaged in attempting to erase our existence. But *AIO* is with us, just as She is with the Maoris in our struggle for life…

Asia

Chapter 10

Voices of Resilience and Resistance: The Ainu Peoples of Hokkaido, Japan

Etsuko Aoki, Kiyoko Kitahara
Kayano Shigeru and Koichi Kaizawa

Introduction

This chapter presents unique voices of the Ainu peoples of Hokkaido, Japan, who are a living symbol of resilience and resistance against the discrimination and prejudice by the Japanese government and society at large. For a long time the Japanese government has perpetuated the myth of a monolithic Japan that is rooted in a single identity, culture, and language, thus forcing the Ainu peoples to assimilate into the dominant culture. This is an Ainu story that captures multiple voices of Ainu men and women expressed in the oral tradition.

The Meaning of Ainu

Ainu is a precious word that means 'human.' This word also represents the name of the people. In addition, it is used as a title of honor with which an elder calls a respectable man as .... *ainu* or ... *aino*. The majority of the Japanese immigrants to Hokkaido, Japan's northern island, had described 'Ainu' as a derogatory term for many generations. Because of this, the Ainu term *Utari,* meaning brothers or fellows, has been used instead of 'Ainu.' But in recent years the Ainu people have again come to use 'Ainu' without a hitch, as an honorable name of the Ainu peoples.

Etsuko Aoki: My Life Story

I was born in Chirotto, a small village near Obihiro in Hokkaido. My parents were Ainu. My father died at a very young age and left my mother with five children to take care of. I had three brothers and a sister. We were a very poor family. Most Ainu families were poor, but I believe that my family was the poorest of them all. Mother worked as a construction worker among men because that was the only job available to most Ainu men and women without education. She would come home exhausted and never had time to speak to us or even teach us the Ainu culture and language although she knew the language and spoke it fluently with the elders. I sometimes asked her why she did not teach us the Ainu language. She told me that there was no use for our language in the Japanese society. As a result we all grew up not knowing the culture or the language. However, I must add that it was not only mother who denied us of our Ainu-ness. This feeling of self-hate was perpetuated across the island by other Ainu families who were convinced by the government that assimilation was the only way for Ainu children to make it in school and in the workplace. Schools were thus another vehicle for the continuation of devaluing our culture and language.

Jobs too were not for the Ainu people. After receiving my high school certificate I decided to come to Tokyo. My mother's friend was not Ainu, but understood our plight and took me under her wing and got me started in Tokyo. She helped me to find a job. My older brother Sakai also decided to join me later in Tokyo. When I came of age I married. I never wanted to marry an Ainu man. Looking back at my path, being Ainu meant that you were under scrutiny all the time. At school we were teased and made fun of, and when searching for a job, we experienced severe discrimination. I was determined to spare my children the pain and anguish I had experienced growing up Ainu by diluting their blood. I know that I was not the only woman who felt this way.

I thought that things would change for the better in Tokyo; however, time proved me wrong. I have many tragic stories to tell, but one that haunts me every day and often leaves me with unanswered questions has to do with the death of my brother, Sakai. Back then jobs were a problem especially for Ainu men. Sakai and many other Ainu men could only find jobs in Sadya, a day-labor district for the homeless. As soon as he got to Tokyo in the early 1980s he joined the Liberation Movement of the Ainu Peoples and Day Laborers. In 1987 he was stopped by a police officer and taken to the police station for questioning. He was told that his name was blacklisted in the computer. As the evening approached and a new shift of private investigators came in, he was harassed and beaten up. He had a broken leg and incurred a cut on his forehead which required four stitches. The following day we went to the police station to look for him. The police denied any violent treatment of Sakai. We were made fun of and told that we were imagining things. He was in and out of jail for questioning during the rest of 1987. By the end of that year he had reached a point where he could care less about what happened to him. Every day I spoke to him, he told me that he could sense death coming. 'I just do not know what day,' he said. Early in 1988, his body was found in a canal in Tokyo. There were no toxins, no alcohol in his blood, and since he was a good swimmer, he could not have drowned in the canal. It has now been more than a decade since Sakai's mysterious and tragic death, and to this day my family does not know what and who is responsible for his death.

The thought of going back to live in Hokkaido sometimes crosses my mind; however, the memories are so sad and painful at this point that I have no intention to move back. I must also mention that although the Ainu people experience discrimination and prejudice in Tokyo, I also feel that here I can be part of a larger group of Ainu as well as non-Ainu political activists who are giving us all the support we need. I currently serve as the President of *Peure Utari no Kai* (Young Utari Association) and am also the secretary of the NGO called Indigenous Peoples Working Group. Being part of these groups is for me an educational process which is helping me reconnect with my authentic Ainu identity.

As I conclude my story, let me share with you one of the well-known sayings by Chin Yukie, an Ainu young woman. She died at an early age and left these words which are a constant reminder of who the Ainu people are and what the island of Hokkaido means to us: 'Once upon a time this huge Hokkaido was a place where our ancestors lived freely and joyfully. Today such memories are a long gone past. We are the disappearing ones.' What a sad name we Ainu peoples have today!

Kiyoko Kitahara: My Life Story

Both my parents came from Sakhalin Island. This island was occupied by Japan around 1904. When Japan was defeated in 1945, all Indigenous peoples were forcibly removed out of the island and relocated in Japan. Along with other Ainu families, my parents settled in Hokkaido. The newly relocated families all tell sad stories of famine, illness, lack of jobs, and above all, gross instances of discrimination and anger from the locals who resented newcomers whom they perceived were coming to take away their jobs. I was born in 1946, a few months after the relocation. My father got seriously ill when I was seventeen, and from then on I had to work while going to school. Many times I was refused jobs not because of my age but because to employ an Ainu person would defile the kimono store or company. That was the remark I heard over and over in my search for a job.

At home we never spoke the Ainu language nor did anything that seriously connected us to the Ainu culture. At an early age, my parents made every effort to send me to colonial Japanese schools. Whenever I wanted or wished to speak the Ainu language or practice our culture mother discouraged me, saying that being Ainu exposes me to discrimination and would bring me more problems than I can imagine. In 1972 I left Hokkaido for Tokyo. At first I was very discouraged that Japanese people around Tokyo had a very subtle way of showing their discrimination against the Ainu peoples. Some of my friends whom I least expected to be so naïve always said that I could not be Ainu because I did not 'act like them.' I know that although in my presence they did not say anything negative about the Ainu, in my absence a lot of derogatory statements were made.

In 1980 a group of Ainu people formed the *Ainu Kanto Utari Kai*. At that time I had my son and attended every meeting with him. At home I have made every effort to teach and sing Ainu songs with him and perform traditional dances. On weekends we attend Ainu language classes here at the Ainu Center. My mother made every effort to hide her identity. From that day on, and whenever we visited, she taught her grandson rituals, songs and words she remembered from her *Sakhil* days. I have never blamed my parents for depriving me of the opportunity to learn my language and tradition. However I would blame myself for doing the same thing to my son and even to myself. Today Ainu parents live under different times and conditions. Although we still experience discrimination, we are in a better position to regain our Ainu-ness than our parents were.

When my son entered elementary school, we used to attend entrance ceremonies. Parents would be sitting at one place while our children were lining up to do some performance. This particular day, a parent who was sitting next to me nudged, and as she was chuckling she said something like, 'Look at that boy'(pointing at my son), 'he sure has thick eyebrows – he looks very much like an Ainu.' I smiled at her, and commented that the boy certainly had very fine eyebrows. Later we discovered that her family lived in the same neighborhood. However, from then onwards, they always avoided crossing paths with us and went to the extent of relocating and pulling their child from that elementary school. Deep down I did not feel sorry for them. I realized that we did not have a problem but they certainly did. Since my many experiences in Hokkaido I learned to develop what I call an 'attitude for survival' and it has helped me overcome many painful situations. Although I have taught my son to speak up in the face of prejudice, I have also taught him that it pays to be slow to anger because anger consumes a person and consequently taints one's judgment. So far he has done just that. When he entered the higher grades the teasing and harassment got worse. Some children would also call him at home using derogatory remarks. He never ran away from his classmates, but confronted them with words rather than violence. He always came home to let out his anger. I would always encourage him to be calm and strong in order to survive, and would always remind him that they – his generation of Ainu children – have it easier than us, their parents. I have also instilled in him a strong sense of being Ainu, unlike our parents as well as teachers who often attributed our mistakes to our ethnicity. At a very young age at home and in school we often heard the statement, "You are no good in anything because you are Ainu." I hated this statement, and unfortunately many of the children I grew up with internalized such feelings of worthlessness. I let my son know that if he failed math, English, or any subject matter it was not because of his being Ainu; rather it was because he did not give it the time and effort it deserved. Ainu families need to play a major role in helping the younger generation regain their Ainu identity, language and culture. The future of the Ainu peoples depends on the social environment of Japan. Lots of Japanese families learned to devalue and disrespect the Ainu people, while some treat us as if we did not exist at all. Such attitudes were instilled in the younger generation. The Japanese government, teachers and the schools also served as conduits to perpetuate such attitudes. It will thus take the government, schools and the society at large to correct the past mistakes. I tend to be pessimistic. While on the one side I realize and appreciate efforts and the strides made by the Ainu people, on the other I see little real change for the better.

I am not sure if the Japanese government and society at large is listening to the Ainu people. Until then we will remain the marginalized and the voiceless on our own land.

My Story: Elder Kayano

Let me begin by presenting what I wrote in my book, *Our Land was a Forest*, published in 1994:

> *With just a glance at that piece of katsura, I, a woodcutter for twenty years, can still conjure up images of the dense woods in the mountains behind Nibutani. It was a forest of katsura, with herds of deer roaming through it. Whenever the Ainu needed meat, they entered the woods with bows and arrows and hunted as many deer as they desired. Sometimes they made sakankekam, or dried venison, and stored it. And in the Saru River, whose pure water flows beneath the mountain with its beautiful katsura woods, salmon struggled upstream in the autumn. The Ainu caught only as many salmon as they needed, and removing the innards, they split the fish open to dry or smoked them for later use. Long before my time, Nibutani was such a fertile region. During the Edo period, however, the shamo (mainland Japanese) came into the area and finding the Ainu living in this vast and rich landscape, forced them to labor as fishermen. Then in the Meiji era the shamo started taking over on a larger scale. Ignoring the ways of the Ainu, who had formulated hunting and woodcutting practices in accordance with the cycles of nature, the shamo came up with arbitrary "laws" that led to the destruction of the beautiful woods of Nibutani for the profit of "the nation of Japan" and the corporate giants. With this, half of the Nibutani region ceased to be a land of natural bounty.*

Japan is made up of many islands, one of the largest being the northernmost island of *Ainu mosir*, also known as Hokkaido. In the southern part of the island on the Pacific side is the Hidaka region. The Shishirimuka River is the longest of rivers running through Hidaka. Until about one hundred years ago, the Ainu were blessed with an abundance of God-given food: the mountains provided them with trees, the forest offered animals, and the rivers provided salmon. Thus, the Ainu considered Nature – mountains, forests, and rivers – as the food source to be shared by everyone.

There are different opinions about how long the Ainu have lived in Hokkaido. Some scholars say that they have lived on the island for ten thousand years, while others say it has only been five or seven thousand years. We, the Ainu people, know that since Indigenous times we lived along the Saru River region with its mild climate and rich supply of food, dotting the landscape with our communities. I believe it is to the Saru that Ainu culture can trace its origins, for the *kamuy yukar* say that the river is the land of *Okikurmikamuy*. This is the god who taught folk wisdom to the Ainu: how to build houses, fish, raise millet, and so forth. We, the Saru River Ainu, pride ourselves on being from the land where the god *Okikurmikamuy* was born. Whenever we greet other Ainu from neighboring hamlets, we first identify ourselves in the following manner: 'I am so-and so, living and working in the village to which *Okikurmikamuy* descended from the heavens and taught us our folk wisdom.' The other person would take a step back and welcome us respectfully, replying, 'Ah, you're so-and-so of the village where the god *Okikurmikamuy* lived.'

It was not until recently that I discovered the origins of the name *Nibutani*, which lies at about the midpoint of the Saru River. An acquaintance by the name of Nagai Hiroshi brought me an 1892 map on which the valley and its surroundings were labeled

Niputay, which must come from *nitay*. *Nitay* means 'woods, forest, or jungle.' It was this map that finally made me realize the evolution of the Japanized name *Nibutani*. Like my ancestors, I was born and raised in the hills about 13 miles (21 kilometers) upriver from the ocean. I was born in 1926 in the country of *Ainu-Nibutani* Village which is the basin of Shishirimuka. We, the Ainu, have lived in the northern part of the Japanese islands – from northern Tohoku on Honshu and Hokkaido to Sakhalin and the Kurile Islands – since ancient times. We spoke the Ainu language, which is completely different from the Japanese language, and cultivated our own distinctive culture. From early childhood, *Huci*, my grandmother, had a great influence on me. I thus draw strength and some of the Ainu folk wisdom I will be sharing with you from her. She had tattoos around her mouth that served as a protection against evil spirits. I learned from her that in early times our ancestors nurtured our culture through a strong respect for and interaction with the environment, and through trading with the Chinese, Koreans, and Russians, the northern Indigenous people of Asia and Alaska, and of course with the Yamato race – ancestors of the majority of Japanese today.

Huci had several grandchildren but I was her favorite. When telling a story she would start by saying my name, but because she had problems pronouncing 'Shigeru,' she would say 'Shimeru.' As soon as I responded she would then begin telling the tale without stopping her work at the spindle. These were great tales that were interwoven with words of wisdom for carrying out daily chores and lessons for life. One of the most interesting tales that she often repeated because she believed that it taught us something was about a young girl who was considerate of the elderly. Her behavior towards the elderly was praised by other people and the gods. She grew up to become a happy and respected adult. Many of the folktales I learnt from *Huci* are told in my book, *The Ainu Uwepekere – Folktales* (1985). I will share with you my favorite one:

Why the Brown Hawk Owl Is Ugly

A long time ago, there was a time when the brown hawk owl was not as ugly as it is today. The hawk owl, forgetting who he was, imagined that he was the most handsome creature in the world and wanted to marry the most beautiful girl in the country, who was the sister of Okikurmi, the god of Culture. The gods came to know this and decided to make fun of him. They told the owl that if he wanted her badly and if he worked hard and made his fortune they would let him marry her.

The owl was delighted to hear this and worked hard because he really wanted to marry the beautiful goddess. He went to the mountains very early in the morning to hunt bears and deer and brought them all to Okikurmi and his sister. However, it did not seem that Okikurmi would give his sister. Nevertheless, believing that his dream would come true some day, he hunted deer day after day, roasting the venison over a fire, catching the drippings in an iron pot and storing them in a wooden bowl called nima.

One day, the owl went to the mountains to hunt animals as usual. When he came home, he found that the fat was all gone. There was none left in the bowl. He asked Okikurmi and his sister whether they knew anything about it or not, but they said they didn't. However, the owl saw a smudge of white fat on her nikotoro, the roof of her mouth. When the owl noticed it, he glared at them fiercely and made a formal complaint, charanke, about it.

Flashing a big smile at him, Okikurmi took a fishing net out of his treasure box. Then he gave it to the owl saying, "You can catch as many fish as you want if you use this magic net. I will give it to you as a token of my heartfelt apology."

The hawk owl was pleased and went down to the river right away. He cast the fishing net over a stretch of water where swarms of fish were swimming, but all the fish scattered and the net was washed away and lost in the water. The owl became angry and complained loudly. This time Okikurmi took a reaping hook out of this treasure box and handed it to him saying, 'This hook can reap thatch reeds all by itself.' Hearing this, the owl took the reaping hook to the thatch reed field and waited for days. But nothing happened. Again, the owl became angry at it and threw it far away over the other side of the mountain. Everybody heard the owl grumbling. Then Okikurmi showed him a broadaxe saying, "If you lay this axe by the root of a tree, it will fell the tree all by itself."

Believing what Okikurmi had told him, the owl took the axe to the mountain and placed it by a tree. The next morning he went back only to find the axe as he had left it. Day after day the axe remained there without felling any trees. The owl became angrier than ever and threw the axe away to the far side of the river. He came back to Okikurmi and again made charanke about it.

Finally Okikurmi, looking serious, said, "I will give you a real nice thing this time," and gave the owl a kind of hood called onanchisapanpe. Then the owl asked Okikurmi, "What is it used for?" The god answered, "If you wear it when it is very cold, it will keep you warm." Delighted to hear this, the owl put on the hood. Certainly, it kept him very warm in the cold wintertime. However, when the hot summer came and the owl wanted to take it off, he could not do so. It was stuck to his head. Alas, the two corners of the deerskin hood had become his long ears.

'This is why I have become as ugly as you see me now. Therefore, I say to all birds, don't strive to marry beyond your position with humans but seek to marry creatures of your own kind," said the afunrasanpe, the brown hawk owl.

Huci taught us how to take care of the forest. She reminded us that plants are not to be killed, but that we need to take good care of them. One must not arbitrarily cut down trees and one must not pollute running water. She added that even beasts and birds will remember kindness and return favors someday. We need to take care of the rivers, the oceans and the mountains that surround us because they are a treasure box which nurture us.

In addition to sharing with us the Ainu folk wisdom and *uwepekere*, *Huci* also told many *kamuy yukar* – tales about the Ainu gods. She revered and showed great respect towards the gods. She told us that gods dwell in each element of the great earth. 'The gods look just like human beings,' she taught, 'they speak the same language, they sleep at night, and work in the land of gods at day time.' As a child, I must admit that I trustingly accepted as truth these tales about gods. At the age of four, we were on our way to visit our relatives. As we approached a little creek below the Nibutani communal graveyard, *Huci* called out, *'Kukor son ponno entere'* (Grandson, wait a moment for me). As I stood still, she put aside her cane, sat down at the edge of the creek, and removed her headdress. Washing her hands and face in the creek, she turned to me and said, 'Wash yourself too, Shimeru.' After I had done as she asked, she said, 'You are going to grow up, and your *Huci* will die. Whenever you pass this creek after I am gone, I want you to remember that this is where you washed with your *Huci.'* Although nowadays the creek no longer exists because the government built a road in that area, I always recall *Huci* whenever I pass that area. I am proud to say that even though more than fifty years have gone by, her wish still lives on in my heart, and I will always fulfill it whenever I go past the area where the creek once was.

The concept of the gods as I learned from *Huci* is different from the god of the Japanese. In the modern time for example, military leaders are worshiped as if they were gods and are often given the status of heroes. In Japan, there is a saying that if you kill a person you are a murderer, however, if you kill a million, you are a hero. Given this understanding, around the Middle Ages the Japanese and Europeans waged military and biological wars that killed millions of Indigenous peoples around the world and thus became 'heroes.' In contrast to this, grandma taught me that we, the Ainu people, believe that all creation – the living and any aspects of nature – have a life and deserve respect. We believe that leaders are not born, but acquire certain leadership skills by living and acting in certain ways. The most important qualities being eloquence, good looks, courage, honesty, knowledge about one's people and culture, respect for humanity, and a great sense of humor. The Ainu people are known for their jokes, which can be dirty sometimes!

Although in the past we had many disputes with the Japanese government, it is time to look forward. Today the Ainu people mainly live in Hokkaido, Japan's northernmost island. While surveys conducted by the Hokkaido government put the Ainu population at 24 000, there are several tens of thousands of Ainu who don't claim to be Ainu because of the fear of discrimination, or who were not included in the government survey because they live in other parts of Japan. Many Ainu are economically disadvantaged due to our ethnic and social background. Today, however, many Ainu have begun to feel pride and confidence in their cultural identity. Like the First Nations of North America, we are trying to preserve and gain respect for our traditional culture and to achieve social and economic independence.

From our conversation, my books, and in the museum you will hear, read and see with your naked eye many aspects of Ainu traditional life, ceremony, and our spiritual culture. However, I want you to understand that in contrast to what anthropologists and other so-called experts say about our ways of life, you should understand that this is not a dead culture, and that our wisdom does not belong to antiquity. For example, contemporary Ainu art, our foods, language, and ways of living are a testimony of the creative strength of the Ainu spirit, and an indicator of a 'living' culture. In addition to the books, the Ainu dictionary and many short stories, I have been a catalyst in the establishment of the Nibutani Ainu Language. There is a school in my backyard. Such schools have since spread to a dozen communities in Hokkaido. I also started the Nibutani Museum of Ainu Cultural Resources. However, after a few years of operation, the Biratori township indicated that it wanted to take it over. Rather than hold onto that collection I decided to donate it to Biratori. Instead I started another one with Ainu folk crafts and collections from other Indigenous peoples around the world. In July 1992, I resigned as a member of the Biratori town council, on which I had served seventeen years and three months over five terms. Having left the town council and having failed to win a seat in the Diet, I am back home to enjoy a freedom I have not known for many years. In the Ainu language there is a saying: 'One should go home while it's light enough to see one's own foot,' and I did just that.

Lungi's story

As we were about to leave, Keibo requested elder Kayano's permission to take pictures. He happily agreed to that. As I got closer to him to pose for the picture with him, I could not resist the temptation of putting my arm on his shoulder. The wisdom he shared with us, and the charm of this seventy-four-year-old man drew me closer to him. After the picture was taken, he said with a naughty smile, 'I hope you realize what you have gotten yourself into, because by touching an Ainu man a woman gets pregnant!' We all burst into laughter. As we were leaving I shook his hand and told him that I would see him the following year. He replied, 'Yes, and carrying my baby on your back!'

We arrived at the Kaizawa's home in Nibutani on the evening of August 14. We were met by his wife Miwako and their daughter Tamami. Koichi and Miwako practice organic farming. I was deeply honored the following morning when they agreed to my request to join them in the cornfield for a harvest, and later that morning to join Miwako in her vegetable garden for weeding. At first they resisted my request saying that I was only a visitor and should not worry about going to the field. To sort of twist their arm to agree to my request I had to bring in folk wisdom from the African culture, which maintains that a visitor is a visitor for a day, after that you give them a hoe. I told them that I was ready for a hoe. On the evening of our arrival they had prepared a delicious meal of well-marinated and seasoned lamb, fresh corn, pumpkin and fresh vegetables that were organically grown from their garden. We enjoyed the meal and a wonderful conversation in their garage while watching the full moon. The following evening, after a full day's work, I had an opportunity to hear Koichi's story.

Koichi's Story

The major issue for me concerns the redress of the unjust past: the Nibutani Saru River Dam Case. I was born here in Nibutani in 1946. 'Ko' which is part of my name Koichi means 'to cultivate.' It was given to me by my grandfather, whose desire was that I become a farmer. Both my grandfather and my father lived during the time of assimilation. My grandfather in particular believed that the way for me to escape prejudice and discrimination was to reject the Ainu traditional ways of hunting and gathering and become a farmer. Farming has been part of my life since childhood, but I am not sure if it has made a big difference in terms of being discriminated against by the Japanese government.

My father, the late Tadashi Kaizawa, was one of the Ainu icons and legends who fought to preserve the Saru River and the lands surrounding Nibutani village. The majority of this land was given to the Ainu as 'allowance land' by the Japanese government in the Meiji period. As my father neared his death he said, '… with this dam as my screen, I can deliver the voices of the Ainu to a country and a government that has never once tried to listen.' He was photographed standing in silent protest in a buckwheat field that is now underwater.

Kayano and my father owned pieces of farmland that were going to be flooded by the construction of the dam. However, for them the issue was not only about the fate of the farmland, but was about the preservation of the land that their ancestors had enjoyed, the culture, Ainu identity, history, and the spiritual nourishment that come from this land. Out of thirty thousand rivers in Japan, only two had not been either dammed or modified in some way. For the Saru Ainu who live on the banks of this river, destroying the river meant the destruction of their livelihood and culture. Nibutani as it is described in the legends and mythology is a sacred Ainu place and it has the largest Ainu population in Hokkaido.

In 1996, ignoring the protests of Ainu and other local residents, the government constructed a dam on the Saru River. Although the dam's efficiency has been questioned and the Sapporo District Court has mandated compensation to the Ainu because their lands and rights were violated by the construction, the existence of the dam is a modern example of continued Japanese violence to Ainu lands and culture. Before the dam was built the river was crystal clear. We could easily see the river bottom more than seven feet, or two meters below, and the clean water also prevented the rocks from getting slippery. During the summer we children often went to the river on our own to play; with 85-degree days few and far between one barely called it 'summer' in Hokkaido. We were nearly always swimming on cold days. We used to gather up driftwood and light a fire so we could warm ourselves after swimming. Tired and hungry, we would sometimes sneak into a nearby field and swipe potatoes and corn to cook over the fire. We grilled fish too, whenever we managed to catch some.

Although less than fifty years have passed since my grandfather harvested lumber in these mountains, nowadays the logging companies use bulldozers and power shovels to cut trees year-round. They tear into the mountainsides and build roads so that their trucks can haul logs from the very tops of the mountains. After the trees have been hauled away the smallest amount of rain washes the soil from the abandoned roads, carrying it down into the river. Such reckless deforestation, combined with the drainage of nonsewage wastewater, has left the Saru River (as the Japanese renamed it Shishirimuka) thoroughly polluted.

In 1996 the central government completed the construction of another dam on the same Saru River. The dam's original purpose was to supply water to a planned industrial sector some 38 miles, or 60 kilometers away in Tomakomai. The proposed industrial development was eventually deemed a mistake, and as the plans for the industrial park underwent thorough reconsideration only the dam was built. Despite having lost its primary purpose, the Nibutani dam was constructed and is now producing 3 000 kilowatts, enough to provide electricity for 1 000 households. It is also destroying some of the surrounding irrigation systems by forcing dam water into them. With only 140 households, the village of Nibutani has a population of just less than 500, more than 70 percent of whom are of Ainu heritage. Nibutani has the densest population of Ainu in the world. It was here that the government chose to build a dam.

In our village we have a ceremony known as the *chip-sanke*. With the government's policies to assimilate the Ainu into Japanese culture and threatening to extinguish Ainu culture, Diet member and Ainu cultural leader Shigeru Kayano endeavored to, at the very least, preserve this custom in the form of a festival. In the Ainu language, *chip* means 'boat,' and *sanke* means 'to bring down.' It was originally a ceremony to mark the first launching of a new boat. Begun twenty-nine years ago, the festival is held to ensure that the boats now being housed in museums are floated upon the river at least once each year. This festival is held not only for us, the Ainu, but for all people.

In August 1996, four months after the dam halted the river's flow, the floodgates were opened one last time for the sake of the festival. With the water draining faster than usual, it took only four days for the river to return to its normal flow. Although the water had been stagnant for only four months, the river bottom was now covered with sludge, four inches (ten centimeters) thick in shallow water and as much as ten inches (thirty centimeters) thick in the deeper areas. A foul smell emanated from the water and drifted throughout the village as the wind changed directions, and the riverbanks were so choked with silt that it was impossible to walk along them. The government hauled away the silt and spread gravel alongside the river. Somehow we managed to hold the *chip-sanke*, but the water level rose to its former height only three days after the festival; thus it would seem that the government's stated alternative purpose for the dam, flood control, is not really the case.

Before his death on 3 February 1992, my father, Tadashi Kaizawa, joined with Shigeru Kayano to oppose the construction of the Nibutani dam. They first filed a legal objection to the confiscation of their land by the Hokkaido Land Expropriation Committee. A total of 15 attorneys assisted them without promise of compensation, and more than 10 000 people showed their support by signing a petition. My father and Kayano argued the following points as they presented their case to the Land Expropriation Committee, the Ministry of Construction, and the Sapporo District court: the Ainu people are historically the Indigenous people of Japan; by failing to consider the needs and wishes of the Ainu people, construction of the dam was illegal; and construction of the dam has robbed those Ainu living in Nibutani of their culture.

My father was given only two opportunities to present his opinion officially, once before the Hokkaido Land Expropriation Committee at its first hearing on 15 February 1988, and again on 26 April of the following year during an on-site inspection. The committee handed down his decision: approval of the forced expropriation, one year later, on 3 February 1989. The plaintiffs quickly filed a request for an investigation with the Minister of Construction, provided under the Land Expropriation Act, but it was another two years before they were able to present statements to the Construction Ministry on a bitterly cold March day in 1991.

By that time my father had undergone surgery for cancer and had suffered a relapse. The doctor informed us that he had only six months to live. We went to a room, one that is not usually open to the public, on the first floor of the Ministry of Construction. We were not served tea and the room was without a heater. It must have been a difficult time for my father. Nevertheless, hiding his pain, he made his appeal:

> This concrete monstrosity has become a symbol of the environmental degradation of the peaceful land around *Nibutani's* Saru River. How, indeed, would it look to the Ainu *ekashi* and *fuchi* [male and female elders] who, since ancient times, lived on this land and thought always of the welfare of their descendants? We, their descendants, have been silent and obedient in the face of these evils of civilization. During this long history, we have lived through struggle and oppression facing one thing after another. No one stops to listen to our voices because those in power want only to see results, and so the building goes on and on. I cannot predict whether or not I will live until the dam is completed, but I have resolved to build a little house on the land my ancestors left to me. When the water is dammed up, I will become a human sacrifice at the bottom of that lake. If I did not do this, I would have no explanation for my ancestors when I join them. Someone must accept responsibility for the destruction of *Aimu mosir.*

My father finished his statement, but even before we left the building he turned to me and said, 'Koichi, take my place.' Exactly one year later on 3 February 1992 my father closed his eyes for the last time at Oji Hospital in Tomakomai. On 27 May 1993 I went with Shigeru Kayano to the Sapporo District Court and together we filed a lawsuit demanding a reversal of the decision by the Hokkaido Land Expropriation Committee. When the court handed down its verdict on 27 March 1997, Judge Ichimiya read from the decision:

> From a historical viewpoint, the Ainu are an Indigenous people and lived here well before our country began its rule. Furthermore, keeping in mind the historical sequence of events that precipitated the decline of the Ainu culture, in a situation where the utmost consideration was called for, there was instead unjust negligence and utter disregard, and it was therefore illegal.

Despite the above ruling the court approved the dam's continued existence, and so from the government's point of view the matter is nearly closed. It is now merely the scurrying to find justification for the completed dam.

The day will come when the folly of the Nibutani dam will finally be acknowledged. They will then open the floodgates, letting the Shishirimuka River return to its original state and the dam will become a 70-billion-yen bridge. It must be left standing though, as proof of the aggression against the Ainu and to symbolize our 'empty inheritance,' if only so that people will understand that all humans are equal!

As we concluded the conversation I asked Koichi, 'What keeps you going?' 'Being an advocate for the Ainu people is the foundation of being human,' he said.

'To be human one does not exist for the pleasure of himself or herself. After all, we are all dependent on one another and on nature that surrounds us. We do not live in isolation, but are interdependent on one another within and outside of Japan. My mission and my calling is to give a voice to the losses and acts of discrimination the Ainu people have suffered in the hands of the Japanese government. I am sharing this information with you this evening so that the whole world that is made up of Indigenous and non-Indigenous peoples may know our plight. We need to keep educating communities in Japan and around the world that the Ainu peoples are still discriminated to the present day. I believe that together with the international community we can make the Japanese government listen to our cause.'

On 27 October 2000, after our visit in Nibutani, we traveled to the eastern part of Hokkaido to the town of Akan that faces Lake Akan. We were met at the train station by Keibo's dear friend Yuriko Takiguch. She had invited her other family members and friends to welcome us at the train station and to join us for lunch. This was another emotional moment that will remain etched in my heart. After lunch we drove to the town of Akan, popular for its hot springs and summer holiday resort for Japanese tourists from the mainland. At the edge of the town there was a section called *Ainu Kotan,* which means Ainu village. The village was set up for the Ainu by a wealthy local landlord and is primarily a tourist attraction. The main street goes up a small hill and on either side are stores with colorful facades, selling everything from highly artistic sculptures and crafts to cheap plastic souvenirs. Many salesclerks dress in traditional Ainu costumes and wear embroidered headbands. At the top of the slope is a large thatched hut where groups from the community perform traditional music and dance at regularly scheduled times.

The Takiguchis own a small craft store on this street. In a way the couple is symbolic of the future of the Ainu. Yuriko, an Ainu woman originally from Tokachi, is an artisan practicing traditional embroidery and knitting and is also active in various communal cultural activities. For our arrival, she had collected all kinds of mountain vegetables and filled the table with incredible dishes. In spite of her limp, she bustled about her house to keep us supplied with food and drink, her large friendly eyes promising to break into laughter. Her husband, Masamitsu or Mas as we called him, a deaf-mute Japanese sculptor, was born in 1941 in Manchuria, the northeastern part of China where Japan had set up a puppet regime during the Second World War. Living conditions were very rough there, thanks to the war, and he developed pneumonia when he was three years old, resulting in his loss of hearing and speech. After his family returned to Japan he entered a school for the deaf and eventually took up crafts, which had became his lifelong passion. At twenty-two he traveled to Hokkaido where he met Yuriko, fell in love, and eventually married. Since then, eastern Hokkaido has been his home. As a wood carver, he has earned many prizes and given exhibitions in both Hokkaido and Tokyo. He narrated the following:

I work only with wood because it has *tamashii* (soul). Each tree has its own personality. I can tell by the texture, hardness, and color. A tree strives to grow, twists, and turns in its struggle. To slice it straight is sad after it tried so hard to grow for many years. If it is crooked there are reasons for it. So each curve is important. When I look at it, I see life and try to imagine why it went like that. When I see the flow of the grain, I could see the wind in it. The series of sculptures I did called 'Kaze' (Wind) was inspired by the wind I saw in the tree. The tree has life. The tree is quiet but it is praying quietly. Maybe I am crazy, but I do believe a soul is there.

To Masamitsu, dead wood is not really dead. He demonstrated this by carving a piece for us. His work never imposes on nature; rather it helps nature express herself. One of the most common images in his pieces was a fairy-tale-like woman. Just like the Chinese folktale in which a baby girl emerges from a bamboo tree, the faces on Takiguchi's figures spring forth from the natural grains and shapes of the weathered driftwood. He would take a large trunk of the dead tree, but would carve only a small section of it. As he showed us, his conservative strokes furnished a beauty and depth to the wood.

Before the end of our visit with the Takiguchis, Mas decided to take us to the Akan National Park and Lake Onneto. This lake lies on the eastern part of Ashoro Town, on the southeast edge of Akan National Park. *Onneto*, which means 'old and large pond' in the Ainu language, was formed long ago when the lava flow blocked a stream. It is particularly breathtaking to watch the bluish greenish water moving up and down the lake. Because of its spectacular and colorful water it is sometimes called a mysterious lake. The looks of the water change with the weather. On the morning of our visit it was a beautiful and sunny day and the water kept changing from a greenish to a sort of bluish color. We were told that the color of the water is especially gorgeous on the cold winter night. As we stood by the lake appreciating this unspoiled beauty we could not help but think that undefiled nature is our precious possession. After we had enjoyed the beauty of the lake to our hearts' content, Mas led us to his 'real home,' the woods. As he led us along the trail, he stopped every time to communicate with us using his hands, lips, and grunts whenever he spotted some tree or piece of wood that attracted his attention and described how he might carve something out of it.

Conclusion

Soon it was time for us to depart and for me to leave my beloved Ainu friends in Japan. I will never forget this very moving experience of realizing the power of Indigenous peoples' knowledge in an industrialized country that clearly did not appreciate the beauty and power of its first people, whose wisdom and life give rich meaning to our existence but are denigrated because they have refused to assimilate. Instead they are just but themselves, as people are in so many other parts of the world.

Chapter 11

Coming Home to the Earth Household: Indigenous Communities and Ecological Citizenship in India

Pramod Parajuli

> Without land, we will float like a tortoise.
> – *Adivasi* folksong in the Jharkhand region, India[1]

Summary

Under the rubric of ecological ethnicities and ecological citizenship, I explain why the resolution of ecological conflicts requires self-governance for the communities who are most affected by the lack of governing power. For what kinds of citizenship rights do they aspire? Have ecological ethnicities enlarged the parameters of nationality and citizenship? Why Indigenous groups fighting to stop the construction of large dams or to gain control over forests and mineral resources pursued the principle, 'our rule in our villages.' Why are ecological movements combined with ethnoregional movements in Jharkhand and other parts of middle India? These issues raise even broader questions: How might ecological issues have changed the patterns of social contradictions in society? As the globalization of the economy shifted the conventional role of the nation-state, how will the issue of governance and autonomy be settled? Have the ecological ethnicities lost faith in the welfare schemes of India? Who are the new social actors and what symbolic productivity have they brought into social movement discourses? Do these actors and movements signify any redefinition of citizenship and nationality? I conclude by exploring plural identities and citizenships in this struggle of ecological ethnicities for life and nationhood in India.

---

1 The word *adivasi* is derived from two Sanskrit words: *adi* (original) and *vasi* (inhabitant). The survey, *People of India's Volume 3* (1994) estimates that India has 461 tribal communities, out of which 174 are subgroups. Throughout the article, I will use the word adivasi instead of 'tribal' unless the word 'tribe' or 'tribal' is used in the original sources.

Coming Home to the Earth Household: Interrogating Ecological Discourses

> Indigenous peoples know their region. They must know where the food is, where water is available, where firewood is found, where the medicinal plants are, where the trees grow that furnish poles for their tents or the wood for their fires.
>
> Thomas Berry[2]

To appreciate the aspirations of ecological ethnicities, I will critically examine each of their ecological discourses, worldviews and strategies. It is important to recognize why the mainstream ecological discourses are incapable of representing the worldviews of these ethnic groups. Within the umbrella of ecological ethnicity, I include a range of agro-ecological worldviews espoused by the world's more than 500 million Indigenous peoples, perhaps 2 billion peasants, and other cultures of habitat such as fisherfolk, seedkeepers, forest dwellers and nomadic shepherds. Combined together, ecological ethnicities actually comprise what Esteva and Prakash call the 'social majorities' of the world.[3] I refer to these communities as ecological ethnicities because the conventional categories based solely on caste, tribe, language or even religion are inadequate to describe their agonies and struggles today. The notion of ecological ethnicity refers to any group of people who derive their livelihood through day-to-day negotiation with their immediate environment.[4]

These ecological ethnicities have their own form of environmentalism. Modern environmentalism as we know it has come of age globally; beginning in 1970, it is more than three decades old. The time is ripe to critically look at what has been said and done in the name of environmentalism, and what has been left out. For the sake of simplicity, I identify three distinct schools of thought, discourses, plans of action, and choices available to us: Earth as wild and sacred, Earth as a factory and Earth as a household.

The first and perhaps the most common-sense view is that the Earth is wild and sacred so we as humans should protect it and revere it. Humans should not be around her except for times of meditation, nature walks, hiking and contemplation. Among others, Henry Thoreau, John Muir, Leo Tolstoy, and Edward Abby are famous for championing such views and are aptly considered the 'bachelors' of nature. The most

---

2   Thomas Berry, *The Great Work: Our Way into the Future*. New York: Bell Tower. p. 99. 2000.

3   Gustavo Esteva and Madhu Sarin Prakash, Grassroots Postmodernism. London: Zed Press. 1997.

4   Pramod Parajuli, "Revisiting Gandhi and Zapata: Motion of Global Capital, Geographies of Difference and the Formation of Ecological Ethnicities" in Mario Blaser et al, *In the way of Development: Indigenous Peoples, Life Projects and Globalization*. London: Zed Press. Chapter 14, pp. 235–255. 2004; "How Can Four Trees Make a Jungle?" *The World and the Wild*. Tucson: The University of Arizona Press, pp. 3–20. 2001, also available at www.terrain.org/essays/14/parajuli.html; "Learning from Ecological Ethnicities: Towards a Plural Political Ecology of Knowledge" in *Indigenous Traditions and Ecology*, John Grim, ed. Harvard University Press, pp. 559–589. 2001.

recent manifestation is the fascination with the idea of wilderness, nature reserves and sanctuaries as a form of saving and protecting nature. This has grown to be a big industry in itself, with the credo: Nature is purer if it is untouched by humans. So as the logic here goes, we should have fewer people and more nature. In an extremist version, this might justify killing, eliminating and displacing people in order to save nature. But the question remains: who is dispensable and who is not?[5]

These are real worldviews informing real people in real time. I am conversing with one of my doctoral students here at Portland State University in Portland, Oregon, who is an avid hiker in the woods and a long-time teacher of outdoors education. She recently reflected: 'the irony is that as I connect more deeply with nature, I become more disconnected from my own species – the humans.' But in her mind she knows that she should be more accepting and loving of humans as another expression of the cosmos's creativity and beauty. How do we recognize and empathize with these sentiments and predicaments as she and many of my students in North America are facing? Perhaps there is a reason why this thinking has a strong hold on my students and many others embedded in the techno-industrial world. Perhaps it is just a natural response. When you don't like this techno-industrial life you want to run away from it and get wild, but that emotional release is achieved only at the expense of escaping from human society. But I wonder rather than embracing life, why should we escape from it at all?

The second view is the extreme antithesis of the first, and I would like to put it within the rubric of 'Earth as a factory.' The idea here is to tame, subdue and extract from nature. We have seen enough of the 'hit and run' model of clear-cutting and monoculture in agriculture, forestry, mining and dam building. This is the story of the all too familiar mainstream techno-industrial worldview which sees nature as an obstacle to progress and the expansion of the frontier. The ideal for this worldview would be if nature could operate in the model of a machine – measurable, quantifiable, predictable and thus controllable. Here the primal desire is to have control and it has been achieved by teasing single variables out of complex natural and human systems. This sort of reductionist science has created a bubble economy while destroying nature's integrity. With clear-cut forestry, large dams, smokestacks and paved roads as their glorious evidence, humanity has come a long way to realize this bad dream. But the agonies brought about by this view abound and are beginning to be felt and seen everywhere. This is no longer a path we can pursue, pleads ecological theologian Thomas Berry. Instead he urges us to create and pursue a new universe story where we change from a human-centered to an Earth-centered frame of reality. Our technologies would mimic nature's technologies, where human activity would create a minimum of entropy, unusable and unfruitful waste.[6]

---

5   For a critical reading of the nature conservation tradition from a peasant perspective, please read Pramod Parajuli, "How can Four Trees Make a Jungle?" available at: www.terrain. org/essays/14/parajuli.html

6   Thomas Berry, *The Great Work*.

How would such a new story look and who will pursue it? In this chapter I open that possibility through the third ecological discourse, and use the rubric of Earth as a household to do so. Interestingly, although espoused by the social majorities of the world, this ecological discourse remains the most often misunderstood and least talked about in the mainstream of ecological discourse. Indian ecological historian Ram Chandra Guha has aptly commented that the Indian environmental debate is an argument in the cities about what is happening in the countryside. How then do ecological ethnicities – those who mostly live in forested and rural areas and who have to establish a healthy relationship with their immediate environment – comprehend nature and define human/nature relationships? What is their stake in nurturing and maintaining biocultural diversity? By biocultural diversity I mean nurturing a totality of species, populations, communities and ecosystems, both wild and domesticated, that constitute the life of any one or overlapping ecosystems. It is not merely the sum of biological ecosystems but also the human modification of this ecological niche – the embedded cultural element, the stories, the rituals, the performance, and the multiversatility of interaction among humans and more than human species. Thus it is not merely the sum of biological ecosystems but also the human modification and nurturing of this ecological niche.[7] This is how we can explain why wherever there are ecological ethnicities there is an abundance of biological and linguistic diversity. As this chapter will show, the ecological view has tremendous significance to chart out a distinct strategy of redefining the realm of governance, the resilience of community, and the promise of ecological citizenship.

The Agro-ecological Earth Household

The soil is the great connector of our lives, the source and destination of all.

Wendell Berry, Farmer-Poet, Port Royal, Kentucky, USA

Let me elaborate a bit more on this agro-ecological worldview of ecological ethnicities. Agro-ecology basically means doing agriculture according to ecological designs and principles. Doing so, you can get agricultural crops without overtaxing and in some cases actually enhancing nature's vital energies. In economic terms, you could say you are using the interest rather than the principal sum of nature in doing agriculture and pursuing your livelihoods. In a nutshell, a move towards

---

7   For an in-depth exploration of biocultural diversity, please read Gary Paul Nabhan, *Cultures of Habitat: On Culture, Nature and Story*. Washington DC: Counterpoint Press, 1987; and Luisa Maffi ed., "Introduction: On the interdependence of biological and cultural diversity" in *On Biocultural Diversity: Linking Language, Knowledge and the Environment*. pp. 1–50. Washington DC: Smithsonian Institution Press, 2001. You can read Nabhan, Maffi and a number of authors working in this tradition at www.terralingua.org.

agro-ecology from this techno-industrial society is a move from an emphasis on the accumulation of 'technomass' to an emphasis on the nurturing of 'biomass.'[8]

Among others, poet and ecological philosopher Gary Snyder eloquently represents this view when he suggests that we find a place, dig in and stay put. This view carves the middle path between the other two views above by overcoming the projection of culture and nature as binary opposites, a deeply entrenched view in the techno-industrial mindset. In the agro-ecological worldview, those who tend the land are considered housewife or househusband who nurture biocultural diversity. The idea of husbandry or housewifery is a mode of using and being in nature that I call the 'moral ecology of using nature.' In this mode there is a possibility of overusing and/or abusing nature but in the majority of the cases ecological ethnicities have been appropriately using nature. A majority of peasant and Indigenous cultures and ecological thinkers and activists, such as Vandana Shiva and Mahatma Gandhi in South Asia and Wendell Berry, Gary Nabhan and Gary Snyder in North America share such views. In some ways Emiliano Zapata's 'land and liberty' in Mexico and Sandino's struggle for land in Nicaragua, and other 'land to the tiller' movements can be recognized in this framework.

The poet-farmer Wendell Berry from Port Royal, Kentucky, firmly believes that the alternative to the techno-industrial culture is not to go wild, nor is it to pursue a hunting-gathering mode of life. The alternative is agro-ecology based on the husbandry and housewifery of land. He farms using horses, following seasons and native plants of the region. Berry urges that before we choose any technology we should always ask: What is possible here? What do we already have here? Let us start with that. What kind of climate is it? What elevation is it? Where is the nearest forest? Where is the river system and what does the river give us? What kinds of birds migrate to and from here? What pollinators serve the flora and fauna freely? What kind of diversity do you have? And most important, will the new technology strengthen or weaken our immediate community?[9]

The option ahead of us, as Wendell Berry aptly says, is not whether to live with or without nature. We can afford to live only with and in nature. But we can choose how, in what scale, in what speed and velocity, with what degrees of reciprocity we want to live in nature. So the division between the wild and domestic is the function of a techno-industrial mindset. The answer is not in creating national parks and sanctuaries; the challenge is in creating different ethics for using nature.[10]

---

8   See my "Homewardbound: Agroecological Civilization and the Quest for a Sustainable Society" available at: http://www.talkingleaves.org/s04homeward.htm

9   There is a rich material available on the internet for Wendell Berry's prolific writings on the agrarian mind. I specially suggest *Home Economics*. San Francisco: North Point Press, 1987.

10 For further discussion on this, please read my article, *"How Can Four Trees Make a Jungle?"* available at: www.terrain.org/essays/14/parajuli.htm).

Nurturing Biocultural Diversity

Among other things, ecological ethnicities have become fairly visible today in the recent phase of the global motion of capital due to their rich biocultural diversity. Recently there was a delegation of Mamallakta people from Ecuador in Portland, Oregon, where I live. They gave lectures and distributed an e-mail defining who they are and what they do. The first paragraph in their e-mail read 'We come from the Ecuadorian Amazon, which is by the way, a cultivated forest (*le silva cultiva*).' I consider this one of the most profound statements in the history of agro-ecology and ecological discourses. In the mainstream discourse, the Amazon is supposed to be the wildest place untouched by humans. Now look at what are the Indigenous people saying: Yes, it's a forest but it is cultivated forest, not only by humans but also cultivated by birds, insects, plants and mammals. No wonder the Kichwa word Mamallakta means 'mother community.'

I myself was born and raised in a mountain village in the Himalayan foothills of Nepal. In that village, we had figured out almost all aspects of what today we know as sustainability and agro-ecological civilization. Except for salt and kerosene oil, the village produced almost everything. People did most of their labor without buying and selling labor, through what was known as *parma*, a form of labor-sharing with your neighbors. Through *parma*, houses, fences, farm terraces and walls were built and repaired, crops were planted, weeded and harvested. Life journeys such as birth, coming of age and death were celebrated without much cash exchange. However, a set of forces unleashed in the early 1960s unsettled our village economy and culture – one of those being my own departure for Kathmandu (the capitol city) and eventually to the United States. While merchant capitalism, trade, marketing of goods, wage labor and English-speaking schools gradually moved in, we witnessed the accelerated erosion of the agro-ecological base and the customary laws that governed it.

Reflecting back on that life system in that mountain village today, I cannot but appreciate the implicit science and knowledge system in a very so-called unscientific world. For example, when I began to develop a multipurpose educational farm in my own land in Chitwan (located south of the mountain village in the plains of Nepal) in 1993–94, I began a systematic study of plants used in the traditional agricultural and medicinal texts and found that there were books and chapters written on the quality of those plants. Some of them are used for manuring, controlling pests and fermenting seedlings. They can cure you when you are sick, and you can brush your teeth with the twigs of at least five plants. Perhaps people there didn't know the term 'nitrogen fixing,' but they knew which tree was beneficial for the soil and which was not, which one needed to be kept near the garden, which one by the end of the field as a windbreak, which trees worked together and which did not.

There were codes of customary usage that regulated the scale and speed of harvesting nature and maintaining the circularity of natural cycles. For example, no one was allowed to cut trees around water sources. I distinctly remember that within a mile of my own house there were about six or seven water places—springs sprouting directly from the earth. They were basically carved-out small places where the spring was just bubbling up. These water sources were either within larger public forests or where there was a thick forest cover around the water sources. Nobody could even think about cutting that forest. That is what we call the sacred, but there is a difference. Our sacredness was understood not outside but inside the realm of basic necessity of the community. Interestingly, lots of deities were placed at the bottom of those trees just so that people would also say that this was not only a watering place but also a place of the *Nagas* (the serpent snakes) who were supposed to be the givers and regulators of water. In each and every source of water the idea was that there was a certain kind of god or goddess living there.

The biocultural diversity in the paddy field nurtured by the South Asian peasants is another illustration of peasant cosmology. According to archeological evidence, rice has been in India since 2 300 BC, making it an ethno-history of about 4 300 years. Its ancestor is a wild aquatic grass and with modifications it has taken the present shape. Just like the corn plant in Mexico, rice in India is a product of hundreds of years of human intervention. That is why with 200 000 varieties of rice available, the diversity of rice types in India is phenomenal. There were 20 000 varieties within the state of Madhya Pradesh alone. Among others, Winin Pereirea has documented the scale and scope of this rice diversity. Some rice grows in 60 days while other kinds take 200 days. Some are grown at sea level and others grow at 2 000 meters (6 000 feet) altitude. Some require water and some don't. They come in various colors, scents, time for cooking, duration of storage, usage, and some even have two to three seeds in one husk. Each variety of rice was identified to be suitable for a certain elevation and soil type. Furthermore, some peasants' own cosmic energy was tied to a certain variety. In the vicinity of Bombay, one particular variety called *Deodan* was called 'god's rice' because it sprang up by itself in the swamps and other marshy places. The other variety, called *ambemhar* costs four to five times higher than the rest. Diversity in rice is cultivated and nurtured not only for their look and taste but also for their medicinal and nutritional properties. For example, a wild rice called *Devobhata* found in swampy areas near Bombay was used for medicine. Another *Kolpi* rice is easy to digest and is eaten by older people. Certain rice is given to lactating mothers because it increases milk.[11] In my own farm in Nepal we have about a dozen varieties, such as *masino, jhinuwa, samjira, mansuli, jureli, anadi* and *ghaiya*, each of which is used in festivities in different seasons of the year.

During my visits to Mexico in 2001 I found a form of what Mexican ethnoecologist Victor Toledo calls 'Zapatista ecologism' alive and well. This current form of agrarianism builds on how Emiliano Zapata dreamt of an agro-ecological civilization for Mexico. This is akin to how India's current peasant and Indigenous movements are inspired by Gandhian legacies of self-reliant village ecologies and economies. In 1996 I found another prophetic example among the peasants in the Peruvian Andes, where a host of grassroots peasant organizations inspired

---

11 Winin Pereira, *Tending the Earth: Traditional Sustainable Agriculture in India.* Bombay: Earthcare Books, 1993.

by Proyecto Andino Tecnologias Campesinas (PRATEC) are revitalizing the age-old practice of exchanging seeds and cultivating biodiversity in the *chacras* (farm fields). They call themselves an agricentric civilization that depends on nurturing nature and being nurtured by nature. Participants associated with PRATEC show that peasants can only function as midwives who work in the *chacra* to please *pacha mama,* the Mother Earth. Julio Valladolid, one of the founding members of PRATEC, eloquently captures this interconnectedness:

> The *chacra* is the piece of land where the peasant lovingly and respectfully nurtures plants, soil, water, micro-climates and animals. In a broad sense, *chacra* is all that is nurtured; thus, the peasants say that the llama is their *chacra* that walks and whereof wool is harvested. We ourselves are the *chacra* of the *Wakas* or deities that care for, teach and accompany us. [12]

Although I am from the Himalayas, I was surprised to find that the Andean peasants were farming at 14 000 feet altitude. I wondered and asked during my visit there, 'Isn't it too much that you are farming on the top of the mountain?' They said, 'No, we are farming in a different way. This farming is for the gods because gods see the top of the mountain. We are farming for them and then by farming at the top of the mountain you get a different kind of potato that is not possible in the lower elevations.' By respecting the ecological niche of the top of the mountain, they are strengthening biodiversity.

Evidence abounds that biocultural diversity has been maintained within the farms and in the intersection of farms and forestry. Actually, high population density and land use do not eliminate wild plant and other biotic species but may instead have led to the incorporation of many of them by protecting them from competition and through conscious cultivation and management. The case of multiuse forest-farms among Indigenous peasants in Mexico illustrates this well. As Victor Toledo identifies, the peasant strategy to enrich biocultural diversity includes a variety of strategies: 1) the Mesoamerican *milpa* system that generally constitutes a polyculture including up to 25 agricultural and forestry species; 2) the extraction of timber and nontimber products from the primary or mature forests and their secondary forests of different ages resulting from the succession process; 3) the manipulation of forests in different stages of anthropic disturbance from which different products are obtained; 4) the management of the home gardens which are agro-forestry systems located close or next to dwellings; 5) the extraction of products from available water bodies (rivers, lakes and swamps); 6) the management of small-scale cattle-raising areas which are generally pasture areas combined with legume species of trees and shrubs;

---

12 Julio Valladolid-Rivera, "Andean Peasant Agriculture: Nurturing a Diversity of Life in the Chacra" *Interculture* 24(2):18–53. 1995. p. 23. Also see Frederique Apffel-Marglin and PRATEC eds, *The Spirit of Regeneration*. London: Zed Press. 1998.

and 7) management of forestry or agricultural plantations for cash crops such as sugarcane, sesame, citrus or rubber.[13]

That is why Mexico hosts 10 per cent of the global flora (26 000 plant species) while occupying merely 1.4 per cent of the global landmass. In Mexico biocultural diversity is nurtured by 54 main Indigenous groups who speak 240 languages and dialects. Let there be no surprise that this is not just a geographic accident; what is involved is centuries of labor of love by Indigenous peasant communities. In one estimate, three million peasant productive units (*ejidos* and *communidades*) own half of the Mexican territory, principally forested areas 70 per cent of the national total and 80 per cent of the nation's agricultural land. It is on the basis of this rich biocultural diversity that Toledo conceives of an alternative modernity for Mexicans identified as the Mexico Profundo (the Authentic Mexico).[14] Furthermore, of the nine countries in which 60 per cent of the world's remaining 6 500 languages are spoken, six of them are also the centers of megadiversity. Those six countries are Mexico, Brazil, Indonesia, India, Zaire and Australia. In geographer David Harmon's overlapping of the top 25 countries with the highest number of endemic languages, 16 also had the highest number of endemic wildlife species.[15]

Political Stirring for Autonomy and Governance

While agro-ecological identity of ecological ethnicities is emerging, we are also witnessing equally strong resurgence of demands for political autonomy and governance. For example, 2 000 *adivasi* villages in India declared that their villages were self-ruled in March 2001. They erected bamboo altars at the gates of each village to declare their intent. In India, about 630 officially recognized tribal groups comprise an estimated 85 million *adivasis*. They span across India's expansive landscape ranging from the Great Andamanese who are left with only 18 surviving members to the Bhils of Rajasthan with 5.2 million, the Gonds of Madhya Pradesh with 4.8 million, and the Santhals with 3.6 million, all spread out over the states of Jharkhand, West Bengal, and Orissa.

Such a declaration was only a small part of the latest strategy to implement the law passed by the Indian parliament on 24 December 1996. This law, *Provision of the Panchayats Extension to Scheduled Areas Act* (1996) extended a scheme of decentralization in areas where adivasi comprise a majority of the population. This act states that, 'in the tribal areas, every *Gramsabha* (the village assembly) shall be competent to safeguard and preserve the traditions and customs of the people, their

---

13 Victor Toledo, "Biocultural Diversity and Local Power in Mexico" in Luisa Maffi ed. *On Bio-Cultural Diversity: Linking Language, Knowledge and the Environment*. Washington DC: Smithsonian Press. pp. 472–488. 2001.

14 Toledo, Ibid.

15 David Harmon, 'On the Meaning and Moral Imperative of Diversity" in Luisa Maffi ed. *On Biocultural Diversity: Linking Language, Knowledge and the Environment.* Smithsonian Press, pp. 53–70. 2001.

cultural identity, community resources and the customary mode of dispute resolution.'
This legal provision constitutes a partial victory for *adivasis* in their long drawn-out
struggle for political autonomy that precedes colonial times. As the narrative in this
chapter attests, *adivasi* communities and several other rural peasant communities
have been at odds with outsiders, including Indian ruling classes as well as British
colonial rulers, throughout their history. While resisting external interference from
the state and outsiders, they have championed the cause of free access to resources
according to their customs and usage.

Perhaps the clue to understand adivasi urge for self-governance lies in the
incongruence they have felt between the ecology in which they are embedded in
and the economy, which is getting farther and farther away from them. I can make
sense of their plight by looking at the cumulative picture of the five-fold crisis they
are facing, namely the crises of nature, of survival, of social justice, of identity,
and of governance. They are facing unprecedented crises in the globalization of the
economy because ecological ethnicities make a careful effort to ensure continuity
in the symbiotic connection between the human economy and nature's economy. In
turn, ecological ethnicities are not only resisting forceful subordination into this new
phase of global capital but are also creating alternative proposals for a sustainable
economy, appropriate technology and community-level political autonomy. What
seems common in all these 'geographies of difference' is a combination of a distinct
geographical and ethnic makeup, resulting in aspiration for varying degrees of
political autonomy.[16]

First let us look at the crisis of nature and survival. While their lands are facing
bio-physical limits due to unlimited extraction of resources for consumption by
people who live far away from them, they also unevenly bear the ecological cost
of contamination of soil and water, displacement, and health risks. The irony is that
those who are rich in nature's wealth (including biodiversity and diversity of cultural
forms) have been unfairly integrated into the market economy and have become its
unwilling victims. For example, the resource-rich adivasi belt in middle India is the
prime target for new economic activities under foreign investment. Consequently, it
will result in accelerated paces of proposed mining, industries, and larger dams. These
in turn will intensify and compound the problems of displacement, submergence, and
forest destruction. By 1998, 13 minerals were identified for exploitation including
iron, gold, diamond, copper, lead, zinc, nickel and platinum. Power generation and
road construction are the other key items for foreign investment being proposed.
The Indian government has identified 27 road projects for investment, involving
a cost of around US $4 billion. In the energy sector, the transnational corporations
(TNCs) have forwarded proposals that include US $23 billion of investment. In a
sense, all these projects are premised upon what Vandana Shiva describes as India's
'environmental subsidy to global commerce.'

---

16 See P. Parajuli, "Revisiting Gandhi and Zapata"; and P. Parajuli and S. Kothari,
"Struggling for Autonomy: The Lessons from Local Governance."
Development: Seeds of Change, pp. 41:3:18–29. 1998.

Second, let us look at the entrenched crisis of social justice. Like everywhere else in the world, while profitable resources are flowing from the poor to the rich, the pollution and contaminated end-products are flowing from the rich to the poor. They are aptly called the effluents of the affluents. Obviously, not all Indians are paying for this 'uneven development' and the burden is heaviest on ecological ethnicities. In India, environmental racism and discrimination has two facets. First, uneven global industrial policies make India a place to locate environmentally hazardous production facilities such as mining, petrochemicals, fertilizer, and pesticides. Secondly, within India, although counting only 8 1/2 per cent of India's population, adivasis comprise half of the total population of those displaced by development projects. In one estimate, at least 10 million out of India's 85 million Indigenous people have already been displaced by one development project or another. However, only one-quarter of them have been rehabilitated properly. The rest of the displaced have become landless laborers or migrated to the cities, or become extinct.[17]

Selective economic growth on the one hand and destitution of the social majorities is an India-wide phenomenon. Political ecologists Madhav Gadgil and Ram Chandra Guha have aptly identified three distinct groups who face each other in an antagonistic relationship regarding resources. They distinguish between the *omnivores*, who shoulder no obligations or responsibilities to replenish nature even though they heavily use natural resources. Comprising one-fifth of India's population, *omnivores* are the sole beneficiaries of the riches achieved by five decades of 'development.' To accomplish this uneven advantage from nature's economy the *omnivore* class has built up an alliance akin to an iron triangle: an alliance of those favored by the state (industry, rich farmers, and city dwellers); those who decide on the size and scale of these favors (politicians); and those who implement their delivery (bureaucrats and technocrats). The providers of natural resources are unfortunately what they call the *ecosystem people* who depend on the natural environments of their own locality to meet most of their subsistence needs. About three-fifths of India's population is still *ecosystems people* who in many ways return to nature what they take out of it. Even worse is the one-third of India's population whom Gadgil and Guha call the *ecological refugees* who have been displaced by the process of capitalist expansion in India. Displaced from their own ecosystems and sources of livelihoods, the ecological refugees live in the margins of rural lands or in the city slums.[18] Analysis of the spatio-ethnic distribution of displacement by mines, industries, and hydropower projects in India shows that most of the *ecological refugees* are adivasis, traditional artisans, fisherfolk, nomadic groups, and small-holdings rural peasants.

---

17 B.D. Sharma, *Globalization and Tribal Encounter.* Delhi: Har-Ananda Publications, 1996; Pramod Parajuli, "Beyond Capitalized Nature: Ecological Ethnicity as a New Arena of Conflict in the Global Capitalist Regime." *Ecumene: A Journal of Environment, Culture, and Meaning,* 5(2):186–217. 1998.

18 Madhav Gadgil and Ram Chandra Guha, *Ecology and Equity: The Use and Abuse of Nature in India.* London: Routledge, 1995.

Fourth is the crisis of their identity, culture and language causing what ethnoecologist Gary Nabhan calls the 'extinction of experience' among the cultures of habitat. For about a decade and a half, I have closely observed the agony caused by the lopsided development in the Jharkhand region in India. Adivasis of the Jharkhand region and elsewhere have experienced this external intervention not only because they are poorer (a class consideration) but also because they are adivasis – Indigenous people with little political or economic power. Their historical ethnicity today is rearmed with ecological loss and a contingent crisis of survival and identity. Small wonder that Jharkhandis describe 'development' as *Diku Chalaki; Diku* is a Jharkhandi word which means 'outsider' or 'exploiter.' *Chalaki* is a Hindi word which means 'cleverness, wiliness, craftiness, the capacity to cheat, to circumvent a rule, to beat the system.' As Gunsi Soren, my Santhal friend puts it, 'the old triumvirate of *Sarkari* (related to government), *Sahukari* (merchants and moneylenders) and *Zamindari* (landlords) are currently being reproduced in the guise of industries, mines, and development projects. Like the *dikus* of yesterday, development programs are also looters, trouble makers and cheaters. This phrase captures at the deepest level not only how 'development' has become a means of exploitation of Jharkhand, but also how Jharkhandis have learned to recognize their own identity by a diminution, if not a negation of their exploiters.[19]

Finally, adivasis in India have come to the conclusion that all their crises cannot be adequately addressed without their say in the governance of their lives and their natural resources. Obviously the scale and scope of autonomy demanded by adivasis are diverse and varied. While some adivasi areas of the northeast have asserted autonomy in the form of independent states outside of the Indian union, adivasis of middle India (covering major parts of Jharkhand, Chhatisgarh, and the tribal belt in Gujarat and Maharashtra) have sought regional autonomy as a separate state within the Indian union. The Jharkhand and Chhatishgarh regions in middle India and the Uttarakhand region in the Himalayas were recently formed as separate states to respond to some of these demands. Yet communities who have declared village self-rule are not content with just carving out a separate state within the Indian union; they propose to change the very relations of ruling, including their rights over resources in their areas. Some others are trying to reject buying seeds from corporations and grow and use their own seeds. Forcing the World Bank and other bilateral and multilateral agencies to withdraw their funding from the multipurpose Narmada Project continues to be the most successful event in the history of struggle of *ecological ethnicities* against large dams in India.

Recognizing their strategic importance in terms of resources, the Movement for Tribal Self-Rule demands that the community ought not possess less than a 51 per cent shareholding in all industries located in adivasi areas. This way, the host community can have full control of the direction of development and can ensure that the people's

---

19 P. Parajuli, "Beyond Capitalized Nature"; *Grassroots Movements and Popular Education in Jharkhand, India.* Unpublished doctoral dissertation, Stanford University, Stanford, Palo Alto, California. 1990.

advancement is central in any development undertaking. Additionally, it demands that the labor of adivasis as a whole ought to have a one-quarter shareholding in the concerned enterprise. Interestingly, the *Mavali Bhata* declaration under the leadership of the National Alliance for Tribal Self-Rule favors that the government undertake the responsibility for capital, technology and management through public sector enterprises. Private enterprise may be allowed only if the government is unable to do so, but the capitalists ought not to have more than a 24 per cent shareholding. [20]

Residual institutions of Governance

Passing of this Act alone has not guaranteed self-rule for these communities but there are indications that it has certainly opened a legal space for contestation for power. Most importantly, the new Act recognized that in the adivasi areas, customary forms of governance such as *Munda-Manki* among Mundas and Hos, and *Manjhi-Praganna* among Santhals will be allowed to oversee local administration.

Such claims for autonomy carry further weight because most of these communities still have modes of local governance that are either functioning or are recoverable. The people of Kolhan in Sighabhum district are sticking to their traditional system of self-management through the *Munda Manki* system and are not prepared to surrender that right in favor of new formal institutions established by the state. The people living within the boundaries of the sanctuaries and national parks are not prepared to move out leaving their homes behind. The *Rai Sabhas* of Adilabad are managing all affairs of the village community on their own. The *Kewats*, fisherfolk residing along the river Ganges are rejecting the rights of *Zamindars* (locally known as water *Zamindars* or landlords) and are struggling to establish their traditional rights over water and fishing.[21]

I will offer a glimpse of the traditions of governance by looking at the customary governance structure among *Santhal* adivasis of the Jharkhand region. Their governing structure starts with what S*anthals* call the *Kulhi*. The village *Manjhi* (head person) has all the records about trees in the forest. He is responsible for administering the protection of the forest. No one has access to the forest except as defined by *Baisi,* the village council. A *Baisi* is composed of five distinct office-bearers who represent various aspects of the village life. Among the *Santhals*, a descendent of the village founder is usually chosen to be the *Manjhi*, the village headman. A village founder is the person who conducted the first labor of clearing forests and making terraces. Land thus cleared belongs to the village community, and individual members gained and inherited only usufructory rights. Some of this original land is separated for the *Manjhi* for his religio-political functions. The *Manjhi* and other village officers symbolically own the land.

---

20 B.D. Sharma, *Globalization and Tribal Encounter*, p. 139.

21 Authors interview with B.D. Sharma and Dr Ram Dayal Munda, leaders of the movement.

The *Manjhi* is usually selected from the lineage of the founders of the village. He is custodian of the village property – the communal wells, roads, *Jahers* and grazing grounds. He is also responsible for taking care of the village *Manjhithan* or founder's shrine, and to administer the *Jaher*, or the sacred grove. It is understood that the *Manjhi* embodies both secular and sacred authority. He in turn is assisted by the *Paranik*, who helps him in securing rents and other economic obligations. The *Jogmanjhi*, on the other hand, is the moral custodian of the village, especially in matters of sexual conduct among the youth. He is the master of ceremonies in the festivals such as *Sohrae,* and during the ceremonies of childbirth, marriage and death. The *Manjhi* is helped by *Godet*, who is his judicial assistant in the sense of implementing the rules. He calls the meetings, informs people about the decisions made and makes sure that they are implemented properly. The *Manjhi* is assisted in the religious functions of the community by two other officials, *Naeke* and *Kudam Naeke.* The *Naeke* officiates at all the public festivals and performs sacrifices, while the *Kudam Naeke* offers his own blood to the *parganna bonga* and the *bongas* of the outskirts.[22]

Symptomatic of a democratic tradition, all the village functionaries are renewed every year on the occasion of *Mage Sim*, a festival held at the end of *Magh*, in February, to give thanks to the millets as well as ancestors. On this occasion the functionaries surrender their respective posts for consideration for renewal to villagers, and villagers surrender their land-use rights to the village headman. If the villagers so wish, both are returned after ten days. There is no doubt that this annual remuneration of office is naturally far more nominal than real. It has a symbolic value in the sense that it emphasizes village approval as the basis for office and provides an annual occasion for the expression of grievances. Theoretically, the people have the authority to expel officials who neglect their work and cause the village to suffer. An annual hunt known as *Bir Seren*, which acts both as a high court and a parliament for the community, is also organized. On this occasion, the ordinary *Santhal,* the *disom hor* (the people of the country) are considered above *manjhis* (village heads) and *praganaits* (regional heads). During *Bir Seren* anyone can complain to the *dihiri* (hunt priest) about the misconduct of their village officials.

Are Ecological Ethnicities the Seam between the Nation and the State?

Are adivasis in India and Indigenous peoples elsewhere experiencing a new degree of confidence on their own autonomous history and cultural domain? Does there exist outside of the state system and political culture a radically different culture with its unique notions of law and order, nation, 'people-nation' and peoplehood? In order to exemplify this, I make a distinction between state and nation, society and culture, citizenship within the state and membership on the basis of ecological ethnicity.

---

22 P. Parajuli, *Grassroots Movements and Popular Education in Jharkhand, India.*

Secondly, is there an increased level of acceptance of the fact that Indigenous people's political culture can be as valid (if not more so) as the modern political culture upon which the nation-states base their international relations? Since the majority of nation-states are multiethnic or multicultural, the power derived from the image of the state is simply coercive and bureaucratic. Where Indigenous peoples are concerned, the state merely aspires to integrate and assimilate them without respecting their deep-rooted differences.[23]

What then is the role of nation-state today vis-à-vis these stirrings of ecological ethnicities? The nation-state was supposed to be the guardian of subalterns against local exploiters, or the liberator from their state of subjugation, underdevelopment, and 'backwardness.' On the contrary, ecological ethnicities find that the state is at the very heart of their subordination, exploitation and deprivation. I was not surprised when I found that adivasis of Jharkhand made distinctions between 'state' and 'nation.' For them citizenship within the Indian State is only one reality. Their own membership on the basis of ecological ethnicity in their own community and the region as described above is another reality. This is how adivasi peasants residing in the Jharkhand region use a distinct notion of *disum* (a word designating their own country) and the *muluk* (referring to areas outside their hilly and forested terrain). Their notion of concepts such as 'nation,' 'territory,' 'community,' 'place' and 'space' are different from the notion of land that is commodified, individualized, and treated as an alienable object in the capitalist marketplace.[24]

What do such claims signify in terms of the relationship of people with the state? Are these social fabrics of institutions and networks of communitarian solidarity integrated into the modern nation-state? Unfortunately, it did not happen. On the contrary; the Indian State, completely absorbed in the task of constituting itself and establishing its own fragile hegemony, considered such institutions of governance, networks and solidarities antithetical to their project. Thus the Indian nation-state has always experienced deficits in its hegemony over ecological ethnicities. As my own research and that of many others shows, the same residual institutions, ignored and abandoned, have functioned as counterpowers and centers of resistance against a state that excluded them.[25]

Emerging Politics of Inhabitation and Community

Building on the new ecological discourse of the Earth household and the aspiration for tribal self-rule, I will project a new citizenship for ecological ethnicities. The twin issues of ecology and democracy can be the locus of this emergent citizenship.

---

23 Frank Wilmer, *The Indigenous Voice in World Politics*. London: Sage Publications; James Scott, *Seeing Like a State: How Certain Schemes to Improve Human Condition have Failed*. New Haven: Yale University Press, 1998.

24 James Scott, Ibid.

25 For a subaltern historian's reading of the deficit of hegemony of the Indian state, see Partha Chatterjee, *Nation and its Fragments*. Princeton University Press, 1993.

I consider ecology as the site for self-organization and self-creation of life. Likewise, democracy can be understood as self-governance at the level of ecosystem-based communities. A community provides both the 'hardware' and 'software' for human relationships. As software, the community provides a sense of place, and networks of connection and relations. As hardware, it facilitates arrangements for organizing units such as watersheds and foodsheds. At the same time, the promise of the community as the new organizing principle lies in the fact that community is Janus-faced. On the one hand it is a site of remembering, restoring and regenerating what is lost from the past. On the other it is a site of constant critique, reform and transformation of existing relations. The starting basis for the recovery of community is in preserving and restoring ecosystems. As I have noted elsewhere:

> I propose that the ethnoecological political organizations uphold two cardinal principles. First, they are based upon "democratic equivalence" between several groups. Secondly, they are premised upon self-management of human relations as well as human-nature relations. What emerges is not another state, but a federation of self-managing communities. The central feature of emergent ethnoecological politics is then self-management of resources and cultures. In essence, they aspire to a different social mode with a view to different development alternatives. In this sense, Indigenous politics seeks a plurality of ways to organize autonomous units without a central authority such as the nation-state or any other uniform model as such. That is why the nation-states whether it is in Mexico or India are so hesitant to offer autonomy to Indigenous peoples.[26]

Now let me try to organize my thoughts about how ethnoecological communities could prepare themselves for a mode of self-governance. I see six distinct tenets of an ecologically organized community: 1) a site of producing livelihoods; 2) a landscape of resistance; 3) a source of regeneration; 4) a site of constant self-critique; 5) a site of organizing; and 6) a site of envisioning and presenting a network of meanings.

Invoking community at the center of new global order entails reenvisioning the very idea of political participation and citizenship. For example, in Europe the state fully enfranchised certain individuals (white males, property holders) while simultaneously disenfranchising others (women, people of color, white men without property). Marx reflected this irony when he divided the French nation into two: the nation of owners and the nation of workers. Thus while those who considered themselves as universal, rational and cultivated claimed to be citizens, those who were local, ethnic and cultural were given no citizenship or were considered second-class citizens.

It is then logical to rethink the imagery of the nation and the state. We could either see the state as the apparatus for hegemonic discourse, or in a more utopian inversion see it as the incipient or emergent expression of the national-popular sentiment. We then have nation as no longer the sign of modernity under which cultural differences are homogenized in the horizontal view of history. Like the re-imagined state, the nation could also reveal in its ambivalent and vacillating

---

26 P. Parajuli, "Revisiting Gandhi and Zapata" p. 248.

representation the ethnography of its own historicity and open up the possibility of other narratives of people and their differences. Then nation-state is something in the making rather than a given, something as a field of contestation rather than fixed and sealed forever.[27]

By arguing for greater autonomy for each community, I do not mean to suggest that these communities are isolated and can function without coordination and exchanges with other communities. Obviously, these communities will need to build linkages with other communities, watersheds, foodsheds, bioregions and nations. However, we cannot construct ecological and cultural democracy within the framework of a homogeneous national community. We need a framework in which each community can exercise enough autonomy to defend their internal solidarity and find some common definition of mutual rights, responsibilities and obligations with others. Through such mutual recognition of identities, all communities can realize themselves.

What emerges through this process is not a matter of establishing a mere alliance between given interests but of actually modifying the very identity of these forces. Thus, essentializing any identity is counterproductive, but recognizing the complexity of discursive surfaces will be useful. For example, if adivasis claim superior citizenship on the basis of 'primal peoples' or 'indigenosity,' such assertions would negate the very idea of democracy. In the same way, Indigenous groups have been either victimized by blaming them as an obstacle in the march of progress or they have been valorized as the 'exotic other' in order to dominate or render them as docile and insignificant. I would rather situate adivasi aspirations within the field of ecology and a sense of the place of inhabitation. Let us see if this departure helps us to resituate the realm of representation and citizenship for ecological ethnicities.

Ecological and Cultural Citizenship?

> The idea of India is not based on language, not on geography, not on ethnicity and not on religion. The idea of India is of one land embracing many.
>
> Shashi Tharoor[28]

Let me again draw insights from the Jharkhand region of India. Perhaps recognizing the limits of essentialized identity politics such as caste or tribe, Jharkhandis are also configuring new identities. For example, Jharkhandis have begun to reflect their identities not in terms of 'tribe' or 'caste' but in terms of an emerging coalition of 'tribals' and 'Indigenous' peoples. A Jharkhandi now is defined not in terms of Indigenous identity alone but in terms of those who share a common territory and a

---

27 For the notion of state as an expression of popular national will, see Antonion Gramsci, *Selections From Prison Notebooks*. Translated by Quintin Hoare and Geoffrey Noel-Smith. New York: International Publishers, 1971; Homi Bhabha ed., *Nation and Narration*. New York: Routledge, 1990.

28 Shashi Tharoor, *India: Midnight to Millennium*. New Delhi: Penguin Books, 1997.

common history, cultural heritage, and experience of exploitation by the *dikus*. Thus besides Indigenous groups, *Sadans* (Hindu communities who comprise at least 55 per cent of population) are considered Jharkhandi. Only those 10 to 15 per cent of the population who have migrated from other places and are in exploitative relations with native Jharkhandis are considered non-Jharkhandis.[29] Some might argue that such new alliances belittle the existing caste and tribal identities. On the contrary, I see its significance in subverting the colonial and nationalist categories designed to divide and rule and in creating an alternative terrain of political participation based on geographic and ecological commonalties. In the Narmada valley, for instance, what we witness is a new configuration of alliances between the land-holding *Patidar* peasants and other ecological ethnicities, adivasis, fisherfolk and other artisan groups who in many respects are dependent on the landholding classes. I am certainly not suggesting that such alliances are 'heavens of harmony and equality' but I would argue that they are indeed the source of ethnoecological formations with new opportunities for internal social critique as well as regeneration. In many ways the conflicts embedded in class, caste and gender relations could be resolved by taking care of the conflict between the imperatives of local ecologies for renewal and regeneration and those of global economies for fast and quick profits.

While deeply grounded in the Earth as a household discourse, claim over ecological and/or cultural citizenship is timely because, although the idea of a modern citizen was indeed crucial for the democratic revolution two hundred years ago in Europe and fifty years ago in India, it constitutes an 'obstacle to its extension' today.[30] The question of 'multiple' citizenship is relevant in India because the multinational Indian State is not unitary but rather made up of many nations, cultures and peoples. In order for multinational states to exist and function in a period in history when identity and autonomy have become the mainstay of cultural praxis, there needs to be at least two routes for consideration. One obvious choice would be to allow the formation of as many states as there are nations. Alternatively, the multinational state could accommodate broader notions of citizenship including cultural, ethnic, linguistic and ecological citizenship. As we saw in the case of biocultural diversity, in many cases those diversities overlap and enrich each other. This means not only giving such groups legal recognition but also accepting their discursive formations that include ways in which various differences can be represented.

Recognizing ecological ethnicities as equal citizens in India is therefore basically about different arrangement, rather than integrating them into the mainstream as if they were second-class citizens or they were protected within the welfare schemes of the State. Through the ecological citizenship, adivasis will seek their recognition, pursue political spaces for expression and assert claims of difference without accepting the imposed social hierarchy in a caste, ethnic and class-ridden society. A

29 Jharkhand Coordination Committee Manifesto, Ranchi, 1987.

30 Chantal Mouffe, "Democratic Citizenship and the Political Community" in Chantal Mouffe, ed. *Dimensions of Radical Democracy*, pp. 225–239. 1992. James Scott, *Seeing Like a State*.

new ecological citizenship could be based on not only the principle of self-rule but also biocultural diversity, self-reliance, respectful participation in national life and most important, equal exchange in the marketplace.

Conclusion: Imagining Plural Societies

The examples from India and various other ecological ethnicities described in this chapter evince that Indigenous communities have survived and thrived, disproving both liberal and Marxist predictions of their imminent demise either by cosmopolitan assimilation into global citizenship or their integration into economic proletarian classes. I hypothesize that their persistence and survival amidst great odds and their resurgence in recent periods is due to their ties with ecology and their deep roots in an agro-ecological household.

Rather than ignoring these new ethnoecological stirrings, a multiethnic and democratic country like India would be better off creating spaces for multiple ecological and cultural citizenships. Ecological ethnicities are coming into focus today because of the biocultural diversities they nurture. This coupling of biological and cultural diversity opens up a very new dimension in ethnoecological politics.

Whatever might be the actual outcome of struggles for governance at the grassroots, I think that this is an indication that social movements in India and elsewhere have shifted from a phase of 'protest' to a phase in which protests are accompanied by proactive 'proposals.' It is palpably clear that as much as the subalterns under the categories of 'Indigenous community,' 'caste' and 'gender' have been historically used in nationalist narratives to subordinate them, the subalterns have also seized these categories, claimed them for themselves and subverted them for their own representation and citizenship. Unequivocally, social movements in India are articulating minor and residual forms of resistances into larger forms of claims and mobilization.

Europe

Chapter 12

Tour in the Old and New Vuornese: A Saami Journey

Asa Virdi Kroik

Introduction

When I was a child I was much like other children. I played in the forest, bathed in the brook and climbed the rocks. I went with my dad to the mountains in the summertime at the period when the calves were marked, and gathered moss in the fall for the hungry reindeer to eat during winter. My friends and I fantasized about fairytale people who lived under big trees or by the brooks or on the high mountain. We played with them and they were real to us. Now, when I am adult, these fantasies have turned into a longing for knowledge of who actually lived in the area before me. Who was born, played, loved, gave birth, struggled and died by these same brooks, swamps and mountains? This chapter represents my journeys of rediscovery of my rich Saami ancestral heritage as I traveled the hills and valleys of the land where my ancestors once thrived in Norway and Sweden. I grew progressively excited as I encountered venerated dwelling places of worship and ceremony which our community intends to preserve amidst the interference of insensitive and thoughtless European tourists who tread ignominiously on our sacred sites.

Inledning

During a summer I took time off from my religious studies and devoted myself to explore the area where I grew up and where my ancestors, practically all on my father's side, lived before me. The area is not known from the oldest sources of the Saami religion and did not make its mark later for any religious event, but it is situated within the larger area where the first missionaries worked and even if it is not mentioned, the missionaries probably met its inhabitants who traveled along the long valleys between Norway and Sweden. For this reason some of the missionaries' stories about the Saamis' faith may be valid here as well. It turned out that despite the fact that the area was not mentioned, there were examples of almost every kind of typical Saami monuments of the past you can find, plus a few more!

I have looked for the history of my ancestors in archives, in books, and have talked to people in the area who have memories and knowledge of the neighborhood. I have also talked to experts on various topics of the Saami culture. I am more familiar with the summer pasture and therefore I have to rely on the narratives of other people with regard to the other parts of the region. There is so much to discover and I have come to understand that I have only scratched the surface, but I have enough to tell to give you a glimpse of an exciting area.

Welcome to Vuornesen, my native place!

Vuornese

Vuornese is a part of Saami. It is situated in southern Lapland, the greater part surrounding what is known today as the Frostvikens Saami village or in Saami Vuornese. A Saami village is a group of reindeer herders who work together in a limited area. I will not limit myself to these frontiers which have been set rather late. Instead I have chosen to explore the area which in a natural way connects to the long valleys where my relatives, ancestors and other people have wandered.

Vuornese is beautifully situated in the interior of Lapland. The winters are harsh with raging storms and temperatures close to 30 degrees Celsius below zero, sometimes colder. The summers are rainy but offer fantastic, warm days as well. Along the long valleys high fern grow, as if in jungles. On the high mountain the vegetation is thrifty. The bare top of the mountain is often imbedded in clouds and spots of snow can still be seen in the summer, to the relief of the reindeer who seek protection from mosquitoes and heat. The Saami village of Frostviken/Vuornese borders on the south on Oredahke, on the north on the Saami village of Vilhelmina and on the east on nostre Namdal in Norway. It is a region of strong Saami tradition and the Saami roots go way back in the history, generation before generation. Less than fifty years ago the people here moved and lived with the reindeer in a way that is quite different from today. This is a vast village and formerly the people here traveled all the way to the district of Sundsvall during the winter. This is a journey of about 500 kilometers, by skiing and walking!

My father tells about living in *gÂetie* (the Saami equivalent to the North American teepee). With a humorous twinkle in his eye he says that when he was born the skis came out first. It's a joke, but somehow serious. Life in this area was and is still hard and if you cannot learn how to use all the utensils you cannot live here. My father grew up with many brothers and sisters in the Eastern Voorjaren, in Vuornesen. The children learned at an early age how to ski; there is still no main road. European colonization was imposed on us as development during my father's lifetime, and as a result the old paths, reindeer fields, and milking places are no longer used. We do not milk the reindeer today. We live in houses, move the reindeer by truck, live much like our Scandinavian neighbors – we are baptized, we get married and are buried according to Christian tradition, but it has not always been like that. Taking a walk about in the surroundings of Vuornese, you will find the traces of Saami life in the old times.

Orresijjiej Dwelling Sites

The climate has not always been the same. Maybe this is why you can see several traces of stationary Saami camps along the road on the high mountain between Klimpfjll and BiÂsjˆn.

Along this road, not far from the stream Gaustdahke with its blue clear water, there is a gathering of five round-shaped sites about one decimeter deep into the ground. These remains are named *jehnah-gÂetie-sijjie*. There is a rich sense of mythological history linked to this place. There are tales of stupid giants named *Stalo,* who caused a great deal of trouble for the Saami people and who with pleasure ate their children. The stories describe a Stalo catching a child to eat it, but the child tricks the Stalo who itself eventually gets into trouble. The following tale is told as an example:

> Once upon a time a Stalo succeeded in catching a Saami boy. Stalo put the boy in a big sack where he also had his money. He carried the sack with him on his back. After *Stalo* had walked for some time, he got tired and wanted to sleep. He took the boy out of the sack and made him collect wood and make a fire. The boy did as Stalo told him but when he passed the sack he took the chance to cut a hole in it. Stalo fell asleep, but when it started to hiss and crunch in the fire the boy shouted 'The snake is coming! The snake is coming!' Stalo quickly stood up and snatched the boy, put him in the sack and ran away. All the Stalo's coins fell out of the sack and so did the boy. The boy screamed in despair, 'The snake has taken me! The snake has taken me!' Stalo heard the calls and then ran as fast as he could without looking back. There stood the boy with Stalo's entire treasure.

In reality the *jehnah-gÂetie-sijjie* are old Saami dwelling places. They are a special kind not used all over Saami. These dwelling places are in fact the ones that are the most southern. Archeological excavations have revealed the hearth in the middle. You can sometimes see it with your bare eyes as a small rise (elevation) in the land. The C-14 archeological dating method used on carbon from the hearths show that these places had been used for decades, sometimes repeatedly. They date back to the Viking Age and the 16th and 17th centuries. Most of the scientists agree that the sites are Saami, but questions arise: Did they milk the tame reindeer, or did they hunt the wild reindeer or did they do both? Exactly what the constructions looked like is unknown and we know only of the ground level round. Why did they build these dwellings on these places and why did they stop building them? *Jehnah-gÂetie-sijjie* are found also at Maskien and on the south side of the lake Voorjaren. None of these places have been examined or excavated.

There are more signs of old Saami dwellings. Many Saami hearths can be seen. They are to be found in the reindeer pasture, often in the pine forest near water and there are usually several of them gathered. They are the remains of camps from 800 to 1200 CE and they were made more or less in the same way they are today: rectangular shaped, ovals, or round circles of stone. At the inner side of the hearth lies a big flat stone used as a table and a storing place. One round circle stone-setting is situated very close to the water, on one side of Gaustdahke, and two stone-settings are on the opposite side of the stream. The former is probably a hearth. I am very soon going to tell you more about the other two.

Between Old and New Faith

It is impossible to say when the Saami people abandoned their old faith and became Christians. The imperial missions that took place in the 18th century were successful from the Christian viewpoint, forcing many Saami people to become Christians by the 19th century. But this was a process and from the Saami perspective a clear disaster because their conception of the world was severely affected. Saami myths and rites were slowly replaced by Christian ones, but some Indigenous religious thoughts and acts remained, albeit in Christian guise. Were the Saami people really Christians at the beginning of the 19th century? Well, perhaps they were, although they interpreted Christianity in their own way and they kept many of the traditional myths, customs and ways of thinking. Tragically they did abandon their old burial customs and adopted the ways of the Christian Church.

Not far from the *jehnah-gÂetie-sijjie*, along the road to Stikkenjokk, closer to the stream, there are two striking stone-settings. They have been registered but not excavated. Stones the size of a fist are visible on the ground on a beautiful plain overgrown by grass. One of the formations is shaped like a boat and the other is rectangular. They are both the size of a man and are reminders of graves. Saami graves are often situated near dwellings. They are not placed in an east-west direction according to Christian burial custom, but lie north-south as is the Saami tradition. There are several theories of how the rocks got there. Maybe it is the result of children playing or maybe it represents the remains of a sacrificial reindeer that has been buried, which is something the oral tradition vividly describes.

Single graves as well as grave fields are pointed out by older Saami people and they can even name the persons who rest there. My grandmother's brother knew where his sister was buried. Grave fields are pointed out at the church place, Ankarede, and at two different places in Storjola. There is a grave field in BÂgede as well. A grave field that is known as well as archeologically excavated is situated on the island of LÂngˆn outside Hoting. The Saamis buried here were well-off and were in frequent contact with people in the east as well as in the west. There were finds of ancient remnants probably manufactured in Russia, and in a man's grave was a purse for fire utensils made of Indian *Varanlizzard*! It is evident that the Saami had interactions, perhaps even trade, with Indigenous peoples in North America and in west Asia.

Formerly, the grave was often placed by the water and on islands to set a boundary between the dead and the living. Rituals of separation were performed to separate the living from the dead. The demand from the Church that the bodies be buried in consecrated ground gave rise to temporary burial grounds. The body was protected as far as possible, preferably on a small island, until it could be transported to the burial ground. According to traditional custom the body should be shroud in birch bark before it was buried. It was common to place the body in an *akkja* (a reindeer sleigh), a boat, or a hollow log. The body could also be buried between two logs and covered with rocks to protect it from wild animals, before the grave was covered with soil. Even the reindeer that pulled the body to the burial site was slaughtered and the bones were buried. The grave goods contained utensils belonging to the dead: axes, knives, bows and arrows, sewing utensils and similar things. In *Mubben·jumuo*, the spirit world where the dead went, the Saami believed that life went on pretty much like before. This is why the dead needed the utensils in their graves. The dead received gifts up to three years after their death, and we were told by our elders that it was customary to place a gift whenever a grave was passed.

The departed stayed in contact with the living. A woman who was pregnant knew the name of the unborn child as an ancestor came to her in a dream. It has been told that ancestors were reincarnated and born again in the world of the living. The *nÂjd*, the Saami shaman, was in close contact with the dead. In a state of trance he could visit them and even hire them to guard the reindeer.

As long as the dead were remembered, they were present and as long as their personal *joik* (musical rendition) sounded they were remembered. In the southern part of Saami the tradition of joik sadly ended about a generation ago, but among the young Saamis the joik has come to life again. At the Saami midsummer festival, still celebrated in Ankarede, there has to be joik at the dance or else it is not a dance. The Saami from the mountains in the area have come together in Ankarede for as long as can be remembered. It has been a natural place to meet when the reindeer move up to the mountains in the summer and it is told the dead were buried there. The small hills and hollows around the *gÂetie* are supposedly the remains of these graves. Many wished to rest their last rest where the reindeer dwelled, for example by the mouth of a brook where the earth is fertile. This is where you could hear the sound of the calves and the snapping of the heel string. Eventually Ankarede became a *kyrkplats* (church place or church camp) and a church was built in 1785. This place has been a distinctive meeting point for the Saami, from the north to the south, until this day.

In the transition between old and new, the Saami did not always think well of burying the dead in the churchyard cemetery. It was by constraint and they had to abide. Jonas IhrÈn lived in Oredahke, a neighboring Saami village south of Vuornese. His memories were published in the 1960s. When he was a child he knew a woman who wanted to be buried on the mountain.

When she found out that it was no longer custom to bury the dead on the mountain, she found this remarkable and wondered why it was not possible to bring consecrated ground to her grave on the mountain. It was common in the old days, she said, to send someone for the three shovels of soil (earth, dust, and stone) from a churchyard in the country. And when the priest had read the rituals the soil was carried to the grave on the mountain and the words of the priest were repeated to the dead.

It is told that the priest could also point in the direction of the mountain where the dead were buried. The soil was then thrown in that direction and the ritual was performed. This was sometimes the procedure in BÂgede.

Hunters and Game

In these areas you had to hunt to survive. The animals provide fur, meat, tendons for sewing and horns for handicraft. In the past, drugs were produced from the body fluids and the fat of animals. Today, Vuornesen has a strong handicraft tradition. Handicraft for household use and for decoration is common.

Although not all of the Saami have traditionally been reindeer breeders, the reindeer is still very much associated with the Saami, but hunting and fishing is equally important in Saami culture. In past times, game, milk, or other food and beverage had to be stored in a way that it would not be destroyed or wasted. For that reason the *bˊrnie* were built, which are storage spaces made with stone. Believing that we would find such *bˊrnie*, my father and I one day climbed the mountain of Borgahllan to see what could be found there. We discovered a single oval shaped stone-setting, and a few kilometers from this site, two circular stone sites situated in the birch forest in the steep hill. They were about one meter in diameter and about the same size in height. They appeared very stable and were very well made. What was this? They seemed too well made to be *bˊrnie*.

On the Norwegian side, one is familiar with the *bogastiller*, which is an old method of hunting where the hunter comes as close to the game as possible. A kind of construction of stone in several levels, half circular-shaped and sometimes with a pillar in the middle was built to hide the hunter. Behind the hiding-place the hunter waited until the animal was close enough for him to attack it. Maybe our stone-sites were kinds of *bogastiller*, I don't know.

In the northern part of Norway there are big stone circles, six to nine meters in diameter and bigger. The walls are about a meter in height, and in the middle of the circle a stone pyramid was built that has kept a stone or wooden deity in place. The deity has received sacrifices and there have been remains of horn and bones found at the place. Our circles do not have that size and there is no place for a holder in the middle. I believe they may have something to do with hunting as they are situated in an area with a lot of elk. In the valley there are still many *fÂngstgropar* (pit traps for catching animals), though many were buried under the water of the dam that was built at the end of the 1940s.

There are also other traces of hunting there. *FÂngstgropar* exist all over Saami. They are situated one by one or several together in a system, often placed in narrow passages, like on a *landtunga* (bridge of dry land between two lakes) or something similar. The pit trap was covered with branches so that the game would not discover it, and the unsuspecting animal brought down in the hole could be taken care of by the hunter. Mostly elk and wild reindeer were caught in this type of trap that was most frequently used late in the summer and in the autumn. This way of hunting was transmitted from Saami hunter-gatherer culture to agriculture, probably during the Iron Age. The pit traps are difficult to date but could be several thousand years old. In 1864 they were forbidden by law. No pit traps have been excavated in the area, and some of them were destroyed when the road between Borgafjll and Storjola was built without any concern for any further historical investigation.

Muadt-aajja ñ the Furman

One of the bigger preys is the bear. The bear once had a very special role in the creation stories among the Saami people. It was holy and a special ceremony was celebrated every time it was hunted. Many scholars believe that this ceremony is among the oldest elements in Saami religion. Two of the very old rock carvings in Alta in Northern Saami show people hunting bears. In connection with the bears, rings are carved. It is believed that the scene depicts a bear ceremony as the ring has a very prominent role in bear rituals. For example, the Saamis decorated the place where the bear was prepared with rings and the women were not allowed to look at the bear hunters except with one eye open holding a ring in front of it.

Similar bear feasts are celebrated by many peoples living in the area around the North Pole, such as in Siberia, or among the Ainu in Japan and the Inuit of Canada. In Siberia the tradition is still alive but tragically among the Saamis it has died out.

The oldest written sources narrate unambiguously that bear bones could not be cut off. If a dog succeeded in stealing a bear bone, he had to pay with one of his own. If there was an injury on one of the bear bones, the animal responsible had to suffer the same injury in the other world. Such mistreatment had to be avoided so that the visited bear could be pleased with the Saamis and send them new bears from the other world.

Bear graves are difficult to find. Several are known around different places in Saami and within our area, there are, strangely enough many. Bear rituals were evidently very alive here. Vuornese is also very rich in bears. A site believed to be a bear grave is situated at LÂngˆn, an island in lake Hotingsjˆn. All bones except the cranium are buried together. The bones have been split to reach the marrow. In the village Grdselet, close to the community of Junsele, are burned bones from a bear, and from the village Avatrsk there are sites where ritually treated bear craniums can be found.

The oldest sources emphasize the importance that all bones must be buried. Still the finds show that body and skull have been separated. Kristoffer Sjulsson, a Saami informant from Vapsten north of Vuornese, narrates that the bear hunters brought in the bear's head through *bÂassjoe*, the holy door, when a bear was killed. If the bear had killed a bear hunter, the head was stuck on a pole. The bear bones found in this account had also been burned and cut in violation of the restrictions in the old sources. Maybe this rule was not so important then or maybe the customs were different from place to place in Saami. Another explanation is that there might have been years of starving and the bones were split and the marrow eaten as the need for food was so serious.

There are not so many memories or old stories about bear rites in Vuornese. But there is a small and detailed trustworthy script that was released in 1755, written by the priest Pehr Fjellstrˆm. Here the ritual, the feast, the conceptions and the ideas connected to bear and the bear hunt are described in detail.

The bears' divine protector was called *Leibolmaiñ*, the Alderman. The Saamis chewed alder and the juice was sprayed over the hunters and the dogs during parts of the bear ceremony. According to the old Saamis, the bear could hear and understand when it was talked about, and it was better to change words about the bear and the bear hunt so that the bear would not be aware when the Saamis would go out and hunt it. Some of these *noa* – words that the scientists call them – are remembered in Vuornese even today. Such a name is *muadtaajja*, a word the children often used. It can be translated to the old *furmanî*. *Muadta kan* means both fur and the black insect that often lives in the bears' fur.

When a bear was killed it was more than a normal hunt. It was a feast, a religious ceremony that could go on for days. It ended with the burial of all bear bones that were placed exactly in the same order as it used to be in the living body. A creature, not only bears, was not considered dead when it stopped breathing. If the bones were placed in the same order as they had been in the living body, new flesh could grow on them. The animal could return to the world behind, where it was believed to once have come from and could send new bears to the Saami. Nobody was totally obliterated and the cycle of life was continuous with that of death, generating ongoing life.

The bear's penis bone was specially powerful. It was kept and hung on the holy drum. It was custom to make a mark in the drum for every bear that was caught. While celebrating bear rituals one was *joiking*. It was an important part of the celebration and in the *joiks* it was illustrated how the bear, satisfied with the Saami's treatment of it, happily walked away to the other world. (The south Saami words in one of the joiks was documented sometime between 1750 and 1780, but it is difficult to understand the words in it.) Different bear joiks, from different places, have been recorded and are kept in archives. Others have survived and are still joiked today. Musicians of today become inspired and create new interpretations of the old joiks in their music compositions.

The Bear from Vuornese's Remarkable Story

At the same time as my father grew up in Eastern Vrjaren, his uncle Anders Andersson lived at the other end of the lake, at Western Vrjaren. There it is told that Anders discovered a human-made mound of stones close to his house. He showed his friend Andersson Smith this cairn about the year 1914. When they lifted the stones they found a skeleton from a bear. Around one of the head bones hung a chain of brass. This was an old bear grave. Later when a man called the *Germanî* came around, Anders sold the bones to him. Then the bear skeleton started a long journey.

Later the archeologist Inger Zachrisson wrote about the first part of this bear's history in a book. Not long after, she received a letter from Germany where a scientist wrote that they had a bear skeleton from Jutland there and one of a bear from Vrjaren. The vertebrae were slipped on a twig that was younger than the bones. The skeleton was lent to Sweden and dated to earlier than 250 years ago. I saw it myself in a box at the historical museum in Stockholm before it was returned to Germany. When Zachrisson and I inspected the find we discovered that only half of the bear's bones were there. Where were the other half of the bear bones? There may be a possible explanation: in the priest Pher Fjellstrˆm's small book, there is a note that Saamis and Swedes sometimes hunted together. The prey was then divided but the Saamis did not have access to all the bones. They still buried the bones they had. But this explanation did not correspond with the information Andersson and Smith gave about the circumstance of the bear grave. They stated that they did not think even one bone was missing in the grave. So either the other half was left in Vrjaren or it was missing from the long journey the skeleton had traveled. Western Vrjaren is today abandoned and the houses are decayed. No person lives there and to find Anders Andersson's cairn would be an impossible task.

Gifts to the Gods

When Christianity occupied Saami land many restrictions were introduced, including a prohibition on making sacrifices to the gods. In opposition to the restrictions, people continued to make sacrifices and the tales about them lived even longer. There are plenty of stories about sacrifice, both oral and written. I get the impression that the habit to sacrifice was widespread and continued long after the Saamis had officially became Christian.

Particularly famous are the sacrificial stones known as *seitar,* but the name belongs to the North Saami territory. More common in the south is the word *Sjielegierkie*. In Vuornese and Vilhelmina variants of the word *tsieggjue* are used, such as *tjekku*, *tsikko*, *sikku* or *tjetteke*. The name of the neighborhood, Gddedes, is said to be the word *tjekkeke* in a Swedish form. *Tsieggjue* originally meant something that stands up and was a term describing the reindeer-sacrifice that was buried standing up (something I will talk about more later). Meanwhile the meaning changed so that even sacrificial stones and woods/trees were included. Similar changes in the language are seen for example in the word *nÂjd*, or more specifically, *nÂejtie*, that was a term restricted to the shaman in the older days but that today includes other healers too.

There were sacrificial stones and woods and trees. Sacrificial woods were formed simply by hand to take the shape of humans. The tree gods are difficult to find today as they decompose with time, but the stones are still there. Sacrifices to a tree god were practiced by people in this region from the beginning of the 19th century. From Marsfjll, the curators from the historical museum in Sweden removed a sacrificial tree that now stands for public viewing in their Saami exhibition in Stockholm.

The sacrificial stone is naturally shaped but still has something that contrasts it with the environment. For example, its color, shape or position were all distinctive. Parts of the hunting prey were sacrificed and the blood from these parts was smeared on the stone. It provided answers to prayers, and if someone asked it something it was believed to give the answer by becoming light or heavy when it was lifted. People sacrificed for their own well-being, for health, successful birth-giving, reindeer hunting, and fishing fortune. A person mostly used several stones. This was so because a stone could vary in power and even lose its power. It was viewed as a ruler over something with a strong connection to a particular area, or as a temple. A way to show respect for the stone was to put fresh branches around it, something called *duorkstith* or *dorg*, the same term which described putting new branches in the *gÂetie*. To worship a sacrificial stone was later called *dorga*.

Such a sacrificial stone is situated at the mountain peak Dajmanjapp. The tradition about this mountain is forgotten but it was alive in 1943 when Levi Johansson compiled an inventory for the Nordic museum in Stockholm. Several people knew by that time that the stone had been a sacrificial stone and they had seen animal bones lying next to it. Nobody made sacrifices then; rather this stone was avoided as it was considered a place of spirits. In 1954 two curators at the museum discovered a collection of stones that seemed to have been placed there by people. It was revealed that the stones covered a large amount of reindeer bones, many split. These in all likelihood pointed to *daktesijej* (bone sites) and *jartesiijej* (earth-sites). The curators drew the conclusion that the bone site had to do with the sacrificial stone. *Daktesijej* are remains of a meal where the animal's bones have been placed in the body's natural order. It derived from the idea that an animal is given a new body as long as it has all its original bones intact. It could then go on living in the other world. Even though the rituals were fragmented and the concepts diminished by the imposition of Christianity, the old way of splitting instead of cutting the animal bones was still preserved. Another *daktesije* was discovered by Birger Isaksson, a local from Borgafjll. It is situated at Garsegaske.

The big stone at Dajmanjapp is isolated and is located at *pÂ fjllkanten* (above the treeline) and has over the years maintained its resemblance to a face although some parts of the stone have cracked. Another strange stone we found on the mountain Borgahllan. *Inlandsisen* (inland ice) has been found placed beautifully on some small rocks and it appears as if somebody had placed it there on purpose! Beside the stone there is a human-made mound of stones. This is possibly a sacrificial stone whose tradition has been largely forgotten. In accordance with the Dajmanjappstone, it is situated on a ground of stone. Nothing could have been buried there, so the bones that might have been placed there are gone without a trace.

In Subpme another sacrificial stone was believed to have been found. It is big with a strange shape, in the middle of an old Saami camp. Astrid Kroik, who has lived a great part of her life in Subpme, speaks with a gleam in her eye that the more tourists that came to see the stone the more the belief grew that it was a sacrificial stone. She remembers that in her youth there were stones placed on the stone, possibly indicating a history of sacrifice.

Silver in the Horns

A common story is about reindeer sacrifice that has been buried so that only the horns are visible above the ground. The sacrifice does not seem to have any connection with sacrificial stones or woods. This is a story from my great-grandfather, Klockar-Ante from Eastern Vrjaren:

There is something mysterious at Leipikvattnet, and I believe that there is such a place of reindeer sacrifice. It is south-west of the lake and not very far from the river, close to the border and higher up, and it was in the middle of the summer that I was there. I found sticks of birch raised and I thought that somebody was hoping to find something there. So I became suspicious and started to look around because I thought there might be silver there. And it probably did exist there! Instead, I found a 15-year-old reindeer ox which had been sacrificed. He was buried in the ground so that only the horns were visible. No silver was on them. I thought I would go back to that place when not too many people were around because there was surely silver in the bottom like old coins and such things.

The sacrificial sites were respected long after the change of religion, but after some time looting became common. From the time when people were tempted to take with them the sacrificial gifts many stories describe what happened in those cases, for example this story from 1928. Olof Persson from Raukasjˆ recalls this account:

> East of the Lake Seunan and east of a small lake on the swamp there, by a frequently used path between Dabbsjˆn and Daima in the older days, lies a Saami sacrificial site. It is like a small open place in the forest there. About 30 years ago it was fully visible, and many people, even Swedes, knew about this sacrificial site. A horn was visible from the ground and in it silver leaves were tied. On the ground lay several little things. People knew that it was dangerous to take things from there and for that reason everyone would lie as to where the silver was. But a defiant man, Klemet Andersson, from Orrnsfjll, decided to take the silver that was there. On the way home to Daima where he lived, he got sick and had to rest as soon as he arrived. He became worse and realized that he would die if he did not return the sacrificial silver. He did so but he never got completely well again. He grew weaker until he died.

At the end of the time of sacrifice, no animal was sacrificed; only small metal objects were used in rituals. One of the most famous sacrificial stones is in Marsfjll on an often used path. Today only the tourists stick coins in the cracks of the stones.

Gievrie gvisare n: An Advisor

In every South Saami valley, there is at least one proud oral tradition about a drum (*gievrie ñ* – something that is bent, and *mievrie ñ* – noise or song) that has been buried in the mountains. The level of truth in the stories is difficult to determine but remains have been found in the ground. As late as 1950 a man from Ankarvattnet found something by coincidence that would prove to be the frame of a 300-year-old drum. He was out working in the mountains and caught sight of something he thought was a riddle or something similar. He left the small objects that lay deeper under the stones, but took the drum with him. When he learned that he had found a drum-frame and that the small objects he left probably belonged to it, he tried to find the place again but in vain. The man died the next year, but the drum remains are still with his widow.

Drums were believed to be quite common in the older days. It is possible that every household had a drum to ask for advice when there was a need for it. During the time when the drums were used in certain ceremonies, a hunt started out for them. The Saami were forced to give away their drums that were buried, essentially destroying an important symbol of their culture. That is why some Saami people chose to hide their treasures in the mountains instead.

The missionaries focused on the drum's religious meaning, but they did not understand that it had many practical meanings and was necessary for the reindeer herding. Jonas IhrÈn tells us that one could find out with the help of the drum whether beasts of prey or even robbers, so-called *tjorie*, were coming. It was possible to see which way was best and least dangerous for the animals and it is even told that the drum could help a lost person find his way. Jonas IhrÈn also says that many Saami, even after becoming Christian, could not understand what was wrong with believing in an almighty God and asking the drum about such things. Even Christian believers had to know this in their daily work with the reindeer. Maybe this is the reason that the drum tradition was so rich in this area and the reason why it was kept for so long. Jonas IhrÈn could name a person who kept his drum up to 1910.

The last person to own a drum (and sometimes mentioned as the last nÂejtieî) in the area is told to be Tomas Nilsson, my grandmother's grandfather. His son, Lars Aron, is told to have hidden the drum in some cave in the valley of Skornjan, or at the east end of Lill Raukasjˆ after his father's death. Whether the statements are true or not is hard to say, but it is possible that Lars Aron hid his father's drum in the neighborhood.

Lately the drums have come into fashion. Handicraft men have learned how to make drums again. They are very beautiful instruments and are mainly sold for decoration purposes. People among the so-called New Age circles have been influenced by shamanism, which has led to a movement called Neo-Shamanism, even though there appears to be significant confusion among many 'New Age' Europeans as to where their spiritual roots lie. Among these people the newly manufactured Saami drums are also very popular. The drum is used for the purpose of reaching a state of trance. The old drum was not traditionally used as a music instrument by the Saami, but has nowadays found its way to the instrumentalists and joiker of today.

Fatmomakkesmycket

At the church place Fatmomakke just north of Vuornese, a strange find was discovered in the spring of 1981. When a grave was dug, two Saami ornaments became visible at a depth of 30 centimeters. One of the ornaments is believed to be an *arpa*. The *arpa* was used by the *nÂjd* of the older days when he was divining with the drum. It was placed on the membrane and the *nÂjd* beat it with the hammer so that the object jumped over the membrane. When the *arpa* stopped on a particular picture, the *nÂjd* could read the answer to his question. This beautiful metal ornament provided inspiration to the goldsmith Tore Davidsson in Vilhelmina to make an ornament collection and a bridal wreath with the *arpa* as a model.

This ornament shape has its roots in Catholic history. It is told by the M-form. This M stands for Maria, mother of Jesus, and was a common symbol in Scandinavia during the early Catholic period when the Maria cult was most alive. The pendant is a variant of an *A* that stands for Anna, Maria's mother. Anna, as well as Maria, fashioned her disciplines and cult during this time. The letters have had their own Saami characteristics and are nowadays very common and popular motifs. On the Fatmomakkesmycket, the *A*-shape looks like a man and thus it is believed that he is a *nÂjd*. Fatmomakkesmycket as it is now called is worn as a brooch or a pendant and signifies a testimony and a greeting from a *nÂjd* who had the ability to move in time and space just like his *arpa* has done. The original is kept at the museum of Vsterbotten in UmeÂ.

The Pictures Narrate...

Lately and thanks to the work of Bernt Ove Wklund, many rock carvings and paintings have been discovered in the area. Wklund has been working in the parish of Ingermanland where a part of the Vuornese Saami village is situated. There is reason to believe that even more rock art remains to be revealed in places other than Ingermanland. The rock art is thousands of years old and difficult to date exactly. It provides us with some idea of the precolonial world that the people lived in before the arrival of missionaries and colonizers. Mostly animals, and among them elk have most frequently been depicted on the rocks, but there are also humans and abstract characters. Why these characters were depicted as such is difficult to fathom. Scientists have suggested that the animal pictures were made with the belief that the animal and its pictorial depiction were connected to each other. By reproducing a successful hunt in art, the same event could actually occur. The opinion that rock art was made for this *jaktmagiskt* (magical hunting) purpose has been criticized. Other scientists suggest that such a hypothesis reflects a view of the people that makes them look ignorant and naive. The pictures should rather be interpreted as a reflection of the shamanistic conception of the world in which they lived. According to this interpretation, the animals could be helping spirits. The last word in this debate has yet to be heard.

Conclusion. Vuornese: A Place with a History and a Site of Indigenous Wisdom

Vuornese is a rich cultural place with a clear continuity of the Saami's life in the region today. What started as a summer project has turned into a systematic research project that has been going on for years. To find all these remnants from the past and their meanings has not been easy. The information in the archives is meager and the region is not fully explored.

The complex question of cultural heritage also is not easy. While the Indigenous people have an interest to know more about their history they are reluctant to dig up their ancestors' graves, as all Indigenous people are. The dead should rest in peace and the Saami people have suffered enough from the dehumanization and humiliation through colonization and imposed religion. This history of domination has led the Saami to keep silent about the precise locations of their holy places. Too many sacred objects and skeletons of ancestors have been lost. The objects have now been squandered in distant and unknown places, shamefully stored in European museums or, sadly, have been destroyed.

Recently, a debate about where these historical Indigenous constructions belong resulted in the Saami Parliament's request that these items be returned to the Saami people, especially the craniums and skeletons stolen from the Saami for archeological investigation and Darwinian science. Some are remnants from people whose names, relatives, and homes are known by living Saami individuals.

Much of the Indigenous religion of the Saami may have been lost, but the Saamis still have their Indigenous dignity. Their historical objects still have a meaning and a value to the contemporary people. Objects and remains link the living to their ancestors who have passed on to the spirit world. It is important that both the Saami and the Scandinavians are able to understand each other's histories, although the Scandinavian subjugation of the Saami must be acknowledged and confronted so that the genocidal past is not repeated. There is certainly reason to be proud of a people like the Saami, who, with plenty of inventive ability and few material resources have managed to survive in a harsh and risky environment for thousands of years and yet left little trace of this vast-reaching history.

The mysterious stones in the ground at Gaustdahke awaken the curiosity, enhance the self-esteem of the Saami as they rediscover their true history and identity, and signify a cultural treasure not only for Saamis but to everybody who lives in the area. It even has a value for the tourists who find their way there. The historical remains that exist there are unique and have to be treated with great care. In spite of this request by the Saami, these remains are treated shabbily by the dominant European culture: the two graves lie just beside a *grustag* (heap of gravel) that the spring's melting water slowly destroys, bringing the gravel closer to the graves with each successive year. The pit traps in Storjola were taken away without permission of the Saami, and the ritually treated bear bones lie in a box in Germany. My request to the curators of the museums and the archeologists who removed these objects is that they return them to their original location in the region so that people here and others can understand the rich history of the Saami people. To protect these sacred remains is an obligation that we have to our precursors, to ourselves, and to our children and future generations.

Africa

Chapter 13

African Indigenous Worldviews and Ancient Wisdom: A Conceptual Framework for Development in Southern Africa

Vimbai Gukwe Chivaura

Introduction

The central concern for us in Southern Africa is to assume full responsibility for our own development. This development process includes material and spiritual aspects which must be in balance with each other. Our development depends on both dimensions of materiality and spirituality. It can only be truly human when the material and spiritual harmonize. The spiritual tempers the material and vice versa; this relationship is mutual.

Indigenous self-propelled development is important in Southern Africa for numerous reasons. We have been dominated by imperialism, ruled by colonialism, exploited by capitalism, oppressed by racism, and humiliated by minority-settler whites longer than most other people on the African continent. The result of this protracted and entrenched European hegemony is that we have been forced to imbibe Western European culture, knowledge systems, languages and worldviews to the extent that we often appear to be more Eurocentric than the Europeans themselves! We derive our standards of development from Europeans. We work for them, wash their clothes, iron their sheets, make their beds, sweep their houses, nurse their children and cook for them while our own starve. We apparently love Western Europeans more than we love ourselves. We certainly care for them more than we care for ourselves!

It can also be argued that we share with Africans in the Diaspora in our alienation and self-denigration. They are away from their home in Africa. They have been uprooted from African knowledge systems and culture through the genocidal history of enslavement by Europeans in the Americas. In the United States (known as Turtle Island by many Indigenous people) Africans have lived long as a minority among their white abductors. They have struggled to connect with Mother Africa in many instances such as during the Back to Africa movement in the 1920s and during the civil rights movement of the 1960s. In Zimbabwe we find ourselves in the curious position of neocolonialism where we often cooperate with whites in our own destruction and have generally capitulated to viewing whites as masters. This may explain why we have been the last to win independence and self-rule in Africa. Even these are a sham. We have not won economic independence since whites still own the most productive lands in Zimbabwe and the bulk of the economy. We have not even won social equality yet since whites are still treated as superior people. We have not won freedom of thought. We use white generally to describe our reality in formal educational settings.

We have not won freedom of expression. We still use European languages as the lingua franca of commerce, education and communication. The media is still in white hands. We are therefore not responsible for our own development and destiny in Southern Africa as Africans. The foreign models we use are hostile to our interests as Africans. We need our own worldview and models of development for us in Southern Africa to be truly independent.

This chapter will critique the Eurocentric philosophies and models of development employed by what the African scholar Chinweizu describes as 'Europhiliac' Africans and argue that our own Indigenous worldviews and models of development will set us free from dehumanization and the barbarism of oppression because our models have the interests of Africans and the humanity of Africans at heart.[1]

An Indigenous African Worldview

The importance of balance in African human development and worldview is clearly explained by Mazisi Kunene in his introduction to *Anthem of the Decades* (1981). This is an epic poem on Zulu cosmology describing the balance between material and the spiritual, the seen and unseen, and the tangible and intangible. According to the Zulu worldview, 'Our world is not the only one.'[2] Other worlds do exist in the universe. 'Some [are] at the stage of completion, some at the stage of unfolding [and] some at the stage of annihilation.'[3] Kunene implies that all worlds are self-sufficient. They have their own moons and suns. They can be known or felt although they are far away. They influence our human world and we must live in harmony with them.

The African worldview declares that our world has two aspects. They are the physical and spiritual. The spiritual manifests itself in various ways. It appears through third parties. It can be experienced as dreams and visions. It can express itself as premonition or intuition. The material and spiritual, therefore, coexist both in human societies and the rest of nature since we are all interwoven into the fabric of the spiritual universe.

Our world therefore contains everything we need, spiritual or material. Our duty is to harness both and enrich our lives. We are buried here on earth when we die.

---

1   Chinweizu, *The West and the Rest of Us*, New York, Random House (1970).

2   Mazisi Kunene, *Introduction to Anthem of the Decades: A Zulu Epic*, London, Heinemann (1981), ix–x.

3   Ibid.

Our spirits are released from our physical bodies. They spend a period among the Ancestors for at least a year. They come back to earth as Ancestors themselves and play their part as advisors and peace brokers in our lives. The balance between the spiritual and the physical in our lives as Africans is, again, in operation here.

The ceremony of return is *ukubuyisa* in Zulu.[4] It is *kurovaguva* in Shona. *Ukubuyisa* is to bring back the Ancestors and integrate them into family and social life. The same applies to *kurovaguva*. It is to summon the ancestors and empower them through ritual to play their part in family and social life.

The ancestors and the living need each other. They are mutual and equal. They are governed by *umthetho wobuntu*, the 'fundamental law of humanity,' and *umthetho wemvelo*, 'the law of origins.'[5] They both must obey *uMvelinqangi umdali wezulu nomhlaba*.[6] This means God, the Creator of heaven, life and all laws, and living in harmony and balance with each other and God and all creation here on earth.

The importance of unity between the living and the ancestors in the African worldview reflects the integration of the spirit-realm and the physical world and the involvement of the spirit world in our social sphere. According to the dominant Western European view, Earth is essentially evil and death is viewed as freedom from hell into heaven or paradise. In the African worldview, paradise is survival of the community and the continuity of the life of one's people here on earth.[7]

The earth-centeredness of the African worldview can be demonstrated with reference to African dance. All African dances are earth-centered. Let's take *Mutshongoyo* or *Isitshikitsha* in Zulu or Ndebele as examples. The stamping of the ground with the staff or feet is the emphatic expression of human beings connecting with the Earth Mother.[8] *Izigi zomhlaba* or 'echoes of the mutual affirmations of earth to that contractual covenant unity between earth and humanity' are foundational in African worldviews.

Earth is the be-all and end-all in African worldviews or dance. She is life. She is paradise. There is no hell in the African worldview. You make hell or heaven here on earth by flouting or obeying the fundamental laws of humanity and origins here on earth. The differences between African and European worldviews concerning earth and heaven relate to differences in their attitudes towards the material and the spiritual. Africans regard them as compatible. They emphasize mutual relationship and harmony. Europeans see them as antagonistic. They emphasize mutual conflict and, therefore, separation.

The danger of adopting the European worldview to solve African problems is therefore obvious. It is hostile to our own worldview and idea of development. African development can only be truly achieved through an African worldview.

---

4   Ibid., xix.
5   Ibid., xxvii.
6   Ibid., xv.
7   Ibid., xviii.
8   Ibid., xix.

That is the way we in Southern Africa can realize our humanity and aspirations as Africans.

African Knowledge Systems

African knowledge systems are the sources of the African worldview. They are ways that Africans use to encode, package, preserve and share information and wisdom and pass it on to future generations. There are various knowledge and information systems in Africa. They include the arts and languages that African people speak in Southern Africa, the African continent and her Diaspora.

Africa as reference point is what defines their identity. That is what Indigenous means. It means roots. All those people who look up to Africa as the source of their lives and ideals share the same worldview and roots. They are all one people. They are all African. Chancellor Williams explains:

> That we are here studying a single race, not races, a single people, not peoples, is a major theory and fact of black history and one of our principal guidelines. We are concerned with things characteristically African, practically universal among them from one end of the continent to the other and an ancient common culture in a common center of Black Civilization. On this we stand.[9]

African wisdom is one for the same reason. It is a body into which African people from the past, present and future pour their observations, knowledge, information and conclusions from their experiences in history. It is open-ended and dynamic. It is passed on from generation to generation. It is adaptable. It is ancient. Men instill discipline while women impart manners. Gayl Jones describes an example:

> My great-grandmam told my grandmama the part she lived through that my grandmama didn't live through and my grandmama told my mama what they both lived through and my mama told me what they all lived through and we were supposed to pass it down like that from generation to generation so we'd never forget.[10]

Maya Angelou provides another anecdote:

> She said that I must always be intolerant of ignorance but understanding of illiteracy. That some people, unable to go to school, were more educated and even more intelligent than college professors. She encouraged me to listen carefully to what people called mother wit. That in those homely sayings was couched the collective wisdom of generations.

> Women in African wisdom hold a special place. They give us birth. They breastfeed us. They provide us with our first food. They look after our health. They teach us manners.

---

9   Williams, Chancellor, *The Destruction of Black Civilization*, Third World Press, Chicago (1987), 161.

10   McKnight, Reginald (ed.), *African American Wisdom*, San Rafael, California, New World Library (1994), 1.

They give us morals and our first 'tongues.' They hold the key to our lives. We may disrespect our fathers but never our mothers.

The disrespect that we see towards women today is not of African teaching nor African in origin. It is from an alien worldview and society. 'Never chide your mother,' we say in Shona. You cannot teach her morals. Nigeria's Chinua Achebe asserts that:

A woman who began cooking before another must have more broken utensils.[11] "A new broom may sweep clean, but an old brush knows the corners."[12] When old people speak, it is not because of the sweetness of words in our mouth; it is because we see something you do not see. Our fathers made a proverb about it. They said when we see an old woman stop in her dance to point again and again in the same direction we can be sure that somewhere there something happened long ago which touched the roots of her life.[13]

Those who flout the wisdom of the elders are like the little bird *Nza* who ate and drank and challenged his personal god to a single combat.[14] They are doomed to suffer the fate of the 'The Chicken in the Well' which reads thus:

"Don't go near the well! Don't play round it!" Mother Hen [had] said to her children. And they never came to the well. But once a little chicken ran to the well and stopped there. "Why is this so bad?" he thought. "I am here and everything is all right with me." "Let me see what is in the well." And he jumped up to look into it. And what did he see there? He saw another chicken. Our chicken turned his head; the chicken in the well did the same. The chicken jumped; so did the chicken in the well. He became angry with the chicken in the well and decided to have a fight with him. He jumped down into the well. But there was no chicken to fight with, only water and water. He cried, "Help me, help me!" But nobody heard him. He went down under the cold water, and nobody saw him again.[15]

That is exactly what the Igbo mean when they say 'A fly that has no one to advise it will follow the corpse to the grave.'[16] '*Unofa senhunzi*,' they say in Shona, which means 'You die like a fly.' But African wisdom will not allow elders to let children meet their tragedy that way. There is a time that children must be disciplined. 'Spare the rod and spoil the child' may be applied here. Children must know that 'A hard

---

11 Chinua Achebe, *Girls at War and other Stories*, Heinemann, London (1977), 100.

12 Cited in Reginald McKnight, *African American Wisdom*, San Rafael, New World Library, California (1994), 64.

13 Chinua Achebe, *Girls at War and other Stories*, Heinemann, London (1977), 14.

14 Chinua Achebe, *Anthills of the Savannah*, Garden City, NY, Anchor Press/Doubleday (1988), 14.

15 MOCKBA, *Tales and Legends of Africa* (1987), 10–11.

16 Chinua Achebe, *Anthills of the Savannah*, Garden City, NY, Anchor Press/Doubleday (1988), 14.

head makes a soft behind.'[17] If your mother can't thrash you herself, your father will!

Wisdom in the African Worldview

African wisdom is not mere information. It is situational. It is knowledge tested by time and long observation, following serious contemplation and reflection on human behavior and nature of things and life. It is the 'rock of ages' and 'ancient of days,' *Chidzivachepo* in Shona or 'Permanent Pool.' It is always there, adjustable and adaptable for all people for all time. We have the following explanations from various African writers to illustrate the power of Indigenous African wisdom. The elder in Achebe's *Arrow of God* has this advice to the confused Western-educated youth of today:

> Look here my son, "This path was here before you were born and before your father was born. The whole life of the village depends on it. Our dead relatives depart by it and our ancestors visit us by it. But most important, it is the path of children coming to be born."[18]

Wole Soyinka emphasizes the nontemporal nature of African worldview and wisdom as follows:

> The expression "the child is father of the man," becomes within the context of this time structure, not merely a metaphor of development rooted in a system of representative individuation, but a proverb of human continuity which is not unidirectional. Neither "child" nor "father" is a closed chronological concept.[19]

Ugandan author Okot p'Bitek explains what history means in African worldview and wisdom:

The African of tradition is not bothered about the beginning of time. He or she is not interested in the least about the end of time. History [to him or her] like all other arts is an integral part of culture and should be carried inside the head to enliven the entire body of the individual in society. But, alas, the history of the books exists only as corpses in the graveyard called the library. Occasionally some curious fellow would refer to them, especially for examination purposes. But this type of history is not lived by people in society. It has no impact, influence or importance for the living of here and now. It is not celebrated in song and dance, nor in poetry or the *Ebivugo* of Western Uganda. In these books there are plenty of pictures, statues, ruins, and old coins bearing the heads of some ancient ruler or other. But they do not

---

17 Cited in Reginald McKnight, *African American Wisdom*, San Rafael, New World Library, California (1994), 64.

18 Chinua Achebe, *Arrow of God*, London, Heinemann (1977), 73–74.

19 Wole Soyinka, *Myth, Literature, and the African World*, Cambridge University Press, New York (1976), 31.

stir me much in the way that a living history does…The African of tradition is not bothered about the distant past. History is strictly a functional business. He or she remembers the past, which is meaningful; that is, those events and personalities that explain, make meaningful and justify the present. To the African of tradition, history is not the record of all events that happened in the past. It is those events; wars, droughts, famines, migrations, eclipses, floods, the founding, flourishing and decline of chiefdoms, shrines, the rise of great doctors, scientists, agriculturalists.[20]

Mazisi Kunene of South Africa says:

> The secret of ancient wisdom lies in the names of things and their forgotten meanings.
> [T]he naming of things follows a principle of describing their function, appearance, sounds and relationships, not merely to identify and label them…it is from such a study that one can amass and trace some of the fundamental philosophies of the culture.[21] The encoding of Indigenous African ancient wisdom is enigmatic to most. Meaning is revealed to those who know the language and worldview it expresses. But depth of the meaning is only bequeathed to the initiated and chosen few. The symbols with which to encode the meaning are organized [in such a way as] to appeal to a complex and varied set of community emotions. [They] carry within [their] inner meanings thoughts which seem simple but grow more complex as one probes deeper into their hidden systems. In the discovery of these meanings lies one of the most amazing experiences one can have. In them is embodied a timeless set of values which by their ethical authority supersede the whims of temporal political power. [22]

When declaiming Zulu heroic poetry or *imbongi,* for instance, the poet addresses not only the living but also those gone before. The address is

> more than a frivolous comment on the heroic deeds of men and women; it is a cosmic address, a prayer to life, a celebration of the accomplishments of all the generations of man. The individuals in the poem become symbols of a greater belief in the national ethic and continuity of life.[23]

The African way of encoding their worldview and philosophy of life and wisdom is vastly different from that of the West. The Western worldview is essentially one-dimensional, materially centered and temporally circumscribed. The Africana view is multidimensional and temporally transcendental. African worldviews and wisdom look like myth and superstitious metaphysics when cast in a Western mold. We must insist on using our own worldview and wisdom as conceptual frameworks for our own development in Southern Africa and Africa as a whole and for the African Diaspora. Ways of encoding and decoding the Diaspora's worldviews and wisdom remain the same even when using other people's languages. Africans in the Diaspora are still informed by their African culture. Examples are African writers in English

---

20 Okot p'Bitek, *Artist, the Ruler*, Nairobi, Kenya, Heinemann (1986), 42–47.

21 Kunene, op. cit., ix.

22 Ibid.

23 Ibid., xi.

or other European languages who are not brainwashed by the West. Mastery of any language that one chooses to speak or write in is applauded in the African worldview. But one's own language comes first. One must take pride in writing and speaking one's own mother tongue and being in control of its nuances at all times. The 'Story about the Tongue' is an example:

> Once a chief told one of his servants to bring him the best meat from the market. The servant brought him a tongue. The next day the chief told the servant to bring him the worst meat from the market. The servant brought a tongue again. "What?" the chief said, "When I ask for the best meat, you bring a tongue and then you bring the same thing for the worst meat." The servant said, "Sometimes a man is very unhappy because of his tongue; and sometimes his tongue makes him very happy." "You are right," the chief said. "Let us be masters of our tongue!"[24]

The following example demonstrates the success in controlling one's language as well as the failure to do so. The first is considered as mature and wise, the second as childish and churlish. It is, therefore, smoothly debunked and exposed for the shallowness of thought and lack of wisdom and mastery of language that characterizes it:

> Once there lived an old woman. She had two donkeys. Every morning she went with them down the street to the fields. One morning two young men saw the old woman with her donkeys and shouted: "Good morning, mother of donkeys!" "Good morning, my sons!" the old woman answered and smiled at them.[25]

African knowledge systems are survival strategies. That is why the deeper meanings of sacred ones are made elusive to grasp fully and interpret by the vulgar as in the story above. Sacred meanings are entrusted only to those who will use them responsibly for the benefit of communities. No amount of outside training or genius can access such meanings. Only knowledge received from upbringing within the worldview and wisdom of African society itself can produce a viable conceptual framework for Africa's true independence and self-determination. Outside knowledge as imposed under colonialism and capitalism has not worked for Africa's development, but instead underdeveloped and arrested her path of autonomous development. Eurocentric knowledge systems have systematically discredited and denied the validity of Indigenous knowledge systems and civilizations. Great Zimbabwe is a classic example. The whole edifice is an enigma to strangers, particularly Europeans:

> In the middle of this country is a fortress… [It] is built of large and heavy stones inside and out, a very curious and well-constructed building according to reports as no lime to join the stones can be seen. In other districts of the said plain there are other fortresses built in the same manner. Over the gate of the building is an inscription neither the Moorish

---

24 *Tales and Legends of Africa*, MOCKBA, 8.
25 Ibid.

[Swahili] traders nor others learned in inscriptions could read, nor does anyone know in what character it is written.[26]

The same happened with visitors to South Africa in 1896. They report the following mystery:

> Lt. Col. E.L. de Cordes, who was in South Africa for three years, informed the writer that in one of the "Ruins" there is a "stone-chamber," with a vast quantity of Papyri, covered with old Egyptian hieroglyphics. A Boer hunter discovered this, and a large quantity was used to light a fire with, and yet still a larger quantity remained there.[27]

African rituals, handcrafts, paintings, arts and architecture are also inscrutable to aliens as knowledge systems. Bent tells of his immense amazement concerning the skills and artistry that went into the construction of Great Zimbabwe:

> Entering from the northern portal, we at once plunge into its intricacies. The great and astounding feature is the long narrow passage leading direct from the main entrance to the sacred enclosure, so narrow in parts that two people cannot walk abreast, whilst on either side of you rise the stupendous walls, thirty feet in height, and built with such evenness of courses and symmetry that as a specimen of the dry builder's art it is without a parallel.[28]

He wonders what all this meant about the worldview and wisdom of the Shona people who constructed the monument:

> Vainly one tries to realize what it must have been like in the days before ruin fell upon it, with its tortuous and well-guarded approaches, its walls bristling with monoliths and round towers, its temple decorated with tall, weird-looking birds, its huge decorated bowls, and in the innermost recesses its busy gold-producing furnace. What was this life like?[29]

The passing of African worldviews and wisdom from generation to generation using various knowledge systems of encoding messages and communicating them is an important part of the heritage of African culture. It is learned through socialization and upbringing. To master one's worldview, knowledge systems, and philosophy of life and wisdom is a responsibility and achievement of the highest order. It is akin to the tortoise. The tortoise never leaves its shell behind. It carries it along wherever it goes. That is why we regard the tortoise as wise. We must carry our worldview wherever we go. It is our humanity. It is our destiny.

---

26 Walker (1999), 105–106.
27 Ibid.
28 Ibid.
29 Ibid.

Development in the African Worldview

Development in the African worldview has two aspects. One is social. The other is technical. The social is spiritual. The technical is economic. These dimensions must balance in African development but cannot be confused as being identical with each other.[30]

While capitalist societies describe social and material progress in identical terms of growth from lower to higher levels, African worldviews separate the two spheres depicting the ethical and the technological in balance with each other. One of the commonly stated ethical judgments in Ndebele society, for instance, illustrates this contradiction: *Banako konke kodwa yizinja*, which translates to 'They have everything material, but they are as contemptible as dogs,' which is to say, human beings have reduced themselves to a predatory existence. This proverb is not mentioned in a flippant vein but rather reflects a serious critique of the violators of the social ethic. Thus a highly ethically advanced society need not necessarily be technologically advanced; conversely, a technologically advanced society does not automatically possess a high ethical quality. Indeed, more often than not, technological advancement tends to demonize society, since by its very nature it implies a high degree of competitiveness for resources. In short, the instruments or tools for fashioning humankind's material environment do not necessarily improve or enhance the ethical quality of the society.

Kenyan author Ngugi wa Thiong'o, in *Writers in Politics*, critiques the United States and Western European model of development:

America has reached hitherto undreamed of heights in the conquest of nature through a fantastic development of instruments of labor (i.e. technology). But America today is a man-eat-man society. In the realm of social nature, America is still in a state of social cannibalism. It eats its own children and the children of other lands especially of Africa, Latin America and Asia. What I have said of America is true of what has been called Western civilization. Some African civilizations had not developed the conquest of nature to a very high degree; but they had developed to a high degree their control of social nature.[31]

Economic development is material. It covers people's physical needs. Examples are homes, food, clothing, transportation and shelter. Tools to produce them are included. The challenge to true human development in African worldview as Ngugi puts it is to strive for a civilization that ensures adequate clothing, shelter and food for everyone. It is to create a society that ensures that all the benefits of modern science and knowledge are made available to all and that social cannibalism on earth is brought to an end.

---

30 Kunene, Mazisi, *The Ancestors and the Sacred Mountain*, Heinemann, London (1982), xi.

31 Ngugi wa Thiong'o, *Writers in Politics*, London, Heinemann (1981), 67.

Such a challenge, Mazisi Kunene argues, compels the ethic of social integration and justice as ultimate in the scheme of development:

[T]he complexity of human relations, their cosmic significance, and their continuity become a much greater criterion of human intellect and history than the faculty that is developed as a result of man's confrontation with his material environment. From this viewpoint the earliest act of civilization was not the creation of a tool but the establishment of a cooperative, interactive, human community. When that human community began to modify its material environment to make life better for succeeding generations, then it began the second most important act of civilization: that of providing for communities beyond its own immediate circumstance.[32]

The provision of material needs of community cannot be done fully through development programs fashioned from outside, but through local innovation, creativity and hard work. Outside models are not for us. They suit the particular conditions for which they were intended to address. Our development projects must be planned, controlled and directed by ourselves.

The dangers of imposing imported development models are real. Recent history substantiates that development programs engineered from outside Africa elude our control. We will have to always seek direction from those who conceptualized them for us. We will always be forced to turn to them for advice and training and continue as dependent slaves on the West. We will continue to have an unhealthy reliance on our former colonizers for maintenance of our borrowed technology. All these services consume time and money. They compromise our dignity as a sovereign people. They are out of step with our aspirations. '*Chinwango choumwe hachina ndima*' we say in Shona, which translates into 'A borrowed hoe has no harvest.'

Among the Zulu and Ndebele, there is a similar caution: *Ingwe idhla ngamabala,* which means 'A tiger uses its colors to catch and eat its prey' or 'The colors of the tiger will eat you.' When foreigners offer their assistance uninvited, the Shona remind us to stop for a moment and ask: *Mwoyochenai jaya kufura mwana wemvana madziwa?* which means, 'When a young man offers to wipe the nose of a young mother's baby, especially the one who is single, he is not being kind; rather he is after you.'

For us to attain true human development in Southern Africa in ways that do not compromise our sovereignty and dignity as African people we must shun our dependence on foreign ideologies, however attractive and magnanimous they may appear. We must turn to our Indigenous worldview and wisdom as our conceptual framework. '*Mudzimu weshiri uri mudendere*' say the Shona, which means 'A bird's soul is in its nest.'

---

32 Kunene, Mazisi, *The Ancestors and the Sacred Mountain*, Heinemann, London (1982), xi–xii.

Conclusion

We have more than enough Indigenous wisdom in Southern Africa to guide us to attain true human development. True development for us can only occur within the context of our own African culture, using Indigenous knowledge systems and worldviews as the conceptual framework. Development inspired by alien worldviews, especially the West, has actually fostered underdevelopment of our people. Our salvation lies within us. We are our own liberators. We must rely on our own wisdom. We must carry our shell like the tortoise.

References

Achebe, Chinua *Arrow of God*, London, Heinemann (1964).
_____, *Girls at War and other Stories*, London, Heinemann (1977).
Kunene, Mazisi, *Anthem of the Decades: A Zulu Epic*, London, Heinemann (1981).
_____, *The Ancestors and the Sacred Mountain*, London, Heinemann (1982).
Ngugi wa Thiong'o, *Writers in Politics*, London, Heinemann (1981).
Okot p'Bitek, *Artist, the Ruler*, Kenya, Nairobi, Heinemann (1986).
Soyinka, Wole, *Myth, Literature and the African World*, London, CUP (1976).
Tales and Legends of Africa, Harare, MOCKBA (1987).
Walker, Robin, *Roots of Black History*, London, Bogle L'Ouveture Press (1999).
Williams, Chancellor, *The Destruction of Black Civilization*, Chicago, Third World
       Press (1987).

Chapter 14

The Nature and Function of *Izibongo-Panegyric Legends: The Case of the Xhosa People of South Africa*

Somadoda Fikeni

On an occasion such as this we should, perhaps, start from the beginning. So let me begin. I am a (Xhosa) African. I owe my being to the hills and the valleys, the mountains and the glades, the rivers, the deserts, the trees, the flowers, the seas and the ever-changing seasons that define the face of our native land . A human presence among all these, a feature on the face of our native land thus defined, I know that none dare to challenge me when I say: I am a (Xhosa) African! I am the grandchild of the warrior men and women that Hintsa and Sekhukhune le, the patriots that Cetshwayo and Mphephu took to battle, the soldiers Moshoeshoe and Ngungunyane taught never to dishonor the cause of freedom.

It rejoices in the diversity of our people and creates the space for all of us voluntarily to define ourselves as one people. As an African this is an achievement of which I am proud, proud without reservation and proud without any feeling of conceit. Our sense of elevation at this moment also derives from the fact that this magnificent product is a unique creation of African hands and African minds, but also constitute a tribute of our loss of vanity that could, despite temptation to treat ourselves as an exceptional fragment of humanity, draw on the accumulated experience and wisdom of all humankind to define for ourselves what we want to be. . . I am an African. Today it feels good to be an African. . . I am an African. I am born of the peoples of the continent of Africa.

"I am an African" speech delivered by Deputy President of South Africa, Thabo Mbeki, on the occasion of the adoption of South Africa's new Constitution by the Constituent Assembly, 8 May 1996 in Cape Town.[1]

This speech by then Deputy President Thabo Mbeki exudes a sense of expansive satisfaction, pride and restorative dignity that is infused when people unequivocally affirm their identity through self-definition, a process which holds the ultimate promise of being in charge of one's own destiny while at the same time embracing the present and connecting with the past. There is no other conceivable form of genuine self-actualization than being able to define oneself. This becomes a highest point in

---

1 Thabo Mbeki, *Africa: the time has come: Selected Speeches-Thabo Mbeki* (1998), pp. 31–35.

one's sense of being, self-understanding, self-love, and ultimately intrinsic human dignity. Throughout history people have gone to wars to defend this ultimate sense of individual and group sovereignty or self-determination. If this timeless search for a sense of self-defined identity and, therefore, dignity and ultimate virtue of being, is denied or frustrated then there is a feeling of incompleteness, disharmony, and discontent which inevitably result from a loss of equilibrium within the human soul.

Introduction

One of the most painful difficulties for those of us who are Indigenous in Africa is writing in the language of the colonizer, and being forced to translate Indigenous concepts in ways that can be understood in European languages and cultures, even though in many instances, African words cannot be directly or precisely translated into European concepts since many European languages may not possess the equivalent. *Izibongo* is one such word.

In this chapter, I describe, classify, analyze and explain *izibongo* with the insights gathered from the Indigenous Xhosa peoples of South Africa, and amplify their voices in reflecting upon the significance of *izibongo*, particularly in its social and religious function. I will also draw from my own experience as an African who observes and lives in this cultural experience enriched with *izibongo*. By allowing these Indigenous voices long silenced in so-called mainstream literature to speak, I am merely engaged in a process of retrieving the wisdom which gives a window of opportunity for those who are genuinely interested in our lives and experiences. By putting myself and my experience at the center I transform that which has hitherto been regarded and studied as an object into a participant subject, affirming authenticity of my experience by holding a mirror to see myself in it.

The Xhosa-speaking Nation

Who are they? Where are they? The Xhosa-speaking nation is one of the Indigenous groups of South Africa. It is the second largest group in South Africa, second only to the Zulu-speaking nation in numbers. Most of AmXhosa are concentrated in the Southeastern region of South Africa in the present day province of the Eastern Cape. This concentration is between the Indian Ocean and *Intaba zoKhahlamba*, otherwise called Drakensberg Mountain Range. There are however, significant numbers of AmaXhosa who are settled in the following provinces of South Africa: the Western Cape, Free State, KwaZulu-Natal, Northern Cape, and Northwest. A few are also settled in Swaziland and Namibia. AmaXhosa are part of the Nguni people and Nguni also include AmaZulu, Amaswati, and AmaNdebele, Nguni people share a lot of cultural traits including mutually intelligible languages. For example, all Nguni people make frequent use of three click consonants derived from the San (Khoisan) languages. Of all these Nguni groups, isiXhosa has the most combinations of click sounds. Miriam Makeba, the renowned South African musician, often used these Xhosa click sounds in her songs. AmaXhosa are further categorized into sub-groups which include Xesibe, Thembu, Mfengu, Bomnvana, Baca, Pondo, Mpondomise, Gcaleka, Rarabe, and Hlubi.

The Meaning of *Izibongo*

Before embarking on a discussion of *izibongo*, it is important to describe this phenomenon of *izibongo* in order to have a sense of what they are and what they are not. From the very onset it should be categorically stated that *izibongo* happens to be one of those words[2] which has no English equivalent. The conventional English term which is often used to refer to *izibongo* is a "praise-poem" but this word is misleading as it only focuses on some aspects, particularly the poetic of *izibongo* while leaving out its nuances and components which are equally important. The use of the term praise-poem tends to obscure rather than illuminate the full meaning of *izibongo*. It is generally true that a textual analysis of *izibongo* as performed by *iimbongi*-court poets or bards will reveal a tendency to minimize criticism and maximize praise but this is only one aspect of a complex phenomenon. The historical, the educational, the spiritual as well as the individual or group identity markers of *izibongo* are not captured in a description that emphasize the "praise" or "boast" aspect to the exclusion of all other vital components. Consequently, simplification and reductionism, whether intended or not, become an inevitable result of this approach to *izibongo*. All indications point to the fact that the use of the terms "praise poetry" for *izibongo*, "praise poem" for *umbongo* and "praise poets" for an *imbongi* were motivated by a search for a Western, and more specifically an English equivalent term where there is none, thus distorting the very meaning of the concept. The pervasive nature of *izibongo* also makes it very difficult to apprehend in any form of a neat definition or conceptualization without oversimplification of what is otherwise a complex phenomenon.

It is therefore necessary to make a cursory reference to the literature's attempts to define *izibongo* while at the same time exposing some limitations of these efforts. Damane and Sanders explain "praise poems" or *izibongo/lithoko* in the following manner:

> They are not historical narratives, but poetry with historical allusions. In general, accuracy and clarity have been sacrificed for the sake of eulogy and aesthetic excellence.[3]

According to Du Toit, *Izibongo*

> ...contain all elements generally found in folk-narrative, it is highly stylized poetic form rendered by a speaker in a chant rather than an ordinary speaking voice and accompanied

---

2   It should be noted that a general survey of the literature on this subject as well as personal encounters reveal widespread use of izibongo in other ethnic societies of the Indigenous peoples of southern Africa.

3   Damane, M., and Sanders, P. (eds), *Lithoko:Sotho praise-poems* (1974), p. 59.

by rhythmic body movements or even wild jumps during which stabbing movements are made with a spear. On the whole words and acts complement each other in the recitation of the *izibongo*.[4]

In describing *izibongo* Coullie makes this observation:

They are more similar to song and music than to a piece to Western poetry which is supposed to be read and appreciated in individual study. They are similar to dance because of their marked rhythm of delivery.[5]

Perhaps a more telling effort is that of Trevor Cope as he grapples with the meaning of *izibongo*.

He reasons that:

Praise-poems are like odes in that they present a single subject for admiration, and like epics in that they record historical events. However, odes incline to philosophical reflection and epics purport to be complete historical records. The praise-poems have neither of these qualities. The praise-poems are therefore eulogies combining some qualities of both the ode and the epic.[6]

To reinforce his own conception of *izibongo*, Cope also cites Lestrade's description of *izibongo* as:

...a type of composition intermediate between the pure mainly narrative epic, and the pure, mainly apostrophic ode, being a combination of exclamatory narration and laudatory apostrophizing.[7]

A strenuous attempt to understand *izibongo* in the context of or in terms of Western paradigm is a common thread that goes through all the above passages. Even these attempts immediately reveal complexities of *izibongo* and the elusiveness of their meaning especially when viewed through the Western literary prism instead of being understood in their own terms. A common feature of the above definitions is that they have isolated only a tiny fraction of *izibongo* which is performed by *imbongi*-court poets in public events where leaders or high profile individuals are eulogized. This leaves out other dimensions of *izibongo* and with it the everyday use of *izibongo* by common people. Scholars such as Nyamande (1988) and Jordan (1973) did not bother looking for a definition; instead they classified and described some features of *izibongo*. Given the complexity of *izibongo* which operates at different levels of Xhosa culture, I will settle for a more modest task of simply describing them in a more general sense and supplementing that with the classifications and illustrations of

---

4   Du Toit, B., *Content & Context of Zulu folk-narratives*, University of Florida Press, Gainesville (1976), p. 11.

5   Brown, D. (ed.), *Oral literature and performance in Southern Africa*, David Phillip, Cape Town (1999), p. 67.

6   Cope, T., *Izibongo: Zulu praise poems*, Cape Town, David Phillip (1968), pp. 33–34.

7   Ibid.

izibongo. In this approach there is no attempt to define *izibongo* except for outlining its broad indicators with the hope that its full meaning will become obvious in the subsequent discussion. Another disclaimer, this chapter will not attempt to juxtapose Western and African cultures as this tends to obscure the meaning and fullness of *izibongo* when understood in its own terms with all its intersections and articulations within the various aspects of its African culture.

Izibongo: The Core of Everyday Narratives of the Xhosa-speaking People

Izibongo form the core of everyday narratives of the Xhosa peoples. They are complex forms of oral narratives with specialized, yet integrated components. *Izibongo* include among other things, oral poetry, oral epics for clans, kinship groups and/or nations, axioms, idioms, salutations, clan names, totems, and eulogies. They are threads weaving together the social, political, economic and spiritual aspects of an African society. *Izangoma*-spiritual healers, *imbongi*-court poets or bard, *abakhwetha*-initiates, *ilima*-work team, kinship groups in ceremonies, *amaxhwele*-herbalists, *ukuteketisa*-parents or caregivers cooing as they nurture babies, a person expressing gratitude, in exclamation or expressing shock, *ukufunga*-in making solemn pledges, in *ukukikizela*-ululating, and *isikhahlelo*-people saluting their traditional leaders.

Izibongo have a number of distinct and yet integrated functions. Just to mention a few, they play a vital role as a spirit medium in connecting the living and the dead as they are used to invoke supernatural forces, *izinyanya*-the ancestors and totems, as well as uQamata-God. They are also used as a historical source of a nation, kinship groups or their leaders thus serving as a key component in fostering positive group and individual identity. This oral history differs from conventional Western history as it weaves together symbolism, mythology, folklore, legends, totems, and historical facts as well as character description of a group or an individual. Most important is the fact that *izibongo* form a collective memory, conscience and soul of an African society, and they are spiritually-centered oral narratives which are repositories of Indigenous wisdom. *Izibongo* also have some strong ecological aspects as they define relationships between peoples and their physical and spiritual environment. Taken together, the above description of *izibongo* gives a holistic view of this phenomenon as observed and lived in an African community, representing a radical departure from the conventional definitions which isolate, or more specifically amputate, public or court poetry from a complex network to which it is inextricably bound.

At this juncture, a brief commentary on the trend of literature on *izibongo* is necessary. Most scholars – Opland, Cope, Damane and Schapera – almost exclusively concentrate on *izibongo* which focus on kings, chiefs and important public figures. They inevitably emphasize the role of the *imbongi*-court poets who recite *izibongo* of these prominent figures. This literature treats *izibongo* as distinct, often unrelated components with an over-emphasis on African poetry. The focus on praise poems and court poets, *imbongi*, often leads to an almost exclusive focus on, and analysis of, the eulogies of kings and leaders, thus marginalizing women, youth, kinship groups, spiritual healers, and the common people who, in real African life, feature prominently in everyday use of *izibongo*. In this way, Euro-centric paradigms have generally stripped *izibongo* of their richness and complexity as they seek to fit them into established perspectives. A critical flaw of this approach is that it fails to see that not everyone in an African setting is an *imbongi*-public poet and yet everyone does use *izibongo* in everyday life, away from the high-profile public ceremonies. The inadequacy of this approach stems from the fact that it is based on the narrow and particular Western experiences with little attempt to understand Indigenous philosophies and ancient wisdom on their own terms.

Another category is that of books which have collected and documented *izibongo* without any interpretive analysis, such as Thamsanqa Sithole' *Izithakazelelo nezibongo zakwaZulu* (1982), Nyembezi's *Izibongo zamakhosi* (1958), Tyatyeka's *Iziduko nezibongo* (1995), and Mkonto's *Amakhikhizela oncwadi lwemveli* (1991). African scholars used *izibongo* extensively in their novels as well as in some writings on the history of an ethnic group or a nation. A.C. Jordan's *Igqumbo Yeminyanya* (1940), Mqhayi's *Ityala Lamawele* (1914), David Makaula's *UMadzikane okanye Imbali yamaBhaca* (1963) are examples of history writing which uses *izibongo* extensively. It is worth noting that the above literature tends to depict the everyday use of *izibongo* in their integrated form. An excerpt from Makaula's novel illustrates this point as he describes an encounter between men from the Baca Chief and the Zulu king, Shaka; *AA! thole lesilo! Ndabezitha! Sivela kwesikaMadzikane kaKhalimeshe kaWabana.*[8] In this case the messengers from the Madzikane people use *isibongo*, *Ndabezitha!* to salute Shaka and proceed to invoke *isibongo* of their own chief when they are tracing their place of origin. This is done in many parts of this novel and by other Xhosa writers. This frequent invocation of *izibongo* in greetings or in different encounters with people is a depiction of real everyday life in a Xhosa community. *Izibongo* cannot be understood simply as expressions; they possess boundless treasures of linguistic styles, expressions, metaphors and grandiloquence. Jordan stresses this point when he asserts:

> To the Bantu-speaking Southern Africans, the praise-poem is their proudest artistic possession. It is in this genre that the greatest possibilities of Bantu language as a medium of literary expression are bound to be found.[9]

The above is an indication of what matters in *izibongo*, it is not just what is being said, but the art of it. Hence in *izibongo* dwell symbols, metaphors, images, idioms and complex prose which are meant to make connections to past immortals, the world beyond, the immediate present and the distant future. Nelson Mandela recalls what he terms a turning point in his life of political consciousness. The setting was his high school where a great Xhosa *imbongi*, Krune Mqhayi, was invited to recite

---

8　　Makaula, D., *UMadzikane okanye Imbali yamaBaca* (1963), p. 5.

9　　Jordan, A.D., *Towards an African Literature: The emergence of literary form in Xhosa* (1972), p. 21.

izibongo. On this day Mandela says that he had never felt so proud to be elevated and defined as an African or Xhosa in such glowing terms. He recalls 'I felt such intense pride at that point. . . I was galvanized.'[10] *Izibongo* have the power to incite and excite. As another *imbongi*, Nomvethe, dramatizes this point in his *umbongo*:

> Igugu leAfrika,
> Kuthi ndingabonga, mandithuke,
> ndinithuke de ndinithunuke.
> Senditshilo!
> Aningabo benu, ningabeAfrika.
> Yeyenu nayo.[11]

In the above inciting *umbongo*, the bard is threatening to insult until it hurts, to insult those he is praising until they feel hurt deep inside. He is reminding them that they are not, and do not live for themselves as they belong to Africa which in turn belongs to them. This again displays the mastery of *izibongo* in manners too mysterious for those who are outside its realm. The word 'hurt' here, taken out of its literal meaning, refers to incitement or whipping up of passion and emotion. In *izibongo* dwells the Xhosa cosmology as they capture the universe in all its dimensions while situating the person concerned at the very center.

Who Am I?

Uqobo olu lwam ndingubani? In essence, who am I? How do I understand and define myself? It is in trying to address these questions that one begins to appreciate the vitality of *izibongo* in the Xhosa Indigenous ecology of identity. It is in answering these questions and in invoking my *izibongo* that I begin to feel flames raging in the belly of my soul. I come alive like no other time as it is the time when I come face to face with the essential me in the best way I understand myself and my universe in a manner that fuses the present, the past and the future. There is no other tool for a Xhosa to interrogate his or her identity and sense of being (*uqobo lwakhe*) without appealing to these greatest tools and treasures, *izibongo*, that have been passed to us from time immemorial. This will soon become obvious as *xa ndizilanda imvelaphi, ndizithutha ndizityibela* (as I begin to trace my roots in the best way I know how). Then I have to contend with a deluge of emotions for I do not take it lightly to invoke and summon the giants and heroes that came before me as mortals and remain enshrined as immortals that never die. I will, however, be mindful of the fact that the reader may easily get lost in the world that I only know and feel in every vein of my body.

I am an Indigenous African of the Xhosa people of South Africa. Throughout my life I have had to deal with what W.E.B. Du Bois (1994) called dual consciousness,

---

10 Mandela, N., *Long Walk to Freedom* (1994), p. 38.

11 Mkhonto, *Amakhikhizela oncwadi lwemveli* (1991), p. 108.

of having to answer the question "who are you?" in both the Indigenous way (when asked by umXhosa) and in the Western way in schools, offices, and so forth. I am often struck by how vastly different my responses are to each of these stimuli. I will juxtapose them for you to understand myself as I respond to my coexisting realities, one being by choice and the other being by prescription, therefore alien to me in all conceivable ways. One (Indigenous) is affective whereas the other(Western) is afflictive. The former allows me to define myself while the latter describes me.

When I meet umXhosa, I am customarily asked A*umngumni? Khawuzithuthe* or *khawuzilande*? The question posed as you meet a new person is Who are you? Some will even specifically ask you to trace yourself. Note that unlike the Western greetings there are no specifications and confines (What is your name? Who are your parents? Where are you from? Where do you live?), the respondent is given leeway or the entire self-definition landscape to decide what and to what extent she or he defines *uqobo lwakhe* (essential self or being). In this Indigenous approach there is no time or space specification. To the question *ungumni* I then respond:

ANdiliXesibe lomthonyama/lomgquba/lothuthu. Ndiphuma kwesikaJongintaba kwisithili saseMaXesibeni(Mount Ayliff) kwinqila yaseNdzongiseni kwilali yaseLugelweni. Mna ndizithutha ngelithi;
NdinguXesibe
UNondzaba
Uradu
Usinama
UMjoli
USomadoda
Umalandelwa yintombi isithi ndizeke
Umatshob=endlovu
Uthanga limenyezela ngokuthanjiswa
Usabela uyabizw=emazibukweni

For a casual outside observer steeped in the Western ways this may look more like a tedious and unnecessarily long response to a simple question. If anything, this is only the beginning. The above response to a question *ungumni*, starts by pointing that I do not just belong to Xesibe people but I am an authentic Xesibe (*elomthonyana/lomgquba/lothuthu*) who traces his roots to the original people or forbears of the group. The use of the metaphor *umthonyana* (literally meaning the decomposed underlayers of cattle deposits, or dry old cow dung found in a cattle byre/kraal-*ubuhlanti*), or *umqguba* (dry cow dung) or *uthuthu* (ash deposits accumulated from one's home hearth (*iziko*) over the years) is meant to indicate authenticity as well as the deep rootedness of one to the group to which he or she belongs. The reference to both *umgquba/umthonyama* and *uthuthu* represents the importance of cattle and kraal as symbols of wealth, and the latter is also a sacred place in which ancestors dwell and it also used to be a burial place. Placing one in *umgquba /umthonyama* is to connect with the spirit world and the distant past. *Uthuthu*, on the other hand, represents that which is central in every Xhosa, for that matter African, home. It is around the fireplace that generations of family members gathered, it is the same place that generates warmth and connection with the ashen deposits from this place connecting one with that history and present every time fire was made and ashes were generated and deposited. There can be no more powerful symbols symbolizing continuity from the past than *umthonyama, umgquba* or *uthuthu.*

I then went on reciting my *isibongo* in which my ancestors were invoked. We trace our roots and ancestry to Xesibe who is the founder-father of this group, Sinama is one of my great grand ancestors who led a section of the Xesibe people during the Mfecane wars and he is a descendant of Radu. Sinama is the father of Mjoli who in turn is the father of Fikeni (which is my surname). This demonstrates that *isibongo* actually invoke the names of selected ancestors who are singled out for their heroic deeds or great achievements in the chronicles of a group. When my *isibongo* goes on to say A*Umalandelwa yintombi isithi ndizeke* (literally meaning the one who is followed by women asking for or pleading for marriage), this is a character description which means that we understand, and we are understood among our people as great charmers with such irresistible magnetism arising from our personality, of handsomeness and beauty or attributes inherent in us. Who can afford to have a low self-esteem or self-doubt when the ones who came before you confer such a confident imprint on you? Who cannot float and soar in the clouds of confidence when you belong to such people? Now one can have a sense of why I feel like I am summoning the galaxies and the constellation of stars when I evoke my *isibongo*. Nothing can better define me. This is the steady reassuring diet of self and group identity that I grew up within my African environment.

When I was born I was given three names: Somadoda, Mayibongwe and Patrick. Somadoda, as you can see, is taken from my *isibongo* thus closely linking me to my origins or it becomes a certification of authenticity. When I say I am Somadoda to Xesibe people they often finish my sentence by invoking the rest of my *isibongo* and nothing makes me feel prouder than that response, for obvious reasons. I come from a Christian family, my parents, therefore, felt it proper to give me a name that reflected this. I was then given the name Mayibongwe, which means "Let the Almighty be praised." It was an expression of deep gratitude to the Creator who blessed them with this child. My parents also felt that I had to be given a third name, a school name, Patrick, which is European. The European colonial system often imposed their names on the Indigenous people. My parents preempted this imposition by giving me one name that would make my life easy at school or in public offices. Growing up I gradually left out both Patrick and Mayibongwe in favor of Somadoda. Somadoda seemed to connect with me in a manner that I can never fully explain, nor do I need to. In addition, many Xhosa people I met and interacted with preferred Somadoda from the very start. I have never bothered understanding the meaning of the name Patrick, all I knew was that it was alien to me, therefore it was doomed to die. Some of my school teachers at Lugelweni Junior Secondary, Colana High and Rode High School, insisted on calling me Patrick, with a perverted understanding that it was my school name. I grudgingly complied. This name is still reflected in some of my official documents even though it sounds strange whenever

I hear anyone calling me by that name. It is just foreign to me as extraterrestrials are to Earth, so in my mind it has always been that other name that was supposed to be mine. I do not use this name anymore unless I am specifically forced to as I outgrew it once I reached the age of reason. Now you know why I fell in love with questions that ask, What are your preferred names?

The history of colonized African people is replete with examples of these imposed European names which often sit like an albatross around my neck. The case of my paternal grandmother and her brother is instructive. My grandmother, Madunjana, often told us, as we squatted around the fire, how she became Nellie. She narrated that on her first day at school they were lined up and asked by a white missionary teacher what their names were. In cases where they did not have European names, as was the case with my grandmother and her brother, they were given what was then called Christian or 'school names.' For those who already had European names, the white teacher exclaimed, Very good! My grandmother was given the name Nellie and her brother who was standing right behind her became Nelson. But the community continued, up to her last days, to call my grandmother by her clan name, Madunjana. She then assumed the same dual existence of an official name and the real Indigenous name. Nelson Mandela, who also acquired the name Nelson under similar circumstances, reflects on this dual-identity when he says, "I am often addressed as Madiba, my clan name, as a sign of respect."[12] He continues in his autobiography:

> That day, Miss Mdingane told me that my new name was Nelson. Why she bestowed this particular name upon me I have no idea. Perhaps it had to do with the British sea captain Lord Nelson, but that would be only a guess. . . Africans of my generation, and even today, generally have both a Western and African name. Whites were either unable or unwilling to pronounce an African name, and considered it uncivilized to have one.[13]

In a more recent history another African becomes a casualty of this identity mutilation, nullification and interposition. Makgoba relates his experience which echoes many others,

> I lost Mampokoro as a name at Medical School in 1972, as my names were considered too long to register, the then registrar, Ms Whitbey would say. However, in my village this remains my name.[14]

Goduka recounts a similar treatment and duality in the Nomalungelo Maqhudeni and the Ivy which had to coexist with unequal weight in terms of self-understanding.

When I went off tangent trying to make a point on the notion of double-identity which Ngubane argues has caused disharmony in the soul of an African, I was still trying to answer the question, who am I in essence (*Uqobo lwam ndingubani*)? When

---

12 Nelson Mandela, *Long Walk to Freedom*, Macdonald, Randburg (1994), p. 4.

13 Ibid., p. 13.

14 Makgoba, M.W., *Mokoko: The Makgoba Affair: A reflection on transformation*, Vivlia Publishers, Florida Hill (1997), p. 12.

I went through an initiation or circumcision school during my early adolescence, I was given yet another chance to define my self and come up with an *isibongo* which I, myself, composed. I then came up with my own individual *isibongo* which was meant to reflect me through my own mirror. Since then, this is my personal *isibongo*:

Umdaka omnyama
Owehlul=isephu zabelungu
Usikhunduva
Bambheka bath=uqumbile kant=unqubile
Umahlamba, ahlanz= asele eNgqubusini
Intw=esithunzi ukwedlul=eseNtsizwa
Umavuk=ajongumsobomvu phezu kwentab=uSimaka-maka
Umakhafula kunyibilike ikhephu likaNolangeni,
Umayokozel= okoMngcunube
Ngumaphiko asith= inkedama
Ungxamtsholo wexhonti werhwanqandini lesilo sikaXesibe
Umabhodl=engqitsh=okwebhubesi
Umabalabala hlosindini
Ngunxelendini ugalela okwezulu
Ngumabatha-bath=otshayel= okwenkanyamba
Myekeni umatshob=endlovu adlokove azidlikidle.
Myekeni akhwitshilik= akhaful= okaMkhwetsho

There is no direct translation of the above *isibongo* into English suffice to say it describes what I understand to be as much as that which I aspire to be. Roughly, it says that I am the dark one whose complexion could not be transformed even by the white man's soap. It goes on to invoke the names of the rivers (*Ngqubusi*) and mountains (*Ntsizwa, Nolangeni* and *Simaka-maka*). It also refers to me as a hairy beast (I am actually hairy and bearded). I also register my desire to be a person who will give shelter and comfort to the orphans or more generally those who are the disadvantaged and the discarded or those mistakenly identified as the least among us in our society. I also make reference to my left-handedness and its stealth in a combat situation. Metaphors are used, and animals such as the lion and the leopard, as well as natural phenomena – tornado, storm and lightning – all used to symbolize some personality traits. I end this *isibongo* by pleading with people to give some space to feel free to sneeze, me-myself the descendent of *Mkhwetsho* (my grandfather).

This process of self-identification in a more personalized manner coexists, as Ngubane has said earlier, with my group or clan identity and these exist in a state of harmony and self-collective sovereignty. In this case there is no duality but infusion as one is given a chance to name himself, thus affirming his sense of being which started from birth and continues as a work in progress in different phases of his life.

This brings us to the philosophical underpinnings of *Ubuntu*, which is used to give a proper context to the subject of this work, *izibongo*. This sense of self-determination and interconnectedness is the essence of an African philosophy of *Ubuntu*, which Ngubane traces to its Sudic and Nudic roots in ancient Egypt. Another African intellectual, Cheik Anta Diop (1974), has demonstrated this link between different regions of Africa and ancient Egyptian ancestry. Ngubane captures this *Buntu* philosophy in the concept of *UQOBO*. He asserts that:

> The central teaching of Buntu is that all things originate from UQOBO and evolve in response to the challenge of their nature; that the person is a self-defining value (umntu ngumntu; umzimba uziwa ngumniniwo; that is: the person is human; it is the person who knows best the workings of his body) and that life's purpose for the person is perpetual evolution (ukuma njalo) . . . Each phenomenon had its UQOBO (reality or value) which was an integral part of the infinite Value.[15]

He goes on to give a compelling link between diversity represented by self-defined individual identities and those of community identity:

> In the preliterate civilization variations had to occur even within each family or nome. But this did not bother the Nguni because Buntu regarded the person as a self-defining value; all self-definitions which served the purpose of the community were simultaneously legitimate. This protean character of Buntu gave flexibility to self-definitions which survived because the collective sovereignty of the group guaranteed the individual sovereignty or primacy of the person . . . The social purpose was the exploration of the person and his environment in order to enable him to discover more satisfying dimensions of being human.[16]

Reinforcing Ngubane's observation on this *Buntu* philosophy of being, you hear umXhosa exclaiming, *luqobo lwam olu okanye ndim uqobo!* which simply translates "this is the quintessential me." This exclamation is invoked when a person feels deeply they are in a state of being that best describes the way they understand themselves.

In yet another context similar to the notion of self-actualization flowing from understanding a sense of being, Thomas Merton describes what he terms 'the gift of self understanding.'

> You seem to be the same person and you are the same person that you have always been: in fact you are more yourself than you have ever been before. You have only just begun to exist. You feel as if you were at last fully born. All that went before was a mistake, a fumbling preparation of birth. Now you have come into your element . . . you have felt the doors fly open into the infinite freedom, into a wealth which is perfect because none of it is yours, and yet it all belongs to you. And now you are free to go in and out of infinity.[17] Xhosa idioms and proverbs, in various forms, demonstrate the rootedness of the philosophy of *Ubuntu* which is grounded on the primacy of interdependence and interconnectedness among people as well as the intricate and intimateness with physical environment and the spiritual world around them. The foremost principle of *Ubuntu* is

---

15 Ngubane, J., *Conflict of Minds*, Books in Focus, Washington, DC (1979), p. 77.
16 Ibid., p. 78.
17 Merton, T., *Seeds of Contemplation*, Dell, New York (1948), pp. 139–140.

expressed in the saying that *umntu ngumntu ngabantu* which simply means you are only human because of others and they are human because of you. This *Ubuntu* principle of mutual interconnectedness and interdependence is eloquently described by Goduka who translates it as meaning I am we; I am because we are.[18] Also closely related to the above idiom is the metaphor *izandla ziyahlambana* literally meaning no hand can, on its own, wash itself, it takes both hands to wash each other. Even political authority of chieftaincy-*ubukhosi* is founded on this principle of interdependence as captured in the Xhosa idiom *inkosi yinkosi ngabantu* which roughly translates into a chief can only be a chief because of the support and legitimacy given or conferred on him by his people. In other words, one can exercise the authority over his subjects only on condition that he has their consent thus instilling the notion of a consensus in governance.

In 1954 Mesatywa compiled some of the commonly used Xhosa proverbs and idioms in which this core principle of interrelatedness of people is immediately revealed. I will present just a few to illustrate this point. There is no accurate translation of these proverbs and idioms; I will therefore settle for giving a rough idea of what they mean. *Ungadinwa nangamso*, even in the future do not tire showing kindness and offering help to people; this is said by Xhosa people as a way of thanking people who have done something good and also inspiring them to do more in the future. *Ukuxhentsa uzombela*, to dance while singing and cheering yourself; this is often invoked to remind people that they cannot do everything by themselves without the help of others. *Ukudla ngamntu*, when a feast is organized because a visitor has come or someone has done something good, those who join them in feasting often thank the visitor or the person for whom the feast is organized for making that occasion possible. AmaXhosa often remind people to treat the people they do not know well for they may find themselves stranded in the land of the very same people, and they capture this in saying *unyawo alunampumlo*, which literally means a foot has no nose (you will travel one day and find yourself at the door of the very person you may have ill-treated). Another idiom, *intaka yokha ngoboya benye*, a bird builds its nest with the feathers of other birds, captures the essence of mutual help and the inadequacy of individuality. Another idiom, *inxeba lendoda alihlekwa*, simply means that one should not laugh or rejoice at someone's misfortunes. This is only a sample of proverbs and idioms in an Indigenous culture so replete with idiomatically expressed principles of *Ubuntu* philosophy. It is in these expressions that the treasures of African Indigenous philosophy and wisdom are entrenched.

Ngubane's work decries the disharmony caused by upsetting this philosophy of *Buntu*, and more specifically the notion of *UQOBO*, discords which inevitably arise from colonial and apartheid imposition of that which is foreign and nullification of that which is an intrinsically Indigenous way of life and wisdom. For Frantz Fanon (1965; 1967), this disharmony, its resultant identity crisis and its manifestation in psychological pathologies are captured in the concept of alienation. We will return to this disharmony concept with concrete illustrations later in this chapter.

---

18 Goduka, M.I., *Affirming unity in diversity in education: Healing with Ubuntu*, Juta & Co. Ltd., Capetown (1999), p. 39.

If one is to understand the core and central fabric of amaXhosa, in general abeNguni people's philosophy of individual and group self-definition and self-identity, one has to understand what *AmaXhosa* call *izibongo* and AmaZulu call *izithakazelelo*, whereas it is known as *lithoko* among the Sotho people. *Izibongo* and *isibongo* actually mean the same thing; the former is the plural form and the latter is the singular form. *Izibongo* penetrate, intersect and articulate with each and every aspect of Xhosa culture, politics, religion and economic transactions, and yet it is not given such prominence in the works of many scholars who study African people of South Africa. This is one of the yawning gaps that exist between the written word and lived experience. This chapter is a partial remedy to this situation as it tries to demonstrate the centrality of *izibongo* in understanding Xhosa Indigenous wisdom and identities. Ngubane affirms the importance of this phenomenon among the Nguni people:

> Our main source of information on these developments is still the body of panegyric poems or patronymic legends (izithakazelelo = words by which one is welcome) which were attached as titles to each family name. These poems which describe the exploits of distinguished ancestors, were passed from generation to generation because in them each family defined itself, stated its interpretation of the Sudic Ideal and preserved its identity and uniqueness.[19]

The above statement does not only allude to the importance of *izibongo/izithakazelelo* but also to the resilience of this phenomenon as an identity marker. *Izibongo* constitute one of the most enduring body of traditions and wisdom by which amaXhosa trace, position and define themselves. It has survived the onslaught of the early European missionaries, colonialism and apartheid. Like a perennial river it has been flowing from generation to generation. The following is Nyamende's impression, which also reinforces the above claim of *izibongo* resilience:

> It is only by mystery of its enchanting nature and the fact that it holds the key to self-identity and self-pride that it continues to be seriously learnt informally, despite the persistence of the school education, and the views that hold its learning a backward practice.[20]

In a qualified sense, Opland echoes the same sentiment of the continued existence and vitality of *imbongi*, the one who recites *izibongo*. He claims that

> The voice of the imbongi is as loud and clear in South Africa today as it was when Stephen Kay first heard it at Hintsa's great place in 1825, as it has been, in all likelihood, for generations and centuries before.[21]

---

19 Ngubane, op cit., p. 82.

20 Nyamende, in Sienaert, E. and Bell, A. (eds), *Catching Winged Words: Oral tradition and education* (1988). pp. 226–227.

21 Opland, J., *The Image of the Book in Xhosa Oral Poetry*, in Brown, D. (ed.) *Oral Literature and Performance in Southern Africa*, David Phillips, Cape Town (1999), p. 108.

The reason I make the observation that Opland's claim of *izibongo* resilience is a qualified one is based on two things: firstly, he uses the witnessing of *imbongi's* performance by a European explorer, Stephen Kay, as a time marker for *izibongo*, thus introducing a subtle European 'discovery' bias. That this explorer witnessed and later reported what he had seen ought not to be such an important phase in the timeless life of *izibongo* as compellingly demonstrated in Ngubane's treatise. Secondly, his use of the term in all likelihood introduces an element of doubt which is certainly not traceable in the works of many African writers. In all likelihood, Opland unwittingly committed these errors in his judgment much because of the limitations of the Western or Eurocentric paradigm from which most of the Western scholars operate. In an Afrocentric paradigm the timeless and certain existence of *izibongo* would be understood as self-evident given the preponderance of evidence as drawn from the Indigenous oral narratives. In all, the survival and continued vitality of *izibongo* attest to the assertion of Indigenous wisdom and an oral narrative that transcend the Western hegemonic cultural impositions.

In this chapter I describe, classify, analyze and explain *izibongo* with the insights gathered from the Indigenous/Xhosa peoples of South Africa.[22] The primary task of this chapter is to bring together Xhosa voices and reflections on *izibongo*. These voices are used to classify aspects of *izibongo*, as well as explain their social, cultural and spiritual roles. I will also draw from my own experience as an African who observes and lives this cultural experience enriched with *izibongo*. By allowing these Indigenous voices long silenced in the mainstream literature I am merely engaged in a process of retrieving the wisdom which gives a window of opportunity for those who are genuinely interested in our lives and experiences. By putting myself and my experience at the center I transform what has hitherto been regarded and studied as an object into a participant subject affirming authenticity of my experience by holding a mirror to see myself on it. This approach has been effectively deployed by Ngubane (1979) and Goduka (1999). This approach is emancipative and therapeutic in as far as it offers a chance for me to define myself and heal the condition described by Du Bois:

> It is a peculiar sensation, this double-consciousness, this sense of always looking at oneself through the eyes of others, of measuring one's soul by the tape of a world that looks on in amused contempt and pity.[23]

This particular approach is Afrocentric, along the lines articulated by Molefi Asante (1990) as it places the African worldview and experience at the center of analysis. The cumulative result of this discourse is not just an affirmation of one's own Indigenous heritage as it also is a dialogical encounter with, and an alternative to, the dominant Western paradigms of knowledge construction. This opening of

---

22　It should be noted that a general survey of literature on this subject as well as personal encounters reveal widespread use of *izibongo* in other ethnic societies of the Bantu-speaking Indigenous peoples of Southern Africa.

23　Du Bois, W.E.B., *The Souls of Black Folk*, Gramercy, New York (1994), p. 5.

other avenues of visiting and understanding human experience, in Mohamed Seedat's statement, locates Euro-America within the framework of epistemological pluralism, without hierarchy, hegemony and arrogance.[24] The chief proponents of this notion of epistemological pluralism are Asante (1990) and Wathiongo (1986). This assertion of Indigenous voices does not only promise to affirm Indigenous heritage and wisdom but also empowers those who are trapped in the hegemonic Western knowledge industries who may have a chance to revisit some of their assumptions about the others, or even about themselves.

At this point it is proper to allude to one more feature or method used in this discussion: since the Xhosa voices are in Indigenous languages, I will translate (as already seen in the foregoing discussion) Xhosa words, idioms and phrases where possible and simply describe those parts whose original intended meaning would be seriously altered if a direct translation was used. The very figurative, idiomatic and metaphoric nature of most of *izibongo* makes it difficult to find some linguistic or semantic equivalents in English, which will become evident in the following discussion. This chapter is steered by the following questions: What are *izibongo*? How can they be classified? What are the various roles of specific types of *izibongo*? How do these types of *izibongo* articulate with each other and with the wider social fabric in an African society?

For illustration let me take another *isibongo* of the Zibula clan as given by Siyanda Mnukwa who belongs to this clan. As a welcome coincidence, this *isibongo* is also my mother's and as such she is called by her clan name, MaZibula. It goes as follows:

OoZibula
OoMhlwane
Oosihlahla somnquma[25]
Oosihlahla Siyagawulwa siyahluma
Osihlahla siyawanqinda amazembe.

Similarly, Zibula and Mhlwane are the prominent selected ancestors of the Zibula clan, as most clans are named after an ancestor who once lived or the one who is thought to have actually given birth to the clan. The character description also features in this *isibongo*:

Osihlahla siyagawula siyahluma (The shrub that is cut down but grows back to life)
Osihlahla siyawanqinda amazembe (The shrub that blunts the axes)

---

24 Seedat, M., 'The quest for liberatory psychology', in *South African Journal of Psychology*, 27(4), (1997), 263.

25 *Umnquma* is a shrub-like tree which grows in semi-desert or dry regions. It is thorny and resistant to fire or drought. It is often sought after as firewood as the coal from this tree is said to be the best and last longer. So the choice of this kind of tree indicates the features of a tree that is both good and stubborn at the same time, something that survives and faces off adversities.

This description emphasizes the stubborn nature of the people of this clan as they bounce back whenever you try to overcome them. A point has to be made here that a careful observation of the members of these clans demonstrates the pervasive effect of these character descriptions in the psyche of a clan. One can often hear a member of the Sinama clan claiming that a partner was attracted to someone because he found her irresistible, hence known as *Oomalandelwa*. Similarly, Siyanda often narrated stories of heroic deeds of his ancestors and family members which demonstrated their stubborn quality: *Uthi kutheni kusithiwa sibosihlahla somnquma nje* (Why do you think we are called *osihlahla somnquma*, it is not for nothing that we are given that name). These perceptions are reinforced by both the members of the clan and those from outside as they invoke these *izibongo* or character descriptions whenever a member of that clan displays what may even remotely resemble the features or characters contained in *isibongo*. The above *izibongo* clearly indicates the historical role and fostering of positive self and group identity. Mathobela Gwiliza gives yet another dimension to the historical character of isibongo of a Ngwane clan. He recites his isibongo:

Oongwane
Oozibovu
Ochachacha
Bona bawela umlamb = iThukela ngentambo yesigcawu kwaze kwathi chacha.

Besides the conventional invocation of ancestral names, this *isibongo* actually traces the migration route of the Ngwane clan as history reveals that they did cross the Tugela river (*umlambo uThukela*). Moreover, the fact that they are descendants of Ngwane points to the fact that they are of Swazi origin. Mathobela Gwiliza claims they trace their lineage back to a region in Swaziland before their migration to the Eastern Cape. Some *izibongo* also include a totem[26] of that clan such as Majola[27] in the case of the Mpondomise royal family.

Out of a clan or kinship group *isibongo* one or two ancestors are often used as *isiduko* identity markers or clan name for a group. For example, when one asks for my own *isiduko* I may respond by simply saying 'I am Sinama' or I may say 'I am Radu' or even better I may just evoke all the names of the ancestors contained in my *isibongo*. *Isiduko* is then used on a daily basis in many aspects of social interaction. The most common of these is to substitute the generic way of saying thank you

---

26 A totem in this particular case is an animal or an object which is taken to represent the ancestor or within which dwells the spirits of the ancestors of a given clan. In my case a bee is my totem. A totem is a revered animal which is protected and cannot be killed by the members of that clan. If killed by accident, a cleansing ritual is performed to appease the ancestors.

27 Majola is a snake that is a totem of the Jola clan of the Mpondomise. It is often said that this snake often appears when a Jola child is born or when a Jola wife is pregnant and this signifies that the ancestors have showered that baby with their blessings thus welcoming the baby to the clan. Clan members are not supposed to chase away the snake or harass it in any form. Instead they must give it an egg or something before it disappears.

in Xhosa which is *Enkosi*, but once the clan name of a person is known, it is used for thanking the person who is rendering help or service. In fact, many Africans who receive help or are touched by the generosity of someone will ask, *ndithini xa ndibonga* (what should I say in thanking you) or will ask *sithini isiduko sakho* (what is your clan name), to which the respondent or person who has helped will say 'I am so and so.' In my case I will say *ndingu Sinama*, Siyanda will say *ndingu Zibula* and Mathobela will say *ndingu Ngwane*, and Ivy Goduka will prefer *Qhudeni*. If really touched, the recipient of help or gift will evoke and recite the whole *isibongo*. Invoking a person's *isibongo* signifies an expression of the deepest sense of gratitude, which is more personalized and deeper than a generic thank you.

When a child is born, *izibongo* are some of their first lessons in a language. When a child learns to talk the notion of saying *isibongo* when accepting a gift from a person is often positively reinforced. In some cases the gift is held back until the child says *isibongo*. This is also taken as a sign of deep respect.

In fact, *izibongo* ring in the ears of a child right from infancy, long before they can make any sense of their language. When a mother or caregiver is nursing or cooing the baby during nurturing they will often evoke *isibongo* of that child's clan. When a baby cries, *isibongo* is also used to calm them down as caregivers say *thula, thula kaloku Sinama/Khumalo/Zibula/Qhudeni*, which simply means be quiet, ooh please be quiet, or whatever *isibongo* might be. In this case *isibongo* is often preferred to an individual's name. These are some of the instances of cultural production and reproduction of *izibongo*. They also have a great value in transmitting Indigenous knowledge systems from one generation to another.

When a person drops something or is shocked by the news, *isibongo* or *isiduko* is evoked as part of an exclamation. It is a way of summoning the ancestors to come and witness, or to help if there is a need. I can still remember those days when I or my siblings came home to report that we had done well at school. The first instinctive or impulsive reaction of a parent or a relative would be to evoke *isibongo*. A person would exclaim *Yho-yho-yho Sinama*! whenever the news was good or bad and unexpected. If a person sneezes they will cry out the name of the ancestor. All these are prayers for help.

In yet another instance of transaction or communication people often swear or make solemn pledges (*isifungo*) by their clan names. This pledge is often taken as an indication that a person is very serious in what they are promising or claiming as they would dare not evoke ancestors when telling a lie. *Ndifunga* ooNgwane (I swear by the Ngwane people), the people of the Gwiliza family and Ngwane clan are often heard as is the case with many Africans. When one enters the gates of a family or comes to join people who are already gathered in a particular place or family they first salute the gathering from a distance and this is done by evoking *isibongo* of the people being approached. The person is then invited to join and food is offered. It is the *ubuntu* tradition among Africans.

Conversations with elders as well as a general survey of oral narratives often reveal the fact that *izibongo* and parents' names were often used instead of surnames, which were imposed by colonial officials for administrative reasons as well as to fit in a Western way of identity. In this case married women did not change their names or assume the surname of their husbands. In a traditional arrangement women were often called by their clan names. MaQhudeni, MaDlamini, MaZibula, MaKhumalo, MaDosini, MaNyawuza, MaNgwanya,[28] these are some of the clan names that married women carried with them to their new homes. In faraway working places migrant workers are known by their clan names instead of their names and this immediately connects them to their relatives who may share the same clan name. They thus treat each other as brothers and sisters even though their actual relationship may be generations and generations back. Among the Xhosa one cannot marry a person unless they have checked that they do not share the same clan name, which would then exclude that person. Should this relationship or marriage occur between people who share clan names it is regarded as incest (*umbulo*) and an elaborate cleansing ritual has to be performed to appease the ancestors who may otherwise frown on this. *Izibongo* have a profoundly spiritual content and role as they link the living and the dead, a clan or an individual connects to the ancestors. When *isibongo* is invoked for a spiritual ritual it is often called *isinqulo* which simply means that an intimate contact is being made with the ancestral spirits. When *idini*-sacrifice is made for a specific religious ceremony *isibongo* is utilized to summon the ancestors. When men are slaughtering an animal for a sacrifice, the sound that animal (often a goat or a cow) makes is followed by an invocation of *isibongo* to signify that the connection with the ancestors has been made, thus blessing the occasion. Xhosa people gathered will, almost in unison, exclaim *icamagu livumile* which simply means that the spirits have heard our plea and therefore bless this event.

Spiritual healers (*izangoma*) are often involved when *isinqulo* is used. In a healing ceremony *izangoma* will recite their own *izibongo* and then recite those of their patients as powers of both the healer and the patient's ancestors have to be involved or summoned to help in the healing process. In this way the patient becomes part of the healing instead of part of the conventional sense of a professional-client interaction. These elaborate rituals also involve the burning of incense (impepho). Even a traditional medicine man or herbalist (*ixhwele*) will often invoke *izibongo* and urge the patient to invoke their ancestors when using the medicine or herbs. An initiate or apprentice of traditional healing (*ucamagu*) is thought to have been selected by the ancestors by calling for spiritual healing. *Izibongo* are utilized throughout the initiation process as only ancestors will guide and empower the person to be a successful *isangoma*.

When young men (*abakhwetha*) go through the initiation process, an important rite of passage from boyhood to manhood, they are asked to compose their own individual *izibongo* to be recited on the day of their initiation ceremony. These *izibongo* are often classified as *ukuzithutha*, which Opland (1999) refers to as boasts. In this case an initiate often mixes their own *izibongo* which involve both ancestral names and their own, which may reflect their self-appraisal. One hears things like

---

28 Note that *ma* is added before the name of a woman to indicate that they are female whereas a man would use the same clan name without this prefix.

Ujuju umaqegu amdaka or *Umdaka omnyama owehlula isephu zabelungu*, all being a reflection of one's self-understanding or identification. It is also important to note that Xhosas also use *izibongo* for the animals and inanimate objects or for incidents. Nyamende list a number of properties such as shops, buses, taxis and houses that are given clan names. It is common to find a person or an owner of an animal or property (be it a dog, a cow, a horse or a car) having a specific *isibongo* for each one of these. At the appearance of, or when approaching or sending away one of these, they will invoke *isibongo* to which some animals have come to identify and respond. An incident such as a war or a disaster will also inspire an *imbongi* to compose *isibongo* as S.E.K. Mqhayi[29] did in *Ukutshona kukaMendi*.

At this juncture I turn to *izibongo* that are dedicated to leaders. There is, as shown earlier in this paper, a considerable amount of literature on this subject as it is the most public and visible form of performance that readily catches the eye of the outsiders. It is also in the public interest of a given group to have *izibongo* publicly performed even in the presence of visitors, for it is also a way of projecting the aura of greatness and power to the subjects and the outside world. *Izibongo zenkokheli zemveli* (traditional leaders) have a public face in the form of *iimbongi* (bards or court poets). These explain considerable interest on this particular aspect of *izibongo* among scholars who study these African communities. The people of prominence among the Nguni are often eulogized in public events, especially before and after they appear or deliver a speech or perform a public function. This task is performed by an *imbongi* (court poet). *Imbongi* is a person who is publicly recognized for his ability and knowledge of the community or nation's history. Each leader usually has an *imbongi* who travels with him to public events. An Indigenous *imbongi* is often dressed in distinct and colorful traditional garments with animal skins and birds' feathers being the favored outfit. An *imbongi* performs with a spear (*umkhonto*), a club (*iqakatha/isagweba*) or a battle axe in his hand and sometimes a shield in the other hand. Some *imbongi* prefer to use *itshoba* (horsetail-end hair stitched or tied to a stick). This somewhat formal performance of a court poet does not preclude spontaneous outbursts from performers who simply take the stage to render their own *umbongo*. These spontaneous performers are usually responding to a particular issue or utterance or moment that has stirred their emotion to an irresistible threshold. *Izibongo* of traditional leaders do not just target the individual leaders in their invocation, they narrate the history of the nation and sometimes urge the nation to stand up and take an action. It is important to note that *umbongo* performed for or in the presence of these public figures more often becomes a way of evaluating, by way of registering concern or commending the leaders. The leader has no control of the content of what is being said. This is in keeping with Ngubane and Goduka's notion of unity in diversity, one of the embedded principles of *Ubuntu* philosophy. In other words, activities that promote social cohesion of a nation are promoted, but not at the expense of an individual's own contribution in defining that reality or ideal. This

---

29 Mkhonto, B., *Amakhikhizela Oncwadi Iwemveli*, Lovedale Press, Alice (1991), p. 98.

is a social equilibrium which, if disturbed, inevitably leads to disharmony at the very core of the nation's soul.

Imbongi and public figures' *izibongo* are not just a thing of the past. More recently, the arrival of the new democratic South Africa in 1994 saw a spectacle of the *imbongi* performing in Mandela's Presidential inauguration as well as in the opening of Parliament. This has since become a ritual in these public ceremonies, a testimony to the fact that our Indigenous African time has come and is resonating in all corners of the country. This along with the increasing frequency in the public burning of Indigenous incense by traditional healers (*izangoma*), the wearing of traditional garments, traditional dances, changing of names to preferred African names, speaking African languages in public places, especially Parliament, marks a season of hope in which Africans are free to define themselves after centuries of oppression, humiliation and dehumanization. This promise of a restoration of dignity is reflected in Thabo Mbeki's statement at the opening of this chapter in which he proudly, publicly and passionately proclaimed his Africanness, a sense of being long-denied but never destroyed. This promise of revival or rebirth has been given a boost and a sense of urgency by the government, particularly with President Mbeki's proclamation of the broad program of African Renaissance which has galvanized South Africans. *Izibongo*, for multiple reasons already stated, will be the main pillar in the cultivation of these new identities as they are the very treasure box of Indigenous wisdom and tradition.

The above discussion illustrates the critical and pervasive role played by *izibongo* in AmaXhosa identity and life in general. *Izibongo* are central in the philosophy of *Ubuntu,* thus making them the social fabric that binds the spiritual, political, cultural and economic life of the Xhosa people. Simultaneous transgenerational production and reproduction of both individual and group identities has been demonstrated and *izibongo* has emerged as a catalyst in this process. One can only part with the reader hoping that we have connected and that the futility of understanding umXhosa or a Xhosa societal identity without intimate understanding of the intricate phenomenon of *izibongo* is clear.

Chapter 15

Human Rights Violation and Indigenous Peoples of Africa: The Case of the Maasai People

Naomi Kipuri

Introduction

Any discussion about 'Indigenous peoples' is essentially one about human rights, democracy, political development and civil society. This has followed continuing human rights abuses and oppression in the political, social, economic and cultural field as well as human rights abuses where Indigenous peoples are the ones most affected.

This chapter represents a brief overview of the human rights situation of Indigenous peoples in Africa, with particular reference to the Maasai people of Kenya. It begins with the definition of who the Indigenous peoples are. This is followed by a discussion of the features that are common to the peoples we refer to as Indigenous peoples and the concerns relating to their human rights situation.

The Concept of Indigenous peoples

In a literal sense, the term 'Indigenous peoples' refers to the original inhabitants of a given territory. This definition has accurately and usefully been adapted to refer to the original inhabitants of the Americas (known as Turtle Island by many Indigenous people), Australia, Aotearoa (New Zealand), the South Pacific, many peoples in Asia, Palestine, and Africa. Following processes of enslavement and colonization, the Indigenous populations in these regions have been marginalized, oppressed and denied certain human rights that are assumed by the dominant groups in the same geographical regions.

This definition however, is not useful for the purposes of identifying poor, marginalized and oppressed peoples in all parts of the world. For this reason, it has been useful to consider the word 'Indigenous' in a broader sense in order to take account of the experiences of other people whose lives reflect similar experiences with those who have been identified as Indigenous peoples and who regard themselves as such.

The International Labour Organization (ILO) in its Convention No. 169, refers among others to 'tribal peoples in independent countries whose social, cultural and economic conditions distinguish them from other sections of the national community, and whose status is regulated wholly or partially by their own customs or traditions or by special laws or regulations.' The definition of the World Bank emphasizes the geographical isolation and nonmonetized aspect of Indigenous peoples. It 'aims to facilitate development of tribes.'

Following various discussions on definitions, certain elements merged to reflect the commonalties of features and experiences of Indigenous peoples all over the world. These have provided useful guidelines and orientations indicating how the term could be applied in other parts of the world including Africa:

- Indigenous peoples have a special attachment to land and territories.
- They have a sense of shared ancestry and a right to self-determination.
- They have their own languages, cultures, spirituality, and knowledge.
- They have their own political, social, and cultural institutions; these include customary law, consensual decision-making processes, community life and collective sharing.
- Their lands and territories, as well as cultural institutions, are violated by states and global forces through acts of domination.[1]

Such an orientation is most useful since it limits the definition to a number of peoples (but not all) in many parts of the world. It will contrast with the earlier connotations that classified almost all African peoples as Indigenous (in a literal sense) or only very few, mostly hunter-gatherer communities, to suggest the very first people in any given territory following evolutionary times.

In Africa the literal meaning of 'Indigenous Peoples' has not been useful in the identification of poor vulnerable communities since most Africans are indigenous to Africa in the sense of having their origins in the continent. This is where the additional connotations that encompass marginality, oppression and denial of human rights have been quite useful. In some parts of Africa, the term 'Indigenous' has been restricted to the literal sense as a mockery to Indigenous peoples in order to suppress their distinctiveness and further oppress them. This is why many marginalized communities had not found it useful to identify themselves as 'Indigenous' except when dealing with people from outside the continent. They do, however, identify with the fact that the problems they are faced with are quite similar to those encountered by other Indigenous peoples in other parts of the world.

Notwithstanding these difficulties, over the last several years, through identification with the situation of other marginalized peoples, an increasing number of peoples who see themselves as oppressed have started calling themselves 'Indigenous' as a label of self-identification. The mockery has also lessened as the focus has shifted from definitional terms to the actual politico-economic and social

---

1   Indigenous Affairs (1995), p. 4.

situation of certain communities in the region. There are also opportunists (from dominant communities) who use the term as a way of attracting donor support since the phrase has become catchy in donor circles over the last few years.

The Human Rights Situation of Indigenous Peoples in Africa

The 1993–94 International Working Group for Indigenous Affairs (IWGIA) Yearbook recognized as Indigenous in Africa the nomads of East Africa and the hunter-gatherer communities of Southern Africa and Botswana. Among the nomadic and pastoral communities who are Indigenous are the camel-keeping Tuaregs and Fulani of West Africa; the Turkana, Rendille, Samburu, Borana, Pokot, Arialal and Somali of northern Kenya, the Maasai of Kenya and Tanzania, and the Himba of Southern Africa. Among the hunter-gatherer Indigenous communities are the Bambhuti and Batwa of central Africa, the Hadzabe of Tanzania and San/Abathwa of Southern Africa.

Although pastoralists are difficult to represent accurately in official statistics since they are dispersed over a wide arid territory with little or no infrastructure, they are estimated to number approximately six million people.[2] They subsist mainly on livestock – cattle, sheep, goats and camels. In Kenya, for instance, they constitute 25 per cent of the country's population and occupy 88 per cent of the arid region of the country. Geographically, the marginal status of the areas occupied by pastoralists is identified by the allocation of a hardship allowance to administrative personnel posted to work in those areas. The colonial connotation of Northern Frontier District typified this concept of geographical isolation of Indigenous peoples. Most of the remote and isolated areas in Africa are occupied by either pastoralists or hunter-gatherer communities. This fact in itself denies them the right to autonomous social and economic development, which further isolates them economically, politically and socially. The denial of the human rights of Indigenous peoples centers around the denial of their humanity and the accompanying expropriation of their resources for other purposes. These are discussed broadly below.

Special Indigenous Attachment to the Land and Territories

In a situation with low technological levels, like that observed in most parts of Africa, livestock herders require large and optimal productivity. The special attachment they have to the land is therefore the need for mobility during different seasons, either as pure nomadic or as practiced by southern pastoralists. Mobility is necessary for the regeneration of the environment for sustainable use and for optimum management of the herds. They feel especially attached to the land because they depend on its resources for the survival of the herds and people and without it they cannot survive, especially since they do not also have the skills necessary for survival outside the

---

2 *The Indigenous World* (1994), p. 95.

pastoral sector. The reason they feel marginalized vis-à-vis land and therefore identify with other Indigenous peoples is because, in most cases, their best grazing and water catchment areas have been alienated for other land uses that benefit others. Conflicts arise between extensive land-use systems (such as pastoralism, hunting, and gathering) and other systems.

Forced relocation, plundering of resources, and destruction of the natural environment in the name of management of those resources are all human rights abuses familiar to Indigenous peoples from their territories. All wildlife parks, particularly in eastern Africa, have been created following evictions of Indigenous peoples. At least 90 per cent of protected areas such as national parks, wildlife reserves, or gazetted forests have been carved out of the best areas occupied by Indigenous peoples. Maasai Mara, including the Serengeti National Park in Tanzania (the largest in the world), Amboseli, Marsabit, Samburu and Turkana National Reserves and others, were all the better-endowed grazing areas for livestock herders. The discovery of oil and precious stones almost always involves violation of the rights of Indigenous peoples in order to benefit from resources in their areas. The case of the dispossession of the Ogoni of Nigeria and the contamination of their water systems by corporations such as Shell Oil is a familiar one. Similarly, where tanzanite has been mined in Tanzania, the Maasai have been pushed out.

Eighty per cent of the area occupied by the Indigenous Samburu has been protected by the state as game park or forest reserve and the remaining 20 per cent is shared with wildlife, 60 per cent of which is outside the designated park or forest areas most of the year. Utilization by pastoralists of any protected area during difficult drought conditions has to be negotiated with the relevant authorities, who often deny them use and impose fines on those found 'poaching.' More serious actions have been taken against Indigenous peoples trying to utilize territories they used to use freely and sustainably. Law enforcement officers take advantage of the ignorance of Indigenous peoples on matters pertaining to their rights to such an extent that they are a law unto themselves. It is common knowledge that the further away people live from the center of administration the more likely they are to have their rights flaunted by the local administration. Illegal arrests by wildlife park and forest officials are common and defense provided within statutory law is inaccessible for those who are not adequately literate to access it.

The highlands of Nairobi and the outlying areas used to be dry-season grazing for the Maasai, but they now have to negotiate the use of open spaces for grazing livestock during drought conditions with the present owners. At the same time, the allocation of land and plots in all areas is done centrally by Ministry of Lands officials who often allocate land to themselves and their friends in order for Indigenous people not to own plots in their own district. This displacement of the Indigenous people from their ancestral lands is ensured by governmental apparatuses. Communities such as the Maasai and the Turkana, for instance, are ignored in decisions affecting their need for access to use their own lands. The Turkana people are not represented in the Ministry of Lands. The same is true of many urban centers where Indigenous peoples find themselves visitors in their own urban centers.

Owing to the ineffectiveness of state management mechanisms, the result of eviction is usually destruction of forests and water catchment areas that are critical for the survival and comfort of Indigenous peoples. While Indigenous peoples use resources sustainable for themselves and for future generations, state-managed bodies do not. Many Indigenous peoples are denied the right to harvest subsistence resources such as fuel wood, water, wildlife products and medicinal plants, which they are accustomed to utilizing without destroying the forests or the environment. Not only does this policy deny Indigenous peoples items necessary for their everyday life, it also seriously undermines the productivity of their economic systems and their ability to feed themselves. The consequence has been serious famines resulting in many lives lost as well as the decimation of herds. The denial of rights to their own resources is often coupled with devaluation of the contribution of Indigenous peoples to the national economies of their countries. In East Africa, the bulk of the profits from tourism derive from pastoral areas as well as from the meat raised by the pastoralists which is consumed in all the urban centers of the republic. Yet pastoralists are often castigated by the authorities and upper classes for failing to contribute productively to the national economy.

Indigenous Africans: A Sense of Shared Ancestry and the Right to Self-determination

It is often said that when northern Kenyan pastoralists go to Nairobi, they say that they are going to Kenya. This is because they are so far removed, physically, culturally and politically, it is as though they are in another country altogether. What goes on in Nairobi is completely alien to them and to other Indigenous peoples who live in remote parts of the countries to which they are supposed to belong. What they do have in common is shared ancestry among themselves and this is disregarded by the authorities in the states in which Indigenous peoples live. Because Africa was geographically divided up by European colonial powers in the 19th century, encounters today between law enforcement officers and Indigenous peoples when they cross national boundaries are often a nightmare. The Somali, for example, have found themselves in six different countries through no fault of their own. The Boran, the Maasai, and the Abathwa, the hunter-gatherers of Southern Africa, have all been split up by international boundaries. Consequently, laws have been promulgated to deny Indigenous people their shared ancestry.

Indigenous Africans: Their Language, Culture, Spirituality, and Knowledge

While national and official languages exist throughout Africa, few Indigenous peoples speak them. This is due to a combination of factors stemming from poor educational systems where there are untrained or poorly trained teachers as well as a lack of teaching equipment and other educational facilities in Indigenous communities. It is common for poor teachers, and those being disciplined, to be sent to remote areas where the Indigenous live. Such teachers generally do not meet Indigenous education needs because they have had no linguistic or cultural training to teach Indigenous children. The result is the widescale failure of Indigenous children in school and their inability to benefit in any form from formal educational structures. Long distances to schools as well as irrelevant curricula also contribute to the lack of effectiveness of the school system to most Indigenous peoples. The net effect is that the Indigenous children are left uninformed and as a result become nonparticipants in the affairs of the state and feel alienated from the instrumentalities of society.

In East Africa it is only Indigenous peoples who display visible culture. The mode of dress, knowledge of the environment, retention of Indigenous political and social institutions, religious ideas and so on are usually telling. Since the region depends a great deal on tourism as the principal foreign exchange earner, Indigenous peoples are forced to sell the distinctiveness of their cultures to tourists for display at airports and hotels frequented by tourists as 'state of the art.' Their art is even on display at the State House. Dances performed by Indigenous peoples in these hotels raise the value of the hotels and make them popular vacation spots. Paradoxically, even though the Indigenous contribute definitively to the enrichment of the national culture, these hotels and such places are out of their reach. Indigenous peoples who insist on retaining their cultures and languages with pride are frowned upon by dominant cultures in Africa, particularly when such dominant cultures have adopted Western European cultural traits and behavior as a result of pressure from colonialist and neocolonialist capitalist social structures.

Political, Social, and Cultural Institutions: Consensual Decision-Making Processes, Community life, and Collective Sharing among Indigenous Communities

Some of these institutions have served Indigenous peoples well over the years, to govern tenure and use of resources, and to regulate human interaction. Although some exist in an attenuated form, little has been developed nationally to replace these institutions or to fill the roles they are meant to perform. Customary law still exists in Kenya but as a junior partner to conventional law, and as long as it does not conflict with statutory law. Although constitutions provide for equal protection under the law, in effect, due to prejudice against Indigenous peoples, equal access to and use of the legal system is difficult and in most circumstances viewed as inaccessible by Indigenous people.

In countries where democratization is being developed, consensual decision-making processes are still being practiced in locally isolated corners by many as part of their cultural heritage to resolve issues and reduce conflicts. These are often set aside and replaced with systems that are neither democratic nor locally sustainable. Were it not for ideological resistance to Indigenous ideas and peoples, some of these institutions would be considered in any discussion on what Africa could offer in terms of democratic ideas and models.

The Violation of Indigenous Cultural Institutions by States and Global Forces Through Acts of Domination

Although colonialism ended over thirty years ago in most parts of Africa, except for Zimbabwe, Namibia, and South Africa, the socio-economic, cultural and political acts of domination that are presently oppressive to many Indigenous peoples are derived from the colonial past; they are imbibed, upheld, and perpetuated by the educated elite following 'independence.' Some of these acts resulted in a lack of recognition of status of Indigenous peoples. Postcolonial Africa, or more accurately neocolonial Africa, is characterized by a struggle to create uniformity and deny differences. When discussing the issue of Indigenous peoples and their rights the argument of 'tribalism' often surfaces, an issue which has absolutely nothing to do with securing the rights of Indigenous people. To this end, the recognition of a status that is different from the mainstream is perceived as allowing 'tribalism' to persist by most pro-capitalist and elitist African governments. Following colonization, Africa has often opted for open democratic parties shaped upon a Western model rather than a situation where common interests are organized by interethnic unity.

Yet in most of Africa differences are acknowledged and somewhat tolerated to a point since administrative regions are often named and represented along ethnic lines. Talking about differences gives the impression that the common interests of all will be represented equally within national structures. But the interests of minority Indigenous peoples isolated in remote parts of countries are suppressed under the guise of 'national unity.' In this way the visible differences and interests reflected by many Indigenous peoples are portrayed as though they have no right to be different. This attitude threatens their very cultural survival and denies them the right to exist. As a result of discrimination and domination, many Indigenous peoples are outnumbered in their own areas to such an extent that they are unable to communicate in their own languages, practice their own religion, and live their own cultures.

Finally, there are conflicts that relate to differing views on development between Indigenous peoples and the nation-states of which they are a part. One example of differing views on development is well illustrated by the Turkwel Gorge hydroelectric power plant built in Turkana territory. Here state interest was directed to meet national electricity supply needs while the pastoral Turkana needed access to the rivers for their livelihood and the survival of their livestock. The interest of the state prevailed over those of the Indigenous peoples whose survival as a viable self-reliant community was made even more vulnerable in the interest of national 'development.' The water from Mount Kilimanjaro crossing Maasai territory is another example. The water flows across some dry plains to the flower gardens and a portion of it reaches the Indigenous peoples of the area, even though it is common knowledge that water is desperately needed there. In both cases, and in many others, 'development' has meant development for others, not for Indigenous peoples.

Lack of Representation of Indigenous Peoples in Political Affairs

Another major problem for Indigenous peoples in Africa is exacerbated by the fact that they are not recognized as Indigenous peoples by the states in which they live. Thus, lack of effective political participation in the political affairs of their countries is a matter of concern for most Indigenous peoples and others, both in Africa and elsewhere. While inadequate political representation at various levels contributes to a certain extent to the marginalization of Indigenous peoples in the political affairs of their countries, the situation is complicated by other factors.

Some Indigenous peoples have parliamentary representation but others do not. Those who do not, find themselves being represented by persons who may not know their problems. At other times, their representative does not speak their language, making communication with the Indigenous peoples minimal at best. The majority of Indigenous peoples are not fluent in the national language, also making communication difficult.

However, despite parliamentary representation, the Indigenous still find themselves unable to effectively participate in active politics. A combination of factors including geographical distance from metropolitan centers, lifestyle of the Indigenous peoples and the style of politics adopted by the respective states have contributed to this situation. Most Indigenous peoples in Africa are either hunter-gatherers or livestock keepers residing far from the metropolitan centers. For pastoralists, whether nomadic or transhumant, this means traveling long distances in search of grazing and water for their livestock. Hunter-gatherers also move to places where wildlife is plentiful. Depending on the season, this could mean being totally engrossed with the survival of herds and people with little time and energy left for involvement in other activities. During the 1997 elections in Kenya, the heavy rains and floods in the North Eastern Province seriously affected both voter registration and the actual voting exercise. It was reported that after the votes had been cast, some ballot boxes along with the officials accompanying them were swept away by heavy floods. Then in mid-2000, at the peak of a most devastating drought causing pastoralists to move far and wide with their herds in search of pastures, voter registration was announced in preparation for the next general elections.

Besides environmental upheavals, insecurity in the form of banditry and cattle rustling (and even wildlife) in some parts of Kenya and Uganda almost always mars elections in pastoralist areas, making it difficult for many people to go out and vote and assert their political rights. This contrasts sharply with areas where settlements are close to each other and near urban centers with better infrastructure and security. The infrastructure permits easier communication and better access to information through the media. This affords urban-based people the opportunity and capability to participate fully in political life, articulate their concerns and express them through the vote without hindrance.

The question of population numbers also plays a role in determining levels of participation in politics. Indigenous peoples are often minorities in contrast with the more dominant groups. The fact that they occupy vast and inaccessible areas creates complications that further hamper their political participation. At the national level, political representatives are drawn from constituencies created on the basis of population numbers. This results in many small Indigenous communities having no representation at the national levels such as the National Assembly, where representation is necessary for matters of community concern to be addressed.

Representation is also complicated by party politics. In East Africa, following independence, some countries have adopted multiparty politics as a method of governance through parliamentary representation as a way of realizing democracy. However, in order to obtain support from the electorate, party leaders, who are usually the urban elite, have to co-opt individuals to rally behind them. Support may be obtained voluntarily or through granting favors and sometimes by gifts of various kinds to the electorate. In this way party politics are manipulated and the electorate finds itself used and misused without participating in any real sense in political decision-making or political action.

In addition to outright buying of votes, there are also more subtle methods of obtaining support. The selling of party membership cards to a largely illiterate electorate without any explanation of what the benefits are is commonly used by all parties to rally support for their parties. While mainstream societies are also manipulated through party politics, Indigenous people are more disadvantaged than the others because illiteracy rates are higher among Indigenous peoples and because the newly emerged opposition parties have taken no interest in garnering support from Indigenous peoples in isolated areas of their countries.

Where there have been attempts to garner opposition support in these areas, opposition supporters are often frustrated not just by the ruling parties, but realizing that perhaps the process of campaigning and seeking votes might cost more than it is worth in terms of actual votes. The distances covered are too long, the infrastructure too poor and the votes too few to make a difference. At the same time, the issues that beset Indigenous peoples might not be of interest to the mainstream communities and in some cases they may even contradict the objectives of opposition parties. For example, with the question of land and economic marginalization, the core complaint of most Indigenous peoples is that dominant communities have through commission or coercion either expropriated Indigenous peoples' land or designed policies that lead to regional disparities and inequity.

So far in East Africa, the primary objective of the opposition parties has been to remove the party in power and not necessarily to institute fairer methods of governance and more equitable distribution of national wealth. Many Indigenous peoples are increasingly dissatisfied with the treatment they receive from the ruling national parties and from the fact that emerging opposition parties have not demonstrated that they are capable of delivering radically different methods of governance that would assuage the ills committed. Indeed more fear, perhaps unfounded, is expressed by Indigenous peoples at the thought of some opposition parties taking over the reins of power than if the status quo is maintained. In the case of Kenya the main opposition party is associated with the Kikuyu, and in Tanzania and Uganda it is associated with the Chagga and Baganda respectively, all of whom are numerous, dominant and perceived to be inward looking in terms of national development. For this reason Indigenous peoples find it easier to accept the 'devil they know' and can continue struggling with rather than the 'angel they do not know' which they suspect will be worse.

It so happened that in Kenya, the first president was Kikuyu and he was expected to favor his own community at the expense of all the other communities, which he promptly did. The same happened in Uganda. In Tanzania, while no person from the Chagga community has ever ruled the country, the promotion of socialist doctrine was accompanied by the suppression of capitalistic tendencies perceived to be exhibited mainly by the Chagga. This history is recalled every five years in political campaigns and election rallies and is often viewed as irrelevant and superficial by Indigenous peoples because the dominant status quo is almost always preserved. This is precisely why support for emerging opposition parties in East Africa comes mainly from mainstream dominant communities and not from marginalized Indigenous peoples.

Conclusion: Indigenous Peoples Organizing Themselves for Liberation and Independence

Ever since the declaration of 1993 as the International Year of Indigenous Peoples and the subsequent declaration of the Decade of Indigenous Peoples, there has been much discussion on the subject. A handful of African Indigenous peoples have attended international forums and have formed small NGOs to address their problems. However the organizations are still few, weak in organization due to lack of material and financial support, and do not encompass all Indigenous communities. At the same time, the organizational skills of peoples working in Western-style structures are limited. Further, they have not formed coordinating umbrella bodies. While a few individuals have attended international conferences on Indigenous peoples, they do not consistently or in any systematic way attend these meetings, generally because they lack the funds. This results in poor representation and a lack of expertise on how to organize and advocate for Indigenous peoples' causes.

There is also little networking among the various Indigenous groups in Africa and, unlike Asia and Latin America, no African regional Indigenous network or organization exists. It is warming to note the recent formation of a regional network, 'Indigenous Peoples of Africa Coordinating Committee,' with an office in South Africa. Another problem is that some NGOs using the name 'Indigenous' have no focused agenda and generally no regular program activities; if they do they are not comprehensive enough to target issues that are critical and of concern to Indigenous peoples in their territories. Others are ad hoc intermediary groups that have developed without involving Indigenous peoples and therefore are not committed to their cause and do not represent them or their views.

It remains to be seen how Indigenous peoples in Africa will organize themselves more effectively in the near future, particularly in the wake of the onslaught of

Western 'globalization' systems which have wreaked havoc on global ecosystems, economies and cultures, particularly decimating Indigenous peoples' already diminished resources. Organizational networking of Indigenous peoples on the African continent and advocacy of Indigenous people's causes is an imperative for the new millennium, albeit a Western-defined one. Failure to address Indigenous African concerns will affect the sustainability of the entire continent and the world. The survival and thriving of Indigenous people is interwoven with that of all peoples.

Chapter 16

Indigenous African Knowledge: Human Rights and Globalization

Julian Kunnie

Introduction

We need to extend our deepest thanks to the Creator, *Umvelinqangi, uModimo, uQamata*, and to the ancestors of Mother Africa and Turtle Island for being able to be here and to pen these words from our hearts. To our grandparents, Marie Christina and Abraham, Barnabas and Ayah, and father, Matthew, we say *Siyabonga kakhulu*, "Thank you very much" for your love and the persistence in the Black struggle of liberation from which we have learned so much and will continue to impart to our children, grandchildren, and future generations.

This chapter will discuss the question of contemporary human and natural rights issues and concerns pertaining to Africa and the globe in the new millennium, particularly in the wake of the imposition of Western European globalization and imperialism, utilizing an Indigenous African philosophical and cultural framework. As legal scholars Sammy Adelman and Abdul Paliwala aptly put it:

> Despite much rhetoric about democracy, the global political economy remains resolutely imperialist. The 1992 Earth Summit in Rio de Janeiro, the Uruguay Round of the General Agreement on Tariffs and Trade (GATT) and Western-dominated institutions such as the International Monetary Fund (IMF) and the World Bank epitomize the enduring structural imbalances in the global economy and the undemocratic nature of the international politico-legal order.[1]

We will demonstrate that human rights observances, protections, and discourses have always been a foundational part of historical African and other Indigenous societies and that there is much within such Indigenous traditions that can inform struggles for human rights, as well as contribute to the shaping of global formulations of human rights platforms, contrary to the exclusivistic and culturally parochial paradigms imposed on groups like the United Nations by Western European cultures and governments. As Pollis has pointed out:

---

1   Sammy Adelman and Abdul Paliwala (eds), *Law and Crisis in the Third World*. London: Hanz Zell Publishers, for the Center of Modern African Studies, University of Warwick, 1993, 1–2.

Most Western-based human rights organizations are, to a greater or lesser degree, political advocates of the West, albeit unconsciously, and often Western concepts of human rights.[2]

This chapter will illumine issues of human rights, with particular regard to women, children, workers, and the poor, with special relevance to the situation of human rights in Africa today, as well as elucidate the intrinsic dimension of ecological and environmental rights and needs.

Indigenous Cosmologies: Interconnectedness of All Life

Among all Indigenous peoples' cosmologies there is the implicit assumption that all life is interwoven and inextricably connected as part of the spiritual web of the universe. Indeed, humans are viewed as an intrinsic element of nature, contiguous with and related to the rest of creation, as Winona La Duke from the North American Indigenous context reminds us in her classic work, *All Our Relations: Native Struggles for Land and Life* (Boston: South End Press, 2000). There is no distinct word for 'nature' among Indigenous peoples because all of life is seen as coterminous with nature.

Western European cosmologies rooted in Platonic-Aristotelian concepts view human beings as separate from the rest of nature, and above a demarcated realm called "nature." This perception has resulted in the conquest of nature by Western European powers, most visibly manifest in the dispossession, colonization, and extermination of millions of Indigenous people in Africa, Asia, the Americas, the Caribbean, and the Pacific. It was educational and touching for me to be a participant at the Second International Tribunal on Africa, held in Los Angeles in February 2000, to hear testimonies from scores of individuals from Africa and the African Diaspora in the Americas, regarding the atrocities perpetrated against Black peoples by European colonialism and the US government, represented by agencies like the World Bank and the International Monetary Fund that further impoverish already poor and hungry people.

Indigenous peoples were and are seen as part of the 'savage wilderness' requiring 'domestication' and 'civilizing' by European humanity. So, too, this objectification of nature evolved into hierarchies of dualism that became institutionalized into systems of racism, patriarchy and sexism, and cultural effacement: male, European, intellectual, and rational on the one side, and female, Indigenous non-European, intuitive, and nonrational (or pre-logical as Levi-Strauss would put it) on the other. Kwame Nkrumah discusses the deleterious effects of Cartesian dualism in his erudite work, *Consciencism* (London: Heinemann, 1964), where he argues for a consciencism that rejects the mind/body dualism, and rooted in the Indigenous African worldview which "...accepts the absolute and independent idea of matter...which is not just

---

2   Cited in Issa Shivji, *The Concept of Human Rights in Africa.* Dakar: CODESRIA, 1988, 51.

dead weight, but alive with forces in tension..."[3] Rosemary Ruether, a religions scholar, has discussed these institutions of hierarchy and subordination in her book, *Sexism and God-Talk* (Philadelphia: Westminister Press, 1983). Today, these same hierarchies and dualisms persist in most parts of the globe, the product of the past five centuries of European hegemony in the world, reflected in the global economy of capitalist monopolies of power, wealth, and resources confined predominantly to the West as a result of Indigenous resources and the confiscation of the value of Indigenous peoples' labor.

The spiritual foundation of life is enshrined among all Indigenous societies. There is no sphere of life that falls outside the realm of spirit, not even law or human rights. Indeed, unlike the Eurocentric ideological imposition on the world which enforces an ostensible sacred/secular dichotomy in sociopolitical life, Indigenous peoples view the arena of politics, economics, social construction, and transformation as directly connected to the Creator; *Onyeame*, in the Akan tradition of Ghana, for instance. The mental universe of Indigenous peoples, including Africans, is foundationally spiritual. Kwame Gyekye, the noted African philosophical thinker, observes:

> Belief in Mystical power is common to all African societies; it is a feature of traditional African religion and worldview. There is a pervasive and resilient belief in the existence of mystical forces or powers in the universe that can be tapped by those human beings who have the knowledge to do so for good or ill ... In traditional African religion, God is the Supreme Being, but not the object of direct 'worship.' Worship is directed to trees, rocks, rivers and mountains ...[4]

It is this all-encompassing aura of spirit that permeates all African and other Indigenous societies, and which was severely threatened by the invasion of European colonialism and militarism in Africa, Asia, the Americas, and the Pacific.

The assertion of this point of *holism* is significant because it suggests an alternative point of departure for the discussion on human rights in Africa and the world: that of Indigenous spiritual and philosophical foundations. The reason for the rejection of Western European-based premises in discourses on human rights is the fundamentally flawed assumption of Western cultures that eschews spirituality and reduces all human activity to solely materialistic and capitalistic proportions, while deriving from a historical colonialist and imperialist cosmology and practice. This paper will demonstrate that the individualistic, competitive, elitist, male-dominated, Judeo-Christian biased, and capitalistic-grounded notions of human rights for the world's peoples have serious problems and ironically have functioned to deprive human rights while simultaneously calling for the preservation of such rights. The rights to freedom of speech and worship, freedom from economic want, and freedom from fear proposed by Franklin D. Roosevelt in 1941 in the United States is empty rhetoric, since the US has never accorded any substantive recognition of human

---

3   Kwame Nkrumah, Consciencism, 97.

4   Kwame Gyekye, *African Cultural Values: An Introduction.* Philadelphia, PA, and Accra, Ghana: Sankofa Publishing Company, 1996, 6.

rights to colonized Native people and descendants of enslaved Africans or poor people, either domestically or globally.[5] The US represents the bastion of Western imperialism and merely echoes such ideological rhetoric to confuse and hoodwink oppressed people into believing that it is serious about the question of human rights. The freedom fighters globally supported by the US have always been puppets and instruments of US political hegemony, as opposed to interventionists on behalf of the human rights of the oppressed, as the US government has ostensibly claimed in southeast Asia, Angola, Nicaragua, the Caribbean, and other parts of Central and South America. As Ngugi wa Thiong'o, the noted Kenyan author says:

> Over the years, the USA became the main agency for the destabilization of any country in Asia and Africa and South America that leaned a bit too heavily on social change; or that wanted to break the neo-colonial chain around its economy, politics and culture. The USA was not even shy of direct invasions as in the case of Grenada in the eighties. But its main means of destabilization in the countries leaning towards fundamental social change was the creation, followed by an active support, of fake freedom fighters like the Nicaraguan Contras and Angolan Unita. Today the U.S. military bases are everywhere in Asia, Africa, and South America, the areas that used to be the sole domain of European capital.[6]

It is equally important to assert that there are some differences between international and national formulations of human rights, albeit nuanced, owing to the complexities and particularities of individual cultures. What may be considered hideous in one culture may be considered sacred in another. However, the question is to attempt to arrive at a universal declaration of rights that all peoples and cultures can uphold, while respecting the distinctive integrity of individual nations and cultures. The question of whether the discussion on human rights ought to be redirected toward the question of meeting fundamental human *needs* is one which will also be entertained in this article.[7]

African Indigenous Systems of Knowledge and Wisdom

Contrary to widespread notions propagated by Western media and educational-socio-political systems, African societies were not devoid of substantive practices, policies, and behaviors that promoted cultures of human and other natural rights.

---

5   Roosevelt's formulation is mentioned and discussed in Lone Lindholt's *Questioning the Universality of Human Rights: The African Charter on Human and People's Rights in Botswana, Malawi, and Mozambique. Aldershot*, UK and Brookfield, Vermont, USA: Ashgate Publishing Limited, 1997, 30.

6   Ngugi wa Thiong'o, *Moving the Center: The Struggle for Cultural Freedoms.* London: James Currey; Nairobi: East African Educational Publishers; and Portsmouth, New Hampshire: Heinemann, 1993, 49.

7   Lone Lindholt's *Questioning the Universality of Human Rights: The African Charter on Human and People's Rights in Botswana, Malawi, and Mozambique. Aldershot*, UK and Brookfield, Vermont, USA: Ashgate Publishing Limited, 1997, 29.

The foremost question of equality was not absent within African legal and moral discourses and practices. For instance, in pre-colonial societies in Southern Africa, such as among the Sotho:

> ...the Basotho courts had well recognized principles of equality. One Basotho customary norm (*Lekhotla ha la nameloe* – the court lends itself to no person) recognized that all had equal rights before traditional courts. The complaints of the poor were heard, and King Moshoeshoe, founder of the Basotho nation was quoted as declaring that the "law knows no one as a 'poor man.'"[8]

So, too, we know that women were given greater opportunities to express themselves and participate in societal decision-making. Abusive men were decried by clans, and women were urged not to marry into such families. Collective sanctions were imposed on abusive men.[9] The kind of male chauvinism embedded in the English language and reflected concretely in female gender subjugation is not reflected within such cultures as the Yoruba and Ibo of Nigeria, the renowned Nigerian writer 'Zulu Sofola, tells us:

> The female as an appendage is evident in the English language. The very words "woman" and "female" derive from masculine nouns: fe-*male*, wo-*man*. And when it is not necessary to specify her at all, the terms man and hu-*man* are used inclusively to refer to both genders. On the contrary, in African languages, to use Igbo and Yoruba languages as examples, a common denominator is used in the constitution of words that represent male and female. For example, in Igbo, the word for child, *nwa*, is used as a root word: *nwa*-oke, male; nwa-nyi, female. In Yoruba, it is *rin*: *Okunrin* (the type that is male), *Obirin* (the type that is female). And to refer to both genders inclusively (human), it is *madu* (Igbo) and *enia* (Yoruba). There is here no hint of the male chauvinism that is enshrined in the English language. The African perception of the gender question is thus more healthy, positive, and allows for a wholesome development of human society. Consequently, the woman has always had a vital place in the scheme of things within the African cosmology, the most relevant to our present discussion being the dual-sex system of socio-political power sharing fully developed by African peoples and based in the following perceptions of womanhood: (1) as the divine equal of man in essence, (2) as a Daughter, (3) as a Mother, (4) as a wife.[10]

The Tuareg of North Africa still practice the tradition of females assuming definitive roles, where women are the constructors of the household tent with men as 'guests'

---

8   David Penn and Patricia Campbell, "Human Rights and Culture: Beyond Universality and Relativism" in *Third World Quarterly*, Vol. 19, No 1, 7–27, 1998.

9   See for instance Brooke Grundfest Schoepf's article, "Gender relations and development: political economy and culture" in *Twenty First Century Africa: Towards a New Vision of Self Sustainable Development* edited by Anne Seidman and Frederick Anang. Trenton, New Jersey: Africa World Press, 1997.

10   'Zulu Sofola, "Feminism and African Womanhood" in *Sisterhood, Feminisms and Power: From Africa to the Diaspora* edited by Obioma Nnaemeka. Trenton, New Jersey and Asmara, Eritrea: Africa World Press, 1998, 51–52.

of the women, and women are the primary educators, musicians and transmitters of tradition.[11] Something for modern *man* to ponder! Patriarchy was not an original human social formation but began to evolve as human societies became more organized when imperialistic formations starting with Babylonian, Mesopotamian, and subsequently Greco-Roman patriarchal imperialism became formalized and imposed on neighboring cultures.[12]

Sharukh Husain confirms this historic fact too,[13] indicating that in the Tassili region of Saharan North Africa, rock paintings depict female figures bearing marks such as crescents, which were associated with goddesses in Egypt and the Near East and the rest of Africa.[14] Husain insightfully points out that this notion of female divinity and Creator being was not confined to Egypt where Isis was viewed as the Mother of the universe. Female images of a bisexual serpent worshipped as a goddess are found in Benin's creation myths, as the self-fertilizing *Mawu Lisa* where both male and female divinities complement one another; among the Minia in southern Algeria; in the renowned story of Amma the great God who has intercourse with the earth in Dogon creation mythology; among the Ndembu in Zambia, where the *Mudyi* tree signifies a multiple symbol, suggesting breast milk, women's wisdom, death, and the continuity of Ndembu society; among the Yoruba, *Oshun,* the goddess of luxury and love is believed to be the ancestor of the Yoruba and the god, *Shango*, is given control over thunder and lightning by his wife and sister, *Oya,* the water goddess of Brazilian *candomble*.[15] Among the Nnobi of Nigeria, femaleness of creator divinity is also extant, noted by Ifi Amadiume in *Afrikan Matriarchal Foundations: The Igbo Case* (London: Karnak House, 1987) where she states:

> ...the female gender had the more prominent place in myth, Indigenous religious and cultural concepts. There was a strong female orientation. The supernatural, a goddess, is female. The stream, Iyi Idemili, is the source of divinity. The cultural result of the mediation of the natural (Aho, the hunter from the wild) and the supernatural (the goddess Idemili from the sacred stream) Edo, is a hard-working woman. Thus both Nnobi and Nwewi inherit industriousness from females. The most praised person in Nnobi is a hard-working woman. Nnobi traces its matrifocal concepts to another myth of origin. In

---

11 This was beautifully depicted in a national African exhibit on Africa traveling through the United States currently, entitled *Africa: One Continent, Many Worlds*. The author was a keynote speaker at an event held at the Denver Museum of Natural History on November 13, 1998, where the exhibit was being held.

12 Monica Sjoo and Barbara Mor, *The Great Cosmic Mother*. San Francisco: Harper & Row, 10.

13 Shahrukh Husain, *The Goddess: Creation, Fertility and Abundance: The Sovereignty of Women Myths and Archetypes.* London: Little Brown and Co., 1997, 31.

14 Sharukh Husain, *The Goddess: Creation, Fertility and Abundance: The Sovereignty of Women Myths and Archetypes,* 30.

15 Sharukh Husain, *The Goddess: Creation, Fertility and Abundance: The Sovereignty of Women Myths and Archetypes,* 30–32. See also J. Murphy, "Oshun the Dancer" in *The Book of the Goddess: Past and Present* edited by Carl Olsen. New York: Crossroads, 1983, 190.

Obiefuna Aho's wife is called Agbala, an Igbo word for female deity.[16] ("The Origin of Nnobi" in *Abalukwu,* Vol. 5, December 1976).

The swearing before the Earth Spirit, *Ala,* by the men of Agbaja Igbo following an influenza epidemic in 1919 was just one instance where men were made to declare loyalty to the community and refrain from unethical actions against individuals.[17]

In her most recent work, *Reinventing Africa: Matriarchy, Religion and Culture* (1997), Amadiume recounts the Merina social structure in West Africa, where she points out that the Vazimba constituted an 'autochthonous category where the original owners of the land and the symbols of natural fertility were all women, who controlled the natural spirits and wild cattle are symbols of the Vazimbas, with women being associated with water, as givers of life.'[18] In the Anlo tradition among Ewe society in Ghana, both male and female deities constitute integral parts of the sacred. Christian Gaba explains:

> The non-human spirit beings are both male and female; so also are the human ones. Out of 105 recitals that form part of the ritual of worship collected from this African society, four have female spirit beings as objects of cultic attention apart from reference made to them in ritual sayings addressed specifically to the male spirit beings. Anlo religious experience also makes mention of the earth, Anyigba, as a deity, as the following passage suggests:
>
> > O Heaven, your attention please.
> > I also invoke the presence of your spouse, Earth.
> >   (LXXVII, 7–8)[19]

It is clear from Christian Gaba's research that in Anlo tradition both female and male deities are worshipped and priestesses and priests function organically as religious intermediaries.

Although these are important indications of the power of women evidenced in African societies prior to the colonial period, we can never romanticize African cultures, or Indigenous cultures when it comes to the experiences of women or any other practice for that matter. Class differentiation and hierarchies of abuse began to emerge just prior to colonialism and became institutionalized under colonial domination, leading to the progressive disempowering of African women. Capitalism assured the degrading of women both within families and in the market

---

16 Ifi Amadiume, *Afrikan Matriarchal Foundations: The Igbo Case.* London: Karnak House, 1987, 41.

17 Ifi Amadiume, *Afrikan Matriarchal Foundations: The Igbo Case.* London: Karnak House, 1987, 28.

18 Ifi Amadiume, *Reinventing Africa: Matriarchy, Religion and Culture.* London: Zed Press, 1997, 45.

19 Christian Gaba, "Women and Religious Experience Among the Anlo of West Africa" in *Women in the World's Religions.* New York: Paragon, 1987, 178.

place, eroding the independent status that women had vis-à-vis men in areas of food production and fertility in pre-colonial societies.[20]

However there are aspects in African societies in which significant checks and balances are evidenced. The rigidity of patriarchy as extant in Western European societies and as imposed in many global societies was not prevalent with the same level of inflexibility and stridence in the latter. With regard to Africa, Margaret Peil writes:

> A society with unilineal descent may trace rights and duties in one line and inheritance in some other way. For example, in a patrilineal society, women may have some inheritance from their mothers and in a basically matrilineal society children may inherit some goods or positions from their fathers. In other words, many supposedly unilineal systems may have some double descent aspects…[21]

The notion and norm of rugged atomistic individualism is absent in all African societies. Children were never seen as parentless or orphans in traditional societies, as they are in Western societies and Western-shaped societies. Peil notes that even in the observance of *lobola,* or bride-wealth, there is the tie to the transfer of sexual rights and rights to children born of marriage.[22] With generational rights,

> a man is socially the father of all children even though he may not be the biological father; he is the *pater* even though he may not be the genitor (summarized by the Asante proverb, "a thief has no child."[23]

Even the widescale use of the terms 'brother' and 'sister' used principally among Africans in the United States and disseminated among numerous other cultures is a direct carryover from the enslaved African experience. Kinship links provide the basis of a communal practice of individual human rights, so that bonds are developed across ethnic and even bloodlines. The notion of *sahwira* in Shona tradition in Southern Africa transcends consanguineous relations, and signifies an extension of this kinship principle. The continent-wide aphorism, "a person is only a person because of others," or "I am Because We are, We are, therefore I am," is yet another basis for the solid establishment of kinship relations across ethnic, clan, geographical, religious and class lines in Africa.

There are two critical areas where Indigenous values assume formative and transformative importance in the question of rights: that of ecological preservation and women. In terms of environmental rights, Indigenous cultures are instructive for understanding and practicing the harmonization of human beings and the rest of creation. African societies have always cherished and observed the principle of

---

20 See for instance, T.W. Bennett, *Human Rights and African Customary Law under the South African Constitution.* Cape Town: Juta & Co., 1995, 84.

21 Margaret Peil, *Consensus and Conflict in African Societies: An Introduction to Sociology.* London: Longman, 1977, 135.

22 Margaret Peil, 139.

23 Ibid.

sustainability of resources, where the protection of the fragile ecological system and the environment have been paramount. Among numerous Tswana villages, for instance, in accordance with the belief that the destruction of certain trees causes ill fortune, the leader of the community prohibits the cutting down of trees and determines when it is appropriate to fell trees for repairing fences, and controls the allocation of natural resources like thatched grass.[24] Within the Shona tradition in Zimbabwe, women determined the time of planting of certain seeds and in which areas (hilly or *vlei*) and which seeds would be planted for agriculture. The practice of *mateka,* to tap precious water resources, conserve them, and prevent further soil erosion was also observed by women.[25]

On questions of sustainability, Indigenous societies epitomize the health and judicious practice of conservation of scarce resources, always collectively utilized and distributed among the needy. The balance of meeting individual needs while sharing collective resources was always maintained, providing for sustenance in times of famine and drought and harsh environmental and climatic conditions. Professor T. Nhlapo, in the *African Law Review*, argues:

> Traditional society might have preferred, as a strategy, to subsume the protection of the group. For example, the main hedge against old age poverty was the upwards distribution of resources from the young to the old through institutions that were notoriously inegalitarian. Yet who is to say that the strategy was unjustified, in societies without state pensions in social welfare? Similarly, in its precapitalist form of chieftainship, entailed as many obligations as it did rights and privileges. The chief's apparent wealth, accumulation from fines, gifts, and various forms of homage represented a community resource in times of famine…Traditional society viewed hunger and destitution as no less undignified than they are considered to be in the West. It was simply 'no way to treat people.' … One does not need to belabor the question whether or not traditional society recognized human rights; it suffices to observe that the societies recognized human dignity and they aspired to its protection no less avidly than did their Western counterparts. That these strategies were driven by a communitarian rather than individualistic ethic does not detract from the fact.[26]

Human rights in African societies were, and are, an intrinsic element of Indigenous cultural and moral values. Kwame Gyekye underscores this point:

> In the traditional African society, there is little need to assert rights – particularly social and economic rights – because the social and moral systems or values created by the

---

24 Emil Holub, *Seven Years in South Africa*, Vol. 1 (London: Sampson Low, Maston, Seale and Rivington, 1981) and Ellenberger, History of the Basuto, 266.

25 Sarah Muvududu, "Gender Concerns in Indigenous Woodland Management" in *Proceedings of the Conference on Indigenous Woodland Management*, compiled and edited by Calvin Nhira. Harare, Zimbabwe: Center for Applied Social Sciences, University of Zimbabwe, January, 1995, 43.

26 T. Nhlapo, "Human Rights—The African Perspective" in *Africa Law Review*, Vol. 6, No. 1, May 1995, Nairobi, 40–41.

traditional society in many ways and quite satisfactorily provide for the fulfillment of these rights. There is probably no need, for instance, for one to assert one's right to food against the society or the community, since access to food is a necessary part of the traditional social arrangement. But inasmuch as a political power, whether in a traditional or a modern context, could become tyrannical or despotic, a notion of human rights sees these rights as rights that are, or need to be, asserted primarily against the community or the state. Thus, in traditional African societies, assertion of rights against the state are often made in matters, not of social and economic rights, but of civil and political rights. This was due not only to the corrupt and arrogant character and unacceptable behavior of some of the chiefs (rulers), but also to the less developed democratic institutions and practices then available. Claims to civil and political rights become compelling when chiefs act unjustly or when their actions are not in harmony with traditional political custom. Insistent claims to political rights can in fact result – and in a number of cases have resulted – in the removal of unjust or corrupt or authoritarian rulers in traditional Africa, pre-colonial, colonial, and post-colonial.[27]

Perhaps the most striking Indigenous religio-cultural maxim is the infinite value attached to humanity, what Xhosa tradition of Azania describes as *ubuntu*, and which is now popularized in post-apartheid societal transformation: the irreducible, priceless value of human beings that cannot be quantified in economic and materialistic proportions.[28] The Akan of Ghana say, "All human beings are children of God; no one is a child of the earth," substantiating the view that human value is immeasurable and that human beings can never be a means to an ends, but are the ends, can never be objects for exploitation and commodification, but are always creative subjects.

Implications of Indigenous African Philosophical and Moral Systems for Human and Natural Rights in Africa and the World

First and foremost, it needs to be asserted that the question of "human rights" ineluctably becomes the question of "natural rights," the right of all natural life to live in dignity and harmony, since all life is interrelated through spirit foundations and interdependent. Indigenous peoples see the preservation of the ecology, the environment, the forests, the rivers, streams, oceans, and the air as an extension of creation and warranting protection. The ecological rights issue is directly implied as a result of Indigenous African cosmologies. Considering the vitiation of Africa by toxic waste products of Western industrialism as well as nuclear

---

27 Kwame Gyekye, *African Cultural Values: An Introduction for Senior Secondary Schools.* Accra: Sankofa Publications, 1998, 115. For an insight into the dynamics of Indigenous Yoruba law, practice and morality, see A. Toriola Oyewo and O.B. Olaoba, *A Survey of African Law and Custom with particular reference to the Yoruba-speaking peoples of South-Western Nigeria.* Ibadan: Jator Publishing Co, 1999, particularly Chapters 4, 5, and 6.

28 See for instance, Desmond Tutu's article, "African Theology/Black Theology: Soul Mates or Antagonists?" in *Black Theology: A Documentary History, 1966–1979*, edited by Gayraud Wilmore and James Cone. Maryknoll, New York: Orbis Books, 1981.

waste and contamination in countries like Nigeria, the Sudan, and South Africa, the despoliation of African timber forests and grasslands by predatory transnational corporations in Cote d'Ivoire, the Cameroon, and Equatorial Guinea, for example, such ecological principles and rights are coterminous with human rights, since Africans, particularly in rural areas, depend on fragile ecological systems for their survival and sustainability. Africa must not end up like Asia, where half of Chinese rivers no longer have edible fish, two thirds of South Korea's rivers have water that is undrinkable, and one third of Taiwan's rice crop is inedible because of mercury, arsenic, and cadmium poisoning.[29]

Second, the discourse on human rights in Africa and the world needs to be sharpened, broadened, and deepened, to include critiques on Western European imperialism, which includes the United States, and the role of Western imperialism in systematic human and ecological rights violations against colonized peoples, as documented for instance by Noam Chomsky and Edward Herman's incisive work, *The Washington Connection and Third World Fascism: The Political Economy of Human Rights, Vol. 1* and in the film, *What I Have Learned About U.S. Foreign Policy: U.S. Covert Action Since World War II*, by Frank Dorrel. These works expose the flagrantly hypocritical and fraudulent character of US calls for human rights observances in light of US military and political abuses around the world. Issa Shivji, member of the faculty of Law at the University of Dar es Salaam, puts this so candidly and lucidly:

> ...the same 'hypocrisy and opportunism' is reproduced within the African scholarship and activity on human rights. The few African NGOS, funded as they are by their Western counterparts or other Western funding agencies, rarely touch on the role of imperialism. They do not even expose the crimes of their own states. Instead much time is spent on refining legal concepts of human rights and the machinery for implementation ... the so-called human rights activity in Africa has largely been dominated by lawyers. Thus even the development of other social scientists have by-passed them. African NGOs that are set up, it would seem, are institutional mechanisms by which to obtain foreign funds; they are what might be called FFUNGOS (Foreign-funded NGOs) rather than grass-roots organizations of the intellectuals and the people to struggle for rights.[30]

Shivji proposes a revolutionary human rights framework, which all theoreticians of human rights cannot ignore:

> ... where right is not theorized simply as a legal right which implies both a static and an absolutist paradigm or in the sense of an entitlement or a claim, but a means of struggle ... in that sense, it is akin to righteousness rather than right ... Seen as a means of struggle, 'right' is therefore not a standard granted as charity from above but a standard-bearer around which people rally to struggle from below. By the same token, the correlation of 'right' is not duty (in the Hohfeldian sense), where duty-holders are identified and held

---

29 Eduardo Galeano, *Upside Down: A Primer for the Looking Glass World*. New York: Metropolitan Books, Henry, Holt and Rinehart, 2000, 225.

30 Issa Shivji, *The Concept of Human Rights in Africa*. Dakar: CODESRIA, 1988, 63.

legally or 'morally responsible but rather the correlate is power/privilege where those who enjoy such power/privilege are the subject of being exposed and struggled against.'[31]

What Shivji's radical injunction admonishes is a qualitatively different paradigm for comprehending human rights, not merely a legal category, but one which

> ... views rights struggle as the assertion of popular politics. They are regarded as symbols around which people may be mobilized. In this sense rights struggle is a constant activity, a vehicle for expression rather than a means of self-censorship.[32]

Rights are thus those human qualities and conditions which are struggled for, earned and possessed by the people, particularly those from the marginalized sectors and working classes. Rights are not awarded or allocated from the tables of the privileged ruling classes or bourgeoisie to people at the bottom, as we see in most African and other societies, many of which have witnessed unprecedented institutionalized abuses of human rights. The country of Kenya and the horrific systematic torture and detention of Maina wa Kenyatti, an academic at the University of Nairobi, immediately comes to mind as an example.[33] It is indeed incredibly ironic that while arap Moi was giving the opening speech at a conference convened by the International Commission of Jurists in Nairobi in December, 1985, discussing the theme 'Human and Peoples' Rights in Africa and the African Charter,' Maina wa Kenyatti was being brutalized and savagely beaten by police under orders of Moi.[34] The examples of flagrant human rights abuses in countries like Sierra Leone, Liberia, the Sudan, Cameroon, Togo, Mauritania, Algeria, Egypt and the Central African Republic are vivid reminders of the need to redirect discussions of human rights in Africa from that of appealing to ruthless rulers to mobilizing the downtrodden for justice and dignity.

What is implied here in this particularist and tendential assertion of human and natural rights is that rights need to be asserted, demanded and obtained by those who are most direly affected by its absence: the disenfranchised, the illiterate, the landless, the impoverished, and the dispossessed, so that the privileged segments of society which deny such rights to the poor are exposed precisely at the point of their injustice and illegitimate roles in determining the very content of human rights. Ruling classes have no moral basis to grant human rights to the poor, because their

---

31 Issa Shivji, *The Concept of Human Rights in Africa.* Dakar: CODESRIA, 1988, 63.

32 Issa Shivji, "Rights-struggle, Class-struggle and The Law" in *Law and Crisis in the Third World*, edited by Sammy Adelman and Abdul Paliwala. London: Hanz Zell Publishers, for the Center of Modern African Studies, University of Warwick, 1993, 144.

33 The traumatic and moving account of Maina wa Kenyatti is told in *Kenya: A Prison Notebook.* London: Vita Books and Jamaica, New York: Mau Mau Research Center, 1991, and is a must for understanding political imprisonment and human dehumanization in neo-colonial Kenya.

34 The report of the ICJ conference is available in the publication, *Human and Peoples Rights in Africa and the African Charter*, published by the ICJ in Geneva, 1986.

fundamental existence is predicated on the denial of the humanity of the poor and oppressed.

Third, Indigenous African philosophical frameworks and their attendant emphasis on collectivism and shared benefit and distribution of resources can strengthen and reinforce the current push toward African continental unity, recently proposed and supported by Muammar Ghaddafi of Libya at the 36th summit of the OAU in Lome, perhaps marking the beginning of the realization of the dream of a United States of Africa as envisioned by Osagyefo Kwame Nkrumah. The cultural unity suggested by the notions of *umoja* (unity) in East Africa and *simunye* (we are one) in Southern Africa, for instance, must assume political and economic concreteness beyond an amorphous united Africa. Pan African integration and unification of the African continent is a precondition for the establishment of a strongly economically and politically independent Africa, where Africa's vast natural, energy, agricultural, and technological resources can be harnessed and equitably shared and redistributed among all African people, particularly the working classes and the poor. In this manner, the struggle for the attainment of fundamental human rights in vital areas such as food, education, employment, housing, and health care can be seriously advanced, undergirded by a united Pan African scientific socialist system, observed in proportions in places like Cuba and Libya.

The Organization of African Unity meeting that was held in Sirte, Libya, in March, 2001, is a promising indicator of the inevitable pendulum swing toward African unity and integration.[35] Neocolonialism has been entrenched in virtually the entire continent with the exception of Libya, with the accompanying impoverishment and extermination of the poorest sectors of African societies induced by most African regimes' active collaboration with the criminal and unjust policies of the World Bank and the International Monetary Fund. These imperialist institutions imposed privatization of Africa's resources and institutionalized open expropriation and theft of Africa's wealth by the predatory Western transnational corporations, confirming a 'Recolonization of Africa,' as predicted by the late *Mwalimu*, Julius Nyerere.[36]

The shocking statistic that 21 million African women, children, and men have died in the past 15 years as a result of 'globalization,' which resulted in the denial of basic human rights of food, employment, shelter, education and health care due to the dismantling of health care and educational systems, demanded by the Bretton Woods institutions and adhered to shamelessly by the neocolonial regimes of Zambia, Malawi, Uganda, Senegal, Mali, Togo and numerous other states in Africa are indicative of the failed human rights programs of African governments. Indigenous African philosophical systems and cosmologies would work to arrest this tide of decay, this maelstrom of economic devastation of Africa, by refocusing development concerns and economic orientations inward, toward Africa, and away from Europe, Westernism, and capitalism. Grassroots consciousness-raising educational organizations are desperately needed throughout Africa to mobilize

---

35 *West Africa*, 24–30 July, 2001.
36 *Weekly Insight*, Wednesday, June 14–20, 2000.

the working classes in the direction of establishing human/natural rights, cultures and societies, where unity, economic justice, and redistribution of land and material resources from the rich to the impoverished and needy can occur.

Finally, Indigenous African philosophical and moral systems can serve to bolster the struggle for the realization of women's basic rights, particularly those from the rural working classes [discussed extensively in chapter 6 of my recently published book, *Is Apartheid Really Dead? Pan Africanist Working Class Cultural Critical Perspectives* (Boulder, Colorado, and Oxford, U.K.: Westview Press/Perseus Books, 2000)]. The tenacity of male dominance and patriarchal structures that ensure domination by men in political, economic, and social spheres in Africa and around the world, has to be broken. The persistence of systematic rape, economic marginalization, lack of prenatal and neonatal care and unemployment has ravaged women in particular and assured their subjugation. Africa's ancient precolonial history of the balance of women's rights with that of men's, as enunciated earlier in this article, is the framework to achieve through relentless revolutionary Indigenous struggle, the balance of the division of labor, the accordance of mutual respect of all women, and the elevating of women to positions of decisive economic, political, and social leadership that serve the neediest of society. The struggle for women's rights is ultimately a human/natural rights struggle.

Bourgeois men in Africa have been in the forefront of political, economic, and social processes as defined by neocolonial African society since the beginning of the past century. It is high time for the working women of Africa, rural and urban, to take their place at the decision-making table so that Africa's entire polity, culture, economy, and society can be revolutionized and transformed. The men have had the opportunity and demonstrated that they are ill-equipped to extirpate the scourge of neocolonialism in Africa. Let us give Africa's women the opportunity to reconfigure the African landscape in harmony with Mother Earth and all of creation.

Conclusion

The new millennium may just be the millennium of Indigenous people. Human/natural rights in Africa and the world must be defined by those whose ancestors have observed such rights for millennia, as opposed by those who derived from Coca-Cola civilizations and whose behavior for the past five centuries has caused more irreparable damage to humans and all life than ever before. Africa, as the birthplace of human civilization, could just be the next place from where such Indigenous knowledge and wisdom can radiate to all of our beautiful but ravaged globe, so that the right to live in peace, justice, harmony, and security can be truly universal and not confined to the privileged minority elites of this world.

Epilogue

Over two decades ago, Philip Deere, a Lakota spiritual leader, noted that at an earlier point in history before colonialism, Europeans possessed the drum as other Indigenous peoples, but lost it on the road to industrialism and what was termed "progress." Following the loss of the drum, Western European civilization has faltered, lost and rootless, because it fell out of harmony with the pulse of Mother Earth and the rhythm of creation. In the film, *Sugar Cane Alley*, a moving drama on the hardships of life in the Caribbean, an elder man wisely informs a young boy prior to the elder's passing on to the next world that human beings can never "improve on" or "better" nature, but can only destroy it in such attempts. True ancestral wisdom from the elders!

In the aftermath of five hundred years of the hegemony of Western European civilization even as we enter a new millennium by Western definitions of time, there is widespread suffering of the vast majority of the world's people, most being of color, and alienated from their Indigenous lands and relations. The Western world has brought technological sophistry, computer wizardry, mass mobility through air and telecommunication, and inventions that make the most complex and time-consuming of tasks simple and convenient. For the West, there has been affluence, prosperity, monetary accumulation, unbridled wealth possession, unrestrained hedonism, and crass consumerism for Western elites, unparalleled in human history, with the leftovers spilling to the middle classes and working classes of the West. The cost of such consumption and materialism to the colored peoples of the world has been genocide, slavery, dispossession, landlessness, impoverishment, cultural despoliation, and the devastation of fragile ecosystems, since the means by which the West has been able to attain such levels of power and "progress" has been through wars of conquest and annihilation, including developing nuclear weapons for containment, erasure of forests, re-diversion of water systems for industry, accompanying contamination of seas, oceans and lakes, and toxic pollution of air. As if the wars of the 20th century have not been enough, it is now anticipated that the next world war will not be over oil, but over water!

Africa's close to 50 wars are being funded through an insane arms procurement, led by the United States, and supported by the fraternal Western imperialist powers. Thanks to globalization processes over the past decade, the richest 16 individuals in the world possess wealth that exceeds that of the poorest 600 million people in the world, and the wealth of the world's 358 billionaires exceeds that of 45 per cent of the world's people! Some progress! In 1980, 1.3 billion individuals were 22 times poorer than the average individual living in the US. By 2000, those 1.3 billion people were 86 times poorer than the average person in the US. In 1980, the income of all impoverished nations was 14 times lower than that of the US. In 1999, the income of these impoverished nations grew to 26 per cent less than that of the US. Since the intensification of privatization, over one billion persons living in the underdeveloped world saw their incomes reduced to one dollar per day.

Tragically, in almost every corner of our precious Mother Earth today, where there are oil and energy resources in plenty, there is war, ethnic conflict, and social devastation. From the Black Hills of South Dakota, where Oglala Lakota people struggle to preserve their ancestral lands and insist in defiance of the energy corporations that the Black Hills are not for sale, to Yucca Mountain where Western Shoshone people are resisting the storage of 77,000 tons of radioactive waste in their sacred space, from the hills of Colombia where Indigenous peoples resist the oil companies' pollution of water systems, to the forests of the Amazon where Yamomami people challenge the gold-mining predators who encroach upon their ancestral lands, from the brush of central and southern Australia where Aboriginal people oppose the mining of minerals in their lands, to the struggles waged by Indigenous Taiwanese people against the dumping of toxic wastes in their waters, from the opposition movements led by Indigenous peoples of north India to the flooding of ancestral lands for hydro-electric power projects and dams, to the Indigenous Arab people struggling for their lives and cultures in the sands of Iraq and Yemen against corrupt oligarchies, from the struggles of the Ogoni people in the Niger Delta against the oil giants like Shell and Chevron whose oil drilling has gutted sensitive ecosystems and destroyed fishing subsistence economies, to the forced removals of Maasai and San people in eastern and southern Africa traditional grazing grounds respectively to pave the way for game reserves for Western tourists, from the struggles waged by Indigenous peoples of Egoli (Johannesburg) against the gold and diamond companies for stealing their land, to the Indigenous people of Zimbabwe resisting the flooding of their lands by the Kariba dam, the stories are similar. Many Indigenous peoples view the presence of oil or gold or coal or natural gas or any other mineral or energy source as a curse in the lands, principally because of the cultural and economic devastation that industries engaged in extraction of such energy resources have caused to their nations and livelihood. Ironically, in places like Somalia, which has been ravaged by wars fought by superpowers and riven by power conflicts, Indigenous peoples have recently fared more successfully without a formal state government in place, utilizing their innovative cultural frameworks to generate sustainable economies, confirming that in many instances the state is highly irrelevant to the well-being of Indigenous peoples.

The principle of greed enshrined in the Western system of capitalism that knows no reasonable bounds has been accorded respectability and valorization while it wreaks havoc on Indigenous peoples. For Indigenous peoples, it appears that the only religion of the West is the idol of money. All other rhetoric of sharing and justice and democracy seems very hollow in our ears.

Indigenous peoples say Enough is Enough! Greed cannot sustain any civilization. Stop before it's too late! The fires of nuclear war and radioactive contamination and disregard of the sacred ways of our ancestors will destroy us all. If we are destroyed, the whole world will be destroyed with us. Now is the time to listen. Perhaps this volume will give us pause to reflect on this Indigenous prophetic wisdom and begin to do things differently…and live according to the pulse of the drum, and walk in harmony with our original Mother, Earth. We must all pray for strength…

Tunkashile wama yanka yo	Grandfather behold me.
Le miye cha nawajin yelo he	This is me, I am standing.
Tunkashila wama yanka yo	Grandfather, behold me,
Le miye cha	This is me
Nawajin yelo he	standing up.

Mitakuye oyasin[1]

---

1 Leonard Crow Dog and Richard Erdoes, *Crow Dog: Four Generations of Sioux Medicine Men*, New York, Harper Collins (1995), p. 243.

Contributors

Etsuko Aoki, Kiyoko Kitahara, Kayano Shigeru and **Koich Kaizawa** are Ainu activists in Nibutani and Tokyo, Japan.

Vimbai Gukwe Chivaura is Lecturer in Literature in English, Indigenous Knowledge Systems, Theatre Arts, Media and Communication, and Comparative Culture at the University of Zimbabwe in Harare, Zimbabwe.

Jennifer Nez Denetdale is a Diné [Navajo] historian who teaches Indigenous history at the University of New Mexico, Albuquerque, New Mexico, USA. Her publications have appeared in *New Mexico Historical Review*, *American Indian Culture and Research Journal*, and the *Journal of Social Archaeology*. Her book on the Diné leaders Manuelito and Juanita is forthcoming from the University of Arizona Press.

Miryam Espinosa-Dulanpo is a Mestiza/Muchik activist teaching in the USA.

Somadoda Fikeni is an Indigenous activist and lecturer in Political Science at the University of Transkei in South Africa/Azania.

Laara Fitznor is an Indigenous Cree educator and teacher who lives in Canada.

Nomalungelo Goduka is Professor of Human Environmental Studies at Central Michigan University in Mount Pleasant, Michigan, USA.

Naomi Kipuri is a leader representing Indigenous peoples' interests in Arid Lands Resource Management in Kenya.

Kora Malele Korawali teaches in the Department of Architecture and Building, University of Technology in Papua New Guinea and is currently completing doctoral research in architectural education on PNG at the University of Newcastle, Australia.

Asa Virdi Kroik is an Indigenous Saami graduate student studying Saami religion who lives in Vuornese, Sweden.

Julian Kunnie is Professor and Director of Africana Studies at the University of Arizona in Tucson, Arizona, USA.

Roxana Ng teaches in Adult Education, Community Development and Counseling Psychology, at the Ontario Institute for Studies in Education at the University of Toronto.

Kxao Moses ≠Oma from the San Nation, and **Axel Thoma** from Germany, are members of the Working Group of Indigenous Minorities in Southern Africa (WIMSA).

Pramod Parajuli is a member of the Social Movements Learning Project in Jharkhand, India.

Rangimarie Turuki (Rose) Pere, an Indigenous Maori educator from Aotearoa (New Zealand) who has been strongly influenced by the teachings that go back over 12 000 years to ancient Hawaiki, held a Visiting Teacher Fellowship at the University of Waikato and is author of the monograph entitled *Ako-Concepts and Learning in the Maori Tradition.*

Lester-Irabbina Rigney is an Indigenous Narrungga Australian who teaches at the Yunggorendi First Nation Centre for Higher Education and Research, Flinders University, Adelaide, Australia.

Dianne Stewart is Assistant Professor of Religious Studies and African American Studies at Emory University in Atlanta, Georgia, USA.

Pat Mamanyjun Torres, a Yawuru, Jabirrjabirr woman is a lecturer in the Indigenous Studies Program at the Centre for Aboriginal Studies at Curtin University, Perth, Australia, and is a renowned Indigenous Australian writer and artist who has won several national and international literary awards.

Index

(Words beginning with non-alphabetical symbols are listed first in the index)